MONARCHY IN THE AGE OF LIBERTY

LUND
UNIVERSITY
PRESS

LUND
UNIVERSITY

Monarchy in the Age of Liberty

Royal power and public life in eighteenth-century Sweden

JONAS NORDIN

TRANSLATED BY LENA OLSSON

Lund University Press

Lund University Press
The Joint Faculties of Humanities and Theology
P.O. Box 192

LUND
UNIVERSITY
PRESS

LUND
UNIVERSITY

SE-221 00 LUND
Sweden
https://lunduniversitypress.lu.se

Lund University Press books are published in collaboration with Manchester University Press.

British Library Cataloguing-in-Publication Data
A catalogue record for this book is available from the British Library

ISBN   978-91-98740-4-3-1   hardback
ISBN   978-91-98740-4-4-8   open access

First published 2026

Lund University Press gratefully acknowledges publication assistance from the Thora Ohlsson Foundation (Thora Ohlssons stiftelse)

EU authorised representative for GPSR:
Easy Access System Europe, Mustamäe tee 50, 10621 Tallinn, Estonia
gpsr.requests@easproject.com

Typeset
by Cheshire Typesetting Ltd, Cuddington, Cheshire

Contents

Contents

List of illustrations

List of diagrams and table

Preface

Writing a book about one of the most central institutions in the history of Europe (monarchy), but on the basis of a peripheral example (Sweden during the so-called Age of Liberty, 1718–1772), comes with certain challenges. This is a book which aims to say something new and substantial about European politics in the eighteenth century in a general sense; but at the same time, history as a subject has deep roots in cultural contexts where general patterns are shaped by unique experiences. Europe is frequently described as a patchwork quilt of states and cultural circles where the variegated pattern determines the character of the quilt. In order to comprehend the multifaceted history of Europe, this variety has to be taken into account; consequently, peripheral experiences are also crucial to an understanding of the whole. This book thus deals with a phenomenon that existed throughout Europe, and it focuses on historical developments in a region that is situated on the outskirts of the continent with regard to both geographical location and population size. In doing so, the discussion in the book proceeds with the same assurance as it would have evinced had the subject been France, Britain or one of Germany's many principalities. To some readers, the empirical instances from a rather unknown horizon will be the most rewarding feature, whereas others will be more interested in what this 'case' contributes to a picture of the whole of Europe. However, I hope that anybody with an interest in the cultural history, social development and politics of the eighteenth century will find something to take with them from the ensuing chapters. After all, the subject has implications that range far beyond kings and royalty.

Since my ambition is to present a wide canvas, methodological considerations have been crucial. The investigations of different aspects study the same basic phenomenon – royal authority as an institution – but they tackle that issue with the aid of distinct links in a classic SMCR chain: Sender, Message, Channel and Receiver.[1] Many historical investigations have contented themselves with studying pairs of these links, usually sender–message or message–channel. In respect of message and channel, a common error, in my view, is to stop at the surface: if, for instance, a message comprises a royalist bias, it is rather too easy to assume that it expresses the intentions of the royal authority. On the contrary, as this book demonstrates, Swedish kings were frequently incapable of exercising control over the images of them that were communicated to the general public. While studying the sender is essential, it is just as important to study the receiver. For reasons to do with the nature of source materials and methodological considerations, this is the factor that is most often lacking in historical investigations. It is, quite simply, hard for us to obtain an idea of how a message was regarded by those receivers to whom it was directed. In the last two chapters, I have attempted to analyse that issue in depth on the basis of source material that turned out to offer an abundance of insights into central political circumstances: trials, hearings and other legal proceedings connected with the crime of lese-majesty.

This book is a revised version of a book which first appeared in Swedish in 2009. In some places it has been shortened, but there are additions, too. When the matter of a translation into English was raised, I had the option of making a thorough-going revision of the Swedish book. After careful consideration, I decided to reject it, mainly for two reasons. First, there has not been a great deal of Swedish scholarship on the type of issues that I address in the book. I found that to be the case twenty years ago, and not much in the way of new research that might have prompted reconsiderations has appeared since. Naturally, international research keeps producing new studies that might have been contemplated alongside the Swedish experience; but I have not come across any investigations that might have modified my over-arching conclusions. If I had included such more recent research in the book, it would mostly have amounted to pointless name-dropping. Second, this book, like all research, naturally participates in an ongoing discussion in a general sense; over the years, it has been used and discussed by

---

1 The SMCR model was developed by the American communications theorist David Berlo in the 1960s. I have not proceeded specifically from his work, but I have gained general inspiration from the analytical method, which has, following on from his research, come to constitute a fundamental tool in communication theory.

Swedish-language scholars and to some extent by foreign research-ers, too.[2] When that happens, a loop is generated where older scholarship inspires new research which generates further investigations, and so on. In order to do this dynamic justice, I should have had to engage in discussion with research that might, or might not, have been influenced by my own work, and that would have generated argumentation where it would be difficult to determine what is the chicken and what is the egg. Instead, I chose a cautiously pragmatic solution, namely that of regarding the book, in all essentials, as a finished entity, work on which was concluded nearly twenty years ago. (The original manuscript was finished in 2007, though the book did not appear until 2009.) Consequently, the bibliography contains few items published after 2007.

There are a handful of exceptions, though, as the attentive reader will observe. In some cases, studies which supplemented my research without contradicting it (if they had, a more profound discussion would have been called for) have been published, and I would like to mention some of the most important ones.

In 2017, Elise Dermineur published a fine study of Louisa Ulrika as a politician. The book does not attempt to constitute a complete biography; it is a presentation which brings certain aspects of her achievements into focus and studies them in depth. In the present context, Dermineur has above all contributed further perspectives on the failed royal coup in 1756, a significant event in this context which received too little attention in the Swedish edition of my book (and about which more remains to be said).[3]

In 2022, Björn Asker brought out a much-needed survey of the development of the Swedish court from the sixteenth century to the 1970s.[4] Royal courts, wherever they exist, are intricate social systems with special codes and incomprehensible titles. Asker's study, which exists only in Swedish, has contributed clarifications of certain individual circumstances in the following chapters.

2 Some of the central results have been summarised in Jonas Nordin, 'The Monarchy in the Swedish Age of Liberty (1719–1772)', in *Scandinavia in the Age of Revolution: Nordic Political Cultures, 1740–1820*, ed. by Pasi Ihalainen, Michael Bregnsbo, Karin Sennefelt and Patrik Winton (Farnham: Ashgate, 2011), pp. 29–40.

3 Elise M. Dermineur, *Gender and Politics in Eighteenth-Century Sweden: Queen Louisa Ulrika (1720–1782)* (London and New York: Routledge, 2017).

4 Björn Asker, *Hovet: Historien om ett kungligt maskineri* (Lund: Historiska media, 2022).

One of the most prolific younger scholars currently studying Swedish eighteenth-century politics in a European context is Ere Nokkala. His research has inspired me more than can be easily accounted for in writing; and in the present book his visible influence is restricted to a small but significant detail which strengthens my argumentation in Chapter 2.[5]

Some further illuminating works from comparatively recent years have been added in order to supply additional guidance for readers who look for deeper analyses of certain aspects that are discussed in the book. That applies, among others, to Rachel Hammersley's fine summary of the development of ideas in republicanism; Bernd Roling's magisterial work about Swedish Gothicism; and Fabian Persson's book about networks within the Swedish court.

The editors of a recent anthology containing several Scandinavian contributions, *Dynasties and State Formation in Early Modern Europe*, assert that princely houses and dynastic networks have been a blind spot in research on this phenomenon. I do not entirely share that view; and I observe that the discussion I attempted to initiate with this book, about the *institutional* role of monarchy in state formation, has passed unnoticed by the editors of and contributors to this volume.[6]

A book with which I came into contact after my manuscript had been revised for this edition, and which would no doubt (despite what has been said above) have enriched my approach if I had known about it before, is Stephanie E. Koscak's excellent *Monarchy, Print Culture, and Reverence in Early Modern England: Picturing Royal Subjects*.[7] Quite apart from the pun in the subtitle, this study contributes thorough-going insights into a topic that plays a crucial role in my own investigation (above all in Chapter 3), namely the ways in which images of kings and royal persons were passed on to their subjects and mediated through different channels. Koscak's conclusions match mine: increased medialisation made royal personages more prominent and added to their importance in the

---

5 Ere Nokkala, 'Rewriting Eighteenth-Century Swedish Republican Political Thought: Heinrich Ludwig von Hess's *Der Republickaner* (1754)', *History of European Ideas*, 42 (2016), 502–15.

6 *Dynasties and State Formation in Early Modern Europe*, ed. by Liesbeth Geevers and Harald Gustafsson (Amsterdam: Amsterdam University Press, 2023).

7 Stephanie E. Koscak, *Monarchy, Print Culture, and Reverence in Early Modern England: Picturing Royal Subjects* (London and New York: Routledge, 2021).

everyday lives of the people, irrespective of the fact that their actual political dominance was diminishing at the same time. In addition, Koscak studies the British monarchy and politics in Britain, that is, the political system which is probably more similar than any other to the Swedish state as it existed during the Age of Liberty. Many striking analogies invite themselves when the two examples are studied; and Koscak establishes that the British royal house – just like that of Sweden – came to constitute a unifying power above party-political conflicts, as well as a basis for the allegiance and obedience of the subjects, thereby possessing a central sociological function beyond mere politics. Even though I was not able to take Koscak's book into account when writing my own, a parallel reading of the two, as different case studies of similar phenomena, would yield real benefits.

Other recent scholarly works have reinforced our empirical knowledge as well as occasionally contributing fresh theoretical perspectives on previously well-studied phenomena. One example is the anthology entitled *Power and Ceremony in European History.*[8] That power and rituals supply vital perspectives in the scholarly study of early modern politics is pointed out in the introductory survey of relevant research in the present book. However, I have not yet seen any other scholar addressing the perspective I am trying to pursue, that of monarchy as an institution in itself, with its own ideational rationality *beyond* power politics, rituals and personal relationships. I hope that this book will form a small contribution to this wide-ranging discussion about a shared European experience which is still awaiting close examination.

---

8 *Power and Ceremony in European History: Rituals, Practices and Representative Bodies since the Late Medieval Age,* ed. by Anna Kalinowska and Jonathan Spangler, with Pawel Tyszka (London: Bloomsbury, 2021).

List of abbreviations

GA   *Generalauditören* – Judge Advocate General
KB   Kungliga biblioteket – National Library of Sweden
RA   Riksarkivet – Swedish National Archives
RF   *regeringsformen* – Instrument of Government
SPA   Svenska porträttarkivet – Swedish Portrait Archive

Author's note

One of the challenges in interpreting the contemporary sources for this book is to understand who the agent behind monarchical decisions is. The sources normally only employ the term *Kungl. Maj:t*, short for *Kunglig Majestät* '[The] Royal Majesty'. This term covered both the personal decisions by the King himself (or, at times, the Queen) and the collective decisions made by the king in Council. In the latter case, the King did not need to be present in order for decisions to be made in his name, and the rulings could even go against his will. The Royal Majesty's decisions were expressions of perpetual state authority and thus too important to be left to the discretion of one person. Conversely, the sempiternal royal office, elevated above partisanship and vested interests, was necessary to secure the impartiality of the government's decisions.

To analyse this relationship is one of the aims of this study. It is therefore necessary to distinguish between the office and the person. To do this I slightly deviate from standard English usage and write 'king', with a lower-case initial letter, when referring to the royal office, and 'King', with a capital K, when referring to the mortal person holding that office. This separation is not always easy to make – among other things, because the sources often deliberately confuse the meanings – but it is nevertheless fundamental to the analysis.

Introduction

This is a book about the monarchy as an institution, not a book about kings. Researchers have studied states, companies and associations as organisations; but the monarchy as an institution has not elicited the same theoretical interest. This is presumably because the monarchy – at least symbolically, and as is already apparent from the word itself – has been embodied by an individual person. For this reason, the interest of European historians has been focused on kings, not on the monarchy. It has been established that the royal authority has been strong during certain historical periods and weak during others; but as an institution the monarchy itself has been seen more or less as a constant, at least from the beginning of the modern age until the emergence of democracy. Consequently, studies of the royal authority have been focused on periods when that authority was at its strongest – when kings were absolute rulers, when they conducted important struggles against other government organs or when they led their troops in the field.

In other words, it is those periods when the political functions of the monarch were at their most significant that have been of the greatest interest to historians. The point of departure for the present book has been the opposite. By studying the monarchy during an epoch when it was, historically speaking, at its weakest, I believe it will be possible to find interesting perspectives regarding its nature and inherent function in earlier periods of history. The underlying and deliberately trenchant question has been, 'What was the function of the monarchy if the king had none?'

In this book I attempt to find an answer to this question by studying three areas: how the royal authority was defined constitutionally, what kind of image of the monarch was conveyed to the population of the kingdom and what perceptions of and expectations from the king existed among his subjects. At the centre of the analysis are public opinion about and advocacy regarding the royal

authority during the era in Swedish history known as the Age of
Liberty (1719–1772). During this time Sweden was a republic in
everything but name. I hope to be able to show that although the
royal authority may appear powerless on paper, it was by no means
superfluous. The monarchs of the Age of Liberty had key constitutional roles, and their sociological significance was perhaps greater
than that of any earlier kings or queens.

Republicanism versus monarchism

During the Age of Liberty – a designation already in use at the
time – there was a widespread understanding that Sweden had
a republican form of government.[1] This statement requires an
explanation and a specification. The concept of a *republic* was
not linked to the role of the head of state in the same way as it is
today.[2] Rather, there were two competing meanings, where one
simply meant 'state' (as in the English word 'commonwealth'),
and the other referred to a 'state with a free constitution'. For
some a republic was simply an empirical observation without any
deeper valuation, while others saw it as a natural ideal to maintain
or strive for. During the eighteenth century people would speak
about monarchical republics, such as Venice, Florence and the
Netherlands, but also about republican monarchies, such as Great
Britain, Poland and Sweden.[3] Even if the concept of the republic

1 See, e.g., *En Ärlig Swensk* (Stockholm: Historiographi regni, 1755), p. 269:
'We have also been fortunate in this respect, that we during the whole Age
of Liberty have had such illustrious rulers, who have loved and been careful
to protect the freedom of the Men of Sweden, and without resistance
or conspiracies given us free hands, so that we in the greatest peace and
quiet have been able to consolidate and safeguard our freedom ever more'
('Lycklige hafwa wi också warit derutinnan, at wi under hela Frihetstiden
haft så Glorwördiga Regenter, som älskat och warit måne om Swea Manna
Frihet, och utan alt motstånd eller stämpling lämnat oss fria händer, at
i största lugn och stillhet få alt mer och mer befästa och omskansa wår
Frihet').
2 See, e.g., Rachel Hammersley, *Republicanism: An Introduction* (Cambridge:
Polity Press, 2020), pp. 1–14.
3 Horst Dreitzel, *Monarchiebegriffe in der Fürstengesellscahft: Semantik
und Theorie der Einherrschaft in Deutschland von der Reformation bis
sum Vormärz*, 2 vols (Cologne, Weimar and Vienna: Böhlau, 1991), I:
Semantik der Monarchie, pp. 43–45, 58–66, 71, 82–84; Bo Lindberg, *Den
antika skevheten: Politiska ord och begrepp i det tidig-moderna Sverige*,

was at bottom fairly value-neutral, it has also had sloganistic connotations throughout European history. Republicanism has been associated with freedom – personal freedom, freedom from tyranny, freedom from foreign domination. The opposite of the free republic was despotism, lawless absolutism.

The good reputation enjoyed by the republic in European constitutional law was inherited from Antiquity. Typically enough, in Rome even the Empire long continued to be described as a republic. The republican form of government remained formally intact; but all the government bodies, which were supposed to balance one another, had been collected in the hands of an absolute ruler: the supreme commander, the censor, the first consul, the plebeian tribune, the leading senator, the high priest – all these roles were combined in the person of the Emperor. According to Roman political mythology, the best of two worlds was thus combined: the freedom of the republic was united with the monarchy's stability and conformity to law, because the threat to the citizens of the republic was the division of parties, factionalism, and oligarchy – i.e. that a few people made themselves masters of the many in order to safeguard their own special interests. In the middle of the eighteenth century, the political philosopher Montesquieu still felt that a government that conformed to law was closer at hand in a monarchy than in a republic. This was frequently used as a defence for governments in strong principalities such as Denmark and Prussia.[4]

Filologiskt arkiv, 45 (Stockholm: Vitterhetsakademien, 2006), pp. 58–65, 88–94. A typical example of the empirical use of the concept of the republic is the following formulation from 1708: 'Was ist eine Monarchie? Wenn nur ein einzige Person in der Republik vorhanden ist, auf welcher die Majestät beruhet'; the upper-secondary-school principal Christian Weise, quoted in *Geschichtliche Grundbegriffe: Historisches Lexikon zur politisch-sozialen Sprache in Deutschland*, ed. by Otto Brunner and others, 8 vols (Stuttgart: Klett-Cotta, 1972–97), IV: *Mi–Pre* (1978), p. 173, n. 207. Supposedly it was not until Montesquieu's *De l'esprit des lois* (1748) that *monarchy* and *republic* became dichotomous concepts; *ibid.*, p. 181.

4 *Geschichtliche Grundbegriffe*, IV, pp. 139–40; Helmut G. Koenigsberger, 'Republicanism, Monarchism and Liberty', in *Royal and Republican Sovereignty in Early Modern Europe: Essays in Memory of Ragnhild Hatton*, ed. by Robert Oresko, G. C. Gibbs and H. M. Scott (Cambridge: Cambridge University Press, 1997), pp. 43–74; David Armitage, 'Empire and Liberty: A Republican Dilemma', in *Republicanism: A Shared European Heritage*, ed. by Martin van Gelderen and Quentin Skinner, 2 vols (Cambridge: Cambridge University Press, 2002), II, pp. 29–46.

In recent years, the history of republicanism has attracted great interest in international research. It has been seen as a central component in European political life since Antiquity, and in one large European research project republicanism was called 'a shared European heritage'.[5] In the present context, the concept *republican* is used analytically, to denote the defence of the prevailing form of government during the Age of Liberty, which was established by means of the Instruments of Government of 1719 and 1720. The fundamental idea in these documents was to maintain the balance among the three governmental entities of the King, the Council and the Estates, but almost immediately the royal authority became far less prominent than the authors of the Constitution had intended. In this study, those who enforced and defended these successive limitations through a change of praxis are referred to as 'republicans'; but their purpose was not to turn Sweden into a regular republic with a deposable head of state. Their goal was to make

---

That the freedom of the people was best defended in a monarchy, where all subjects were equals before the ruler, was the fundamental idea of the English political philosopher Robert Filmer (1588–1653), one of the most consistent defenders of absolutism: 'The greatest liberty in the world (if it be duly considered) is for people to live under a monarch. [...] All other shows or pretexts of liberty are but several degrees of slavery, and liberty only to destroy liberty'; see Robert Filmer, *Patriarcha and Other Writings*, ed. by Johann P. Sommerville (Cambridge: Cambridge University Press, 1991), p. 4. For similar ideas in the Scandinavian context, see, e.g., Erich Pontoppidan, *Den danske Atlas eller Konge-Riget Dannemark, med dets naturlige Egenskaber, Elementer, Jndbyggere, Væxter, Dyr og andre Affødninger, [...]*, 7 vols (Copenhagen: Godiche, 1763–81), I (1763), chapter 10, 'Om den Danske Nations nærværende Lyksalighed, og sande Friheds-Stand, under et faderligt Regimente', pp. 174–98. See also Dreitzel, *Monarchiebegriffe*, I, pp. 63–65, Henrik Horstbøll, 'Defending Monarchism in Denmark-Norway in the Eighteenth Century', and Simone Zurbuchen, 'Theorizing Enlightened Absolutism: The Swiss Republican Origins of Prussian Monarchism', the latter two in *Monarchisms in the Age of Enlightenment: Liberty, Patriotism and the Common Good*, ed. by Hans Blom, John Christian Laursen and Luisa Simonutti (Toronto, Buffalo and London: Toronto University Press, 2007), pp. 175–93, 240–66.

5 *Republicanism: A Shared European Heritage*, ed. by Martin van Gelderen and Quentin Skinner, 2 vols (Cambridge: Cambridge University Press, 2002), I: *Republicanism and Constitutionalism in Early Modern Europe*; II: *The Values of Republicanism in Early Modern Europe*. See also *Republiken und Republikanismus im Europa der frühen Neuzeit*, ed. by Helmut G. Koenigsberger and Elisabeth Müller-Luckner, Schriften des Historischen Kollegs, Kolloquien, 11 (Munich: Oldenbourg, 1988).

executive power impersonal and, as far as possible, to subject it to the control of the people.[6] But this, it was thought, could also be accomplished with a non-deposable monarch as head of state. Few, if any, in eighteenth-century Sweden were prepared to go as far as wanting to abolish the monarchy. The monarchy possessed certain indispensable values and functions that could not be relinquished, and my aim is to examine what these consisted of and how they were expressed.

There thus exists extensive international research on republicanism, where a great deal of attention has been devoted to the history of its roots and to the rhetoric and symbolism surrounding republican ideas.[7] I would argue that the monarchy, to an even greater extent than the republic, can be considered a shared historical heritage. For this reason, each case study that contributes to a better understanding of the monarchy as an institution is a contribution to a common European history of political ideas. Even though the republic and the monarchy are traditionally regarded as each other's antitheses, it is significant for the attitude to the latter that *monarchism* is rarely spoken of in the same way as *republicanism*.[8] The monarchy is not considered to rest on any

---

6   Fredrik Lagerroth, *Frihetstidens författning: En studie i den svenska konstitutionalismens historia* (Stockholm: Bonniers, 1915), pp. 403–17.

7   Inspiration for the following line of reasoning has been taken from the editorial introduction by Blom, Laursen and Simonutti, in *Monarchisms in the Age of Enlightenment*, ed. by Blom, Laursen and Simonutti, pp. 3–16.

8   One example of many that can be mentioned is Quentin Skinner's influential work *The Foundations of Modern Political Thought*, 2 vols (Cambridge: Cambridge University Press, 1978), I: *The Renaissance*; II: *The Age of Reformation*. The index supplies fifteen references to the word 'republicanism', which is discussed on a total of seventy-one pages in the two volumes. A corresponding search for 'king', 'kingship', 'monarchy', 'royalty', etc. generates no hits. The only entries that provide information about the concept of the monarchy are to be found under 'absolutism' and 'Imperium'.

 The article 'Monarchie' in the standard work *Geschichtliche Grundbegriffe*, IV, opens with the statement that there are too few preliminary studies to provide an exhaustive historical background for this concept. Otherwise, it is German historians who have devoted the greatest attention to the monarchy. As Horst Dreitzel has explained in a study inspired by the research gap pointed out in *Geschichtliche Grundbegriffe*, this is because the unique construction of the Holy Roman Empire with its many self-governing state entities created what came close to being a *Fürstengesellschaft* ('community of princes') or even a *Fürstenstand* ('a princely estate')

consistent ideological foundation. It has been seen as a source for the exercise of power, and less commonly as an institution with its own rationality and traditions of ideas. An exception to this is research on the Middle Ages, within which many important studies on the history of ideas have been conducted which are also fundamental to understanding later eras.[9] During the Middle Ages religion, political symbolism and dynastic mysticism were directly interwoven with the royal exercise of power. In the early modern age, these became ever more separate spheres which certainly could put a tradition-laden imprint on the monarchy as an institution, but of which all the elements were not equally important for the legitimisation of power, nor were they all given a literal meaning. No doubt a deep religiousness still prevailed among eighteenth-century Europeans; but it is equally certain that the importance of religion as an instrument of political legitimisation decreased during the same century.[10]

Some main lines in the research: the power perspective and the ritual perspective

It is not possible to describe here in detail everything that has been written in international research about the monarchy – obviously this is quite a lot. However, two main lines that recur in the treatment of the early modern circumstances will be briefly outlined in order to provide a context for my points of departure. The first of these deals with investigations of the power of kings and its extent,

---

which, like other important social groups, requires independent socio-economic analysis; Dreitzel, *Monarchiebegriffe*, I, pp. 9–10.

9 To mention only a few examples, see Fritz Kern, *Gottesgnadentum und Widerstandsrecht im früheren Mittelalter: Zur Entwicklungsgeschichte der Monarchie* (1914), edited and translated into English under the title *Kingship and Law in the Middle Ages*, trans. by S. B. Chrimes, 2 vols (Oxford: Basil Blackwell, 1956), I: *The Divine Right of Kings and the Right of Resistance in the Early Middle Ages*; II: *Law and Constitution in the Middle Ages*; Ernst H. Kantorowicz, *The King's Two Bodies: A Study in Mediaeval Political Theology*, with a new preface by William Chester Jordan (Princeton: Princeton University Press, 1997 [1957]); Sergio Bertelli, *The King's Body: Sacred Rituals of Power in Medieval and Early Modern Europe* (University Park: Pennsylvania State University Press, 2001).

10 *Geschichtliche Grundbegriffe*, IV, pp. 180–89; Paul Kléber Monod, *The Power of Kings: Monarchy and Religion in Europe 1589–1715* (New Haven and London: Yale University Press, 1999).

and the second concerns investigations of how this power has been portrayed and legitimised through symbols and rituals.

When historians have looked at the monarchy in the early modern era, their investigations have had a clear bias towards studying the strong, *absolute*, royal authority. The major topic of discussion has been whether the concept of absolutism describes an empirical experience at all, and whether it is relevant as an analytical tool. The dominant view is that the power of the supposedly absolute monarchs was in reality dependent on the efficiency of the administrative organs these kings had at their disposal, and that the more efficient these administrative organs were, the better they also were at asserting their independence against princely intervention.[11] This description points to something essential, and from the perspective of European modernisation it is possible to see that at a certain point in history, those strong principalities that had established rational bureaucracies were forced to abolish the executive royal authority, because it was thought to be in conflict with the very rationality of the bureaucracy. This happened in most European states in the nineteenth or early twentieth centuries.

What these studies have investigated is primarily an institution of power and the degree of its intervention. Conceptual content has not been the primary issue; and as a result, when the historical institution has been drained of power, it is also considered to have lost all its content and, consequently, its relevance for historians. Power becomes the essence of the monarchy, and the institution is only interesting to study when its holders – the kings – have been

---

11 For this discussion, see, e.g., Perry Anderson, *Lineages of the Absolutist State* (London: NLB, 1974); Roland Mousnier, *La monarchie absolue en Europe du Vᵉ siècle à nos jours* (Paris: Presses universitaires de France, 1982); *Absolutism in Seventeenth Century Europe*, ed. John Miller (Basingstoke: Macmillan, 1990); Horst Dreitzel, *Absolutismus und ständische Verfassung in Deutschland: Ein Beitrag zu Kontinuität und Diskontinuität der politischen Theorie in der frühen Neuzeit*, Veröffentlichungen des Instituts für Europäische Geschichte Mainz, 24: Abteilung Universalgeschicht (Mainz: Philipp von Zabern, 1992); Nicholas Henshall, *The Myth of Absolutism: Change and Continuity in Early Modern European Monarchy* (London and New York: Longman, 1992); *Der Absolutismus – ein Mythos? Strukturwandel monarchischer Herrschaft in West- und Mitteleuropa (ca. 1550–1700)*, ed. by Ronald G. Asch and Heinz Duchhardt, Münstersche historische Forschungen, 9 (Cologne: Böhlau, 1996); Ernst Hinrichs, *Fürsten und Mächte: Zum Problem des europäischen Absolutismus* (Göttingen: Vandenhoeck & Ruprecht, 2000).

able to hold and exercise power. Research has therefore inevitably come to focus on the individual and not on the institution.

In reality, however, the institution was something far greater and more important than the individual; this is shown not least by the not entirely uncommon cases when monarchs were considered incapable of ruling on their own, and for this reason were removed from power or were compelled to see power exercised by others in their name. Peter III of Russia, Philip V of Spain, Frederick V and Christian VII of Denmark, as well as George III of Great Britain, are only a few examples from the eighteenth century. In a hereditary kingdom, which was the dominant form of monarchy in early modern Europe, the executive power was ultimately dependent on agreements under family law and on royal personages having adequate capacities.[12] Even at this point in time, it was considered obvious that the state could not be exclusively dependent on a single individual and his or her qualities. The monarchy was quite simply too important to be entrusted solely to the king. By studying the period in the early modern era when the Swedish executive royal authority was at its weakest, I believe that we improve the prospects of understanding its true core, its essence. Then power will no longer stand in the way of content.

The second dominant theme in the study of the monarchy is research on rituals. The basic assumption is that early modern statecraft had a different rationality and basis for legitimisation from the political institutions of today. In current democratic forms of government, the legitimacy of politics ultimately rests on popular sanction. Today's Swedish Instrument of Government from 1974 begins with the words, 'All public power in Sweden proceeds from the people.' When interpretation is in dispute, the decision is ultimately made by the electorate through general elections or public referendums.

By contrast, early modern statecraft was based on authority rather than on consent. Nevertheless, the will and welfare of the people were not absent factors in politics – on the contrary. *Salus populi, suprema lex esto*, 'the welfare of the people is the supreme law', was a common maxim. The quotation is from Cicero and was held up as the most important principle of government by

12 Cf. Dreitzel, *Monarchiebegriffe*, II, pp. 844–49, and Yves-Marie Bercé, 'Les monarchies de l'âge moderne', in *Les monarchies*, ed. by Yves-Marie Bercé, Histoire générale des systèmes politiques (Paris: Presses universitaires de France, 1997), pp. 227–322 (pp. 235–37, 269–71).

John Locke among others.[13] Nevertheless, the attitude to politics was qualitatively different from today's situation, when citizens call for civil, political and social rights that were alien to the early modern subject. The welfare of the people could not be determined by the subjects themselves: it was the duty of those in power to make the correct political decisions. Power radiated downwards from the top, and because it was not adjudicated by popular mandate, it required a different form of legitimacy that presented the right to govern as self-evident. This made ceremonies, rituals and manifestations an integral part of politics. They were evidence of the incontestability of power.

In memoirs intended for his successor, Louis XIV of France stressed that the ceremonies surrounding him were in no way an empty façade. For the people he ruled over, their subservience was in proportion to the exaltedness of their ruler, and because only one person could embody the state, it was important that this person be above all comparison.[14] The existence of such views obviously means that it is important to study rituals and symbols as a part of a political language. Precisely this aspect has garnered increased interest among researchers, and scholars seem to have identified two different approaches: on the one hand they identify heads of state who constructed an image of openness and availability around themselves, and on the other hand focus is placed on those who expressed an elevated distance by isolating themselves within the narrow circle of the court.[15] Louis XIV himself considered the

---

13 Cicero, *De legibus*, book III, chapter 3:8. '*Salus Populi Suprema Lex*, is certainly so just and fundamental Rule, that he, who sincerely follows it, cannot dangerously err', wrote John Locke in *Two Treatises of Government*, ed. Peter Laslett, Cambridge Texts in the History of Political Thought (Cambridge: Cambridge University Press, 1988), II, § 158, p. 373. Cf. the Swedish translation, *Oförgripelige tankar om werldslig regerings rätta ursprung, gräntsor och ändamål*; trans. by Hans Harmens (Stockholm: Kungl. tryckeriet, 1726), p. 244.

14 Appendix to Louis XIV's so-called *mémoires* for the year 1666, in *Mémoires de Louis XIV pour l'instruction du Dauphin*, ed. by Charles Dreyss, 2 vols (Paris: Didier, 1860), II, p. 15.

15 For various perspectives on rituals, court life and ceremonies, see *The Courts of Europe: Politics, Patronage and Royalty, 1400–1800*, ed. by A. G. Dickens (London: Thames and Hudson, 1977); Samuel John Klingensmith, *The Utility of Splendor: Ceremony, Social Life, and Architecture at the Court of Bavaria, 1600–1800* (Chicago: University of Chicago Press, 1993); *Iconography, Propaganda, and Legitimation*, ed. by Allan Ellenius (Oxford: Clarendon Press, 1998); *The Princely Courts of Europe: Ritual*,

French monarchy to be of the open type, and the Scandinavian courts have also been characterised as open by scholars.[16]

But even within research on rituals, the emphasis has been on power rather than on the institutions that were to be manifested. It is almost an *a priori* assumption that it was precisely royal power that was manifested, which means that most of the attention has been devoted to the rituals surrounding the strong monarchs of history. In this context, a royal ceremony may be considered a confirmation of an established power relationship or as an instrument in a struggle to achieve increased power. Here, too, Louis XIV is the typical example. During his minority France underwent several revolts by the nobility; and after the declaration of his majority, the coronation, carousels and spectacles, construction activities and court ceremonials became the methods he used in order to gradually assume, and then retain, control of governance.[17]

The form taken by similar processes in Sweden has been charted in two investigations. Malin Grundberg has described royal

---

Politics and Culture under the Ancien Régime 1500–1750, ed. by John Adamson (London: Weidenfeld & Nicolson, 1999); Jonathan Brown and John Huxtable Elliott, *A Palace for a King: The Buen Retiro and the Court of Philip IV*, rev. and expanded edn (New Haven and London: Yale University Press, 2003); Jeroen Duindam, *Vienna and Versailles: The Courts of Europe's Dynastic Rivals, 1550–1780* (Cambridge: Cambridge University Press, 2003).

16 '[D]'aussi loin que nos histoires nous en peuvent instruire, s'il y a quelque caractère singulier dans cette monarchie, c'est l'accès libre et facile des sujets au prince', claimed Louis XIV. In some countries kings safeguarded their majesty by isolating themselves from the people, 'mais ce n'est pas le génie de nos Français', he maintained; *Mémoires de Louis XIV*, II, p. 567. Cf. Duindam, pp. 166–67. The archetype of the closed court was found in the Spanish monarchy; see John Huxtable Elliott, 'Philip IV of Spain: Prisoner of Ceremony', in *The Courts of Europe: Politics, Patronage and Royalty, 1400–1800*, ed. by A. G. Dickens (London: Thames and Hudson, 1977), pp. 169–90, and Glyn Redworth and Fernando Checa, 'The Courts of the Spanish Habsburgs, 1500–1700', in *The Princely Courts of Europe*, ed. by Adamson, pp. 43–65. On the Scandinavian courts, see Peter Burke, 'State-Making, King-Making and Image-Making from Renaissance to Baroque: Scandinavia in a European Context', *Scandinavian Journal of History*, 22 (1997), 1–8.

17 Norbert Elias, *The Court Society* (New York: Pantheon, 1983); Peter Burke, *The Fabrication of Louis XIV* (New Haven and London: Yale University Press, 1992); T. C. W. Blanning, *The Culture of Power and the Power of Culture: Old Regime Europe 1660–1789* (Oxford: Oxford University Press, 2002), chapter 1, 'Louis XIV and Versailles'.

ceremonies during the Vasa era (1523–1654), and Mårten Snickare has discussed the rituals of the Caroline absolutism (1680–1718). In both of the periods investigated, centralised and royal authority was extremely expansive. These studies are cogent and interesting, but I believe that they should be complemented with investigations into what forms the same ceremonies took and what function they filled when the institution they were meant to represent was no longer increasing in power. If the manifestations were exclusively an expression of power, then how are the costly royal ceremonies of the Age of Liberty to be explained? The perspectives outlined above are noteworthy, and many of these investigations have been useful for the present study. In addition, I hope to be able to add further aspects by studying points of intersection between these two fields. I wish to study a monarchy emptied of potency, and I wish to investigate public rituals that perhaps obscured rather than manifested relationships of power. In both cases this involves an inversion of the prevalent approaches.

Previous Swedish research

The constitutional history of Sweden, including the development of the royal authority, up to the eighteenth century has been discussed in many important studies, but there is no reason to delve into this research in detail here. I will only note that this literature, in the ways mentioned above, discusses the distribution and execution of power rather than the institutional rationality of the monarchy.[18]

The political scientist Fredrik Lagerroth is the only scholar who has tried to apply a comprehensive approach to the historical changes in the Swedish monarchy from the Middle Ages to the modern era. In one of his last texts, *Den svenska monarkin inför rätta* ('The Swedish monarchy on trial') from 1972, he presented an elegant and personal summary of a lifelong research achievement and continued promoting ideas that he had defended as early

---

18 See, e.g., Kerstin Strömberg-Back, *Lagen, rätten, läran: Politisk och kyrklig idédebatt i Sverige under Johan III:s tid*, Bibliotheca historica Lundensis, 11 (Lund: Gleerups, 1963), and Nils Runeby, *Monarchia mixta: Maktfördelningsdebatt i Sverige under den tidigare stormaktstiden*, Studia historica Upsaliensia, 6 (Stockholm: Svenska bokförlaget, 1962). For literature on absolutism in the Swedish Caroline era, see, e.g., Anthony F. Upton, *Charles XI and Swedish Absolutism* (Cambridge: Cambridge University Press, 1998).

as his doctoral dissertation in 1915. The subtitle of his book on the monarchy – *En författningshistorisk exposé* ('A constitutional historical exposé') – reveals the boundaries of the subject. Lagerroth saw the constitutional development of Sweden as a struggle through the centuries between an expansive and absolute royal authority and an aristocracy which, in defending its own freedoms and rights, also safeguarded the idea of balance in the Constitution and was the foremost advocate of popular power. According to Lagerroth, the Constitution of the Age of Liberty was an outcome of this struggle and primarily completed a domestic legal development. During the Age of Liberty political participation expanded and the parliamentary system gradually matured. It was the aristocracy, not some benevolent royal authority, that had educated subjects to become citizens, and the barriers that were established for the autocrat during the Age of Liberty were necessary for the political maturation of the people. In other words, Lagerroth's views do not chime in with the condemnation of aristocrats and the glorification of the royal authority which had long prevailed in Swedish historiography.

Even though there is a good deal of research on the Age of Liberty, the issue of the status and importance of the monarchy cannot be considered to have been exhaustively discussed. The monarch is generally spoken of as a fairly insignificant actor; and except for the many works by Lagerroth, some popular biographical works and a few special studies on well-defined problems, not much has been written about the royal authority. In addition, the focus tends to be almost exclusively on constitutional or personal historical aspects.[19] This state of affairs is particularly true when it comes to the Age of Liberty, but research on the monarchy is rare with respect to other periods as well.

---

19 See, e.g., Walfrid Holst, *Ulrika Eleonora d.y.: Karl XII:s syster* (Stockholm: Wahlström & Widstrand, 1956); Walfrid Holst, *Fredrik I* (Stockholm: Wahlström & Widstrand, 1953); *Friedrich, König von Schweden, Landgraf von Hessen-Kassel: Studien zu Leben und Wirken eines umstrittenen Fürsten (1676–1751)*, ed. by Helmut Burmeister (Hofgeismar: Verein für hessische Geschichte und Landeskunde, 2003); Helmut Burmeister, *Der unbekannte König: Friedrich von Schweden* (Hofgeismar: Verein für hessische Geschichte und Landeskunde, 2012 [2003]); Olof Jägerskiöld, *Lovisa Ulrika* (Stockholm: Wahlström & Widstrand, 1945); Olof Jägerskiöld, *Hovet och författningsfrågan 1760–1766* (Uppsala: Almqvist & Wiksell, 1943); Marie-Christine Skuncke, *Gustaf III – Det offentliga barnet: En prins retoriska och politiska fostran* (Stockholm: Atlantis, 1993).

Even so, an interesting contribution to the discussion has been made by the historian of ideas Karin Tegenborg Falkdalen in a study of female rulers of the early modern era, both in general and with respect to the two Swedish ones in particular. It is true that her investigation is confined to ruling Queens, which means that it is to a certain extent centred on individuals; but she nevertheless provides many valuable comments on the institutional changes in the monarchy during the sixteenth and seventeenth centuries. One important conclusion she reaches is that gender aspects were indeed important in the patriarchal order of the time – it was believed that women were not created for ruling – but even more important was the issue of royal distinctiveness, which was cultivated through princely kinship ties. The leadership qualities of rulers were inherited within dynasties in mysterious ways, and female relatives were also capable of possessing them.[20]

In this connection, the historian Mikael Alm's doctoral thesis on the political rhetoric of the Gustavian absolutism (1772–1809) should also be mentioned. He makes the recurring observation that Gustav III reconnected to a traditional image of the royal authority, but chose or was forced to adapt his rhetoric to the political language developed during the Age of Liberty. His image as a monarch therefore became a hybrid between the politics of the seventeenth century and the radical political language of the late eighteenth century. He became the patriotic citizen king with despotic traits.[21]

It should be emphasised that this unconventional mixture can be studied in many other places in eighteenth-century Europe; comparisons with, for instance, Denmark and Great Britain, in spite of their essentially disparate forms of government, are close at hand in this context. However, these countries had undergone a linear constitutional development since the second half of the seventeenth century, and the rhetorical radicalism that was expressed had developed organically from two stable constitutional systems. In contrast, the kingship of Gustav III appears oddly anachronistic because it formed such an abrupt break with the previous political

---

20 Karin Tegenborg Falkdalen, *Kungen är en kvinna: Retorik och praktik kring kvinnliga monarker under tidigmodern tid*, Skrifter från institutionen för historiska studier, 5 (Umeå: Institutionen för historiska studier, 2003).

21 Mikael Alm, *Kungsord i elfte timmen: Språk och självbild i det gustavianska enväldets legitimitetskamp 1772–1809* (Stockholm: Atlantis, 2002).

order and linked up with both the constitutions of the early seventeenth century and the rhetorical figures of the Age of Liberty.

That the royal authority is nevertheless central to the study of the Age of Liberty, and that many other studies have been significant for my investigation both broadly and in detail, will be clear from what follows. This literature is best presented in its relevant place in the following discussion. Nevertheless, Carl Gustaf Malmström's six-volume work *Sveriges politiska historia från konung Karl XII:s död till statshvälfningen 1772* ('The political history of Sweden from the death of Charles XII to the revolution of 1772') should be given particular emphasis. This magisterial work, whose first edition was published in 1855–77 and followed by a revised edition in 1893–1901, is probably one of the most enduring accomplishments of Swedish historical research. Most of the central political events mentioned below have been discussed by Malmström; and for those who wish to acquire more detailed knowledge of the relevant circumstances, his work is the first port of call.

Outline and analytical structure

A fundamental idea behind the present book is that rulers, including those that governed pre-modern and pre-democratic societies, have both wanted and been obliged to anchor their policies among their subjects. Their motivations may be interpreted from a perspective of either confrontation or consensus. Attempts to create support for political goals and institutions can be seen as an endeavour on the part of rulers to attain normative resources of power, where the content of policies is formulated by rulers but approved by those being ruled. This aspect may also be seen as part of a political culture of negotiation which engendered a relatively broad consensus concerning the goals and content of the politics. In both cases, manifestations of power and communication with subjects may be considered important means of gaining political legitimacy. These means will be studied together with perceptions held by those target groups towards which the image of the monarch was communicated, primarily the common subjects. The effect of public propaganda on the intended target groups is the element most often missing in studies of this type, the reason being a problematic situation as regards sources. The present book attempts to identify popular attitudes to the royal authority via legal documents. It makes a loose analytical division into three sections: function, communication and opinion. The first section discusses the concepts surrounding the monarchy and the constitutional content and function of the royal authority (Chapter 1). It is followed by a number of studies that show how the image of the king and of the royal authority was communicated to the subjects through various channels (Chapters 2–4). Finally, an attempt is made to identify perceptions about and emotional attitudes towards the king and the monarchy that were present among the population of Sweden during the eighteenth century (Chapters 5–6).

The basic idea behind this study is that during the eighteenth century, there was still a monarchical mentality that made the royal authority an indispensable part of the state and of the power of the government. This mentality was ubiquitous and was embraced by high and low, educated and uneducated alike. It was so well established that even those who emphasised the republican principles of the Swedish form of government most assiduously imagined a king as the head of state. The rationality of the royal authority had been handed down from generation to generation. Frequently unreflected on and patently emotional, it was also formally expressed in constitutional documents. I have chosen to call this time-honoured and official function the *ethos* of the royal authority.

Even though everyone cherished the basic principle of this ethos, there were varying ideas about the extent of the royal authority and the role of the king. Royalist attitudes were in conflict with anti-royalist views, absolutist positions with anti-absolutist ones, and so on. During the Age of Liberty, an anti-royalist – in the analytical sense – was not a revolutionary advocating the abolition of the monarchy, but someone who wanted to reduce the influence of the court on politics and to limit the king's room to manoeuvre as much as possible. A royalist was the opposite, but did not necessarily advocate absolutism. In other words, there were numerous emotions and attitudes towards the king and the scope of his authority which were not necessarily in tune with the ethos of the monarchy as it had traditionally been formulated.

In reality, there was a great, and over time increasing, distance between the status of the king in established doctrine and the attitudes surrounding him. What the royal authority was and what it was perceived to be were far apart in a variety of ways. The idea of a divine order, of a kingship by the grace of God, remained as a formula throughout the entire period; but this was not an image that was given real credence. During the eighteenth century, the king began to be described as the foremost citizen among a free people, someone whose power was dependent on the approval of this same people. These changing attitudes eventually gave rise to a new ethos. How these mentalities and attitudes were spoken of and justified varied with the context. The ethos of the royal authority was a basic part of the legitimisation of power, and because of the tenacity of the mental structures involved it could only change slowly. The attitude of the ruling class to the royal authority might hence be far more radical than the ethos, and the discrepancy between the two may be studied by examining how the royal authority was spoken of in various contexts and circumstances. Popular opinion also displayed varying ideas about the royal authority, and this issue will be studied below.

Concepts

Certain recurring concepts in the present investigation should be explained. Most of them occur in identical or closely related synonymous forms in the contemporaneous historical sources; but even when they – as a rule – thus possess empirical relevance, they will primarily be understood as analytically determined for the purposes of the current investigation.

As explained in the 'Author's note' above, in this book I use 'king', with a lower-case k, to denote the royal office, whereas 'King' (or 'Queen') refers to the temporal person who sat on the throne.[22] The concept of His Royal Majesty (*Kungl. Maj:t*, short for *Kunglig Majestät*) refers to governmental power as a whole, i.e. the king in Council. In analogy with the main argument of this book, it is necessary to distinguish between the individual and the office; but sometimes it is difficult or impossible to differentiate among all the capacities and guises of the king/the King/His Royal Majesty. In several cases, the use of these concepts is therefore arbitrary. Nor, for obvious reasons, is this analytic separation adhered to in the quotations.

In the present study, the concept of *the lords (herrarna)* refers to the members of the Magistracy other than the king. During the Age of Liberty, executive power was vested in His Royal Majesty, i.e. the king together with the sixteen Councillors of the Realm and the governors general. This group of men was often called *överheten*;

---

22 This practice is inspired by Ernst Kantorowicz, who also distinguished between 'king' and 'King', although the other way around; he wrote about 'those clarifying, if sometimes confusing, distinctions between the King's sempiternity and the king's temporariness'. Kantorowicz, p. 20.

on the basis of John Locke, among others, I have chosen to translate this with 'the Magistracy'.[23] In the strictest sense, only the king was included in the Magistracy, while other state functionaries – from the Councillors of the Realm to the lowest officials – were servants of the Magistracy. However, these concepts were rarely that rigorously applied; and 'the Magistracy', sometimes 'the exalted Magistracy' (*höga överheten*), usually meant the highest governing strata of society. This body of people may be collectively designated by the contemporaneous critical concept *the lords*, and they were often thought to be in opposition to the king or believed to hold the monarch as a political hostage. A common perception was that whereas the king represented the common good, the lords represented their own personal interests.

This book also speaks about *the common people* without providing a detailed definition of this concept. The term denotes, without any profound attempts at delimitation, peasants, workers, and soldiers, servants and poor widows, vagrants and criminals, and many, many others. Contemporaries used concepts such as the *common* or *ordinary peasantry* (*meniga allmogen* or *gemena allmogen*) as a collective term for these groups.

---

23 *Överheten* (*Obrigkeit* in German) was a fundamental concept in early modern Swedish Lutheran political culture. Somewhat surprisingly, it does not seem to have had the same central importance in English Protestant culture, and there are few correlations where the term can be substantiated in, for instance, English and Swedish Bible translations. Where the Swedish Bible uses *överheten*, the English Bible often uses 'the power'; but I have found this term too vague or too general in the present context. However, in his *Two Treatises on Government*, John Locke applied the concept *magistrate/magistrates* in a way that was both concrete and abstract, referring both to persons in power and to the ruling authorities in general, in the same way that *överheten* was used in Swedish. To point out just a few examples: Locke, *Two Treatises on Government*, I: §§ 66, 92, 129; II: § 2, pp. 188, 210, 236, 268. An English–Swedish dictionary from 1757 supplies this translation: 'MAGISTRATE, S. *öfwerhet, som har att bjuda och befalla*' ('[one] who orders and commands'); Jacob Serenius, *An English and Swedish Dictionary: [...]* (Harg and Stenbro: Peter Momma, 1757), no pagination. The term was also used in the same meaning in French, e.g. by Voltaire: 'Leur [the Swedes'] premier magistrat eut le nom de roi, titre qui, en différent pays, se donne à des puissances bien différentes; car en France, en Espagne, il signifie un homme absolu; et en Pologne, en Suède, en Angleterre, l'homme de la république.' Voltaire, 'Histoire de Charles XII, roi de Suède' (1731), in *Œuvres historiques*, ed. by René Pomeau, Bibliotheque de la Pléiade, 128 (Paris: Gallimard, 1957), p. 58.

The common people held as great a variety of opinions as the lords, and as a group they evinced quite as heterogeneous a composition. It is therefore impossible to say that the common people held particular opinions. Nevertheless, what unites all those who are more or less intuitively relegated to this category is the fact that they were usually the object rather than the subject of policy. Another important concept is *majesty* (*majestät*), from Latin *majestas*, 'exaltedness'. It is not possible to impose a concise and complete definition on this concept. Instead it may be said that one partial goal of the present investigation is to move closer to a definition that can be understood by today's readership. The concept was a central one in the eighteenth-century political vocabulary, but not even legal scholars could easily summarise its meaning. The professor of law David Nehrman (Ehrenstråle) of Lund University reasoned in the following manner on this issue:

> The word Majestas is used by all Scriptoribus Jur. Naturæ et publici, but few explain it clearly. I consider it unnecessary to detail the opinions of others, I will only state my own.
>
> I understand Majestas to mean the highest dignity, right, and power of the ruler, through the capacity of which he is the very highest, and has the right to govern the realm and exercise the rights that belong thereto in the way and manner that he has pledged in his Accession Charter, or that the established form of government allows.[24]

The concept of majesty was closely connected with, but not identical to, the *sovereignty* of the realm, its independence of other powers. Majesty was a symbolic means of sovereignty; but while the king could both have majesty and be sovereign, the state could be sovereign but not in itself have majesty. In monarchies, the king's majesty was therefore the primary expression of state sovereignty. In Sweden the concept of sovereignty became associated with royal absolutism, and it was therefore only used sparingly

---

24 [David Nehrman (Ehrenstråle)], 'Inledning till Jus Publicum, eller Swenska Etats Lagfarenheten', B 766, Kungliga biblioteket/National Library of Sweden, Stockholm (KB), 2:V, § 1 and § 3 ('Thet ordet Majestas brukas af alla Scriptoribus Jur. Naturæ et publici, men få förklara thet tydeligen. Jag håller för onödigt wara, at upräkna andras meningar, Jag will allenast säija min egen. Igenom Majestas förstår jag the regerandes högsta wärdighet, rätt och wälde, i förmågo hwaraf han är then alldrahögste, och äger styra Riket och öfwa the rättigheter, som thertill höra på sätt och wis, som han i sin försäkring utfäst, eller thet wedertagne Regieringssättet medgifwer').

during the Age of Liberty.[25] Conversely, the highness or majesty of the king was afforded a central position already in the Instrument of Government. The powers of the king were summed up in the *jura majestatica*, also called the king's *regal rights* or *regalities*. In European public law, decision-making power in a number of issues traditionally belonged to the sovereign. The components of these regal rights were relatively enduring. The regal rights concerning foreign policy included the right to start wars and conclude peace, as well as to enter into alliances and appoint envoys, while the domestic rights included collecting taxes, making laws, appointing officials, supervising the administration of justice and coining money.[26] These regal rights were an expression of the sovereignty of the state and could be exercised by the king, either alone or in collective and mediated forms established in the Constitution.

Finally, three additional concepts are important in order for us to understand the political mentality of the seventeenth and eighteenth centuries: *corporations*, *privileges* and *immunities*. Before the emergence of liberal individualism at the beginning of the nineteenth century (but with forerunners during the eighteenth century), politics was often considered a zero-sum game between the various interest groups of a society. These groups are usually referred to as *corporations*, and they might in concrete terms be estates of the realm – nobles, clergy, burghers and in Sweden also peasants – or, for instance, professional associations, such as trade guilds. Corporatist notions originated in Aristotelian ideas, but they were also fundamental in the ecclesiastical view of society. Each individual had his or her place in a collective unit – a household or a

---

25 Lindberg, pp. 88–94 (pp. 89–90).
26 See, e.g., the so-called 'Zedler's Lexikon': *Grosses vollständiges Universal-Lexicon aller Wissenschaften und Künste, welche bishero durch menschlichen Verstand und Witz erfunden und verbessert worden*, ed. by Jacob August Franckenstein and others, 68 vols (Leipzig and Halle: Johann Heinrich Zedler, 1731–54), XXI: *Mi–Mt* (1739), 'Monarch', column 996; *Encyclopédie, ou Dictionnaire raisonné des sciences, des arts et des métiers, par une société de gens de lettres*, 35 vols (Paris: Briasson, David, Le Breton, Durand, Panckoucke, Stoupe & Brunet; Neuchatel: Faulche; Amsterdam: Rey, 1751–80), V: *Do–Esy* (1765), 'Droits régaliens', p. 144; [David Nehrman (Ehrenstråle)], 'Inledning till Thet Swenska Jus Publicum Förklaradt i Publiques Lectioner', B 762, KB, § 2, chapter 7: 'Om Juribis Majestatis eller de höga Rättigheter som till den Kongl: Myndigheten höra'.

corporation. The household was governed by a master or guardian, and the interests of the corporation always took precedence over those of the individual. The corporation then protected the individual within its boundaries.

The interests of corporations were to a great extent maintained through *privileges*, a term originally from Latin that literally means 'private law'. Since at least the mid-fourteenth century, Sweden had been a unitary state in the sense that the same laws applied throughout the realm. In addition to this shared guiding principle, however, there were a large number of exceptional provisions – privileges – that could be awarded to a single individual or a corporation. The privileges of the nobility form one example of these exceptional benefits. All subjects were, in principle, obliged to pay taxes; but in practice, the nobility was exempted from this legal provision. (In reality, the nobility paid taxes, too; but this is partly a different issue.)

Corporatist thinking was thus based on the idea that society was made up of a number of collectives that safeguarded their own special interests. Here were analogies to the so-called humoral pathology, the medical theory of the four cardinal humours, a theory which also had its roots in Antiquity. In the body there were four fluids – blood, phlegm, choler or yellow bile, and melancholy or black bile – and human disease was caused by an imbalance among them. For example, too much blood led to sanguinity, which was cured by blood-letting. In the same way, harmony in a society was based on ideas of balance. In order to avoid one corporation dominating the others and thus upsetting the balance, corporate privileges had to be safeguarded from trespass by others through *immunities*. No outsider was allowed to influence the privileges of a group without its consent. According to natural law, humans were by origin independent individuals who were completely free from the interference of others. (Natural law was also an antique, originally Roman, concept based on the idea that there were certain innate or 'natural' legal provisions that were common to all people.) The original human condition without laws had led to insecurity for the weak and defenceless, and therefore it was believed that humans had given up some of their original liberty in exchange for protection. This surrender had been implemented by means of a social contract, which was handed down from one generation to the next. Even so, the basic theoretical position was that humans were immune from every form of external influence, and consent was required each time any part of their natural liberty was surrendered. Subsequent generations were then bound by this agreement.

The concepts of corporation, privilege and immunity are essential in the presentation below. They are to a certain extent analytical – the same ideas were frequently expressed by means of varying terminology; for instance, immunity might be phrased as *protection (from intrusion)* – but they were active and central components in eighteenth-century political thought. At the same time these concepts were, as has already been implied, on their way to being replaced by others. The emerging liberal ideas led to the individual being prioritised at the expense of the corporation, and in social thought the welfare of the individual came to be seen as a prerequisite for the welfare of the collective instead of the other way around. The perhaps most obvious rhetorical expression of this change is the fact that the concept of *subject* was increasingly replaced by *citizen* during the eighteenth century. This movement was not unambiguous, though, and as will be seen below, the monarchy was very much an institution that drew its historical nourishment from the political ideas of the past.

1
The royal authority

Since the days of Gustav II Adolf and the Thirty Years War, Sweden had been one of the great powers of Europe. This position of power, which lasted for a few generations, was lost in the protracted Great Northern War of 1700–1721. All of Sweden's neighbouring states joined Sweden's enemies at one time or another, but Charles XII (1682–1718) stubbornly refused to conclude a compromise peace. When he was killed at Fredrikshald in Norway late in the autumn of 1718, there was still no peace in sight, and trust in the highest political leadership was almost exhausted at all levels of society. Eighteen years of war had depleted the economic resources of the realm, and significant attrition in the ranks had had serious consequences for the entire population. Even if people in general had little insight into the larger political game, many people in the inner circles of the kingdom saw one tentative peace proposal after the other rejected by the King. In addition, from 1710 the enemies of Sweden had begun to encroach on the realm itself. In Scania in southern Sweden, the progress of the invading Danish army was successfully checked; but the occupation of Finland had been completed by 1714, and in the summer of 1719 pillaging enemy forces had reached the Swedish Baltic Sea coast.

Sweden had been governed as a royal absolutist state since 1680, and the Riksdag, the national parliamentary assembly with its four Estates – Nobles, Clergy, Burghers and Peasants – had been transformed into an exclusively consultative body. Charles XI, who ruled from 1672 to 1697, continued to regularly summon the Riksdag in order to explain and obtain support for his decisions; but it no longer had any decision-making powers. It briefly regained its authority when, after the untimely death of Charles XI in 1697, it declared the fifteen-year-old Charles XII to be legally competent; but after this declaration, the new King saw no reason to summon the Estates again. In both 1710 and 1714, the Estates made a few attempts to organise themselves after the fortunes of war had turned against Sweden, another reason being that Charles XII was far away from the realm; but these meetings were dissolved through royal decrees. The form of government did not offer any channels for criticising the political leadership. This was in itself not characteristic of the Caroline absolutism but of Aristotelian-Lutheran political culture as such, a culture that prescribed a statically hierarchical and corporate order in which the duty of obedience towards all authority was of fundamental importance. An obvious consequence was that the royal authority was above all questioning.

That conflicts and opposition could not be articulated does not mean that they did not exist. Within the machinery of the state, various groups safeguarded their own interests: civil servants, military commanders, the Council aristocracy, the ancient nobility and so on. Each of these groups had various reasons for opposing absolutism, which had few natural allies. In Denmark, for instance, the absolute kings were able to use a divide-and-conquer method that was based on support from both the Nobility and the Burghers and that relied on a large number of foreign advisers and officials. Conversely, the landed aristocracy in Sweden had seen their properties shrink through the Great Reduction (*reduktionen*) and to an increasing degree competed with Burghers and 'commoner persons of quality' (*ofrälse ståndspersoner*) for government posts. These latter groups were in their turn excluded from top positions, which were still reserved for the Nobility. The Clergy had long provided ideological support for the royal authority, but were basically dissatisfied with the church regime of the absolutism. At the 1714 Riksdag the Clergy, together with the Burghers, eagerly promoted the issue of peace negotiations with or without the approval of the king, and on this issue they had growing support from the military commanders. The Peasants had also supported the royal authority, but continual conscription and raised taxes, as well as a never-ending war, made even their loyalty wear thin.[1]

---

1 The Caroline form of government is discussed in Anthony F. Upton, *Charles XI and Swedish Absolutism* (Cambridge: Cambridge University Press, 1998). The best biography of Charles XII is still Ragnhild Marie Hatton, *Charles XII of Sweden* (London: Weidenfeld & Nicolson, 1968). On the 1710 and 1714 assemblies of the Estates, see Sven Grauers, *Riksdagen under den karolinska tiden*, Sveriges riksdag, I:4 (Stockholm: Victor Pettersons, 1932), pp. 126–43.

The divisions and disagreements among the different Estates were still too great for the formation of a real resistance party during the lifetime of Charles XII. At both of the two assemblies of the Estates that were convened during the war, distrust towards the Council was still considerable. The memory of aristocratic rule during the regency governments of the seventeenth century was still fresh in people's minds. What is certain, however, is that plans for constitutional change were already beginning to be formulated in several quarters while Charles XII was still alive. Oppositional expressions had been voiced at the 1710 committee meeting and the 1714 Riksdag. After the King's death in November 1718, discontent was immediately reflected in the measures taken against the primary representative of the absolutism: Georg Heinrich von Goertz, First Minister at the discretion of Charles XII. The person of the King was beyond reach; however, it was clear that the office in its Caroline form would not long survive his demise. The question that presents itself is how the monarchy could survive the death of Charles XII when this absolute ruler had destroyed all confidence in the royal authority during his twenty-one-year rule.

The question appears to have an obvious answer: of course the royal authority could not be abolished. The details surrounding the accession of a new monarch and the constitutional transformation that followed the death of Charles XII have been carefully investigated by the historian Lennart Thanner. The change was so sudden and dramatic that he has called it a revolution; but no alternatives to monarchy as a form of government seem to have been suggested, not even in passing.[2] The Swedish form of government is traditionally regulated in the Instrument of Government (*regeringsformen*). The current Instrument of Government from 1974 replaced an older one that had been in force since 1809. Before that, new Instruments of Government had been adopted every one or two generations: in 1634, 1660, 1719, 1720, 1772 and 1789 (during the absolutism of 1680–1718, the Instrument of Government was suspended). That Sweden was to be governed by a king was not explicitly stipulated until 1809. In all previous Instruments of Government it was too obvious to need articulation. But why was monarchy as a form of government so self-evident? What functions of the monarchy made it indispensable to the authors of the Constitution of 1719, even

---

2 Lennart Thanner, *Revolutionen i Sverige efter Karl XII:s död: Den inre-politiska maktkampen under tidigare delen av Ulrika Eleonora d.y:s regering* (Uppsala: Almqvist & Wiksell, 1953).

though the aim of their endeavour was to stymie the monarch's actual room to manoeuvre as far as possible?

When the sequence of events at the dissolution of the absolutism and the beginning of the Age of Liberty is analysed, abolition of the monarchy can be dismissed as a realistic alternative. In 1719 David Silvius, Secretary of the National Board of Trade (*kommerskollegium*), wrote what was to become the manifesto of the revolution. In this document he presented a formula that became axiomatic later in the Age of Liberty, namely that the Word of God prescribed an unconditional duty of obedience for the subjects, but not to any particular form of government. On the contrary, people lived under different forms of government: on the one hand republican (either democratic or aristocratic), and on the other monarchical (either limited or unlimited).[3] It was only the monarchical forms of government that were discussed in Sweden, and even if the dangers of absolutism had become apparent during the wars of Charles XII, people in leading circles wanted to preserve certain symbolic functions linked to the monarchy. What these functions were is the subject of this chapter.

Initially, the formal extent and capabilities of the royal authority will be investigated as they were expressed in the constitutional documents. Next, the symbolic appearances of the monarch in a number of areas will be discussed: religion, the administration of justice and the question of the sovereignty and continuity of the government authority.

The monarchs we will encounter are the following. Ulrika Eleonora, sister of Charles XII, who – although she lacked a formal right of succession – was appointed queen regnant after the death of her brother. She abdicated after just one year and handed over the throne to her husband, Prince Frederick of Hesse-Kassel, in

---

3 [David Silvius], 'Oförgripelige påminnelser angående Successions Rättigheten i Sweriges rike', D 837, KB, §§ 3, 20; the petition was printed in the following year. See also Jonas Nordin, *Ett fattigt men fritt folk: Nationell och politisk självbild i det svenska riket från sen stormaktstid till slutet av frihetstiden* (Eslöv: Symposion, 2000), p. 230; Per Nilsén, 'Die problematische königliche Alleinherrschaft und die verständnislosen Ausländer: Über die Bedeutung Jacob Wildes (1679–1755) für die Entwicklung des schwedischen Staatsrechts bis 1772', in *Geschichte und Perspektiven des Rechts im Ostseeraum: Erster Rechtshistorikertag im Ostseeraum 8.–12. März 2000*, ed. by Jörn Eckert and Kjell Å. Modéer, Rechtshistorische Reihe, 251 (Frankfurt am Main: Peter Lang, 2002), pp. 45–58.

February 1720. The couple's marriage was childless, and in 1744 Prince-Bishop Adolf Frederick of Holstein-Gottorp was elected heir to the throne of Sweden. With Louisa Ulrika of Prussia by his side, he reigned from 1751 to 1771, when their son Gustav III inherited the throne. On 19 August 1772, Gustav III staged a coup d'état which restored royal power and brought the Age of Liberty to an end.

The practical ambit of the royal authority

The documents that regulated the status of the royal authority at the beginning of the Age of Liberty were primarily the Instruments of Government, the Accession Charters and the Royal Elections Acts of 1719 and 1720, respectively. In addition there was Frederick's affirmation of 27 February 1720 where he, in the event that he was to be elected holder of the Crown, promised to adopt the Lutheran doctrine, defend the law and the liberty of the Estates, shun absolutist ways and not employ foreign advisers. The amended documents of 1720 were based on the corresponding documents from the year before; but regarding the status of the royal authority, they were more stringent on several important points.[4]

The constitutional additions and amendments that were made during the Age of Liberty were presented in the Royal Elections Act of 1743, the Accession Charters of 1751 and 1772 and the decisions of the Riksdag. They included successive restrictions of the exercise of executive royal authority; but they did not in any fundamental way alter the character of the monarchy, its ethos, which remained all but unchanged throughout the entire Age of Liberty.

The core of the Age of Liberty form of government was summarised in the preamble to the two versions of the Instrument of Government of 1719 and 1720: that the highness of His or Her Royal Majesty remain inviolate, the Council of the Realm be supported in its proper authority and the rights and liberties of the Estates be maintained. The wording harked back to the preface to the 1634 Instrument of Government, and continuity with this document was asserted, especially at the beginning of

---

4 All these documents are included in *Frihetstidens grundlagar och konstitutionella stadgar*, ed. by Axel Brusewitz (Stockholm: Norstedts, 1916).

the Age of Liberty.[5] The expression 'the rights and liberties of the Estates' referred to their participation in the making of laws and the drawing up of the Estimates (the national budget), as well as to the safeguarding of the immunities guaranteed in the Estate privileges. The relationship between the highness of the king and the authority of the Council was established in the crucial section 13, which remained unchanged between 1719 and 1720: 'The king shall govern his realm with, and thus not without, much less against, the counsel of the Council of the Realm.'[6] What these sections meant for the executive royal authority was, in brief, as follows.[7] All decisions made in the Council were to be majority decisions. The king (konungen) – the only concept used in the legal sources, notwithstanding the fact that the first monarch of the Age of Liberty was a queen – had the deciding vote when there was a minority of up to two votes. In fact, the relative weight of the King's vote increased between 1719 and 1720 because the number of Councillors was reduced from twenty-four to sixteen. When there was a full Council, as was required for dealing with urgent general matters of great importance to the welfare of the realm, the King's will was thus enforced with the approval of seven Councillors. Normally, however, the Council was split into two divisions, one of which dealt with matters of law and foreign policy, the other with matters of war and domestic civil matters. The former operated under the name of the Judicial Review Division (Justitierevisionen),

---

5 Lennart Linnarsson, 'Sveriges statsskick under frihetstiden: Några teser ur professor skytteanus Hermanssons föreläsningar i statskunskap på 1720-talet', in Festskrift till professor Skytteanus Axel Brusewitz utgiven till 60-årsdagen den 9 juni 1941, Skrifter utgivna av Statsvetenskapliga föreningen i Uppsala, 12 (Uppsala and Stockholm: Almqvist & Wiksell, 1941), pp. 3–19 (pp. 11–19).

6 Frihetstidens grundlagar, pp. 8, 27 ('Konunger äger styra rike sino med och således icke utom, mindre emot riksens råds råde').

7 See Alfred Bernhard Carlsson, Den svenska centralförvaltningen 1521–1809: En historisk öfversikt (Stockholm: K. L. Beckmans, 1913), pp. 118–20, 129–31; Fredrik Lagerroth, Frihetstidens maktägande ständer 1719–1772, Sveriges riksdag, I:5–6, 2 vols (Stockholm: Victor Pettersons, 1934), II: pp. 175–80; Fredrik Lagerroth, Den svenska monarkin inför rätta: En författningshistorisk exposé (Stockholm: Rabén & Sjögren, 1972), pp. 107–15; Per Nilsén, Att 'stoppa munnen till på bespottare': Den akademiska undervisningen i svensk statsrätt under frihetstiden, Rättshistoriskt bibliotek, I:59 (Lund: Institutet för rättshistorisk forskning, 2001), pp. 102–07.

and served as the highest court of appeal in the realm. In daily activities, the King's influence thus increased significantly because the quorum for each Council division was seven members (as stipulated in *regeringsformen* or Instrument of Government (RF) 1720, § 15). Thus, the King's policy prevailed with the approval of only three Councillors. In return, it was stipulated that the presence of the King was not absolutely necessary. If the King was indisposed or travelling, the kingdom was governed through the majority decisions of the Council (RF 1720, § 16).

There was a potential for a more personal type of influence in so-called Cabinet matters (RF 1720, § 20). These included individual applications that did not concern the realm or the justice system, as well as confirmations of the decisions of administrative boards and appointments of lesser officials. Matters of this kind were decided without voting and in the presence of only two Councillors. If the King in Cabinet dissented from the opinion of the administrative boards or nominated a different appointee than the one being proposed, the matter would be referred to the king in Council. Although the King actually almost always confirmed the decisions already made by the government offices, there were double control functions that were meant to prevent the formation of an inner ministry consisting of royal favourites.[8] The two Councillors were appointed according to a rolling schedule, and decisions were recorded and verified by the larger Council. In the event that the King might suddenly be overcome by a desire to make decisions while travelling or in the field, he was always to be accompanied by two Councillors.

His Royal Majesty's Councillors were a kind of supervisors or ephors who did not only have a right but also an express obligation to control and aid the King. They were to 'voluntarily, without waiting until they are consulted and summoned, call attention to the law of the realm' and, with a wording that originated in the 1602 Riksdag decision, 'advise as required by their office, but not rule' (RF 1720, § 14). The control function was guaranteed in part by the Estates participating in the appointment of the Council – the King had the right to choose, without taking a vote, from a proposed trio of men drawn up by the Estates (RF 1720, § 12); but

---

8 Cf. Samuel Åkerhielm's comments on this section in the acts of 1720, vol. 1, R 2392, Riksarkivet/Swedish National Archives, Stockholm (RA), fols 105^r–106^v.

this limited right of choice was soon even further reduced through various adjustments – and in part by the impossibility of removing Councillors.[9] This protection for the Council had been introduced as a safeguard against absolutism, but there was a contradiction here that would soon prove vexingly impractical. In order to obtain a strong mandate against the king, the inviolability of the Council was a prerequisite. In order to be able, in return, to control Councillors in their task as representatives of the Estates, some form of accountability was necessary. The Instrument of Government presupposed such accountability on the basis of criminal law, but not on political grounds.[10] As long as the Council was engaged in a power struggle with the King – that is, until the Riksdag of 1726–1727 – this was expedient; but when developments led to a form of parliamentary government, the inviolability of the Council turned out to be a major inconvenience. A Councillor could not be removed from his office unless he had violated laws or statutes. From 1738–1739 until the end of the Age of Liberty, so-called licentiation (*licentiering*) was therefore used as a permanent emergency solution. This procedure allowed a Councillor to be separated from the exercise of his office while still maintaining the formal dignity prescribed by the Instrument of Government.

There were two areas where the King could act independently without obtaining the consent of the Council. One was questions regarding the court and its staff, and the other was the right to grant noble status.

The court was the household of the King, and as its master he was able to govern servants independently and freely dispose of the funds allocated by the Riksdag for the court budget.[11] The court consisted of two parts, though: attendants, who were noble functionaries with real or titular duties, and domestics, who were commoner servants who performed the actual household labour. As has been pointed out by the historian Björn Asker, there was a porous boundary between the attendants and the machinery

---

9 For the procedure of selecting Councillors, see Lagerroth, *Frihetstidens maktägande ständer*, II, pp. 181–86.

10 The Council's accountability to the Estates was regulated to an even greater extent in the Riksdag Act (*riksdagsordningen*) of 1723, § 13.

11 The Instrument of Government (RF) of 1720, § 20; Karl Åmark, *Sveriges statsfinanser 1719–1809* (Stockholm: Norstedts, 1961), pp. 313–40.

of the state: the Marshal of the Realm (*överstemarskalken*), for instance, who was head of the court administration, became a Councillor of the Realm as a matter of course.[12] Court etiquette could also be a cause of rank-related quarrels which had political consequences. Such a conflict occurred in 1754, a few months after the royal family had moved into their new palace in Stockholm. On that occasion, the coach of the wife of the Chancery President was refused entry to the courtyard of the palace, in violation of the new court protocol and despite the fact that the authority of the Council, according to the Instrument of Government, was inseparable from that of the Crown. As a consequence, the measures adopted by Adolf Frederick in this matter were revoked, and he had to submit to being lectured on the limits of royal power before the sitting Council.[13]

This matter is characteristic of the position of the king during the Age of Liberty. The Council made an effort to maintain his symbolic highness as far as possible, and his consent was necessary even in the most trivial government matters. In the event that an interpretation was in dispute between the King and the Council, however, the latter held all the resources of power and commanded a varied set of means for enforcing its decisions in a way that also produced the appearance of formal correctness. The King's greatest asset in such conflicts was the sympathy of the general public, and the Council was hence anxious to prevent attention being drawn to these conflicts.

The area other than the court where the King was allowed independence was when he was granting noble status and when promoting someone to the rank of baron (*friherre*) or count (*greve*). The Instrument of Government called for the king, in a

---

12 Björn Asker, *Hovet: Historien om ett kungligt maskineri* (Lund: Historiska media, 2022) pp. 31–43. For the court, see also Fabian Persson, *Survival and Revival in Sweden's Court and Monarchy, 1718–1930* (Cham: Palgrave Macmillan, [2020]).

13 For this episode, which attracted a good deal of attention at the time, see Anders Johan von Höpken, *Riksrådet grefve Anders Johan von Höpkens skrifter*, ed. by Carl Silfverstolpe, 2 vols (Stockholm: Norstedts, 1890–93), I: *Minnes-anteckningar, tal, bref*, pp. 97–105; Louis De Geer, 'Minne af Anders Johan von Höpken: Uppläst i Svenska Akademien den 20 december 1881', in *Valda skrifter*, 2 vols (Stockholm: Norstedts, 1892), I, pp. 60–188 (pp. 90–96); Carl Gustaf Malmström, *Sveriges politiska historia från konung Karl XII:s död till statshvälfningen 1772*, 2nd edn, 6 vols (Stockholm: Norstedts, 1893–1901), IV, pp. 112–17.

strangely specific wording in what was supposed to be an eternally valid constitution, to limit these elevations to 'merely a few at his coronation [...] and thereafter no noblemen shall be created until the realm can permit such things'.[14] The latter diffuse qualifier is also surprising in this context. In practice, the interpretation of how many nobles the realm could permit was made within the House of Nobility, and quite a number of new noblemen were created during the reigns of both Frederick and Adolf Frederick (152 and 201 new noble families, respectively).

Formally, the King could decide on ennoblements without their having been proposed by the Council and without hearing the Council. Although the laws were seemingly clear on this point, it was a regality encumbered by much ambiguity throughout the period. It became the established practice for the King to ennoble people in a number determined by the Estates, and often according to their recommendations. The ennoblement progressed through four steps: a recommendation by the King, approval by the Nobility, the issuing by the King of a patent of nobility creating the new nobleman, and the induction of the newly ennobled family into the House of Nobility. Because the King and the corporation of the Nobility balanced each other in this manner, the question of when a person had actually achieved noble status became a subject of contention from time to time. A person who had been appointed by

---

14 RF 1720, § 44 ('allenast några få vid des kröning [...] och blifva sedermera inga adelsmän giorde, till des riket sådant kan tillåta'); this was an addition conditional on the situation in comparison to the more generally held wording of RF 1719, § 35. The Burgher and Peasant Estates protested against the unusual subclause, which they claimed to have deleted when the Instrument of Government was examined within their Estates; *Borgarståndets riksdagsprotokoll från frihetstidens början*, ed. by Nils Staf and others, 12 vols (Uppsala: Almqvist & Wiksell; Stockholm, Riksdagsförvaltningen, 1945–), I: *1719–1720* (1945), appendix 20, pp. 510–11. Nothing was said in the privileges of the Nobility of 1723 concerning the regulations for creating new noble titles. See also [David Nehrman (Ehrenstråle)], 'Inledning till Thet Swenska Jus Publicum Förklaradt i Publiques Lectioner', B 762, KB, 2:VII, §§ 33–34, fols 89–90, cf. *ibid.*, §§ 38–39. For more information on this issue, see Hugo Valentin, *Frihetstidens riddarhus: Några bidrag till dess karakteristik* (Stockholm: Gebers, 1915), pp. 237–52, 258–85; Erik Naumann, 'Adeln som riksstånd under 1700- och 1800-talen', in *Sveriges riddarhus: Ridderskapet och adeln och dess riddarhus*, ed. by Carl Hallendorf (Stockholm: Historiska förlaget, 1926), pp. 314–16.

the King might still be denied induction into the House of Nobility and thus lack representation even though he had obtained noble privileges. He thus had the capacity of a nobleman in an economic and legal, but not in a political, sense.

The legal status in this case was complicated, something that may have contributed to the issue never having received a well-thought-out formal solution. Nobility was to be considered an official reward, and for this reason it could not be left to the discretion of the Nobility themselves; that would amount to leaving the power of public appointment in the hands of a corporation. In return, the appointments were a means of recruiting favourites and modifying the balance among the Estates; therefore, the power of appointment could not be left to the free disposition of the King. It is true that at the drawing up of the 1719 Instrument of Government, it was stated that the monarch would not be deprived of the right of rewarding and of doing good; but Ulrika Eleonora made too extensive use of this right, appointing no fewer than 190 new noble families during her single year as ruler (Figure 1).[15]

That the rights of the King – at least formally speaking – were not balanced by the power of the Council in this issue may possibly have been because the Council itself could also be considered a corporation of the Nobility, which made it biased in this context. A certain analogy may be found here in the fact that the Councillors lacked the right to vote in the House of Nobility: as Councillors they were the representatives of the Estates and thus could not act as eligents (electors) for themselves. Nevertheless, the creation of new noblemen seems to have occurred according to a praxis that was acceptable to most of the stakeholders involved: the House of Nobility was successful in safeguarding their benches against overwhelming encroachment; there were certain openings for commoners who aspired to be raised to the Nobility; and the king maintained his nominal influence over the process.[16]

---

15 Cf. *En Ärlig Swensk* (Stockholm: Historiographi regni, 1755), pp. 871–75.

16 When, in 1762, the Nobility eventually completely refused to introduce newly ennobled families, this had far-reaching consequences for politics in the last decade of the Age of Liberty. For more information on this issue, see Nordin, *Ett fattigt men fritt folk*, p. 393, and the literature referred to therein. On the representation of the State Councillors, see Valentin, pp. 177–83.

ULRICA ELEONORA
Sweriges, Göthes och Wändes Drottning etc. Landt-Grefwinna til Hesfen etc.
Född d. 23 Jan. 1688. Död d. 24. Nov. 1741.
Schröder Pinxit. *Cura et Impenfis Direct. Petri Momma .* *Bergqvist Sculpsit*

Figure 1 The sovereign Queen. Ulrika Eleonora the Younger. Engraving by Carl Erik Bergqvist after Georg Engelhardt Schröder. Engraved after 1741 at the Royal Printer Peter Momma's own expense. Photo: Björn Green, Kungliga biblioteket/National Library of Sweden (KB).

The constitutional function of the king

As was shown above, the Council was in all essential political functions on an equal footing with the king, whose closest comparison would be to a chairman of the board. Gustav III identified the crux of the matter when he supposedly once said that the Council was in reality the king of Sweden – 'le senat a été effectivement roi de Suède'.[17] In spite of the king thus being non-essential for governmental power, it can immediately be noted that he was in no way non-essential in the state. The kingdom could not be governed without a king. In a proposal for a constitution drawn up soon after the death of Charles XII, the Supreme Power (*Högsta Väldet*) was said to consist of eight main elements, both foreign (to conduct wars, negotiate peace, enter into alliances and appoint emissaries) and domestic (to levy taxes, make laws, administer justice and appoint officials).[18] These functions may be recognised as the traditional regalities. The Supreme Power was, according to the not fully developed constitutional proposal, the aggregate of the government authorities, i.e., the king, the Council and the Estates. Although the royal authority obviously had to be balanced so that all governmental functions rested primarily either with the Council or with the Estates, the king's participation was nevertheless necessary in all respects. The proposal pinpoints the indispensable roles of the king within the kingdom and outside it, as well as the dualism between concrete and transcendent ideas that characterised these roles. If the individual elements of the Supreme Power could be expressed in tangible points that together constituted the government authority, the king was a symbolic incarnation of the impartiality and independence of the state.

In a document commissioned by the ruling Hat party from the middle of the Age of Liberty, Birger Frondin, University Librarian in Uppsala, classified forms of governments as aristocracies (council governments), democracies (estate governments) and monarchies. The fundamentals of this classification are derived from Aristotle,

---

17 Quoted in Gudmund Göran Adlerbeth, *Historiska anteckningar*, ed. by [Elof Tegnér], 2 vols (Stockholm: Beijers, 1892), I, p. 109n.

18 *Handlingar angående revolutionen i Sverige 1718–1719*, ed. by Lennart Thanner, Historiska handlingar, 36:1 (Stockholm: Kungl. Samfundet för utgifvande af handskrifter rörande Skandinaviens historia, 1954), p. 6. For the attribution of this project and other related matters, see Thanner, *Revolutionen i Sverige*, pp. 53–54.

but the line of reasoning and the choice of words display great similarities to the lectures of David Nehrman, professor of law at Lund
University.[19] From these so-called simple forms of government,
Frondin then derived mixed or composite forms of government,
where the three 'moral entities' ('moraliska personerna', i.e. 'the
bodies of the state') counterbalanced one another to varying
degrees. This made the designation of these forms of government
arbitrary. 'Thus if a Council should share the Supreme Authority
with a King, one can, without making an error in the main, call this
form of government an aristocracy mixed with a monarchy as well
as the other way around.' But, Frondin continued, because one of
the state bodies usually tended to have precedence over the others,
it was reasonable to name that form of government after the one
entity that possessed the greatest privileges. 'This notwithstanding,
the veneration of crowned heads, both in our own and in earlier
times, has resulted in a form of government usually having been
called a monarchy wherever there is a King present, even if the
Council or the Estates have in reality possessed the most prominent
rights of the Supreme Power in this respect.' Frondin emphasised
that 'the splendour of the crown and the lustre of the sceptre, as
well as the glorious names and the preference that by honour and
dignity are usually, even in the most limited monarchies, given to
kings' should not lead to the erroneous conclusion that the king for
this reason possesses the greatest power. The Supreme Authority
may instead rest with the Council or the Estates 'although they
do not bear the name of Magistrates and governing persons, nor do
they allow laws and regulations to be issued in their name, but to
be signed and issued by the king.'[20]

---

19 [Nehrman], 'Inledning till Thet Swenska Jus Publicum', B 762, KB. Aristotle
divided the forms of government according to a trichotomy with the good
forms of government, monarchy, aristocracy and constitutional order
(*politeia*) on the one hand and their degenerate forms, tyranny, oligarchy
and democracy, on the other; Aristotle, *Politics*, with an English translation
by H. Rackham (Cambridge, MA, and London: Harvard University Press,
1944), e.g., book IV:II, pp. 280–85.

20 [Birger Frondin], *Riksdags-manna rätt: Til dess grund och beskaffenhet
föreställd* (Stockholm: Lars Salvius, 1747), § 5, quotations on pp. 28–29, 32
('Således om ett Råd är med en Konung deltagande uti den Högsta
Magten, kan man, utan fel i hufvud-saken, kalla Regerings-sättet så väl en
Aristocratie blandad med Monarchie, som tvärtom'; 'Men detta oaktadt,
har dock vördnaden för krönta Hufvuden både i våra och föregående tider
gjort, at ehvarest en Konung varit, har Regerings-sättet merendels blifvit

It was unusual for somebody to speak so plainly about the rights and highness of the king during the Age of Liberty. In most contexts, the indispensable role of the king in the state system was emphatically foregrounded, but it was above all the immaterial and symbolic functions that were pursued. These were representations of the highness and inviolability of the government authority and were especially important in two areas: within the realm they were manifested in the enforcement of the law, and in international relations the supreme majesty was a symbol of the sovereign kingdom. In both cases, the essential aspects were thus security and protection – the original and most basic functions of a government authority. The law and sovereignty will be discussed below, as the two most important spheres of activity of the royal authority; but first a few words about religion.

Religion

The basic foundation of the realm was generally thought to be the perpetuation of the true religion. The Instruments of Government from 1634 to 1809 presented religious unity as the primary source of the unity of the kingdom in the very first section. This is worth emphasising because religion was an area where the Instrument of Government in the Age of Liberty did not attribute an inherent function to the king. Nor were religious issues usually included among the regalities in foreign constitutional law. In the Instrument of Government, in which the basic social contract for Sweden was formulated, the Lutheran faith was a necessary prerequisite for the king; but the king was not a necessary prerequisite for the true faith. The Lutheran confession was a condition for the king's being inaugurated into his office, and he was bound to safeguard the pure Evangelical faith. However, he was unable to affect the articles of faith and was governed by their principles in the same way as were his

---

kalladt en Monarchie, fast än ock Rådet eller Ständerne i sjelfva verket ägt de förnämsta rättigheter af den Högsta Magten derutinnan'; 'Kronas prakt och Spirans glants, samt de äre-namn och det företräde af heder och värdighet, som i alla, äfven de mäst inskränkta Monarchier pläga lämnas Konungarne'; 'fastän de icke bära namnet af Öfverhet och regerande Personer, ej eller låta Lagar och Förordningar utgå i sit namn, utan af Konungen underteknas och utfärdas').

subjects.[21] The official duties of the king belonged to the temporal plane. This dimension is also interesting when studying the coronation ritual, which will be discussed in the next chapter. The act of anointing was important for inaugurating the king into his office, but it was not a confirmation of any exalted religious obligations. How slight the importance of the royal authority was to religion is clearly illustrated by the fact that the Reformist Frederick – in spite of his, to all appearances, long-standing aspirations towards the Crown of Sweden – did not think it worth his while to convert until one week before acceding to the throne.

Even during the Caroline era religion took precedence, so to speak, over the king. This was the single area where the Law Commission, appointed in 1686 in order to draw up a replacement for the medieval Law of the Realm (*Landslagen*), had ventured to suggest limitations to the absolute monarchy. When working on the Royal Code, the officials involved approved of a formulation that said that the king should profess the Lutheran faith; and they also discussed a limitation on the rights of royal children to marry outside their own denomination.[22] The Swedish absolute monarchs were subordinated to religion in a stricter sense than, for instance, those of Denmark. In Denmark, the monarch was Lutheran by tradition and conviction. The first paragraph in the Danish Royal Law (*Kongeloven*), by which the absolute monarchy was formalised in 1665, decreed that the Augsburg Confession would endure for a thousand generations in the realms of the Danish king. Both Frederick IV and Christian VI were, however, drawn to a Pietism that was partly in opposition to the state church; nor could anything or anyone prevent the Kings of the country from marrying Queens of other faiths, as the marriage of Christian V to the intractably Reformist Charlotte Amalie demonstrates. Even during the Age of Liberty in Sweden, a King's marriage was considered to be his own private affair, something in which the Estates did not formally interfere. They did, however, retain the right of veto,

21 [Nehrman], 'Inledning till Thet Swenska Jus Publicum', B 762, KB, 1:IV, §§ 36–42, fols 33–35.
22 *Förarbetena till Sveriges rikes lag 1686–1736*, ed. by Wilhelm Sjögren, 8 vols (Uppsala: Almqvist & Wiksell, 1900–09), II: *Lagkommissionens protokoll 1694–1711* (1901), p. 86; [Nehrman], 'Inledning till Thet Swenska Jus Publicum', B 762, KB, 2:IX, § 21, 2:X, §§ 19, 22–23, fols 110, 114–15.

votum exclusivum, in the event that the intended queen was of the wrong religious persuasion.[23]

During the Age of Liberty, the highest practical ecclesiastical authority rested with the Estate of the Clergy in the Riksdag, the so-called *consistorium regni* (consistory of the realm). The Clergy not only exercised control over the Word and the sacraments, but also regained much of the ecclesiastical right of appointment that had been expropriated by the absolute monarchs. All the parishes that had been declared royal were once again subordinated to the respective diocesan board. The exclusive power of the king over the appointment of bishops was abolished. Instead, the dioceses nominated three candidates from among whom the king in Council made his choice, in the same manner as with other high offices.[24]

The king in Council was formally the head of the temporal church – even though that was of decreasing practical importance – but the King as a person was, like the rest of the general public, subject to religion. It is true that the three opening sections of all Accession Charters between 1719 and 1772 prescribed in detail, and at length, that the king should safeguard the pure clear Word of God and protect the Lutheran faith of his subjects. However, these may be considered to be safeguard provisions in the defence of the spiritual welfare of the realm and its subjects rather than an area where the king had special tasks to perform. That is particularly apparent in the affirmation of Frederick, in which he pledged not to lead anybody to apostasy of religion by 'enticement or persuasion' ('lockande eller trugande'). On religious matters the king was not above his subjects, and he had no preferential right of interpretation; on the other hand, he did have control of the means to promote the proper faith, and through his example he could contribute to keeping the Evangelical faith pure and unadulterated.[25] The king 'has many millions of people to protect', said the political

23 [Nehrman], 'Inledning till Thet Swenska Jus Publicum', B 762, KB, 2:VIII, §§ 4–6, fol. 106.
24 Hilding Pleijel, *Karolinsk kyrkofromhet, pietism och herrnhutism 1680–1772*, Svenska kyrkans historia, 5 (Stockholm: Svenska kyrkans diakonistyrelses bokförlag, 1935), pp. 246–52, 392–97; Harry Lenhammar, *Individualismens och upplysningens tid*, Sveriges kyrkohistoria, 5 (Stockholm: Verbum, 2000), pp. 34–42.
25 See, e.g., Carl Fredrik Scheffer's exposition in Fredrik Lagerroth, 'En frihetstida lärobok i gällande svensk statsrätt', *Statsvetenskaplig tidskrift för politik, statistik, ekonomi*, 40 (1937), 185–211 (p. 189); Christian König,

periodical *En Ärlig Swensk* ('An Honest Swede'), which presented the views of the ruling Hat party on the form of government. 'He should provide for their temporal, and especially eternal, happiness.' A political handbook written by the attorney counsel (*advokatfiskalen*) Isac Faggot maintained that the 'most prominent part of ecclesiastical governance is wielded by the king, because through his officials he provides the strictest supervision, so that his subjects, for the good of their souls, conduct themselves well'.[26] In some respects, this state of affairs resembled the king's role in the nation's defence: he had a duty to protect and save his kingdom if it was attacked, but he did not have the right to start a war of aggression (RF 1720, §§ 5–6).

The fact that the king often made generally formulated religious references when addressing his subjects did not mean that he had any special or indispensable responsibility for the spiritual welfare of the realm.[27] This was only a part of the dominant political rhetoric – and it was probably to a large extent based on sincere religious convictions.

Lärdoms-öfning: Tredje tomen angående lagfarenheten i kyrko-saker, *bergs-saker och några missgerningsmål* (Stockholm: Lars Salvius, 1746), chapter 2, 'Om Regeringen i andeliga saker', esp. pp. 8–12.
26 *En Ärlig Swensk,* p. 262 ('[Konungen] har många millioner menniskor at wårda [...] Han bör sörja för deras timeliga, och i synnerhet ewiga lycksalighet.'); see also pp. 336–44 and subsequent pages; [Isac Faggot], *Swea rikes styrelse efter grund-lagarne* (Stockholm: Johan Georg Lange, 1768). p. 75 ('[den] förnämsta delen af Kyrkostyrelsen utöfwar Konungen, då han genom sine Ämbets-Män, håller den strängaste wård, at Undersåtarne på själenes wägnar hafwa sin rätta skötsel').
27 It is precisely the spiritual responsibilities of the kings of the Age of Liberty that have been foregrounded by Göran Malmstedt. I feel that Malmstedt's representation is a simplified interpretation of formulaic rhetoric. See Göran Malmstedt, 'Frihetstidens karismatiska kungar', in *Maktens skiftande skepnader: Studier i makt, legitimitet och inflytande i det tidigmoderna Sverige,* ed. by Börje Harnesk (Umeå: Institutionen för historiska studier, 2003), pp. 75–89 (pp. 81, 86). See also Elisabeth Reuterswärd, *Ett massmedium för folket: Studier i de allmänna kungörelsernas funktion i 1700-talets samhälle,* Studia historica Lundensia, 2 (Lund: Historiska institutionen, 2001), p. 122, for a similar line of reasoning. The Swedish kings as Evangelical princes are also discussed by Pasi Ihalainen, *Protestant Nations Redefined: Changing Perceptions of National Identity in the Rhetoric of the English, Dutch and Swedish Public Churches, 1685–1772,* Studies in Medieval and Reformation Traditions: History, Culture, Religion, Ideas, 109 (Leiden and Boston: Brill, 2005), pp. 360–66.

The professor of law David Nehrman clarified the limits of the king's supervision of religion:

That which is internal [to man] in this as well as in several other matters, does not belong under the eminent governance of the King, it cannot be governed through advice and power; nor does it create a disturbance in the Republic; but external disturbances and madness can and should be controlled.[28]

In other words, the king had no control over personal faith; but when religious schismatics created social unrest, it was his duty and responsibility to intervene. He was to govern on issues of public order but not on issues of private conscience.

The connection between religion and the royal authority may be viewed from the opposite perspective as well, being regarded as an instrument of legitimation. Even so, ideas concerning the divine origin of the power of the Magistracy, expressed as a royal authority by the grace of God, form an issue connected to ways in which the image of the king was conveyed, and will hence be discussed in a later context. Here, it should only be briefly observed that the historian Mikael Alm – in general terms, and without reference to a particular time – speaks of a 'divine element' in the royal authority. However, he refers primarily to an inherited symbolic language, maintaining that the religious element declined significantly in this area as well during the eighteenth century. In addition, the rhetoric appears to have varied depending on the target group, and religious connections were at their most prominent in media and contexts that included broader social groups. Towards the end of the century, Alm argues, religion had largely lost its politically legitimising potential.[29] This tendency can be discerned already during the Age of Liberty. Pure Evangelical doctrine was emphasised formulaically in connection with the royal authority, but no obligations to protect religion in legislation and in constitutional law were articulated. In the royal ordinances, it was

28 [Nehrman], 'Inledning till Thet Swenska Jus Publicum', B 762, KB, 2:VII, § 9, fol. 82 ('Thet som inwärtes är så wäl i thetta som flere ärender, hörer eij under Konungens höga styrssel, det kan eij genom råd och macht regeras; det oroar eij [h]eller Republiquen; Men utwärtes oro och galenskap kan och bör styras').

29 Mikael Alm, *Kungsord i elfte timmen: Språk och självbild i det gustavianska enväldets legitimitetskamp 1772–1809* (Stockholm: Atlantis, 2002), pp. 40–41, 165–73, 349.

also natural for the king as a benign ruler to provide paternalistic exhortations about religion, but he was not closer to God than any other person in the priesthood of all believers.

The law

After the opening section of the Instrument of Government – which established the central importance of religion, but did not assign any specific responsibilities in that respect to the king – came the almost equally central statement that 'it is incumbent on His Royal Majesty to fortify, love, and protect law, justice and truth' ('Kongl. Maij:t tilhörer lag, rätt och sanning at styrckia, älska och giöma'). This wording harked back to the Royal Code in the Law of the Realm and had been part of the Coronation Oath since the Middle Ages. Expressed here was a regality that summed up the key role of the king in domestic affairs.[30]

Law and justice were among the more tangible branches of state governance, but they were also an idea. The law as an idea may be said to be a covenant on the forms of interpersonal coexistence, and it gains legitimacy through its origin, function and permanence. The idea thus presupposes that the law has been accepted by way of general agreement; that it is applied without arbitrariness; and – in part as a consequence of the former – that it is permanent. In Sweden during the Age of Liberty, the king functioned as the guarantor of this idea. Free of Estate-related interests and personally elevated above law and justice, he saw to it that the administration of justice in the realm was characterised by impartiality. This was to a large extent accomplished on a symbolic level. In reality the King – the physical individual – had little control over the administration of justice, but through the Judicial Review Division His Royal Majesty – the king in Council – was the highest court of appeal and thus in fact the highest interpreter of law in the realm. Consequently, contempt of court and lack of respect

---

30 Nordin, *Ett fattigt men fritt folk*, pp. 115–18. For the Crown and the law, see [Nehrman], 'Inledning till Thet Swenska Jus Publicum', B 762, KB, 2:VII, §§ 17–27, fols 84–88. For a position contrary to this, see Joachim Östlund, *Lyckolandet: Maktens legitimering i officiell retorik från stormaktstid till demokratins genombrott* (Lund: Sekel, 2007), pp. 139–40, 143. Östlund feels that the Riksdag during the Age of Liberty took over the king's role as the ultimate legal guarantor. As will be made clear below, I believe that this idea is incorrect.

for the judicial system were crimes of lese-majesty. In a report by
the Judicial Review Division concerning a case where the accused
had refused to abide by the decision of the Finance Chamber (*kammarkollegiet*) and by the ordinance issued by the late Charles XI,
it was, for instance, said that 'he has failed to show the deference
of a loyal subject and has transgressed against the power, honour
and sovereignty of the most illustrious King and thereby committed
Crimen læsæ Maj:tis [the crime of lese-majesty]'.[31]

In purely practical terms, though, the supervision of justice
could have been performed by the Council without interference
from the king. What was troublesome according to the typical
Age of Liberty way of looking at things was that the highest judges
were themselves subject to the law, and in addition to that they
could be replaced. The Council could function only as the guardian
of the original agreement on the law, while the majesty of the king
was the primary – or indeed the only – safeguard against imperma-
nence and an arbitrary administration of justice. By requiring the
king's signature for ratification, the incorruptibility of the decisions
was thus confirmed.[32]

The combination of symbolism and reality permeated the entire
Instrument of Government. The king symbolically reinforced law,

---

31 Justititerevisionen/Judicial Review Division to Svea Court of Appeal, 1
   July 1725, in the 1725 registry of the Judicial Review Division, RA, fols
   693ʳ-693ᵛ ('han sin undersåtelige wördnad utur acht låtit, och sig, emot
   Högstb:te Konungs macht, heder och wälde swårl. förgripit samt därmedelst
   Crimen læsæ Maj:tis begått'). Similar examples: Judicial Review Division
   to Göta Court of Appeal, 19 February 1724; Judicial Review Division to
   Åbo Court of Appeal, 11 February 1726; Judicial Review Division to Åbo
   Court of Appeal, 18 August 1731. All cases according to the registry of the
   Judicial Review Division, RA.
     The lines of reasoning here and in the rest of this chapter are based
   on Ernst Kantorowicz's rich exposé on the double forms of manifestation of the (English) royal authority to a greater extent than is possible
   to support with examples in footnotes. His extensive and inspiring
   work – originally published in 1957 – is indispensable to anyone wishing
   to understand the ancient and medieval roots of pre-modern European
   constitutional law: Ernst H. Kantorowicz, *The King's Two Bodies: A Study
   in Mediaeval Political Theology*, with a new preface by William Chester
   Jordan (Princeton: Princeton University Press, 1997 [1957]).
32 See, e.g., Christian König, *Lärdoms öfning; sjunde tomen, om stats-
   kunskapen, Swerges rikes ungdom, til tjenst* (Stockholm: Lars Salvius,
   1748), pp. 91, 136–37; *En Ärlig Swensk*, pp. 150–52, 169–73, 836–37;
   C. F. Scheffer in Lagerroth, 'En frihetstida lärobok', pp. 189–91.

justice and truth, which were actually maintained by the Judicial Review Division. By and large, the King in Cabinet was merely able to confirm the decisions already made by government offices; but both symbolically and in reality, the function of the Cabinet was that His Royal Majesty controlled the work of the government offices without requiring the attention of the entire Council. According to *En Ärlig Swensk*, the second section of the Instrument of Government gave the king of Sweden greater power than the most absolute monarch. In order to reinforce law and justice, he had the highest degree of punitive authority. No absolute monarch could demand greater authority without being called a tyrant. This line of reasoning invites comparison with Montesquieu's discussion of the status of laws in a monarchical form of government. In a monarchy, he claimed, the prince was the source ('la source') of all political and civil power. The existence of intermediary powers ('pouvoirs intermédiaires', 'subordonnés et dépendants') did not alter this state of affairs.[33]

The king's role was primarily that of an administrator of justice, not a creator of laws; but this was an idea that only slowly took root. In actuality, the Instrument of Government of the Age of Liberty had an unclear line of demarcation between judicial and legislative powers, and His Royal Majesty was very much involved in the latter. According to the fourth section of the Instrument of Government, laws could not 'be passed and imposed on the Estates against their consent, acceptance, and approval' ('stifftas och ständerne påträngas emot deras ja, samtycke och vedertagande'). In exceptional circumstances, such a procedure might be permitted between the sessions of the Riksdag; but such decisions would then have to be approved at the next Estate Assembly. From the wording

---

33 *En Ärlig Swensk*, pp. 286–87, 290–99, see also pp. 328–29; Montesquieu, *De l'esprit des lois* (1748), book 2, chapter 4. The role of the king as the guardian of the law was emphasised, for instance, by 'Eudippes' in a polemic against 'Aristides' in a widely circulated polemical pamphlet from 1722, which defended the restrictions on the royal authority; see the transcript in the Engeströmska handskriftsamlingen/Engeström manuscript collection, Handlingar rörande konung Fredriks regering/Documents regarding the reign of King Frederick, 1, B.II.2.19, KB, fols 88[r], 93[v], 101[v] and elsewhere. See also Ingemar Carlsson, *Frihetstidens handskrivna politiska litteratur: En bibliografi*, Acta bibliothecae universitatis Gothoburgensis, 9 (Gothenburg: Göteborgs universitetsbibliotek, 1967), no. 62, which lists more than twenty contemporaneous copies.

of the Accession Charter of 1720, however, one gets the impression that this legislative procedure was in fact considered to be the norm, i.e. that the initiative came from the king and that the Estates merely looked out for their own immunities:

> I shall [...] make no new law or impose it on the Estates, nor transform or repeal any old and established law without the advice of the Council of the Realm and the consent and acceptance of the lower Estates[.][34]

This unclear division between executive and judicial powers would be adjusted through shifts in praxis over the course of the Age of Liberty. In several theoretical expositions it was explained that the Estates alone had the right to make laws. The role of the king was merely to safeguard the laws that in reality proceeded from the people. But even on the basis of new fundamental motives and with an altered decision-making procedure, the laws continued to be issued in the name of His Royal Majesty and enter into force through his command.[35]

A common misunderstanding regarding the Age of Liberty is that the almost sacrosanct nature of the Instrument of Government excluded all constitutional revision. This idea is based on the dictum, often repeated during this period, that the fundamental laws could not be *changed*, only *improved*.[36] To be sure, the Instrument of Government was never adjusted as far as its content was concerned; but because decisions of the Riksdag were placed on an equal footing with the Constitution, this put the Estates in a position to interpret the Instrument of Government, and these interpretations functioned as constitutional improvements. (Here, a comparison with the unchangeable Constitution of the United

---

34 Accession Charter (*Konungaförsäkran*), 22 March 1720, § 18. Cf. Accession Charter 1751, § 17, and Accession Charter 1771, § 17 ('Jag skall [...] ingen ny lag göra eller ständerne påtränga, eij heller någon gammal och vedertagen lag förvandla eller afskaffa förutan riksens råds råde samt menige ständernes ja och samtycke'). Christian König avoided this issue by locating the power of legislation in the 'Supreme Authority', which was not clearly specified; König, *Lärdoms öfning; sjunde tomen*, p. 91.

35 Lagerroth, *Frihetstidens maktägande ständer*, II, pp. 236–53; Lagerroth, *Den svenska monarkin*, pp. 108–09; the petition of Bishop Johan Browallius of 1752, in Malmström, *Sveriges politiska historia*, IV, p. 455; *En Ärlig Swensk*, e.g. pp. 379, 381, 387, 898, 962–63.

36 See, for instance, Michael Roberts, *The Age of Liberty: Sweden 1719–1772* (Cambridge: Cambridge University Press, 1986), pp. 61–62, 66–67.

States and its amendments lies close at hand.) The Instrument of Government, like the medieval Law of the Realm and its 1734 successor, were thus simply foundational legislative documents. When necessary, they were explained through royal ordinances, letters patent and resolutions; but it would be a long time before such additions to the law of 1734 were entered directly into the statute book, which was not supposed to be subject to change. (For this reason, the Law Commission had deliberately excluded policy ordinances and economic ordinances, which were considered more dependent on current circumstances, from the statute book.) Through parliamentary decisions and in other ways, the Age of Liberty therefore saw a continuous revision of the Constitution. The legal interpretations that His Royal Majesty was for practical reasons allowed to make between parliamentary sessions would then require subsequent approval by the Estates in order to remain in force. While it was the Estates that actually made the laws, these laws were always presented to the king for signature and issued in his name. In other words, the king continued to be the symbolic guarantor of the laws.[37]

Sovereignty

The exaltedness of the king was a guarantee not only for impartiality in the administration of justice, but also for the independence of the realm.[38] This was the king's most important function and the

---

37 On the power of legislation, see RF 1719, § 4; RF 1720, § 4; Accession Charter 1720, § 6; Accession Charter 1751, § 5; Riksdag Act 1723, § 20; 'Kongl. Maj:ts Förordning, til befrämjande af Lagarnes behöriga werkställighet bland Rikets Embetsmän och öfriga Undersåtare', in *Utdrag utur alle ifrån den 7. decemb. 1718.[–1794] utkomne publique handlingar, placater, förordningar, resolutioner och publicationer, [...]*, ed. by Reinhold Gustaf Modée, 15 vols (Stockholm: Lorentz Ludwig Grefing; Kungl. tryckeriet, 1742–1829), VIII (1795), pp. 274–313.

38 [Nehrman], 'Inledning till Thet Swenska Jus Publicum', B 762, KB, 2:V, §§ 3–9. '[I]n being governed by the king the realm governed itself', writes J. G. A. Pocock, words that apply equally well to the Swedish and to the British monarchies; J. G. A. Pocock, 'Monarchy in the Name of Britain: The Case of George III', in *Monarchisms in the Age of Enlightenment: Liberty, Patriotism and the Common Good*, ed. by Hans Blom, John Christian Laursen and Luisa Simonutti (Toronto, Buffalo and London: Toronto University Press, 2007), pp. 285–302 (p. 287).

one that was hardest to replace. Still, compared with the administration of justice the actual intervention of the king was even slighter, while his symbolic role was all the more important. This state of affairs was complex and could not be explained in rational terms alone. Here functioning constitutional law mixed with considerations of prestige based in historical argumentation (Figure 2). The major difference between the *highness* (in the sense of 'eminence') of the king and the *authority* of the Council was that the former was not criminally accountable for his acts.[39] The ephoral function of the Council was a prerequisite for bestowing this elevated status upon the king. The key sentence was found in the fifteenth section of the Instrument of Government. When there was a difference of more than two votes,

> His Royal Majesty will always adopt that advice which a majority of the Councillors of the Realm claim to be of the greatest advantage, being according to all expectation the safest and the best; *all the more so because* if [actually 'when'] some harmful consequence were to ensue as a result thereof, those Councillors of the Realm who through pernicious advice have occasioned this development, will be held accountable before the Estates [italics added].[40]

This wording was actually very clever, because it on the one hand preserved the most important function of His Majesty – being a symbolic guarantor for the outward inviolability of the kingdom – while it on the other hand guaranteed the inward inviolability of the kingdom (in the sense of the Estates or the people). It was established that the king was elevated, inviolable and infallible; but he was not allowed to act against the counsel of his councillors, especially since they were held accountable before the Estates for any political errors of judgement. In this way, the highest governmental power was

---

39 See, e.g., [Nehrman], 'Inledning till Thet Swenska Jus Publicum', B 762, KB, 2:V, § 13, fol. 68; *En Ärlig Swensk*, pp. 237–38, 465; C. F. Scheffer in Lagerroth, 'En frihetstida lärobok', pp. 191, 193, 197. Cf. Fredrik Lagerroth, 'Det svenska statsrådets ansvarighet i rättshistorisk belysning', *Scandia: Tidskrift för historisk forskning*, 12 (1939), 32–98 (pp. 43–54, 56–60).

40 *Frihetstidens grundlagar*, p. 28 ('antager Kongl. Maij:t alltid det rådet, som de fleste av riksens råd förklarat vara nyttigast, såsom effter all förmodan det säkraste och bästa, *hälst som* när någon skadelig effterföljd deraf hända skulle, de af riksens råd, som igenom fördärfvlige därtill varit vållande, komma at stå ständerne derföre till Ansvar').

Figure 2 The sovereign King 'Frederick, by the Grace of God King of
the Swedes, the Goths, and the Wends and Landgrave of Hesse-Kassel,
born on 28 April 1676, crowned on 14 May 1720. Married to Ulrika
Eleonora, daughter of Charles XI King of Sweden, born on 23 January
1688, married on 4 April 1715, crowned on 28 March 1719'. Engraving
by Martin Engelbrecht, Augsburg. Photo: Björn Green, KB.

controlled by its subjects, but without their being able to question the highness of the king, and thereby of the kingdom. The kingdom had a bulwark against foreign countries in the form of an inviolable majesty, and against absolutism the same kingdom had a bulwark in the form of the Council's accountability. The infallibility of the king was a guarantee of the impartiality of government decisions: *rex non potest errare*, the king can do no wrong. Therefore, only the advisers could be blamed for incorrect decisions. At the same time, the king was made constitutionally incapable of acting without them. In retrospect, this can be seen as a transitional constitutional-historical solution. Above all, it purported to make a distinction between *rex* and *regnum*, king and kingdom, a distinction that had been central and debated in constitutional development since the Middle Ages. During the Age of Liberty, though, the accountability of the Council became crucial, while the role of the king became ever more redundant. This development was hardly one that had been envisioned by the authors of the Constitution.[41]

In a case of presumed lese-majesty considered by the Judicial Review Division in 1725, the infallibility of royal decisions was clearly illustrated. The delinquent, secretary and notary Johan Jacob Pfeif had had the temerity to 'make pronouncements, with less consideration for and submission to the person of Your Royal Majesty than is permissible and proper for a subject, no matter his rank'. The crime consisted of Pfeif having challenged, by way of a supplication, an appointment for which he believed himself to have been passed over:

> which is nothing other than declaring his displeasure with what Your Royal Majesty, not only by royal power and authority, but also according to the requested opinion of the Chancery College, to the best service and advantage of Your Royal Majesty and your kingdom, has done and decreed.[42]

---

41 David Silvius, *Påminnelser angående successions-rättigheten i Sweriges rike, samt det så kallade souveraine wäldet, upsatte i januarii månad 1719* (Stockholm: Johan Henrik Werner, 1720), § 27; C. F. Scheffer in Lagerroth, 'En frihetstida lärobok', pp. 196, 198. Cf. Kantorowicz, pp. 151–59; Horst Dreitzel, *Monarchiebegriffe in der Fürstengesellschaft: Semantik und Theorie der Einherrschaft in Deutschland von der Reformation bis zum Vormärz*, 2 vols (Cologne, Weimar and Vienna: Böhlau, 1991), I: *Semantik der Monarchie*, pp. 48–50.

42 Chancellor of Justice Thomas Fehman's humble petition, in Justitierevisionen/ Judicial Review Division, Besvärs- och ansökningsmål (utslagshandlingar)/

The well-qualified Pfeif, who had nineteen years of service in the Chancery College, the central administrative authority, seems to have had cause for his discontent; but a decision once made was, by definition, irreproachable. Any challenge undermined royal authority, even if – as was the case here – it was actually Chancery President Arvid Horn who decided the matter. Symbolically, it was the king who ultimately guaranteed the impartiality of the administration of justice. His Royal Majesty also had the privilege of tempering justice with mercy, and after Pfeif had apologised, the Judicial Review Division decided to return his supplication as though it had never been written.

This way of mixing the symbolic and the real exercise of power was not unique to Sweden; it had been characteristic of the development of European constitutions since Antiquity. In fifteenth-century France, for example, the parliament in Paris, being the highest court in the kingdom, had declared that its interpretation of the law was inseparable from the majesty of the king. There was a duality between the person of the King and his office, and Parliament was able to provide an equally true, or even truer, representation of the king as interpreter of the law than what the King as a person might offer.[43]

The king's authority for the administration of justice was given its agency because he was himself legally unaccountable; but this idea was, as the professor of political science Fredrik Lagerroth has pointed out, not particularly old in Sweden. The first time it was expressed in a Swedish legal document was in the abdication letter of Queen Christina from 1654. The idea of the prince as unrestrained by law, *princeps legibus solutus*, drew its inspiration from Roman law. In contradistinction, Swedish law at the time of the elective monarchy had rested on what was long perceived as a Germanic idea of justice, i.e. that a king could be justly deposed if

---

Cases of appeal and application (adjudication documents), 26 May 1725, no. 58, RA ('att med mindre warsamhet och submission Emot Eders Kongl. Maij:tt Sielf, sig uthlåta, än Een Undersåtare, af hwad qualité han ock wore, är tillåteligit och anständigt'; 'hwilcket ju intet annat är, än uppenbarl:n förklara sitt missnöje öfver det, som Eders Kongl. Maij:tt, icke allenast af konungzlig mackt och myndighet, uthan ock efter Kongl. Collegii infordrade uthlåtelse, till Eder Kongl. Maij:ttz, och dess Rikes bästa tienst och nytta, giordt och förordnat hafwer'). See also Justitierevisionen, Besvärs- och ansökningsmål (utslagshandlingar), 1 July 1725, no. 1, RA.
43 Kantorowicz, pp. 220–21.

he broke his oath.[44] As late as the 1560s, the hereditary King Eric XIV was dethroned by the Estates acting in their capacity as a court. The possibility of again establishing a similar extraordinary Estate institution that no one, 'regardless of his status' ('ehuru hög han är'), had the right to evade was provided in the 1634 Instrument of Government (§ 9). Conversely, Queen Christina, who did not recognise the Instrument of Government any more than any other legally competent monarch did, demanded the right as a crowned head to be free from accountability before all temporal courts, both for actions already carried out and any future actions. After her abdication it was acknowledged that she did have this sovereign right, as acknowledged not only by the Estates of Sweden but also by the Pope and the Holy Roman Emperor as well as by the kings of Spain and France.[45] The king's unaccountability was established yet again during the reign of Charles XI, and repeated in the 1809 Instrument of Government (§ 3), although it is reasonable to assume that it had lost its historical justifications by that time. The principle still survives in the current Instrument of Government (RF 1974, 5:8).

Nevertheless, this inviolability had its limitations during the Age of Liberty. In certain respects, the king was merely an official who could be removed on the same grounds as lower civil servants. If the king violated the Constitution, or in any way tried to increase

---

44 Fritz Kern, *Kingship and Law in the Middle Ages*, trans. by S. B. Chrimes (Oxford: Basil Blackwell, 1956), pp. 85–97. That there was a special 'germanische Treue' connected to specific ideas of justice has been called into dispute by modern research. However, for historical reasons, different legal systems have developed different views on loyalty and treason; Angela Rustemeyer, *Dissens und Ehre: Majestätsverbrechen in Russland (1600–1800)*, Forschungen zur osteuropäischen Geschichte, 69 (Wiesbaden: Harrassowitz, 2006), pp. 34–37. Cf. also Yves-Marie Bercé, 'Les monarchies de l'âge moderne', in *Les monarchies*, ed. by Yves-Marie Bercé, Histoire générale des systèmes politiques (Paris: Presses universitaires de France, 1997), pp. 227–322 (pp. 271–92).

45 Lagerroth, *Den svenska monarkin*, pp. 91–92, 108; Kantorowicz, e.g. pp. 94–97, 131–32. Queen Christina's letter of abdication, 1 June 1654, § 1, in *Alla riksdagars och mötens besluth, samt arfföreningar, regementsformer, försäkringar och bewillningar, som, på allmenna riksdagar och möten, ifrån år 1521. intil år 1727. giorde, stadgade och bewiljade äro; med the för hwart och ett stånd utfärdade allmenna resolutioner*, ed. by Anders Anton Stiernman, 3 vols (Stockholm: Johan Henrik Werner, 1728–33), II (1729), p. 1209.

his power, his subjects were automatically released from their oath of allegiance. The Accession Charter committed the monarch to renounce absolutism and any attempts to increase his power. That was a necessary condition for obtaining the royal office, and in this respect the king's oath was in substance identical to and referred to ordinary oaths of office, where violations of these sections were sufficient grounds for removal and prosecution.[46] The prohibition in the Coronation Oath against the expansion of power amounted to an inverted form of the Danish Royal Law (*Kongeloven*), in which the only political limitation on the king was that he was not allowed to reduce his omnipotence.

However, no punishment according to penal law was stipulated in the event that the king violated his oath. Charles I of England, who was decapitated by his former subjects, was the great memento of European princes prior to the French Revolution. Adolf Frederick feared he could suffer the same fate after the failed attempt at a royalist coup in 1756; but it is unlikely that things would have gone that far, even if it had been possible to establish a more tangible royal involvement in the scheme.

The attempted coup d'état of 1756

In the summer of 1756 confidants of the royal couple carried out a failed coup. It was the most serious attempt to restore strong royal authority during the Age of Liberty, but it was poorly prepared and badly executed. None of Sweden's foreign allies, and even less its enemies, wanted to see a change of the country's form of government, so the plan lacked both money and backing. In order to avoid placing the royal couple in jeopardy, they were kept out of its direct execution, which meant that the coup also lacked natural leadership. The exact degree of involvement of the royal couple is difficult to reconstruct on the basis of the surviving sources, but they were no doubt informed of the plans, and it has generally been accepted that the Queen was the more active party of the two. The conspirators who resolved to stage the coup were a group of officers and courtiers from the high nobility. The plan was to arrest the Councillors of the Realm and the Speakers of the Riksdag with

---

46 Accession Charter 1719, § 6; Accession Charter 1720, §§ 6–7, 22; Accession Charter 1751, §§ 6, 23; Accession Charter 1772, §§ 6, 23. See also C. F. Scheffer in Lagerroth, 'En frihetstida lärobok', pp. 193–94.

the aid of the Royal Guards, then to gain the support of the closest provincial regiments, dissolve the Riksdag and convene a new one elsewhere in the country where the Instrument of Government could be changed by acclamation. In spite of the conspirators' lack of both money and weapons, as well as the fact that they had insufficient support among the soldiers they intended to rely on, they assumed that the revolt would quickly gain its own momentum through support from the royalist populace of the capital. The lengthy and clumsy preparations had already raised the suspicions of the Council, though; and when, owing to a lack of coordination, the plan was put into effect before everything was in place, it was easy to nip the revolt in the bud. At a critical juncture, too, Adolf Frederick displayed an absence of resolve.[47]

The entire venture was terminated in just a couple of days in June 1756. In the aftermath, eight of the conspirators were executed; some had had time to escape abroad, while a few others were put in prison or had to resign their military commissions. As was mentioned above, Adolf Frederick also feared for his life during these critical days. During the trials, however, the imprisoned conspirators identified the Queen as the driving force behind the attempted coup. The historian Elise Dermineur has emphasised that this presented the Council and the Estates with a problem. The Queen was compromised while the King's lack of initiative resulted in his role remaining unclear, which meant that no severe measures could be implemented. But punishing the Queen alone was hardly possible; and if the entire family had been exiled, it would have created a constitutional crisis and threatened Sweden's relationship with Prussia and other neighbouring states.[48] The solution was to give the King a strongly worded written reprimand.

The so-called National Act (riksakten) opened with the truth, recognised among 'all free peoples', that 'the king is for the kingdom, the kingdom is not for the king', whereupon followed an enumeration of all of Adolf Frederick's transgressions in office. Because of these transgressions, the Estates had been released from their oaths of allegiance; but because of the King's apology and

47 Malmström, Sveriges politiska historia, IV, pp. 203–42; Elise M. Dermineur, Gender and Politics in Eighteenth-century Sweden: Queen Louisa Ulrika (1720–1782) (London and New York: Routledge, 2017), chapter 4, esp. pp. 124–28, 142–49.
48 Dermineur, pp. 148–49.

the nation's traditional affection for its rulers, they had this time refrained from implementing more serious remedies. 'But if His Royal Majesty, to the distress of his subjects, were to persevere with the aforesaid intent', the Estates would be forced to 'take such a step to remove a King whom they had desired to have as their head and defender'.[49] The consequences were left unspecified, but would probably have consisted of the exile of the royal family rather than their execution – that the Estates would 'punish the person they have previously recognised as their king, is inconceivable', David Nehrman emphasised.[50] Another question is whether the Swedish Estates would also – just as the English parliament had previously done – have abandoned the monarchy in connection with executing their threat. The republicanism of the Age of Liberty, which primarily sought to make executive power impersonal, was in the mid-1750s – unlike at the time of the death of Charles XII – so well established that it would have been easy for the Council to continue ruling the country without any major practical or symbolic problems. Still, it is far from obvious what the outcome would have been; and the question, which never needed to be tested, can only be the subject of counterfactual speculation.

The National Act was read to the King, who was in bed with a fever at the time, by the Council of the Realm and a large delegation from the four Estates, whereupon it was sealed. It was never proclaimed to the general public, and in reality circumstances for Adolf Frederick and Louisa Ulrika changed very little. Within a few years, they were actually able to enhance their reputations (Figures 3 and 4). The National Act was also destroyed at the next session of the Riksdag without breaking its seal. Thus it soon became

49 The National Act is printed as an annex in Fredrik Axel von Fersen, *Historiska skrifter*, ed. by R. M. Klinckowström, 2nd edn, 8 vols (Stockholm: Norstedts, 1867–72), II (1868), pp. 205–14, quotes on pp. 205, 213–14 ('alla fria folkslag'; 'att Konungen är för Riket och ej Riket för Konungen'; 'Men skulle Kongl. Maj:t, till undersåtarnes bedröfvelse, fortfara uti det förra uppsåt [så måste ständerna] skrida till ett sådant steg att skilja sig vid en Konung, hvilken de önskat, såsom sitt hufvud och försvar'); cf. Louisa Ulrika's own description of the circumstances surrounding this Act as well as its contents, *ibid.*, pp. 303–04.
50 [Nehrman], 'Inledning till Thet Swenska Jus Publicum', B 762, KB, 2:X, § 22, fol. 115 ('straffa then tillförene erkjändt för Konung, är högst orimmeligit').

Figure 3 Louisa Ulrika as Crown Princess. Engraving by Georg Paul Busch after Antoine Pesne, 1740s. Photo: Björn Green, KB.

ADOLPH FRIEDRICH.
Der Schweden Gothen und Wenden Koenig.
Sieht Adolph Friedrichs Blick gantz Schweden gnädigst an
So beugt sich auch für Ihm ein treuer Unterthan.
Halle, Verlegts der Universitäts Kupferstecher Liebe

Figure 4 'Adolf Frederick, King of the Swedes, the Goths, and the Wends. Behold the gaze of Adolf Frederick which looks benevolently on all of Sweden. Thus every loyal subject will also bow to him.' Undated engraving by Christian Gottlob Liebe the Elder, Halle. Photo: Björn Green, KB.

uninteresting to speculate on the fates of miscreant kings, and royal authority continued to be outwardly maintained as before.[51] The reprimanding of the King could not be made public, because it would have undermined his role as a unifying symbol. However, the Riksdag took measures to strengthen the republican spirit of the people. A special medal was struck in commemoration of the event. On it, below the text *Libertas manens*, 'Freedom preserved', the goddess of Liberty is shown leaning on a column with the Constitution sealed by the four Estates. The text on the obverse runs, in translation, 'A decree for public thanksgiving to God Almighty, who has averted misfortune in Sweden, in addition to the annual feast of thanksgiving of 1756' (Figure 5a and b). Furthermore, on the initiative of the Riksdag's Secret Committee, the Estates decided that Midsummer Day – one of the great popular feast days in Sweden – would in future be celebrated as a national holiday for the preservation of liberty. 'We recognise the harmfulness of absolutism', said the prescribed prayer, 'and taste the noble fruits of freedom. Therefore we ask of you with all our heart, to consent to reinforce and preserve our adopted form of government, for the joy of the present time and the bliss of future ages!'[52]

This feast of liberty was an educational project that never gained popularity among the people. At the Riksdag of 1765 the Clergy,

---

51 Adolf Frederick's affirmation as a successor to the throne on 17 October 1743, § 16; his abjuration of absolutism at his accession to government on 26 March 1751; Accession Charter 25 November 1751, §§ 23–24; *En Ärlig Swensk*, pp. 882, 885–87, 892–93, 952–54; Malmström, *Sveriges politiska historia*, IV (1899), pp. 232–39; *ibid.*, V (1900), pp. 187–93; Marc Serge Rivière, '"The Pallas of Stockholm": Louisa Ulrica of Prussia and the Swedish Crown', in *Queenship in Europe 1660–1815: The Role of the Consort*, ed. by Clarissa Campbell Orr (Cambridge: Cambridge University Press, 2004), pp. 322–43 (pp. 328–38). Cf. the republican justifications in 'An Act for the Abolishing the Kingly Office in England and Ireland, and the Dominions thereunto Belonging', issued on 17 March 1649. The document has been published in, e.g., *Divine Right and Democracy: An Anthology of Political Writing in Stuart England*, ed. by David Wootton (Harmondsworth: Penguin Classics, 1986), pp. 355–57.

52 *Tacksägelse och bön, at alla midsommars dagar upläsas i församlingarne öfwer hela riket* (Stockholm: Kongl. tryckeriet, [1757]) (official proclamation, annual print series) ('Wi känne Enwäldets olycksalighet och smake

Figure 5a and b. Silver medal struck in celebration of the averted royal coup in 1756. The obverse shows the goddess of liberty and the text *Libertas manens*, 'freedom preserved'. The text on the reverse reads: 'A decree for public thanksgiving to God Almighty, who has averted misfortune in Sweden, in addition to the annual feat of thanksgiving of 1756.' Diameter 78 mm. Uppsala University Coin Cabinet.

who were most immediately responsible for implementing it, petitioned that the public thanksgiving should be abolished because Midsummer Day, which has been a day of joy in Sweden ever since the time of the Great King Gustav Ericsson, who on that same day first entered into Stockholm, has now become a day of mourning through the commemoration of the unfortunate escapade here in Stockholm at the Riksdag of 1756, which is all too well noticed in the displeasure of the general public to hear such things repeated every year from the pulpits, when the ordinary service, to everyone's chagrin, is interrupted and people leave the churches in droves.[53]

The Nobility felt that the word 'escapade' (*upptåg*) was inappropriate to describe the unfortunate events of 1756, but they agreed with the conclusion that the Constitution was now secure and that the unity of the realm was restored. The joint decision of the Estates was to abolish the day of thanksgiving and set aside the punishments hanging over the heads of those conspirators who had fled the country and been deprived of their rights as citizens.

<hr/>

Frihetens ädla frukter. Therföre bedje wi Tig af alt hjerta, at Tu wärdes stärka och wid magt hålla wårt antagna Regeringssätt til närwarande tiders glädje och the följandes sällhet!'). See also 'Kongl. Maj:ts Kungörelse til hämmande af de falska och ogrundade ryckten, som, angående det nyligen förehafda upror, blifwit utspridde, twert emot hwad Riksdags-Tidningarne derom innehålla', 9 July 1756, in *Utdrag utur*, VI (1761), pp. 3954–55; [Carl Christoffer Gjörwell], 'Anteckningar af Carl Christopher Gjörwell om sig sjelf, samtida personer och händelser 1731–1757', in *Samlingar utgifna för De skånska landskapens historiska och arkeologiska förening*, ed. by Martin Weibull, 9 vols (Lund: Berlings, 1874–80), III: *1875* (1874), pp. 31–142 (pp. 101–15); *Bondeståndets riksdagsprotokoll*, ed. by Sten Landahl, 13 vols (Uppsala: Almqvist & Wiksell; Stockholm: Gernandts; Bok- och reklamtryck; Norstedts, 1939–86), VII: *1751–1756* (1963), pp. 670–71. See also Malmström, *Sveriges politiska historia*, IV, pp. 203–42.

53 'Prästeståndets protokollsutdrag 27 mars 1765 om midsommardagens firande och benådning av vissa personer', in *Prästeståndets riksdagsprotokoll*, ed. by Lennart Thanner and others, 16 vols (Stockholm: Riksdagsförvaltningen, 1949–), XVI:2: *1765–1766* (2022), p. 1524 ('midsommarsdagen, som waret en glädjedag i Swerige, allt ifrån den Store Konungens Gustav Ericssons tid, hwilken på den samma gjorde sitt första intåg i Stockholm, nu mera är worden en sorgedag, igenom åminnelsen af det olyckeliga uptåget här i Stockholm wid 1756 års riksdag, hvilket nogsamt förmärkes uti allmänhetens misshag, att höra sådant årligen af predikostolarne uprepas, då den ordinaira gudstjänsten, till allmän förargelse, afbrytas och folket hopetals går ut ur kyrkorna').

At the same time, the names and honour of the people who had been executed were restored.[54]

The signature stamp

It may be appropriate to say something here about what has to later ages been the most infamous element of the Age of Liberty: the royal signature stamp. The existence of a stamp bearing the signature of the King that could be used should he refuse to sign the decisions of the Council has stood out in popular perceptions of history as the primary symbol of the powerlessness of monarchs during the Age of Liberty. As reflected in the literature, it sometimes seems as though this stamp was used regularly, unreflectingly and against the King's express will. The latter happened only in exceptional cases, though, and when the stamp was used, it was done in accordance with careful regulations.[55]

The first signature stamp was introduced at the end of 1741 or the beginning of 1742 following a French model. King Frederick had complained that an endless signing of routine official letters prevented him from dealing with more important tasks. The Greater Secret Deputation, a parliamentary committee composed of representatives from all four Estates, was given the task of looking into the issue. In this connection, it was recalled that simpler circular letters of the French king were stamped with his signature after being countersigned by a state secretary. It was felt that a similar practice could be introduced in Sweden, too. The adopted routine became that the King only signed a single copy when circular letters were to be sent out, while the others were stamped.

54 *Sveriges ridderskaps och adels riksdags-protokoll från och med år 1719*, 32 vols (Stockholm: Norstedts, 1875–1982), XXIV:1: *1765–1766* (1958), pp. 143–46 and Appendix 23; *Prästeståndets riksdagsprotokoll*, XVI:2: *1765–1766* (2022), pp. 132, 141, 177, 214, 251; *Bondeståndets riksdagsprotokoll*, X: *1765–1766* (1973), pp. 72–73, 140.
55 Regarding what is said in the following and about the signature stamp in general, see Birger Wedberg, '"Kongl. Maj:ts höga namns stämpel": Några anteckningar', *Statsvetenskaplig tidskrift för politik, statistik, ekonomi*, 27 (1924), 369–87; Folke Ludwigs, 'Namnstämplarna från frihetstiden', *Arkivvetenskapliga studier*, 6, ed. by Lars Otto Berg, James Cavallie, Claes Gränström and Nils Nilsson ([Uppsala]: Landsarkivet i Uppsala, 1987), 247–53; Malmström, *Sveriges politiska historia*, III, pp. 446–47; IV pp. 190–91.

After a few years of this praxis Frederick wished to reduce his workload even more, and from the end of 1747 lists of routine matters were drawn up instead. The King then signed these lists while the outgoing decisions were stamped. Following the King's stroke in February 1748, the use of the stamp expanded even further, and sometimes the lists were instead signed by the Crown Prince or by the Council acting as a single body. This procedure became habitual during the King's final three years; and many matters that had accumulated over time were also stamped, with the approval of his successor Adolf Frederick, after the death of King Frederick.[56]

The Instrument of Government and the Riksdag Act (*riksdagsordningen*) had in fact already opened the door for the Council to make decisions without the King's signature in certain circumstances (RF 1720, § 16; the Riksdag Act of 1723, § 20). The intention was to allow the government to continue to function in the event of the King's illness or absence, but these terms could easily be interpreted in a broader sense than was originally intended.

After the accession of the new King in 1751 the use of the stamp was discontinued, and Adolf Frederick signed all documents himself. However, conflicts soon arose between the Council and Adolf Frederick because he found it harder to adapt to the form of government than his predecessor had done. The King felt he had the right to review the Council's majority decisions, and by delaying his signing of documents he was able to postpone the issuing of urgent decisions. In some cases, decrees had therefore been circulated without the King's signature; but this practice was not sustainable in the long run, in part because it reduced the legal force of the decrees and in part because it might reveal to the public which decisions had obtained the King's approval and which had not. Such a difference of opinions within the government could only have an unfavourable effect on public opinion; and the King's civil disobedience might increase – or indeed reduce – popular support for him in inappropriate ways.

A suggestion to reintroduce the royal signature stamp was raised within the Greater Secret Deputation in April 1756. After having been subjected to review by the Riksdag, the motion was adopted

---

56 Two such lists with over fifty-odd cases, some more than two years old, were signed by Adolf Frederick on 25 April and 1 May 1751, respectively; Handlingar angående Fredrik I:s och Adolf Fredriks namnstämplar/Documents regarding the signature stamps of Frederick I and Adolf Frederick, vol. 9, RA.

unanimously by the four Estates. The use that was suggested for the stamp had primarily to do with matters concerning appointments. If the King, after one or two reminders, delayed in providing his signature – eight days appears to have been the usual time limit – or if he refused to carry out a decision in protest against an appointment, and instead put forward a candidate of his own who had not been proposed by the Council, the stamp could be used. Once again, circular letters also came to be signed in this manner. The actual stamping of the documents was done by an official at the Chancery College. His work was normally supervised by the Court Chancellor (*hovkanslern*) and the most senior officer of the Chancery, and the stamping could be performed only upon presentation of the minutes of the Council.[57] Detailed lists were to be drawn up of the documents that had been stamped, stating their total number. When the stamp was not being used, it had to be kept under cover and closed with the seals of the Court Chancellor and the officer of the Chancery. The Estates had decided that it should be kept on the premises of the Chancery College.

The excerpts from the minutes or the lists that were drawn up would be signed in good order by the King, and thus the conditions for the stamping were the same as those that had applied during Frederick's time. On the basis of the lists that have been preserved from 1767, the legal historian Birger Wedberg has calculated that of the almost 800 stamped official documents that were issued during that year, no more than around ten concerned matters which the King had refused to approve. Whether this number is to be deemed low or high is a matter of judgement. In percentage terms it is a negligible amount. Conversely, it may be noted that the King was overruled in this way almost once a month. Another aspect with a bearing on the issue is that the King himself had created a precedent for this procedure by repeatedly asking for documents to be stamped which did not fulfil the prerequisites that had been established. Indeed, the very first time Adolf Frederick's signature stamp was used it was done on the King's own orders.[58]

---

57 A large collection of such extracts from the minutes has been preserved for the years 1767–1769: Handlingar angående Fredrik I:s och Adolf Fredriks namnstämplar, vol. 9, RA. The volume also contains lists of stamped documents from the final years of Frederick's reign. The preceding eight volumes of this series of records contain a large amount of similar material.
58 Wedberg, '"Kongl. Maj:ts höga namns stämpel"', p. 377; Malmström, *Sveriges politiska historia*, IV, pp. 285, 352, 356.

When used routinely, the stamp was employed without creating any conflicts between King and Council. On at least some occasions, the Council seems to have been inclined to accept the King's prohibition on using the stamp; but on closer consideration the Councillors found that the commands of the Estates carried greater weight.[59] One of the patent advantages of introducing the signature stamp was that the Estates thus acquired a means of taking measures to counter delays in the decision-making. If the implementation of governmental decisions was dependent on the King's signature, no parliamentary accountability could be established because he was above all judicial review. If, on the other hand, the Council had the means to – on its own, and after necessary reminders – implement actions that had been delayed for various reasons, it could also be held accountable in cases where this was not done.[60] As much as the signature stamp gave the Council the means to control the royal authority, it was to an equal extent an opportunity for the Estates to control the Council. Being the delegates of the Estates, the Councillors had limited room for action.

The use of the signature stamp was thus carefully regulated, and even if it did not correspond to the letter of the Instrument of Government, it was entirely in line with its spirit. It was not a question of wanton stamping without consideration. It was far more common for the stamping to be performed at the King's own

---

59 Malmström, *Sveriges politiska historia*, VI, p. 23; Wedberg, '"Kongl. Maj:ts höga namns stämpel"', p. 380.

60 'The stamp is suitable for everything, letters of commission as well as other things, while on the other hand the signature of the Council has formerly been possible to use only on certain occasions, while other matters have had to be left unimplemented; In this way Their Lords the Councillors of the Realm are also made accountable, not only for the decisions, but also for the implementation thereof, if delays should occur regarding this, and not only for certain matters but for government matters in general, an accountability which is completely in accordance with the principles of the constitution' ('Stämpelen är lämpelig til alla så Fullmackter som andra, tå theremot Rådets underskrift tilförene allenast kunnat brukas wid wissa tilfällen, och andra mål åter måst lemnas oexpedierade; Therigenom bindas och Herrar Riksens Råd wid answar, icke allenast för Besluten, utan ock för wärckställigheten, om therwid drögsmål sig förete, och thet icke för wissa utan för Regerings ärender i gemen, hwilket answar aldeles instämmer med principen af Grundlagarne'); the four Speakers' letter to His Royal Majesty, 26 May 1756, quoted in *Riksdags-Tidningar*, no. 12 (17 June 1756). See also *Bondeståndets riksdagsprotokoll*, VII: *1751–1756*, p. 620.

request than against his will. Nor was it the case that this powerful instrument of the Council was kept secret. On the contrary, it was announced with open emphasis on the composite character of government power, where the king was merely one party, albeit an important one. The decisions of the Estates regarding the signature stamp were printed in *Riksdags-Tidningar*, and there it was stated 'that the King's illustrious name gives commands and official documents greater emphasis, and subjects are reminded that they should show the King the proper and most sincere fidelity by their obedience to the law'. In other words, this was true even when the signature was stamped; and according to official doctrine, it was not thought to deprive the king of his highness. The King of Sweden possessed majesty and glory, wrote Isac Faggot, for instance; and the rights belonging to his exalted position included affixing 'the signature of his illustrious name' to all governmental decisions. 'But should His Majesty not condescend to affix his illustrious name', he declared candidly, 'then the instituted stamp is used'.[61]

A not entirely insignificant aspect of this issue is that the signature stamp, in its own way, actually safeguarded the monarchy as an institution, a circumstance which is indicated by the two quotations from *Riksdags-Tidningar* and Faggot above. Under certain conditions, the Council had both the ability and the legal right to govern the kingdom without sanction from the king. Adolf Frederick's obstruction of governmental affairs could hence have been dealt with in a practical manner and without any formal solution; that is to say, governmental decisions could have been issued in the Council's name alone, and the king would simply have been circumvented. That would in reality have amounted to the introduction of a republic. By using the signature stamp, however, the central role of the king when it came to imparting dignity and force to decisions continued to be symbolically foregrounded in spite of everything. And this in itself was an emphatic recognition of the justification for and indispensability of the monarchy.[62]

---

61 The four Speakers' letter to His Royal Majesty, 26 May 1756, quoted in *Riksdags-Tidningar*, no. 12 (17 June 1756) ('at Konungens Höga Namn gifwer befallningar och Expeditioner mera eftertryck, samt undersåtare then påminnelse, at the med sin Laglydnad wisa Konungen then rätta och upriktigaste trohet'); [Faggot], pp. 61–62 ('med dess höga Namns under-skrift'; 'Men skulle Hans Maj:t icke behaga lemna sit Höga Namn, då brukas den inrättade stämpelen').

62 Cf. Alm, p. 423, n. 203, who has made a similar observation.

Immediately after the death of Adolf Frederick, the Council
ordered the stamp to be broken up; this was hence not done in
vengeful rage by Gustav III, as is sometimes claimed. No new
signature stamp was created for the new King.[63]

In summary, one may say that the signature stamp was a genuine
instrument of power, but one that was used with care. The conflicts
that led to the stamp being employed usually concerned appointments or other matters involving few persons; they rarely or never
concerned the foundations of the state. It must nevertheless be
emphasised – as Wedberg has done – that the Council probably
never deviated from a decision simply because the King had refused
to affix his signature or forbidden the use of the stamp. During the
royal strike of 1768, when the Council tried to expand the limits
that had been agreed on and actually endeavoured to rule using the
stamp, that attempt encountered opposition.

The royal strike of 1768

The confrontations in connection with the introduction of the
signature stamp and the averted coup of 1756 had shown that
the Hat party was prepared to make generous interpretations of the
Constitution in order to eliminate the executive royal authority. At
the next major constitutional crisis, it was instead the Cap party
that was in power; but they adopted an equally generous reading
of the Instrument of Government in their attempt to govern the
kingdom without a king. In December 1768, Adolf Frederick
threatened to abdicate unless an extraordinary session of the
Riksdag was immediately convened; the specific issue in this case

---

63 It can be added, as a parenthesis, that Gustav III himself introduced a
procedure reminiscent of the signature stamps of the Age of Liberty. In
1784 he ordered, following an earlier attempt at simplification during his
journey abroad from the previous year, that some government decisions
could be issued under a royal seal alone and without the signature of
the King, so that he would not have to be bothered with certain routine
matters. The procedure for these decisions using 'His Royal Majesty's seal'
('Kungl. Maj:ts secret') was to a rather significant degree the same as for the
use of the signature stamp during the Age of Liberty. However, in this case
it was a matter of delegating certain decision-making while maintaining
royal control; see Clas Theodor Odhner, *Sveriges politiska historia under
konung Gustaf III:s regering*, 2 vols (Stockholm: Norstedts, 1885–96), II:
1779–1787 (1896), pp. 260, 418–19; Carlsson, *Den svenska centralförvaltningen*, pp. 175–76.

had to do with the Council's power over the government offices and thus also with the balance of power between the King and the Council. The Council was given three days to consider the issue, and during this period the King's name could not be used for any decision-making. The immediate response of the government was to resort to the signature stamp. The Hats had previously used it as an exceptional solution when the King was being intractable, but now the Caps tried to transform it into a permanent instrument in order to be able to rule without the cooperation of the monarch. Here, however, they overstepped the limits of what was acceptable. Because of the Hats' long time in government between 1738 and 1765, the administration was dominated by their sympathisers. Four of the central government offices united in refusing, as a matter of principle, to follow government decisions that had been made without cooperation of the King. The form of government rested on the highness of the king, the authority of the Council and the liberty of the Estates, they insisted; and when one of these elements was missing, the balance was disrupted. The highness of the king, they further claimed, was indispensably connected to the person of the King: no one but he could uphold the regalities.

Here the impartiality of the royal office thus became a direct argument in an actual constitutional matter, not just in a theoretical exposition. In a political culture where conflicts between parties were still seen as a frightening abnormality by many people, this imbalance among the government authorities could feel quite tangible. At the same time, a continual pattern characteristic of the Age of Liberty recurs in this conflict: the court was supported by the party in opposition for only as long as it remained in opposition. As an ally against the government, the King was important in influencing opinion and providing leverage; but he was a partner who was difficult to control for the party in government. That the constitutional crisis of 1768 was mainly a conflict between parties, and that it was the strong position of the Hats in the government offices that decided the matter, is shown by the fact that the King did not gain any support whatsoever for his constitutional proposals once the extraordinary session of the Riksdag had been convened.[64]

---

64 For the details of this constitutional crisis, see Malmström, *Sveriges politiska historia*, VI, pp. 60–80; see esp. p. 73 on the positions of the government offices. See also Maria Cavallin, *I kungens och folkets tjänst: Synen på den svenske ämbetsmannen 1750–1780* (Gothenburg: Historiska institutionen,

It is interesting to see that the Caps reacted during the crisis with the same ingrained republicanism that had previously distinguished the Hats. To be sure, the President of the National Board of Trade, Niclas von Oelreich – one of the founders of the Hat periodical *En Ärlig Swensk*, who had now switched his party sympathies – emphasised, in a polemical pamphlet directed against the four government offices, that 'it is of the utmost importance that official documents be issued in the name of the King, because the highness of the King gives the decisions efficacy and force'. In spite of this, he provided detailed references to the constitutional documents showing that there were no obstacles to the Council's ruling without a king.[65] In addition, he maintained that the King was

2003), pp. 136–45; Dermineur, pp. 109, 117–19, 189–91. The crisis lasted from 12 to 19 December, when the summons to the Riksdag was issued. The sole order signed with the signature stamp during this period was a circular to province governors, consistories and regimental commanders telling them to be extra vigilant in 'maintaining a general peace and quiet' ('en allmän ro och stillhets bibehållande'). This was sent in eighty-two stamped copies; excerpt from the minutes of the Council of the Realm of 14 December 1768, in Handlingar angående Fredrik I:s och Adolf Fredriks namnstämplar, vol. 9, RA. The circular is not found in the Council's regular registry for this week, but its contents are clear from the printed Council minutes of 13 December; see Registratur, huvudserien/Registry, main series, vol. 70, 1768, Inrikes civilexpeditionen/Office for domestic civil matters, B 1 a, RA. All Council minutes in domestic civil matters for these days were published before 13 January 1769, and the printed minutes have been substituted for the regular fair copies in the original volume; Rådsprotokoll i renskrift, huvudserie/Fair copies of Council minutes, main series, vol. 87, September–December 1768, Inrikes civilexpeditionen, A 1 a, RA.

65 [Niclas von Oelreich], *Tankar öfwer et högmål uti swenska jure-publico, eller rikets styrelse-lagar, nämligen om Kongl. Maj:t med regeringens nedläggande imellan riksdagarne försätter kongl. collegier och kronans ämbetsmän uti en fullkomlig inactivité och det i stöd af rikets grundlagar, med mera* (Stockholm: Carl Stolpe, 1769), quotation on p. 8 ('Det är högst angelägit, at Expeditionerne uti Konungens namn utfärdas, emedan Konungens Höghet gifwer Besluten drift och styrka'). The legal sections referred to were RF 1720, §§ 13, 15–16; Adolf Frederick's affirmation of 1743, § 4; Accession Charter 1751, §§ 7, 15; Riksdag Act 1723, § 20, and the four Speakers' letter to His Royal Majesty, 26 May 1756, printed in *Riksdags-Tidningar* no. 12 (17 June 1756). Cf. to this the Council's humble petition of 3 November 1755 and other related documents in *Handlingar om grundlagarnes wärkställighet, tryckte på riksens högloflige ständers befalning wid riksdagen år 1756* (Stockholm: Kungl. tryckeriet, [n.d.]). See also Karl-Elof Rudelius, 'Författningsfrågan i de förenade deputationerna

merely the holder of an office and was therefore replaceable. If the King were to suspend 'the governance of the kingdom, where then is the person owing to whose highness the ancient Kingdom of the Swedes and the Goths retains its designation as a kingdom, its prerogative, and its reputation?' he asked. The answer was a given:

> The King cannot relinquish more than his personal rights; but the King cannot surrender the ancient Kingdom of the Swedes and the Goths, nor its prerogative and reputation, for that is the property of the Kingdom and not the personal property of the King. [...] The King, indeed, represents this kingdom, and for this reason he bears the name of King; he can also relinquish the representative, or the personal royal name, but not the Kingdom itself, of which he is merely the representative.[66]

But if the King were to renounce the right to the personal, representative office of the king, where would this personal right go? Well, it would revert to the Council, 'because the Council represents the *jura majestatica realia* of the Estates of the Realm, being their representative, and consequently it also represents the Kingdom of the Realm'. On the same occasion, State Councillor Pehr Kalling stated that 'a king may die, a king may be absent, but the royal authority is always present in the Council chamber'.[67]

This was the Republicanism of the Age of Liberty taken to its logical extreme: the King was an interchangeable holder of an office that represented the independent Kingdom of Sweden, but he did not represent or exert any personal power.

1769', *Statsvetenskaplig tidskrift för politik, statistik, ekonomi*, 38 (1935), 331–65 (pp. 331–32).

66 [Oelreich], p. 28 ('Riksstyrelsen, hwar är då den Person, för hwilkens höghet det urgamla Swea- och Götha-Riket behåller sitt namn af Rike, sin rättighet och anseende?'; 'Konungen kan icke nedlägga mer, än sina Personliga Rättigheter; men det urgamla Swea- och Götha-Konunga-döme, kan Konungen icke lägga neder, ej heller dess rättighet och anseende, ty det är Rikets och icke Konungens Personliga tilhörighet. [...] Wäl representerar Konungen detta Konunga-döme, och bär derföre namn utaf Konung; han kan ock nedlägga det representativa, eller det Personliga Konunga-namnet, men icke sjelfwa Konunga-dömet, hwilket han allena representerar').

67 *Ibid.*, pp. 28–29 ('emedan Rådet representerar Riksens Ständers *jura majestatica realia*, såsom dessas Fullmägtige, och följakteligen representera de äfwen Riksens Konunga-döme'). Kalling quoted in Malmström, *Sveriges politiska historia*, VI, p. 69 ('En konung kan dö, en konung kan vara frånvarande, men konungamakten är alltid närvarande i rådkammaren').

The royal authority and the continuity of the state

A few additional things should be observed about the king's personal lack of accountability and its connection to the continuity of the state, because here was one of the keys to the symbolic power that was attributed to the royal office. That the monarch stood above the law was a European idea many centuries old; but as has already been pointed out, in Sweden that view did not in fact extend further back than to the mid-seventeenth century. The notions held by Queen Christina and her contemporaries concerning the importance of royal majesty were based on medieval continental constitutional law and its interpretation of Roman law. Scholars of the Middle Ages had wrestled with the problem of uniting a secularised, originally pagan constitutional law with a Christian dogmatism for which life after death was the one truly important thing. On the threshold of the High Middle Ages, an idea began to take shape concerning the kingdoms of the earth as temporal equivalents of the Kingdom of Heaven, with kings as gods on earth. Models could be found in the deified emperors of Rome and Byzantium.

The historian Ernst Kantorowicz has described the emerging view of the majesty of kings. His discursive and evocative presentation is not easy to summarise, and it can hardly be done full justice here. However, he identifies a few central ideas that became ever more concentrated over time: the idea of the king's domain (*demesne*) as indivisible; that this territory was above the king's personal control and thereby represented an unbroken context that became something more, and more exalted, than merely an accumulation of land; and that the same continuous connection was transferred to political and collective entities or commonweals – *regnum*, *res publica*, *populus* – that became the bearers of continuity. This continuity was as important to the royal majesty (the sovereignty) as it was to the Law. Only God was timeless and possessed of an eternity that existed outside time; but in earthly existence the Church was a religious, and (the idea of) Rome a secular, bearer of a kind of temporal eternity, *aevum*. During the fourteenth century, the omnipotence and immortality of Rome were transferred to the individual kingdoms of Europe. A kingdom was an independent political body where the people had a right to appoint their kings. Such a king possessed royal majesty and was therefore not subject to anyone else, neither Pope nor Emperor. In this way, the independent kingdom harboured (the idea of) Rome within itself. *Rex imperator in regno suo* – the king is like an emperor in his own realm.[68]

The unaccountability of the king was closely connected to the issue of continuity. A state or a kingdom possessed continuity through succession. As a political body the state was unchanging, even though the individuals who constituted it changed over generations. The same applied to the royal office. In a kingdom the king was the head and the people were the limbs, and one part could not survive without the other. When individual Kings died, the office lived on. Nothing else was possible, because if the King was bound to the kingdom, the kingdom would otherwise die with him, and it would have to be reconstructed every time a new King succeeded to the throne. For similar reasons, the royal office had to be legally unaccountable and possess *dignitas*, highness. Because the office, which was personal, was perpetual, the legal responsibility for misdeeds committed by a predecessor would otherwise be inherited by the new monarch. Now the responsibility was instead borne by the entire political body, that is to say, the realm.[69]

From such origins the image of the royal office, the realm and the majesty developed during the late Middle Ages and the early modern period. There was hardly any general, standard European view on these matters, and in national laws the relationship between the king and the people was always influenced by practical political circumstances. At any rate, the idea of the theoretical unaccountability of the monarch was very important at this stage of European history. During the permanent state of war in the 1600s, lawlessness was elevated to political practice, and dynastic speculations and conjectures regarding constitutional law became a method for reducing the arbitrariness of international relations. Conflicts regarding rank could, paradoxically enough, have a levelling effect because diplomatic protocol was governed not only by the political strength of the states involved, but also by such things as the age

---

68 Kantorowicz, pp. 273–313, esp. pp. 284, 298–99. See also Kern, p. 68; Quentin Skinner, *The Foundations of Modern Political Thought*, 2 vols (Cambridge: Cambridge University Press, 1978), I: *The Renaissance*, pp. ix–x; II: *The Age of Reformation*, pp. 351–52; Dreitzel, *Monarchiebegriffe*, I, pp. 50–53; Bercé, pp. 249–59; André Krischer, 'Das diplomatische Zeremoniell der Reichsstädte, oder: Was heißt Stadtfreiheit in der Fürstengesellschaft?', *Historische Zeitschrift*, 284 (2007), 1–30 (pp. 4–11).

69 Cf. Kantorowicz, pp. 304–06, 314–15, 386–87, 399–401, 418–19.

of a kingdom and the number of titles borne by its ruler. As the great theorist of the state at that time, Samuel Pufendorf, noted, diplomacy was therefore open to interpretation, compromise, and bargaining. Claims that were recognised in one context were not automatically accepted in any other:

> Amongst *Princes* and *Independent States*, they usually alledge for *Honour and Precedence*, the Antiquity of their Kingdoms and Families; the Extent and Richness of their Territories, their Power abroad and at home, and the Splendour of their Styles. Yet neither will all these pretences beget a *perfect Right* in any Prince or State to have the Precedence of others, unless the same has been first obtain'd by Concession or Treaty.[70]

International relations were thus also influenced by practical politics. The mystical-religious qualities ascribed to kings during the Middle Ages began to give way to more secular ideas. The German philosopher Gottfried Wilhelm Leibniz expressed a more pragmatic or sociological definition: a king was a person who was designated as such and treated as such by the people around him. This was true within the individual kingdom as well as outside it. The philosopher David Hume rejected both acts of Providence and contract-theoretical justifications, but supported the royal authority for practical reasons. Even that which had arisen by coincidence was quickly established as tradition, he explained.[71] A typical formulation that alluded to the king of Sweden as a symbol of the political independence of the realm was expressed by the Lord Marshal, the Speaker of the Nobility, at the Riksdag of 1751:

---

70 Samuel Pufendorf, *The Whole Duty of Man According to the Law of Nature*, 2nd edn (London: Motte/Harper, 1698 [1673]), book II, XIV:15, p. 313.

71 Leibniz: Barbara Stollberg-Rilinger, 'Honores regii: Die Königswürde im zeremoniellen Zeichensystem der frühen Neuzeit', in *Dreihundert Jahre preußische Königskrönung: Eine Tagungsdokumentation*, ed. by Johannes Kunisch, Forschungen zur brandenburgischen und preussischen Geschichte, 6 (Berlin: Duncker & Humblot, 2002), pp. 1–26 (pp. 5–16); cf. also, e.g., Jeroen Duindam, *Vienna and Versailles: The Courts of Europe's Dynastic Rivals, 1550–1780* (Cambridge: Cambridge University Press, 2003), pp. 198–200. Hume: Sally Jenkinson, 'Bayle and Hume on Monarchy, Scepticism, and Forms of Government', in *Monarchisms in the Age of Enlightenment*, ed. by Blom, Laursen and Simonutti, pp. 60–77 (pp. 64, 68–69).

Under Your Royal Majesty's vigilant eye, the kingdom possesses a secure calmness: in your manliness and bravery lies its strength: in your loyalty to your word lie the respect and confidence of its friends.[72]

The king safeguarded the honour and independence of the realm, and even though the martial skills of the monarch had been reduced to a formula by the mid-eighteenth century, it was still necessary to emphasise them. Many contemporaneous state formations aspired to be elevated to kingdoms in order to obtain a confirmation of their independent status. The princes of Brandenburg and Savoy let themselves be crowned kings, but the steward (stadtholder) of the Netherlands, and republics such as Venice and Genoa, also wished to be assigned a rank equal to that of a king and given the right to include a royal crown in their coats of arms. For such ambitions to meet with success, some type of formal rationality was always required: an alliance by marriage, a conquest, a historical claim or something similar. Above all, however, the position needed to gain diplomatic recognition. If the practical political circumstances were right, pragmatism might defeat issues of protocol. Still, of the examples mentioned here it was only Brandenburg that managed to attain undisputed royal status, but then as the Kingdom of Prussia, that is, the Brandenburg dependency that was situated outside the Holy Roman Empire. These aspirations nevertheless indicate the great importance attached to the sovereignty that was inherent in a kingdom.[73]

72 Til Hans Kongl. Maj:t[.] Landt-marskalkens, högwälborne grefwe Henning Adolph Gyllenborgs tal, hållit then 12. Octobr. 1751. å riksens samteliga ständers wägnar, uti theras wid samma tilfälle utsedde deputations närwaro ([Stockholm]: Kongl. Tryckeriet, [n.d.] (official ordinance). In the speech, Gyllenborg alternates between using direct and indirect address, and the pronoun thess (its/his/your) in this context refers to the king ('Uti Eder Kongl. Maj:ts waksamhet äger Riket et trygt lugn: uti thess Mandom och Tapperhet sin styrka: uti Thess Ordhållighet vänners aktning och Förtroende').

73 See Robert Oresko, 'The House of Savoy in Search for a Royal Crown in the Seventeenth Century', in Royal and Republican Sovereignty in Early Modern Europe: Essays in Memory of Ragnhild Hatton, ed. by Robert Oresko, G. C. Gibbs and H. M. Scott (Cambridge: Cambridge University Press 1997), pp. 272–350 (on Venice and Genoa: pp. 288–89, 294–301); Jonathan Israel, The Dutch Republic: Its Rise, Greatness and Fall 1477–1806

Denmark provides another relevant example. In the Danish elective monarchy there had been no title of majesty, and the king was referred to as His Princely Grace (*Hans fyrstelige Nåde*). The province councils confirmed the elections of kings, and in relation to the domestic nobility the Oldenburg dynasty was first among equals. In the ideology of the Nobility, the Council was the actual holder of the Crown, which it conferred on the king or the holder of the office. It is worth noting that the medieval provision on the right to revolt made an appearance in a modified form in the last and strictest *haandfaestning* (a form of accession charter) of 1648. Clearly, then, as long as the Danish kings depended on the approval and discretion of the Nobility, their claims to majesty could hardly gain recognition. Not until 1655 did Frederick III demand that the title His Royal Highness (*Hans kongelige Højhed*) should be recognised for his son Christian (V), the heir to the throne. In international relations, however, there were no changes, not even with the introduction of the hereditary kingdom and the absolute monarchy in 1660. The legal basis for the claim of royal power was once considered to have been conferred by the Holy Roman Emperor (who had crowned Danish kings in 1134 and 1152), and Denmark was reduced to a vassal state. Not until 1727 did the Most Christian King of France recognise his Danish colleague as an equal, while the Holy Roman Emperor waited a further twenty-five years before confirming the title of majesty.[74]

(Oxford: Clarendon Press, 1995), pp. 537–38; Hans Blom, 'Spinoza on *Res Publica*, Republics, and Monarchies', in *Monarchisms in the Age of Enlightenment*, ed. by Blom, Laursen and Simonutti, pp. 19–44 (p. 36), and Jenkinson, pp. 72–73.

74 Henning Matzen, *Danske Kongers Haandfæstninger: Indledende Under-søgelser*, Indbydelsesskrift til Kjøbenhavns Universitets Aarsfest til Erindring om Kirkens Reformation (Copenhagen: J. H. Schultz, 1889; reprint 1977), pp. 90–94; Jean Bodin, *Les six livres de la repubiqve* (Lyon [= Geneva]: Gabriel Cartier, 1593 [1576]), p. 145; Edvard Holm, *Danmark-Norges Historie fra den Store Nordiske Krigs Slutning til Rigernes adskillelse (1720–1814)*, 7 vols (Copenhagen: Gad, 1890–1912), I: *Frederiks IV's sidste ti Regeringsaar (1720–1730)* (1891), pp. 89–90, 169–70, 173; III: *Under Frederik V (1746–1766)* (1897), p. 162; Leon Jespersen, 'Teokrati og kontraktlære: Et aspekt af de statsretlige brydninger ved Frederik 3.s kroning', in *Struktur og Funktion: Festskrift til Erling Ladewig Petersen*, ed. by Carsten Due-Nielsen, Knud J. V. Jespersen, Leon Jespersen and Anders Monrad Møller (Odense: Odense Universitetsforlag, 1994), pp. 169–86. See the *haandfæstning* of May/June 1648, art. 55, in

The Swedish statesmen at the beginning of the Age of Liberty were of course eager to avoid such an ignominious situation, especially in such dire military circumstances where the Swedish kingdom was threatened with being obliterated not only on paper, but also to some extent in reality. After the peace with Hanover in 1720, it was enough for Ulrika Eleonora to use a simplified form of address by eliminating all the names of the foreign provinces, whether lost or retained. As an expression of the claims Sweden's national dignity carried with it, it was sufficient to write 'Queen of Sweden, the Goths, and the Wends, etc.' ('Sveriges, Götes och Vendes drottning etc.'). This title was confirmed by Frederick for all time in a special supplementary agreement with Russia in the following year.[75]

In the seventeenth-century constitutional conflicts in Sweden, the aristocracy had upheld the difference between *majestas realis* and *majestas personalis*. True majesty was the equivalent of the state (which in its turn might be given different representations), whereas the kingdom was a body included in the state. This interpretation had been rejected during the absolute monarchy, when the king represented all functions of the state.[76]

In the constitutions of the Age of Liberty, the idea of the royal majesty – that is to say, the idea of the king's independence and elevation above the law – was retained. The king alone possessed *majestas*, but *potestas* – authority – rested with the king in Council. The king thus represented the independence of the state, but the Council in its turn represented the state's independence from the king. In reality, the king was thereby reduced to the holder of an

---

Samling af danske Kongers Haandfæstninger og andre lignende Acter (Copenhagen: Bianco Luno, 1856–58), pp. 119, 121. Cf. the discussions in the Swedish Council on 1 October and 5 December 1650, *Svenska riksrådets protokoll*, ed. by Severin Bergh, Handlingar rörande Sveriges historia, 3rd series, 12 vols (Stockholm: Norstedts, 1886–1920), XIV: *1650* (1916), pp. 321–22, 419–23. Cf. also [Nehrman], 'Inledning till Thet Swenska Jus Publicum', B 762, KB, 2:V, § 2, fol. 65.

75 Rådsprotokoll (det odelade kansliet)/Council minutes (undivided chancery), 17 February, 8 March, 14 March 1720, vol. 131, RA, fols 330–31, 549, 608; 'Acte angående Swenske Konunga-Tituln', 30 August 1721, in *Utdrag af de emellan Hans Konglige Majestät och cronan Swerige å ena och utrikes magter å andra sidan sedan 1718 slutna alliance-tractater och afhandlingar*, ed. by Gustaf Reinhold Modée (Stockholm: Lorentz Ludwig Grefing, 1761), pp. 123–24; Nordin, *Ett fattigt men fritt folk*, pp. 182–83.

76 Lagerroth, *Den svenska monarkin*, pp. 96–97.

office, a representative of the Kingdom of Sweden. But it was the *office*, not the person, that was the symbolic guarantor of the sovereignty of the realm; and this sovereignty could not be borne by a Council, however complete its legal competence.[77]

The symbolic elevation represented by the royal office may seem difficult to comprehend given that the monarchs of the Age of Liberty appear to have been treated with so little deference by the subjects who held the seats on the Council. But that the Estates were able to elevate the respected but frail *man* Frederick of Hesse to be the *king* of Sweden, supreme and above the law, was not in any way remarkable in a society where people knew that Christ was both God and man. Similar forms of symbolic transformations belonged, if not to everyday life, then at least to holidays. According to the Lutheran doctrine of divine omnipresence, Holy Communion was no longer an actual transubstantiation of bread into body and wine into blood, but it nevertheless signified the presence of the true body and blood of Christ. The question is not *whether* people believed in the sacrament of Holy Communion, or the majesty of the king; the fact is that people *needed* to rely on these conditions in order to have a fixed and unchanging system intended to fortify, in the one case, the community of faith, and in the other, the law and the realm.

It is true that faith in such mysticism was, in practice, on the wane in society. This development has been described in different ways by researchers: as the decline of magic (Keith Thomas), as a secularisation and demystification of the world (Max Weber) or as a crisis of representations based on failing organic analogies (Peter Burke). But while no radical external circumstances forced changes to occur, archaic institutions could continue with an eroded but nevertheless undiminished symbolic power.[78]

---

77 Fredrik Lagerroth, *Frihetstidens författning: En studie i den svenska konstitutionalismens historia* (Stockholm: Bonniers, 1915), pp. 210–11, 442–43; Jean Braconier, 'Suveränitetsbegreppets betydelse för det karolinska enväldet', in *Technica & humaniora: Festskrift till Anders Nevsten 1885 18/3 1950* (Malmö: Landby & Lundgrens boktryckeri, 1951), pp. 48–75; Thanner, p. 136.

78 Cf. Peter Burke, *The Fabrication of Louis XIV* (New Haven and London: Yale University Press, 1992), pp. 125–30; Linda Colley, *Britons: Forging the Nation 1707–1837* (London: Pimlico, 1994), pp. 228–36; Hannah Smith, *Georgian Monarchy: Politics and Culture, 1714–1760* (Cambridge: Cambridge University Press, 2006), pp. 95–104.

A thoroughly investigated custom may be cited to exemplify this phenomenon. Since the Middle Ages, French kings had used their alleged holiness to cure skin diseases through the royal touch in an annually recurring ritual. This tradition has been carefully analysed by the French historian of the Middle Ages Marc Bloch. During the eighteenth century, there was no longer anyone who believed in these magical qualities of the king – except perhaps a superstitious peasantry. In spite of this, the custom continued until the French Revolution. It had become an important ritual that changed only slowly and was considered significant because of that which in sociological terms is called 'cultural lag', i.e., the idea that norms and behaviours change more slowly than material and social circumstances. The ceremony of the royal touch was therefore a solemn and essential ritual during *l'ancien régime*. But when Charles X tried to revive the custom after the Bourbon Restoration he was met with ridicule, and the press scornfully called him 'premier médecin de son royaume' – for several reasons an unthinkable occurrence fifty years earlier.[79] A ritual can be extended and can successively renew its content just because it has been established as a tradition. If the continuity ceases, the spell that has been developed by the habit is also broken. Even though the ceremonial royal touch was as anachronistic in 1789 as it was in 1823, it was not until its attempted resumption that it revealed itself as an atavistic, empty ritual, like the emperor's new clothes: it had lost the legitimacy of the continuing context.[80]

---

79 Marc Bloch, *Les rois thaumaturges: Étude sur le caractère surnaturel attribué à la puissance royale particulièrment en France et en Angleterre*, preface by Jacques Le Goff, 2nd edn (Paris: Gallimard, 1983 [1924]), pp. 402–05.

80 The thesis of the importance of broken continuity gains support from the English example. There the practice of the royal touch was discontinued in connection with the change in circumstances brought about by the Hanoverian dynasty succeeding to the throne in 1714; David J. Sturdy, 'The Royal Touch in England', in *European Monarchy: Its Evolution and Practice from Roman Antiquity to Modern Times*, ed. by Heinz Duchhardt, Richard A. Jackson and David Sturdy (Stuttgart: Franz Steiner, 1992), pp. 171–84. Cf. also the *pedilavium*, the ritual washing of the feet of twelve paupers, which was a common Maundy Thursday custom among many Catholic rulers. The ritual referred to John 13. 1–20, and expressed the humility of the ruler while at the same time associating him with the figure of Christ. Franz Joseph I still observed this custom at the beginning of the twentieth century, and as a late representative of an unbroken line of

Such cultural lag can be studied in many situations. The transfers that were made during Antiquity and the Middle Ages between the king's symbolic and the factual qualities, and the union between monarch and state, did not gain the same credence during the eighteenth century, not even at a theoretical level. Even so, the theoretical explanations of the status of the king lived on to a certain degree; but this was true to an even greater extent for the ceremonial customs, which were developed according to traditional patterns. This was, first of all, because there was – as is the case with all cultural processes – a certain inertia built into the system; secondly, because they were, if not a symbolic, then at least a social indication of the king's elevation, the cost more than the content testifying to the monarch's status; and thirdly, because a new regime to a great extent builds its legitimacy on that of the old one: through contrast if the upheaval is revolutionary, through redefinition if it is evolutionary. That is to say, in the former case new forms must be invented that are qualitatively different from the old ones, which have become dysfunctional. In the latter case, well-known figures of thought, which as far as possible combine new content with previously established rhetoric, continue to be built upon. The bloodless Swedish revolution after the death of Charles XII was revolutionary in a constitutional sense but evolutionary in its symbolic expressions. For the new people in power – who immediately following the revolution could most often be found among the Councillors of the Realm – it was most prudent to leave the official appearances of the king as unchanged as possible. In the Council chamber they had full control of the monarch, while the public – who had greater faith in the impartiality of the king than in that of the aristocratic Council – could at best be appeased if the external structures were kept untouched. In addition, royal pomp provided legitimacy for the entire state, not least because of its antiquity. The representational or legitimacy-related crises of the kings during changing political and social circumstances have been investigated by Peter Burke with respect to late seventeenth-century France, and by Mikael Alm with respect to the late eighteenth-century Gustavian era in Sweden. At the beginning of the Age of Liberty, the task for the people in power was rather to provide legitimacy

---

Habsburg emperors since the fifteenth century, he is an example that confirms the rule about the importance of continuity; Duindam, pp. 142–43, 211–12, illustration 40.

for the new political situation by borrowing representative forms from the previous, royal regime. The king was allowed to represent the continuity both within the realm and outside it.

At the constitutional revolution of 1719–1720, royal power was broken up completely. It was therefore important to maintain symbolic legitimacy, because the king as such was intimately associated with the state. It is not the case that the king *was* the state, but he *symbolised* it, and this tendency was to become ever more evident as the Age of Liberty wore on. The perhaps single most important ritual for the manifestation of the status of the king was his coronation, which will be discussed in the following chapter.

2
Manifestation of power

One conclusion that has been proposed in iconographic studies and in research on rituals is that coronations and public ceremonies provided a language that was decipherable by the audience. The ceremony functioned in interaction with the spectator and could also be communicated to larger groups through printed accounts. A ceremony was also important because it conveyed a more direct message to the spectator than theoretical tracts, however numerous they were. Small changes in the ceremonial might represent major political changes. One prominent example that has been fore-grounded in research is that of the Danish kings, who ceased to be crowned after the introduction of the absolute monarchy and the hereditary succession in 1660. An essential general function of the coronation ceremony was the element of reciprocity that bound the king and the people together by means of mutual assurances. With an absolute monarchy, the king became independent of the will of his subjects; and the coronation ceremony was replaced by an anointing that only symbolically illustrated the selection already made by God. At the same moment as the old monarch breathed his last, Providence made his successor king without the mediating intervention of his subjects.[1]

---

1 Sebastian Olden-Jørgensen, '"At vi maa frycte dig af idel kjærlighed": Magdudøvelse og magtiscensættelse under den ældre danske enevælde', *Fortid og Nutid: Tidsskrift for kulturhistorie og lokalhistorie* (1997), 239–53. See also Gérard Sabatier, 'Beneath the Ceilings of Versailles: Towards an Archaeology and Anthropology of the Use of the King's Signs during the Absolute Monarchy', in *Iconography, Propaganda, and Legitimation*, ed. by Allan Ellenius (Oxford: Clarendon Press, 1998), pp. 217–42 (pp. 200–01); Barbara Stollberg-Rilinger, 'Honores regii: Die Königswürde im zeremoniellen Zeichensystem der Frühen Neuzeit', in *Dreihundert Jahre preußische Königskrönung: Eine Tagungsdokumentation*, ed. by Johannes

Another, somewhat different, way of looking at the symbols and public ceremonies of power is to emphasise the character of their manifestations. The iconographic elements should not, according to this way of looking at it, be overemphasised, because the symbolic imagery was so complex that it was barely understood by even the most learned spectators. What instead made the coronation ceremony significant was the display of power. Even if the more profound allegorical implications were reserved for a few, no one could avoid understanding the symbolism of the extravagance involved. Gold, pearls and expensive fabrics, music and solemn speeches, a plethora of people in choreographed roles, commemorative coins and feeding the public – all these contributed to a *Gesamtkunstwerk* that was focused on a single person and that conveyed the unambiguous message that this person was superior to all others.[2]

The question is whether any of these things could be seen in the coronations of Ulrika Eleonora and Frederick in 1719 and 1720, respectively. After all, if an increase in royal power was manifested publicly, then limitations to that power should also be displayed symbolically. One problem when an analysis of this issue is conducted is that the coronations, in spite of their alleged antiquity and tradition-bound character, were essentially unique events. The list of Swedish kings, from Gustav I (r. 1523–1560) onwards, had been a long line of anomalies where the succession of almost every new ruler involved dynastic complications. The progenitor of the Vasa dynasty, Gustav I, could, like his sons John III and Charles IX, be considered a usurper. The same was true of Gustav II Adolf, who lived his entire life in parallel with the deposed Sigismund, and who, to ensure the survival of the domestic dynasty, had to be succeeded by his under-age daughter. She, in turn, somewhat reluctantly entrusted the throne to her cousin, whose son and grandson were both in their minority when they became kings. It is well known that Ulrika Eleonora's claim to the throne was disputed, and Frederick had no right whatsoever to the Swedish Crown.

Kunisch, *Forschungen zur brandenburgischen und preussischen Geschichte*, 6 (Berlin: Duncker & Humblot, 2002), pp. 1–26 (pp. 3–4).

2 Cf. Theodore K. Rabb., 'Politics and the Arts in the Age of Christina', in *Politics and Culture in the Age of Christina: Acta from a Conference Held at the Wenner-Gren Center in Stockholm, May 4–6, 1995*, ed. by Marie-Louise Rodén, Suecoromana, 4 (Stockholm: Swedish Institute in Rome, 1997), pp. 9–22.

In spite of the fact that the royal authority, and especially the hereditary kingdom, were meant to represent stability and continuity, the so-called Gustavian dynasty had also been characterised by a number of *ad hoc* solutions. Consequently, a constitutional and dynastic situation of normalcy that might form the basis for comparisons hardly existed. As the analysis below will show, there is also reason to be cautious about interpreting individual ceremonial changes as politically significant. When individual examples are discussed, a single detail may seem noteworthy and dependent on the specific situation; but in comparisons across a longer period of time, this same detail may turn out to have functioned equally well, and possibly to have been interpreted in another way, in a completely different political context. The basic features of the ceremonial remained the same from the coronation of Eric XIV in 1561 to that of Oscar II in 1873; but changes, adjustments and additions nevertheless made every ceremony unique.[3] The most immediate models for the ritual available at the beginning of the Age of Liberty were the coronations of Charles XI and Ulrika Eleonora the Elder in 1674. The fully developed absolute monarchy, on the other hand, had its own ceremonial.

The acts of tribute and anointing during the absolute monarchy

Charles XII is the only Swedish ruler to have been born an absolute monarch. He did not believe a coronation was necessary for confirming his status, but at the initiative of a few loyal advisers he participated in an improvised act of tribute and anointing that took place over two days in Stockholm. On the first day, the Council and the Estates swore their oaths of allegiance in the courtyard of the Wrangel Palace, or 'Kungshuset' ('the King's House'), which functioned as a temporary royal residence. The King did not agree to any Accession Charter, which made the obligations between king and subjects unilateral. On the second day, the anointing took place in St Nicholas Church (Storkyrkan) (Figure 6). The King wore a crown and carried a sceptre already upon his arrival at the church, he dispensed with the customary coronation oath, and he did not

---

3 Malin Grundberg, *Ceremoniernas makt: Maktöverföring och genus i Vasatidens kungliga ceremonier* (Lund: Nordic Academic Press, 2005), p. 19.

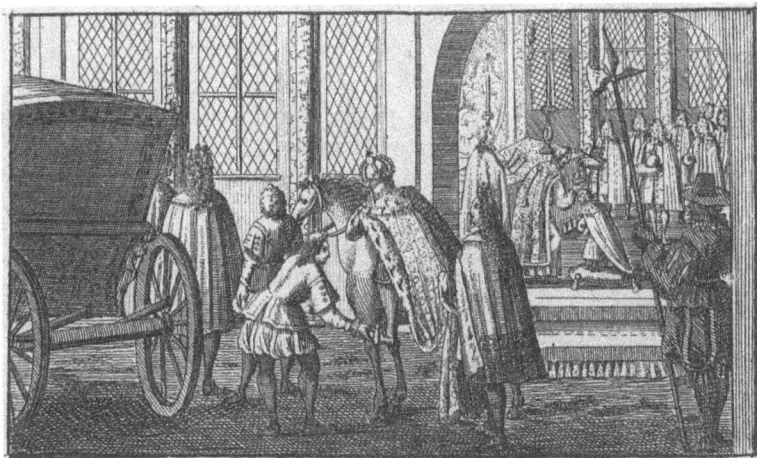

Figure 6 The anointing of Charles XII. This image, a pure fantasy, represents the actual coronation as well as the moment when the King mounts his horse to ride in the procession. Just before his ride to the church, the King had ominously dropped the crown on settling into the saddle. Engraving from *Leben und Tod Carls des XII* (Nuremberg, 1719). The artist failed to grasp the point made in that text about the King himself placing the crown on his head 'thereby signalling that he is the sovereign King' ('als welches eine Marque seyn sollte, daß Er ein souverainer König seye'). Photo: Karina Pettersson, KB.

make any other commitment to his subjects. Because of this unorthodox procedure, even King Charles's contemporaries questioned whether the ceremony could be characterised as a coronation at all. Even though that word was eschewed in the official account, the basic function was nevertheless such that the distinction between an act of coronation and an act of anointing seems to have escaped most people. Both the occasion on which the act took place and the regalia used corresponded to those of regular coronations; and even Voltaire, who conducted an independent analysis of the symbolic significance of the event, called the whole affair a coronation, a *couronnement*.[4]

---

4 Voltaire, 'Histoire de Charles XII, roi de Suède' (1731), in *Œuvres historiques*, ed. by René Pomeau, Bibliotheque de la Pléiade, 128 (Paris: Gallimard, 1957), p. 65. See also, e.g., *Sveriges ridderskaps och adels riksdags-protokoll från och med år 1719*, 32 vols (Stockholm: Norstedts, 1875–1982), XIII:1: *1742–1743* (1890), p. 12.

A not unimportant formality which is known to have been
conceived by Charles XII himself was that all participants in the
tribute should wear mourning for the young King's father, Charles
XI. In this way emphasis was placed on the dynastic continuity
which alone, through divine Providence, was the foundation for the
royal elevation. At the tribute paid in the courtyard of Kungshuset
there were also representations of a Phoenix, the bird whose day
of death was also its day of birth. Ever since the Middle Ages, the
Phoenix had been a symbol of a self-engendering kingdom that
never perished.[5]

The art historian Mårten Snickare has produced a fine summary
of the significance of continuity and change, respectively, in this
ceremony.[6] In the legally binding elements – the paying of tribute
and the swearing of oaths – everything was arranged so that
the king alone was an active subject whereas his subjects were
passive objects. The most sensational element was that the subjects,
in contrast to traditional customs, paid their tributes *before* the

---

5 *Kort berättelse om Hans Kongl. May:tz wår allernådigste konungs och*
   herres konüg Carl den tolftes, Sweriges, Giöthes och Wändes konungz,
   &c. kongl. hyldningh, ock der på följande smörielse-act, med heela
   rijkets, sampt alla trogne och redelige undersåtare största hugnad och
   förnöyelse, anstäld och begången uti kongl. residentz-staden Stockholm
   den 13 och 14 decembr. åhr 1697 (Stockholm: Kungl. tryckeriet, [n.d.]);
   Gunnar Carlquist, 'Karl XII:s ungdom och första regeringsår', in *Karl*
   XII: Till 200-årsdagen av hans död, ed. by Samuel E. Bring (Stockholm:
   Norstedts, 1918), pp. 43–86 (p. 69); Ernst Kantorowicz, *The King's Two*
   Bodies: A Study in Mediaeval Political Theology, with a new preface
   by William Chester Jordan (Princeton: Princeton University Press, 1997
   [1957]), p. 391; Ragnhild Marie Hatton, *Charles XII of Sweden* (London:
   Weidenfeld & Nicolson, 1968), pp. 78–81; Mårten Snickare, *Enväldets*
   riter: Kungliga fester och ceremonier i gestaltning av Nicodemus Tessin
   den yngre (Stockholm: Raster, 1999), pp. 129–40. The ceremony is
   referred to as a coronation in, e.g., Rådsprotokoll (det odeladed kansliet)/
   Council minutes (undivided chancery), 8 December 1718, vol. 127, RA,
   fol. 41; see also Iselin Gundermann, '"Ob die Salbung einem Könige
   nothwendig sey"', in *Dreihundert Jahre preußische Königskrönung:*
   Eine Tagungsdokumentation, ed. by Johannes Kunisch, Forschungen zur
   brandenburgischen und preussischen Geschichte, 6 (Berlin: Duncker &
   Humblot, 2002), pp. 115–34 (p. 120, n.16).
6 Snickare, *Enväldets riter*, pp. 140–46. See also Snickare's discussion of
   the royal rituals of the Age of Liberty: 'Kungliga fester och ceremonier',
   in *Carl Hårleman: Människan och verket*, ed. by Göran Alm and others
   (Stockholm: Byggförlaget, 2000), pp. 252–63 (pp. 259–60).

anointing, and that the King did not swear any oaths or give any assurances at all. In the ritual parts, on the other hand, the old ceremonies were followed as closely as possible. Because the novelties were limited, the political changes stood out all the more clearly, while the continuity with earlier ceremonies contributed to increasing the magnificence of the acts in other ways. The similarities with the contemporary procedures in Denmark are striking in this respect. The Danish coronations, which had lost all legal significance, were abolished at the very first accession of a new monarch after the introduction of absolutism in 1660. By way of compensation, Christian V arranged for an act of anointing in which the ceremonial adhered to the old coronation ritual to the greatest degree possible, but which also exhibited a notable absence of any elements of legal obligation in the form of the swearing of oaths or accession charters (*haandfæstninger*) that had previously been an important part of the proceedings. While the King had formerly had the regalia brought to him and had been adorned in them by the Council of the Realm, the regalia were now already worn by the absolute monarch when he entered the chapel. One interesting detail, which was never tested in Sweden, is that a Danish King would place the crown on the Queen's head in private before she entered the chapel to receive the anointing.[7]

The origin of coronations

At the beginning of the Age of Liberty, there were two coronation ceremonies in quick succession: that of Ulrika Eleonora in 1719 and that of Frederick in 1720. There is no reason to describe these in detail. When compared with other coronations they demonstrate great similarities both to each other and to older ceremonies. It is more important to point out the patent changes that occurred, the significance those changes may have had and how they were perceived by contemporaries. First, however, a few words about the basic meaning of coronations.

---

7 Knud Banning, 'Fra symbol til antikvitet: En oversigt over symboltolkningen i danske kroningsprædikener 1537–1815', in *Kongens makt og ære: Skandinaviske herskersymboler gjennom 1000 år*, ed. by Martin Blindheim, Per Gjærder and Dag Sæverud (Oslo: Universitetets Oldsaksamling, 1985), pp. 123–28; Gudmund Boesen, *Danmarks riges regalier* (Copenhagen: Gyldendal, 1986), pp. 109–22 (pp. 116–17); Olden-Jørgensen, pp. 239–53.

Coronations had their origin in the Eastern Roman Empire in the middle of the fifth century, when the emperor began to be blessed by the patriarchs. According to the so-called Donation of Constantine, *Constitutum Constantini*, a forged document which formed the basis of the secular authority of the popes from the end of the eighth century onwards, Constantine the Great had bestowed dominion over all of Italy upon the bishops of Rome, together with all imperial attributes. Originally, only the pope could administer the anointing, which gave the ruler divine confirmation and distinguished him from other mortals. In parallel with Christianity, the custom of being crowned spread across all of Western Europe during the early Middle Ages. The crowned emperor had the power to appoint his vassals as kings, and in a similar way national bishops came to wield an indirect right to crown kings in the pope's stead.

In the beginning, the ecclesiastical sanction was a way to impart increased legitimacy to rulers. As dynasties became gradually more established, however, they experienced a growing need for distancing themselves from the Church. The kings, who attempted to liberate themselves from competing institutions of power, did not wish to allow their status to be conditional on an ecclesiastical confirmation. The process was accelerated in the Scandinavian countries by the Reformation, which subjected the church to the secular Magistracy. That the coronation should imply any particular elevation was seen as a papal deception. 'Yes! the shameless superstition went so far', wrote an early historian of coronations, 'that the Royal Crown, and in consequence thereof the royal authority and office, were believed to be a gift from the spiritual fathers during the papal era.'[8] After the Reformation, the confirmation of the Church was no longer a necessary condition for royal status in Sweden; but the coronation continued to be important, in part as a rite of passage and initiation, in part and above all for the commitments that were then entered into under oath and that were a remnant of the elective monarchy. In addition, the coronation was a profession of piety, an act of

---

8 [Johan B. Busser], *Historisk berättelse, om alla kongliga kröningar uti Swerige* (Stockholm: Wennberg & Nordström, 1771), p. 7 ('Ja! oblyga widskepelsen gick så långt, at Konungsliga Kronan, och i följe däraf Konunga-magten och wärdigheten ansågs för en skänk af de Andeliga Fäderna under den Påfwiska tiden').

devotion, where the king displayed humility before his calling and the heavenly majesty.[9] The fundamental structure of the coronation ritual remained fairly unchanged through the centuries after the Reformation: mass, coronation oath, anointing, investiture of the regalia, enthronement, blessing, oath of allegiance. The *anointing* provided the religious confirmation; through the *investiture* the king was arrayed in the royal symbols; and the *enthronement* was the formal proclamation of the king.

At the beginning of the Age of Liberty, coronations were regulated in chapter 7 of the Royal Code, 'How kings shall be installed and crowned' ('Huru Konunger wighias skal och krönas'), and in section 3 of the 1719 and 1720 Instruments of Government. The text of the Law of the Realm is concise:

> When the king so desires he shall be anointed and crowned in Uppsala, or elsewhere in his kingdom, as he wishes and finds fitting, though preferably by the archbishop for the sake of the dignities of them both.[10]

---

9 Åke Andrén, 'Kungakröningar och kröningsmässor', *Svensk teologisk kvartalskrift*, 34 (1958), 153–77 (pp. 154–57, 168–69); *Kulturhistoriskt lexikon för nordisk medeltid från vikingatid till reformationstid*, 22 vols (Malmö: Allhems, 1956–78), IX: *Konge–Kyrkorummet* (1964), s.v. 'Kröning'; Edward Francis Twining, *European Regalia* (London: B. T. Batsford, 1967), pp. 71–84; Roland Mousnier, *La monarchie absolue en Europe du Ve siècle à nos jours* (Paris: Presses universitaires de France, 1982), pp. 147–48; Erich Hoffmann, 'Coronation and Coronation Ordines in Medieval Scandinavia', in *Coronations: Medieval and Early Modern Monarchic Ritual*, ed. by János M. Bak (Berkeley, Los Angeles and Oxford: University of California Press, 1990), pp. 125–51.

10 *Swerikes rijkes lands-lag, som af rijksens råd blef öfwersedd och förbättrat: Och af k. Christofer, Swerikes, Danmarks, Norikes, Wendes och Götha konung, palatz-grefwe widh Reen, och hertigh af Beijeren, årom efter C. b. 1442. Stadfäst* [with commentaries by Petter Abrahamsson] (Stockholm: Johan Henrik Werner, 1726), hereafter Landslagen, p. 159 ('NV tha Konunger wil, tha skal han i Upsalom wighias och krönas, eller och annarstadz i Rijke sino efter wilia och fallom sinom: Tho af Erchebiscope hälst, for wärdogheet skuld bäggia thera'). The English rendition given here follows the corresponding paragraph in a translation of chapter 8 in the older law edition: *King Magnus Eriksson's Law of the Realm: A Medieval Swedish Code*, trans. and ed. by Ruth Donner, Acta Societatis Fennicae Iuris Gentium, 2 (Helsinki: Ius Gentium Association, 2000), p. 6.

The 1634 Instrument of Government and the 1660 Supplement had
nothing to say about these issues, and the vague formulations in
the Law of the Realm made it possible to have a fairly long interval
between the accession to the throne and the coronation – six years
with respect to Gustav II Adolf and Christina, three years with
respect to Charles XI. In the Instruments of Government of the
Age of Liberty, the requirements were somewhat more specific and
expanded. None of the male direct heirs of the royal couple were
allowed to accede to the throne

> before he has reached his twenty-first year, has at the assembly of the
> Estates confirmed his Accession Charter, has let himself be crowned
> and has sworn his oaths, in accordance with the laws of Sweden.[11]

In other words, there were to be no long delays. The Accession
Charter, coronation and swearing of the oath were now integrated
into a single process without which formal accession to the throne
was considered incomplete. Even though the coronation with the
anointing may be perceived as an essentially religious ceremony,
the sacred elements were not decisive. In spite of the ecclesiastical framing, this was primarily a secular procedure in which the
king's Accession Charter and the reciprocal oaths were the central
and legally binding elements of the ritual. After all, the Instrument
of Government stated that the King was not allowed to 'assume
government until he has let himself be crowned, which presumably
was prescribed for the sake of the oath', guessed David Nehrman,
'otherwise this would not be so necessary'.[12]

The blessing of the Church gave increased force to the allegiance between the Magistracy and its subjects, but was not in
itself necessary in order to consolidate this bond. In the decision
adopted by the Riksdag in Linköping in 1600, the Estates had
established the importance of the religious orthodoxy of the
temporal Magistracy: 'No one shall after this day assume the royal
crown and government in this kingdom who is not in agreement
with us regarding the pure doctrine of the Christian gospels.'

11 RF 1720, § 3 ('innan han sine et och tiugu år upfylt, vid ständernes sam-
    mankomst sin försäkring ifrån sig gifvit, sig kröna låtit och eda sina gångit,
    som Sveriges lag säger'); cf. RF 1719, § 3.
12 [David Nehrman (Ehrenstråle)], 'Inledning till Thet Swenska Jus Publicum
    Förklaradt i Publiques Lectioner', B 762, KB, 2:IV, § 10, fol. 59 ('tillträda
    Regeringen, för än han sig Cröna låtit, hwilket förmodeligen för Edens skull
    stadgat är, elljest woro det eij så nödigt').

The formulation was directed against the deposed King Sigismund, who still kept his Polish crown; but religious orthodoxy was something that did not require any ceremonial confirmation, in spite of the importance of safeguarding it. Although Duke Charles 'has refused to let himself be crowned', the same Riksdag declared him alone their Lord and Magistrate, and promised him 'that all royal right and obedience would be fulfilled and proven'. As was previously mentioned, Gustav II Adolf, Christina and Charles XI had also, despite many years' lack of ecclesiastical sanction, ruled without any limitations on their offices.[13] Nor was the coronation a necessary condition for royal status in an international context. In Spain and Portugal, both the coronation and the anointing had been abolished as early as the sixteenth century. On the other hand, reciprocal oaths were sworn when their kings were installed. In France during the Middle Ages, the reign of a formally elected king had been counted from his coronation; but as the seventeenth century approached, the coronation was no longer considered a necessary requirement for royal status, and the accession to the throne and the coronation came to be ever more separated in time. Louis XIV became king in 1643 and attained his majority in 1651, but he was not crowned until 1654.[14] The young Prussian monarchy – which had been founded in 1701 and which, because of the lack of tradition, might seem to have

---

13 The Linköping Riksdag resolution of 19 March 1600, in *Alla riksdagars och mötens besluth, samt arfföreningar, regements-former, försäkringar och bewillningar, som, på allmenna riksdagar och möten, ifrån år 1521. intil år 1727. giorde, stadgade och bewiljade äro; med the för hwart och ett stånd utfärdade allmenna resolutioner*, ed. by Anders Anton Stiernman, 3 vols (Stockholm: Johan Henrik Werner, 1728–33), I, pp. 502–04 ('ingeen skal effter thenne Dagh til then Konunglige Crono och Regemente här i Rijket komme, som icke medh oss eenig är vthi then Christelige reene Evangelii Lähre', 'haffuer förwägret sigh at late Cröne', and 'allom Konungzligom Rätt och Lydno hålle och bewijse'). Cf. the Norrköping Riksdag resolution of 22 March 1604, *ibid.*, p. 545. Cf. also the Royal Code (*konungabalken*), Landslagen, chapter 3, § 9; Torsten Lenk, 'Karl IX:s regalier', in *Karl IX*, ed. by Boo von Malmborg, Småskrifter utgivna av Svenska Porträttarkivet, Nationalmuseum, 2 (Stockholm: Nordisk Rotogravyr, 1959), pp. 41–43. Cf. also Andrén, pp. 168–74. [Nehrman], 'Inledning till Thet Swenska Jus Publicum', B 762, KB, 2:IV, §§ 29–31, fols 64–65.

14 Richard A. Jackson, *Vive le roi! A History of the French Coronation from Charles V to Charles X* (Chapel Hill and London: University of North Carolina Press, 1984), pp. 6, 10–11.

needed all conceivable ceremonial confirmation – experienced only one royal coronation. As early as 1714, its second king, Frederick William I, was content to have only an act of tribute and the appurtenant swearing of oaths; and his successor, Frederick II, in a 1740 letter to Voltaire attributed the useless coronation ceremony to superstition.[15] In most cases, the sacred elements of the coronation were thus fraught with tradition and had a ceremonial significance; but on the other hand the coronation had no actual legal effect. The emphasis during the Age of Liberty on the accession to the throne and the coronation as coordinated procedures aimed above all at preventing a repetition of the despotism of Charles XII, and at demanding legal commitments by a monarch before he or she was granted royal powers.

The coronation of Ulrika Eleonora

For all Swedish coronations since that of Christina in 1650, there are official printed descriptions of the ceremonial. Up to and including the rule of Charles XI, these were mostly written in German; but thereafter they are found in Swedish among the Royal Ordinances and were hence intended to be read out as proclamations in the churches.[16] The descriptions of the coronations of Ulrika Eleonora the Younger and Frederick are identical on many points. One difference, though, is that the former is written in the preterite and the latter in the future tense: in other words, in one case an event was

---

15 Where appropriate, a coronation could nevertheless be of importance for diplomatic interaction. For example, the emissary of Francis I of France refused to give precedence to the ambassador of Charles V before Charles V had been duly anointed as emperor; Gundermann, pp. 128–33.

16 This is confirmed by a passage in the minutes of the Peasant Estate of 19 November 1751, where reference is made to the impression given to the peasantry in the country by what is written in the 'coronation ceremonial, which is being disseminated around the country' ('[krönings]ceremonielet, som kommer omkring i landet'); *Bondeståndets riksdagsprotokoll*, ed. by Sten Landahl, 13 vols (Uppsala: Almqvist & Wiksell; Stockholm: Gernandts; Bok- och reklamtryck; Norstedts, 1939–86), VII: *1751–1756* (1963), p. 70. The necessity of the burial and coronation ceremonials 'soon being sent to the printer's and then disseminated around the countryside' ('snart gifvas til trycket och sedan blifva i landsorterne kringsände') is mentioned also in the minutes of the Nobility of 9 November 1751; *Sveriges ridderskaps och adels riksdags-protokoll*, XVIII:1: *1751–1752* (1911), p. 173.

proclaimed that had already occurred, whereas the other referred to an event that was yet to take place. However, this fact hardly alters the value of these descriptions as sources: both cases were examples of prepared programmes that were printed, not narrations from eyewitnesses. Both the act of tribute of Charles XII and the coronation of Frederick I were planned by the Superintendent of the King's Buildings (*överintendenten*), Nicodemus Tessin the Younger. However, because of Tessin's illness the programme at the coronation of Ulrika Eleonora had to be prepared by the city architect of Stockholm, Göran Josuæ Adelcrantz, though the two architects probably cooperated closely.[17]

Ulrika Eleonora was determined that her coronation should take place in Uppsala in spite of the Council having firmly advised against it (Figure 7). Since the city fire of 1702, there had been a shortage of assembly rooms for the Estates; and moving the entire Riksdag from the capital was difficult during the winter and would place additional stress on the already strained war economy. It is not known what the Queen's reasons were, but she would primarily have looked at tradition and the ceremonial weight of the city. The Council stressed that both the Queen's mother and brother had been crowned in the capital; but there were less flattering forerunners as well. Both of the two last kings of the Kalmar Union had been crowned in Stockholm, and already Bishop Hans Brask had, for this reason, firmly advised Gustav (I) Vasa against doing the same thing. However, before the coronation of Christina, the Queen herself had gone against the 'opinion that the common people have of Uppsala' and claimed that her fortune depended on God and not on the place where she was crowned. It is possible that

17 *Berättelse om Hännes Kongl. Maj:ts wår regerande allernådigste drottnings, drottning Ulricæ Eleonoræ Sweriges, Giöthes och Wändes drottning &c. &c. &c. smörjelse- och krönings-act, med allmän fägnad begången uti Upsala dom-kyrkia, den 17. martii, åhr 1719* (Stockholm: Kungl. tryckeriet, [n.d.]); *En noga underrättelse om alt hwad, som wijd Hans Kongl. Maj:ts wår allernådigste konungs och herres, konung Friedrich den förstes, Swerjes, Göthes och Wändes konung &c. &c. krönings-act, j acht tahgas bör, så i det Kongl. Palais, som wijd processen til och ifrån Store Kyrkian, samt ceremonierna uti sielfwa kyrkian, uppå krönings-dagen här i Stockholm, den [3] maji, åhr 1720* (Stockholm: Kungl. tryckeriet, 1720). According to Ulrika Eleonora's own collated copy of the ceremonial, Tessin also failed to appear at the coronation of Frederick, where his functions were filled by State Councillor Axel Banér; D 845, Hist. Sv., Fredrik I., 'Försäkr. til Swea rikes ständer' [title on spine], KB.

Figure 7 The coronation of Ulrika Eleonora the Younger in Uppsala Cathedral. Engraving by an unknown artist. The schematic image supplies a highly approximate rendering of the event. As so often, though, it is possible to identify Queen Christina's silver throne. Photo: Björn Green, KB.

the fact that the ill-fated Christina of all people had been crowned in Stockholm contributed to Ulrika Eleonora's 'repugnance'.[18]

In spite of resistance from the Council, the Queen had her way; and the act of coronation itself happened in the same manner that, with minor variations, had been in use since 1561.[19]

---

18 Council minutes of 30 May 1650, *Svenska riksrådets protokoll*, ed. by Severin Bergh, Handlingar rörande Sveriges historia, 3rd series, 12 vols (Stockholm: Norstedts, 1886–1920), XIV: *1650* (1916), p. 177 ('opinion vulgus hafver om Ubsala'); Council minutes, 8 December 1718, 11 December 1718, 4 March 1719 7 March 1719, vol. 127, RA, fols 41–42, 111, 750–51, 755, 827–28, 842–43. [Busser], *Historisk berättelse*, pp. 13, 18–19; Rudolf Cederström, *De svenska riksregalierna och kungliga värdighetstecknen* (Stockholm: Livrustkammaren, 1942), pp. 15–18; Lennart Thanner, *Revolutionen i Sverige efter Karl XII:s död: Den inrepolitiska maktkampen under tidigare delen av Ulrika Eleonora d.y:s regering* (Uppsala: Almqvist & Wiksell, 1953), p. 292.
19 Council minutes, 22 December 1718, vol. 127, RA, fols 249–50. A handwritten narrative about the coronation, more detailed than the printed version, can be found in the Engeströmska handskriftsamlingen/Engeström manuscript collection, Handlingar rörande drottning Ulrika Eleonoras regering/

The coronation of Charles XI provided the primary model, but the ceremonials of Christina, Hedvig Eleonora and Ulrika Eleonora the Elder had been consulted, too. Once more, the monarch entered the church with the regalia borne before her, not already wearing them as in the act of anointing of Charles XII. After the opening prayers, the Queen swore her oath with her hand on the Bible. The oath was based on chapter 4 of the Royal Code, 'The oath that the king shall swear' ('Eedha som Konunger swäria skal'); but to this was added 'everything that is written in Her Royal Majesty's most graciously established Instrument of Government, and Her Royal Majesty's most graciously confirmed Accession Charter, both dated the 21st of February last'. The Archbishop then performed the anointing and, with the aid of the most senior Councillor of the Realm present, placed the crown on the Queen's head. (Previously the Lord High Steward (*drots*), the foremost of the five Great Offices of the Realm, had overseen the crown, but the Great Offices had been abolished by Charles XI in the 1680s.) The other regalia were presented in the traditional order (the so-called investiture). After the Queen had been declared duly crowned (the enthronement), a salute was fired, and finally the Councillors of the Realm swore their oaths.[20]

Documents regarding the reign of Queen Ulrika Eleonora, B.II.2.14, KB, fols 84–91: 'Kort berättelse om Hennes Maijttz wår [aller]nådigste drottningz Ulricæ Eleonoræ Crönin[gsfesti]vitet, som skedde i Upsala d: 17 Martij [1719]' ('A short narration of the coronation festivities of Her Majesty our most gracious Queen Ulrika Eleonora, which took place in Uppsala on 17 March [1719]'). Aubret de La Motraye has also provided a detailed account: Aubret de la Motraye, *Travels through Europe, Asia, and into Part of Africa; with Proper Cutts and Maps* (London: Printed for the Author, 1723), pp. 365–69; *Voyages du sr. A. de La Motraye, en Europe, Asie & Afrique*, 2 vols (The Hague: T. Johnson & J. van Duren, 1727), II pp. 432–39. La Motraye's description of Frederick's coronation is not as extensive. See also Walfrid Holst, *Ulrika Eleonora d.y.: Karl XII:s syster* (Stockholm: Wahlström & Widstrand, 1956), pp. 186–89.

20 Quoted in *Berättelse om Hännes Kongl. Maj:ts [...] smörjelse- och krönings-act*, p. 13 ('alt hwad i Kongl. Maj:ts allernådigst confirmerade Regerings-Form, samt Kongl Maj:ts allernådigst gifne Försäkring, bägge af den 21 sidtsl. Febr. war författadt'). On the oaths sworn at coronations, see Fredrik Lagerroth, *Frihetstidens maktägande ständer 1719–1772*, Sveriges riksdag, I:5–6 (Stockholm: Victor Pettersons, 1934), II, pp. 176–77; Jonas Nordin, *Ett fattigt men fritt folk: Nationell och politisk självbild i Sverige från sen stormaktstid till slutet av frihetstiden* (Eslöv: Symposion, 2000), pp. 104, 115–18.

It is worth noting that Ulrika Eleonora, just like Christina, was declared *king* of Sweden on completion of the coronation. The formula was as follows:

> Now Queen ULRICA ELEONORA has been crowned King of the lands of the Swedes and the Goths and the provinces belonging to them, she and no one else.[21]

This formula has most recently been interpreted by the historian of ideas Karin Tegenborg Falkdalen. The pronouncement underlines, she says, the contradictory phenomenon where a queen is a ruler and not simply a queen consort.[22] The proclamation is interesting for two reasons: first, because it had an important legal function; and second, because not even this purely legal aspect of the coronation ritual seems to have been completely clear at the time. When the matter was deliberated in the Council, the formulation 'crowned Queen of Sweden' had initially been mentioned without reflection. State Secretary (*statssekreterare*) Samuel Bark then objected that Christina had been declared king, whereafter some confusion arose about what had been meant by this. Chancery President Arvid Horn on his part believed that *if* the formulation really was used, it *should* have been precisely for the purpose of distinguishing between a ruling queen and a queen consort. For safety's sake, a notary was sent to investigate the correctness of this information. After it had been verified, a decision was made to follow the existing model.[23]

---

21 *Berättelse om Hännes Kongl. Maj:ts [...] smörjelse- och krönings-act*, p. 16 ['Nu är Drottning ULRICA ELEONORA krönter Konung öfwer Swea och Giötha Landom och des underliggiande Provincier, Hon och ingen annan').

22 Karin Tegenborg Falkdalen, *Kungen är en kvinna: Retorik och praktik kring kvinnliga monarker under tidigmodern tid*, Skrifter från institutionen för historiska studier, 5 (Umeå: Institutionen för historiska studier, 2003), pp. 133–34. See also Kari Elisabeth Børresen, who makes comparisons with the princely titles of Margaret I of Denmark; Kari Elisabeth Borresen, 'Christina's Discourse on God and Humanity', in *Politics and Culture in the Age of Christina: Acta from a Conference Held at the Wenner-Gren Center in Stockholm, May 4–6, 1995*, ed. by Marie-Louise Rodén, Suecoromana, 4 (Stockholm: Swedish Institute in Rome, 1997), pp. 43–53 (p. 46). The relationship between masculinity, femininity and royalty is also discussed by Grundberg, pp. 190–95.

23 Council minutes, 14 March 1719, vol. 127, fols 910–11, RA ('krönter till Sweriges dråttning'). The rough draft for this day is less detailed than the fair copy of the minutes; Rådsprotokoll i koncept/Rough draft of Council minutes, January–June 1719, vol. 27, RA.

A rather detailed account of the discussions before the coronation of Christina is provided in the Council minutes, but about
this particular issue the documents are silent. The most relevant
information that can be found is that Chancellor of the Realm Axel
Oxenstierna drew up the outline for the procedure in the church,
'following to the greatest extent possible the previous ceremonial at
the coronation of the late King'.[24] According to Johan Arckenholtz,
biographer of the Queen, the Chancellor of the Realm had felt
already during Christina's minority that Christina should and must
be respected as a king because her sex could not be changed. That
Christina should be crowned as a king and not as a queen was also
her own wish.[25] The gender aspect thus probably played a part, at
least when it came to the general view of the monarch.

However, the formulation of the enthronement must have had a
more elementary formal background. The same formula was used
at the coronation of kings, and the basic function must reasonably
have been the same with a female monarch. If the intention had been
merely to differentiate between various types of queens, it would have
been sufficient to add the word 'reigning', as was done in the decision
of the Riksdag and as Petter Abrahamsson had done in his legal
comments.[26] The key phrase when Christina and Ulrika Eleonora
were crowned kings was rather the final words: 'she and no one else'.
The intention was thus to remove all doubt that Ulrika Eleonora was
the legally crowned monarch in the sense of the Royal Code:

> Over the whole of Sweden there shall not be more than one crowned
> head or king.[27]

---

24 Council minutes of 19 July 1650, also 31 July 1650, *Svenska riksrådets
protokoll*, XIV, pp. 232, 247–48 ('fölliandes så mychitt möjel. är dhe förre
cerem. vidh sahl. Kongens chröningh'). The coronation of Queen Christina
was discussed in the Council on 10, 24 and 31 January; 4, 7 and 14 February;
21 March; 9 April; 6, 8 and 29 May; 26 June; 19, 22, 29 and 31 July; 1, 2
and 30 August; 4, 27 and 30 September; and 3, 8 and 12 October 1650.
25 Johan Arckenholtz, *Memoires concernant Christine, reine de Suede, pour
servir d'eclaircissement a l'histoire de son regne et principalement de sa
vie privee, et aux evenemens de l'histoire de son tems civile et literaire*,
4 vols (Amsterdam and Leipzig: Jean Schreuder & Pierre Mortier le Jeune,
1751–60), I (1751), p. 121; *ibid.*, III (1759), pp. 202, 216.
26 Resolution of the Riksdag of 30 May 1719, § 1, in *Alla riksdagars och
mötens besluth*, III, pp. 1338–39; Petter Abrahamsson in Landslagen, p. 87.
27 The Royal Code, Landslagen, chapter 2, p. 2 ('ÖFwer alt Swerike skal
ey Konungsligh Krona eller Konunger wara, vtan en'). *King Magnus
Eriksson's Law of the Realm*, p. 1.

There could only be *one* ruling royal person, and for this person the law text had no gender-neutral designation, knowing only the formal title of 'king', *konung*. As previously discussed, being above parties was in the nature of the royal role, and all forms of shared regencies were in direct opposition to the idea of unity. The lesson of history was that two monarchs almost infallibly implied two parties; this was the reason behind the categorical rejection of Ulrika Eleonora's idea of jointly ruling with Frederick, and even that of including him in the Council.[28] It was probably considered extra important to emphasise the single rulership against the background of Ulrika Eleonora's endeavours in this respect, as well as Frederick's well-known ambition for power; but the phrase was thus not unique. In this context, it should be remembered that a strict boundary had also been drawn against Duke Charles Gustav at Christina's coronation. True, he was the designated successor; but he was allowed to be involved in governmental matters only at the Queen's sufferance.[29]

Furthermore, it seems only to have been at the enthronement that the female monarchs of Sweden officially bore the title of king. Already during the coronation of Ulrika Eleonora, hymn 311 was sung, 'God give our king and all Magistracy peace and good rule!' ('Gudh gifwe wårom Konung och all Öfwerhet, Frijd och godt regement!'), with 'our king' ('wårom Konung') replaced by 'our queen' ('wåre Drottning'), and normally the designation 'Her Majesty the Queen' was used.[30] However, for the remainder of the

28 Cf. 'Ofögripeligt betänkiande' ('Deferential report [re. Frederick's candidacy for the Swedish crown])', Engeströmska handskriftsamlingen, Anmärkningar över tillståndet och förändringen i Sverige efter konung Karl XII:s död/Observations on the situation and change in Sweden following the death of Charles XII, B.II.2.13, KB, fols 303^v–304^r.
29 Council minutes of 8 October 1650, *Svenska riksrådets protokoll*, XIV, pp. 334–35.
30 Cf., e.g., Carl Ernst Klein, *Samtal emellan afledne deras Kongl. Majestäter, Hennes Maj:t drottning Ulrica Eleonora Sweriges, Göthes, och Wendes drottning &c. &c. &c. landt-grefwinna til Hessen &c. &c. &c. som sidstledne d. 24. novembr. här i Stockholm j herranom afsomnade; och dess fru moder, Hennes Maj:t drottning Ulrica Eleonora Sweriges, Göthes och Wendes drottning &c. &c. &c. arf-printzessa til Dannemark och Norrige &c. &c. &c. hwilken högstsaligen afled d. 26. julii 1693 på Carlbergs slott; hwarutinnan bägge deras Kongl. Majestäter hwarannan berätta den mycket märkwärdige historien af deras lefwerne* (Stockholm: Lars Salvius, 1742), pp. 63, 71. Christina herself possibly preferred 'Rex Svecorum' to 'Regina Svecorum'

coronation the Queen was also assigned all the masculine attributes that belonged to the royal office. At the presentation of the sword of the realm, for instance, the customary hope was expressed 'that you may always be fearless and with free and good courage do battle in a manly manner'.[31] The same highness was attributed to a queen consort as to a king, and his subjects were also hers. However, it was made clear that she had no share in government authority except with the consent of the Estates, for example when Ulrika Eleonora temporarily resumed governance of the kingdom during Frederick's journey to Hesse in 1731.[32] The royal status that accrued to women was therefore qualitatively different from that accruing to men. A queen was normally the daughter of a prince, but was elevated to queen only when she entered into marriage. Men who were predestined to be kings usually bore their royal status as an inherent quality, while this was only exceptionally the case for the women who became queens. The office of the king was the one that had constitutional significance, even if it should happen to be held by a woman. With the introduction of the hereditary kingdom, though, the survival of the office rested on an agreement under private law – the marriage – in which the woman or queen was an important party. The king, he and no one else, held an office, while the queen normally only guaranteed its survival. For this reason there could be only one king representing the Crown on any given occasion, while there was in theory no limit to the number of queens. The fact that Louisa Ulrika at one point in her life was simultaneously the daughter, mother and sister of a king did not add to her preferential status before her daughter-in-law Sophia Magdalena, whose primary capacity was to be the mother of the Crown Prince – the titles of queens were not cumulative in the same way as were the titles of kings.[33]

in unofficial contexts; see Børresen, p. 46. Cf. Sven Stolpe, *Drottning Kristina: Efter tronavsägelsen* (Stockholm: Bonniers, 1961), pp. 103–04. See also Tegenborg Falkdalen, pp. 122, 144, who refers to a couple of obscure passages where Christina is called 'king'; cf. pp. 146, 157, 172.
31 *Berättelse om Hännes Kongl. Maj:ts* [...] *smörjelse- och krönings-act*, p. 15 ('att J altid må wara tröst och wid ett fritt och godt mod, til att manligen strida').
32 [Nehrman], 'Inledning till Thet Swenska Jus Publicum', B 762, KB, 2:IX, §§ 8–12, fols 107–08.
33 Cf. Theresa Earenfight, 'Without the Persona of the Prince: Kings, Queens and the Idea of Monarchy in Late Medieval Europe', *Gender & History*,

That the interpretation of the coronation formula presented here, which has due support in the legal texts of the time, nevertheless did not appear unambiguous even to contemporary observers has already been shown. This is emphasised to an even greater degree by the fact that the final subclause in particular – here elevated to the actual main clause – was left out in a detailed unpublished description of the progress of the coronation.[34] On the one hand, this narrative, as well as the eyewitness account by the French traveller Aubry de La Motraye, overlooked the subtlety of the Queen being declared king.[35] On the other hand, this is highlighted in Major Johan Henrik Schildte's depiction of the coronation. He lets Fama, floating next to the canopy, trumpet forth, 'VLRICA ELEONORA crowned King of the Swedes and the Goths and the provinces belonging to them. She and no one else' (Figure 8). It can be added that at the double coronation of 1751, Adolf Frederick was 'crowned king' ('krönter Konung') and Louisa Ulrika was 'crowned queen' ('krönter Drottning').[36]

It is clear that this proclamation attracted attention while leaving room for different interpretations. Nor is there any reason to doubt the fact that female monarchs in themselves also represented an anomaly. Even so, the misgivings were not so great that the sister of Charles XII could not be preferred over his nephew, whose claim to the throne was on a par with hers.

Duke Charles Frederick, Ulrika Eleonora's nephew and earlier rival for the throne, was present at her coronation, and the printed account puts particular emphasis on his leaving Uppsala Cathedral

19 (2007), 1–21 (pp. 6–10), who draws partly different conclusions from similar observations, although primarily with respect to a medieval context.
34 'Kort berättelse om Hennes Maijttz wår [aller]nådigste drottningz Ulricæ Eleonoræ Crönin[gsfesti]vitet, som skedde i Upsala d: 17 Martij [1719]', Engeströmska handskriftsamlingen, Handlingar rörande drottning Ulrika Eleonoras regering, B.II.2.14, KB, fol. 88ᵛ.
35 La Motraye, *Travels*, p. 368; La Motraye, *Voyages*, p. 427.
36 *Wid theras Kongl. Majestäters, Hans Kongl. Maj:ts, wår allernådigste konungs, konung Adolph Friedrichs, Sweriges, Göthes och Wendes konungs &c. &c. &c. samt thess högtälskelige gemåls, Hennes Kongl. Maj:ts, wår allernådigsta drottnings, drottning Lovisæ Ulricæ kröning, som sker then 26. november 1751. kommer följande at i akt tagas* ([Stockholm]: Kungl. tryckeriet, [n.d.]) (official proclamation, annual print series) ('VLRICA ELEONORA Krönter Suea, giöta Konung, och underliggande Provincier. Hon och ingen annan').

Figure 8 The coronation of Ulrika Eleonora the Younger in 1719. Archbishop Mathias Steuchius and, behind him, Councillor of the Realm Nils Gyllenstierna places the crown on the Queen's head under the watchful eyes of the lords of the Council and, up in the gallery, the members of the Riksdag and the ladies of the court. The Queen's consort Frederick and her nephew Charles Frederick view the scene from the balcony above the regalia to the right. Gouache on parchment by Johan Henrik Schildte. Compare Figure 7. Photo: The art collections of the University of Uppsala.

when it was time to swear the oaths. This was completely in accordance with the programme and should most reasonably be explained by his being a ruling prince, who could not be placed in a subject-like relationship to the queen of Sweden. It was a different matter with Frederick, who was of princely birth as well, but who also had an official position in the Swedish state and who swore an oath of allegiance as 'generalissimus'. As the husband of Ulrika Eleonora, he would normally have been her lord and master; it was therefore important to emphasise the order of precedence between them. This basic hierarchy between the sexes is presumably also the reason why Frederick, unlike queens who were not rulers, was not crowned in spite of being the royal consort. On the other hand, it was probably for the purpose of emphasising the difference in rank downwards that he, too, immediately thereafter left the cathedral while the Councillors swore their oaths.[37] To be sure, Frederick was subject to the authority of the Queen; but he was not bound by any other Swedish persons of influence.

Because of the lack of suitable premises in Uppsala, the Estates could not pay their tributes and swear their oaths until around three weeks later at a special ceremony in the Hall of Knights at Kungshuset in Stockholm. During these proceedings, the Councillors of the Realm sat in rows on either side of the throne. The Estates swore their oaths of allegiance, confirmed the Instrument of Government and renounced all absolutism by way of the so-called oath of sovereignty. The counts and the barons were then allowed to kiss the Queen's hand while the untitled nobility and the commoner Estates had to make do with the hem of her skirt.[38] At the tributes to both Charles XI and Charles XII, all four Estates had been allowed to kiss the royal hand. Frederick's act of tribute took place three days after his coronation, but it has not been possible to find a ceremonial for this among the royal ordinances (Figure 9). At the later coronations of Adolf Frederick and Gustav III, however, hand-kissing was common practice.

The coronation of Frederick

A year and a week after the coronation of Ulrika Eleonora, Frederick was declared king and immediate successor. Directly after his accession to the throne, he began a charm offensive in which he displayed great diligence during the administration of government matters. He also requested that the Instrument of Government should always be available in the Council chamber, and that the Chancellor of Justice should remind the King about its content on any occasion when he, out of ignorance, happened to go against his sworn oath. When the coronation ceremonial was to be discussed in the Council a few weeks later, Frederick displayed a demonstrative lack of interest, wished to deal with other more urgent matters

---

37 *Berättelse om Hännes Kongl. Maj:[ts] [...] smörjelse- och krönings-act*, p. 19.
38 Council minutes, 14 March 1719, vol. 127, RA, fol. 912; 'Relation om Hennes Kongl. Maij:[tz] wår allernådigste Drottningz Ulricae Eleonorae Huldningz act uppå Rijkzdagen i Stockholm d: 11 April 1719', Engeströmska handskriftsamlingen, Handlingar rörande drottning Ulrika Eleonoras regering, B.II.2.14, KB, fols 97–99.

De hulding der Koning van Sweden FREDERIK de | Inauguratio FREDERICI I Regis Sueciae per
eerste, door de Ryke-Stenden; op den 17 May 1720. | proceres Regni habita 17 Maji 1720.

Pet. Schenk Exc: Amst: C.Pr.

Figure 9 King Frederick I hailed by the Estates of Sweden on 17 May 1720. The engraving was made by Peter Schenck of Amsterdam and bears little resemblance to what actually took place. Photo: Jens Gustafsson, KB.

first, then said he was happy with anything the Councillors might decide and thereafter left the Council chamber.[39]

By and large, the ritual was copied from the previous year; but there were two major changes: the coronation took place in Stockholm, and the Queen entered the church accompanied by a complete set of regalia, wearing her crown and holding her sceptre (Figures 10 and 11).

What did these changes mean? It is probably not necessary to attach too much significance to the choice of location for the coronation. The Queen's coronation in Uppsala had already provoked opposition, and there was no reason to give in to royal caprice once again. Since Frederick's coronation, the St Nicholas

---

39 Council minutes, 28 March 1720, vol. 131, RA, fol. 705ʳ; *ibid.*, 21 April 1720, vol. 132, RA, fols 265, 267–68.

Figure 10 The coronation of Frederick I in the St Nicholas Church of Stockholm. The King, sceptre in hand, is having the crown placed on his head by the Archbishop and a member of the Council of the Realm. On the right the national banner, which was in reality adorned by the Great National Coat of Arms incorporating the arms of the dynasty; compare Figure 11. Engraving by an unknown artist. Photo: Björn Green, KB.

Church in Stockholm has been the site for every Swedish coronation except for that of Gustav IV Adolf in 1800, which took place in Norrköping.

Still, the fact that the Queen was adorned in a full set of regalia had a significance that she herself was quick to emphasise. The Council had no particular opinion on how the ceremonial should be designed and gladly handed this issue over to Superintendent Tessin, 'who best understands such matters', and to the royal couple themselves. After Tessin's proposal Ulrika Eleonora wrote to her husband a few weeks before the coronation, maintaining that her presence required certain arrangements. Frederick's elevation to the throne was personal, and only his direct male heirs by the Queen would be entitled to succeed him. If Frederick were to be the first of the spouses to die, Ulrika Eleonora would be reinstated as ruler. For this reason, no formal abdication took place; but her subjects had been released from their oaths to the Queen on 24 March, i.e. the same day as the signing of Frederick's act of election. In order to accentuate the fact that Ulrika Eleonora would be reinstated as head of the

Figure 11 The coronation of Frederick I in the St Nicholas Church of Stockholm in 1720. The Archbishop, together with Councillor of the Realm Carl Gustaf Rehnskiöld, places the crown on the King's head. Fama, above right, heralds 'FREDERICK. I. Crowned King of Sweden and subservient provinces. He and none other. VIVAT VIVAT VIVAT' ('FRIEDRICH. I. Krönter Swea och götha Konung och så des underliggiande Provincier. han och ingen annan. VIUAT VIUAT VIUAT'). The Bible before the King is open at the first chapter of the Book of Joshua. The Queen watches the proceedings in full royal dress. Gouache on parchment by Johan Henrik Schildte. Compare Figure 10. Photo: The art collections of the University of Uppsala.

realm in the case of Frederick's unexpected demise, she demanded that the same number of regalia would be carried before both of them. On the whole, the Queen wished to adhere to the ritual from the coronation of Ulrika Eleonora the Elder; however, each spouse, instead of going there on foot, rode to the church in his or her own coach and entered under his or her own canopy.[40]

---

40 Council minutes, 14 April 1720, vol. 132, RA, fols 220–24, quotation on fol. 223 ('som bäst förstår detta'); Ulrika Eleonora's letter to Frederick

As a result of this procedure, Frederick would be crowned with the royal crown of Gustav II Adolf's consort Maria Eleonora (which had also been worn by her daughter Christina), because the traditional royal crown of Eric XIV had already been given to the Queen. From the opening of the 1731 session of the Riksdag, Frederick nevertheless began using Eric's crown, because he thought the other one was too unwieldy. At the two subsequent coronations during the Age of Liberty, Maria Eleonora's crown was again worn by the King. This procedure shows that no special qualities were attributed to individual regalia. With few exceptions, such as the Hungarian Crown of St Stephen, that has been the rule in the princely houses of Europe. Of course, tradition meant that certain objects might be preferred; but it was rare for any intrinsic magical powers to be attributed to them. Unless an object had had the time to reach a particularly reverent age, or become in some other way fraught with tradition, it was also common for them to change with the vagaries of fashion. The individual regalia were all symbolic representations; but their significance was not so great that both their order of preference and number could not vary from the normal five – crown, sceptre, sword, apple and key – to at most ten (for the coronation of Charles XI). Certain standard attributes that were not included among the regalia were added: banner, canopy, mantle, anointing horn and so on. In any case, there were a large number of them. In most European countries, princes were content to have three or four regalia. On the eve of Frederick's coronation there were already several sets of all these objects, with the exception of the key of the realm. Consequently, an almost identical copy of the key of Eric XIV was made. Incidentally, this sign of rank is unique to the regalia of Sweden and is comparable only to the keys of St Peter, which symbolise the temporal power of the pope (Figure 12).[41]

---

of 15 April 1720, printed in *Tidningar utgifne i Upsala år 1774*, second annual volume (Uppsala: Johan Edman, 1774), pp. 164–65.

41 Johannes Hermansson (*praeses*) and Christopher J. Brehmer (respondent), *Dissertatio historico-politica, de regalibus regni Sveo-Gothici* (Stockholm: Johan Henrik Werner, 1733), p. 70; Johann Georg Peter Möller, 'Historische Nachricht [...] der vornehmsten königlichen schwedischen Krönungsinsignien', in Johann Georg Peter Möller, *Die Verdienste der königlichen schwedischen Gustave aus dem Wasastamm* (Stralsund: Christian Lorenz Struck, 1772), p. 47; [Nehrman], 'Inledning till Thet Swenska Jus Publicum', B 762, KB, 2:IV, §§ 17–22, fols 60–63; [Busser],

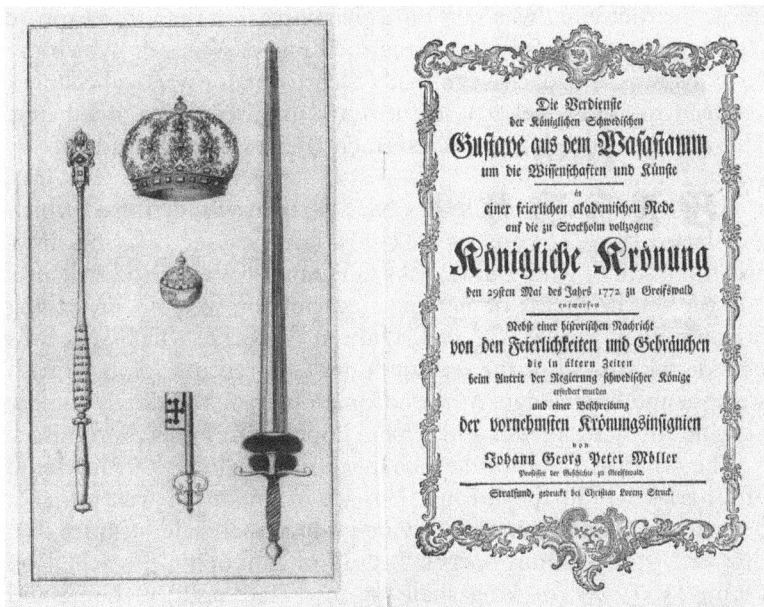

Figure 12 Patriotic tribute to the king from the Swedish provinces. The academic celebratory speech by Greifswald Professor of History Johann Georg Peter Möller about the achievements of the Vasa Kings in the fields of science and the arts was delivered in connection with the coronation of Gustav III in 1772. Facing the title page: the regalia of Sweden. Photo: Björn Green, KB.

The coronation sermons, which were usually delivered by the Bishop of Linköping, were of particular significance. The entire coronation ceremony was framed by a mass, and even though the sermon had no legal function, it was of course important at a time of deep religious convictions. Besides, the spoken word had an immediate and persuasive potential that visual representations lacked. The visible rituals were open to various interpretations, while a sermon had an explanatory power because of its being spoken directly to the audience. True for the period in question, that rule applied to posterity, too. It is usually easier for historians

---

Historisk berättelse, p. 16; Cederström, pp. 21–23, 119; Twining, pp. 21–22, 268; Hoffmann, pp. 130, 136–37, 139. Grundberg, pp. 176, 192–93, discusses Christina's choice to use Maria Eleonora's crown when she was crowned.

to reconstruct what was said on a given occasion than to recapture visual appearances. By comparing the Bible passages on which the sermons were based, one can easily identify major political changes between the late Age of Greatness and the early Age of Liberty. These changes cannot be as conveniently assessed with reference to visible forms.

At the coronation of Charles XI, a sermon was delivered which was based on II Chronicles 1. 1–11. This passage describes how Solomon, son of King David, asks God not for wealth and treasure, nor for the downfall of his enemies, but for wisdom in leading his numerous people of Israel. Only in verse 12, which was thus outside the subject of the sermon, does God reward Solomon with wisdom and knowledge. At the coronation, then, the King's humble petition for wisdom was still a mere hope, an unfulfilled promise.

The political situation had changed drastically at the accession of Charles XII to the throne. His act of anointing was rather a dramatic culmination of the divinely sanctioned rule of kings. On that occasion, Haquin Spegel, Bishop of Linköping, preached on Psalm 21. 1–3: 'The king shall joy in thy strength, O Lord; and in thy salvation how greatly shall he rejoice!' Spegel's sermon has been subjected to a thorough analysis by the literary scholar Nils Ekedahl, who argues that this biblical passage was obviously 'chosen to demonstrate the claims of the Palatinate dynasty to be appointed by God to rule over Sweden'.[42]

At the coronation of Charles XI, the chief message of the sermon had involved the relationship between the king and the people. A monarch would seek the wisdom and power required to govern his kingdom, and support from God would serve this purpose. Spegel's sermon on the other hand focused on the king's relationship to God, his subjects becoming more secondary. Ekedahl shows how Spegel's reading of the text legitimised the self-coronation of Charles XII and made the crown a symbol of the divine nature of the royal office.[43] In this way, Charles XII never had to ask God for

---

42 Nils Ekedahl, *Det svenska Israel: Myt och retorik i Haquin Spegels predikokonst*, Studia rhetorica Upsaliensia, 2 (Uppsala: Gidlunds, 1999), pp. 109–18, quotation on p. 111 ('vald för att demonstrera den pfalziska dynastins pretentioner på att vara utsedd av Gud till att härska över Sverige'). All Bible quotations are taken from *The Bible: Authorized King James Version*, ed. by Robert Carroll and Stephen Prickett (Oxford: Oxford University Press, 1997; 2008 reissue).
43 Ekedahl, p. 116.

wisdom and strength; these qualities had already been conferred on
him when he was designated as king.

At the coronation of Ulrika Eleonora, the hour-long sermon of
Torsten Rudeen, Bishop of Linköping, seems to have been particularly influenced by the troubled situation of the kingdom. The text
was from I Kings 8. 57–58, the prayer of Solomon: 'The LORD our
God be with us, as he was with our fathers: let him not leave us,
nor forsake us.' The same bishop's sermon at the coronation of
Frederick one year later was all the more clearly addressed to the
King. This time, the text was based on Deuteronomy 17. 18–20. In
the ceremonial, it was stressed that Rudeen would deliver 'a short
sermon', but the text from the Bible alone spoke volumes:

> And it shall be, when he sitteth upon the throne of his kingdom, that
> he shall write him a copy of this law in a book out of *that which is*
> before the priests the Levites: And it shall be with him, and he shall
> read therein all the days of his life: that he may learn to fear the
> LORD his God, to keep all the words of this law and these statutes,
> to do them: That his heart be not lifted up above his brethren, and
> that he turn not aside from the commandment, *to* the right hand, or
> *to* the left: to the end that he may prolong *his* days in his kingdom,
> he, and his children, in the midst of Israel.[44]

It could hardly be said any more emphatically. If Frederick himself
had not, at his induction into the Council, made the comment
about having the Instrument of Government read out, he was now
reminded of it at his coronation. The final verse also implies that
observance of the law was a condition of his rule over Sweden.
The king's discharge from liability did not include breaches of the
Constitution, and there were certainly methods for keeping him
within constitutional bounds.

The same passage had already been identified in the previous
year as an expression of the true rights of kings in the great
manifesto of the revolution, written by David Silvius and distributed with the semi-official *Posttidningar*. This is yet another proof

---

44 Deuteronomy 17. 18–20. Incidentally, referring to Sweden as Israel was
an old and well-established metaphor. See also Pasi Ihalainen, *Protestant
Nations Redefined: Changing Perceptions of National Identity in the
Rhetoric of the English, Dutch and Swedish Public Churches, 1685–1772*,
Studies in Medieval and Reformation Traditions: History, Culture, Religion,
Ideas, 109 (Leiden and Boston: Brill, 2005), pp. 154–55.

of how influential his text was.[45] Silvius had also recommended verses 14–17, but possibly the line 'thou mayest not set a stranger over thee' was felt to be somewhat inopportune when the realm had just acquired a German-born King who did not speak Swedish. Another permanent feature at the coronations were the proclamations of pardons (*pardonsplakat*). The king pardoned malefactors from temporal punishment; but the obvious public penance (*kyrkoplikt*), which returned criminals to society after their punishments had been completed, was retained. This gesture was a manifestation both of the king's benevolence and of his role as the highest administrator of justice. The proclamations of pardon were perceived to be a remnant of the medieval royal accession tours of the realm (*eriksgator*), during which the king had pardoned three criminals in each province. Serious criminals were not considered, and the pardon was implemented at the king's pleasure and was not to be understood as a right. Charles XII had not issued any proclamations of pardon.[46]

The significance of the coronation ceremony

What was politically essential about these acts of coronation? We may remind ourselves that the changes regarding the swearing

---

45 David Silvius, *Påminnelser angående successions-rättigheten i Sweriges rike, samt det så kallade souveraine wäldet, upsatte i januarii månad 1719* (Stockholm: Johan Henrik Werner, 1720), § 21. Silvius's original manuscript is kept at KB, D 837: [David Silvius], 'Oförgripelige påminnelser angående Successions Rättigheten i Sweriges rike'. The pamphlet was printed with minor changes and was enclosed with *Stockholmiske Post-Tidender*, no. 4 (26 January 1720).

On Silvius's pamphlet, see Simon Johannes Boëthius, 'Några anmärkningar om uppkomsten och karaktären af Frihetstidens författning', *Historisk tidskrift*, 11 (1891), 233–70 (p. 257); Fredrik Lagerroth, *Frihetstidens författning: En studie i den svenska konstitutionalismens historia* (Stockholm: Bonniers, 1915), pp. 252–54; Carl-E. Normann, *Prästerskapet och det karolinska enväldet: Studier över det svenska prästerskapets statsuppfattning under stormaktstidens slutskede*, Samlingar och studier till Svenska kyrkans historia, 17 (Stockholm: Svenska kyrkans diakonistyrelses bokförlag, 1948), pp. 290, 294, 296; Thanner, pp. 195–97; Per Nilsén, *Att 'stoppa munnen till på bespottare': Den akademiska undervisningen i svensk statsrätt under frihetstiden*, Rättshistoriskt bibliotek, I:59 (Lund: Institutet för rättshistorisk forskning, 2001), pp. 97–99.
46 Landslagen, pp. 158–59.

of oaths had been evident when Charles XII, elder brother to the Queen, acceded to the throne: the subjects swore an oath to their King, while the King did not swear any oath at all. This was important mainly because the oaths had legal force. The rest of the ceremonial displayed the prevailing power relationships more or less clearly, but had no legal effect. Here the variations could therefore be more arbitrary. The only conspicuously altered symbolic act was the King's arbitrary conduct with respect to the crown; otherwise tradition was followed rather closely. One should thus not overemphasise the significance of iconography and other visual details. In addition, changes appear to be truly important symbolic expressions only when they must be abolished under new political circumstances, and that was, on the whole, not the case.

For these reasons, it is best to be cautious about reading any deep situationally determined symbolism into Ulrika Eleonora's coronation ritual. Her and her brother's ceremonials were in that respect variations on a theme. With both of them, the predominant visual expression was pomp and magnificence. What was *said* was, on the other hand, all the more important. At the coronation of Ulrika Eleonora, the old ceremonial order had been restored: first the coronation oath was sworn, then the anointing and the coronation were performed, and finally the Councillors swore their oaths. As usual, the Estates swore their oaths and paid their tributes on a separate occasion.[47]

Even though the political importance of iconography and rituals in connection with coronations has been toned down here, that is a conclusion that must be justified at a deeper level. At this sort of event, all details had of course a history and their own significance, and in this respect nothing was left to chance. However, one should be careful not to read too much into elements that were not legally binding. True, a coronation ritual might illustrate real power relations; but it could also be used to conceal them. In the situation that prevailed at the overthrow of absolutism, the Council and other central political actors had to act with caution for several reasons. The royal authority had been pushed back, but this must not be manifested in a confrontational manner. A provocation might reinforce the determination of the royal family

---

47 *Berättelse om Hännes Kongl. Maj:ts [...] smörjelse- och krönings-act*, p. 13. The Queen took her oath with three fingers on the Bible, which was open to the first chapter of the Book of Joshua.

to reassume the initiative; it might invigorate the supporters of the court; and it might diminish the value of the symbolically important role that the royal family was supposed to play, both within the kingdom and abroad. Thus, the wisest thing to do was to adhere to traditional models as far as possible, allowing the monarch to appear with customary pomp and circumstance. This line of reasoning is possibly also supported by the fact that Ulrika Eleonora's and Frederick's coronations are known through a couple of paintings and half a dozen contemporary engravings, while that of Charles XII is known only from one contemporary and one somewhat later image (1719; Figure 6). The greater the actual power, the less need for manifesting it, and vice versa.[48]

Yet again it should be emphasised that the coronations followed a template with a clear continuity while being unique events at the same time. Small alterations in the ceremonial occurred all the time, and they were not necessarily meaningful. That Charles XII himself placed the crown on his head was no doubt of great symbolic significance, but other elements in the act of tribute to him might continue to be used because they were not perceived as essential or could easily be given a different meaning. Examples may be taken from a comparison between the two final coronation rituals of the Age of Greatness and the two first ones of the Age of Liberty.

At the act of anointing of Charles XII, the royal Councillors were given the task of lifting the canopy in the church and serving the King at the subsequent public evening meal. Scholars – and the French and Danish envoys at the time – have interpreted this feature as a way of illustrating the new social structure of the absolute monarchy. At the coronation of Charles XI, the canopy had been carried by four province governors and four generals, i.e. officials of a somewhat lower rank. It is true that the King sat alone at a raised table at the evening meal; but the Council, the generals, and the entire nobility dined in the same room. In contradistinction, Queen Christina, who was also a constitutionally bound monarch, had even wished to be served in a princely fashion by the Dukes

---

48 See the image in Snickare, *Enväldets riter*, p. 141. David Cannadine has pointed out that societies in a state of transformation are more dependent on rituals in order to legitimise power relationships, and that they are happy to fall back on older models to give an impression of continuity; David Cannadine, 'Introduction: Divine Rites of Kings', in *Rituals of Royalty: Power and Ceremonial in Traditional Societies*, ed. by David Cannadine and Simon Price (Cambridge: Cambridge University Press, 1992), pp. 1–19.

Charles Gustav and Adolf John at her coronation, 'not for the sake of vanity, but that Her Royal Majesty on that day may show her royal power'.[49] At the coronations of Ulrika Eleonora and Frederick, the Councillors of the Realm returned as bearers of the canopy, and the newly crowned couple ate at a separate table and were attended by the Councillors. The official account of Frederick's coronation even stated that when the Councillors of the Realm performed these functions, this was done 'according to custom' ('efter wanligheten'). Small changes had been made successively, but there was nevertheless perceived to be continuity both in the whole and in individual details. What had been considered a strong symbolic expression of the social order of the absolute monarchy was in fact practised in varying forms during both the constitutional monarchy of the seventeenth century and the limited monarchy of the Age of Liberty. (Incidentally, the procedure of the Councillors of the Realm attending the royals at the meal was the same as in the coronation ceremonial of Adolf Frederick, where it was specified in even greater detail.)

This contradiction requires no profound explanation: First of all, the spectators rarely had any points of comparison. Royal coronations normally occurred only once per generation, and they always comprised elements of both continuity and renewal. It was rarely possible for an individual spectator to determine the degree to which the ceremonial had been changed, and whether such changes were politically significant. Secondly, a spectator always interprets an act on the basis of pre-understanding and context. The spectator's interpretation of an event may impart a deeper significance to something that may actually be a chance occurrence. With insufficient knowledge of previous ceremonials, the spectator might interpret the Councillors waiting on the royal couple as a marked expression

49 Council minutes of 2 August 1650, *Svenska riksrådets protokoll*, XIV, p. 251 ('inthet för högfärdh schull, men effter H. M:t på den dagen måtte visa sin kongl. macht'), cf. p. 290. See also Grundberg, p. 182. See, moreover, Snickare, *Enväldets riter*, pp. 139, 145, and *Kurtze Beschreibung wie Jhr. Königl. Majest. zu Schweden Carolus XI zu Upsahl ist gekrönet worden. Aus dem schwedischen verdeutschet* ([n.p.]: [n. pub.], 1676). Variant edition with a depiction of one of the coronation medals: *Kurtze Beschreibung wie Jhre Königliche Mayt. zu Schweden Carolus XI. zu Upsahl ist gekrönet worden. Auß dem schwedischen ins hoch-teutsche übersetzet. Anno M. DC. LXXVI* ([n.p.]: [n. pub.], [n.d.]).

of the defeat of constitutionalism and the victory of absolutism. In another context, the same attendance could instead be interpreted as an act of symbolic deference and respect. In the evaluation of the foreign ministers' interpretation of the episode, one should bear in mind partly their lack of knowledge of previous ceremonials, partly certain tendencies in their interpretation and reporting of the event and partly inevitable comparisons to the corresponding rituals in their native countries. Thirdly, the same symbolism may deliberately be used in order to express different things in dissimilar political contexts. Rituals may sometimes manifest a political state of affairs, but they do not always have to support it. The Council waiting on Charles XII can be seen as an expression of the hierarchy of absolute monarchy. At the coronation of Frederick, the same element may have expressed something completely different.

In the political trench warfare at the beginning of the Age of Liberty it was important to maintain the respect of the subjects (here symbolised by the Council) for the Magistracy. The king represented the top of the pyramid that constituted the entire Lutheran interpretation of society; it was therefore by extension important to all collective relations. The possible symbolic connotations of the Council of the Realm waiting on His Majesty in a free society were not particularly important. The symbolic subservience lacked legal force; and although the monarch's coronation meal was a public act, it was not directed at the common people. It was probably primarily among these that the situation might be misunderstood.

Even at the time, his contemporaries seem to have read a good deal of symbolism into the ceremonies during the act of anointing of Charles XII. The unorthodox self-coronation, like the fact that the archbishop dropped the horn at the anointing, and the King his crown during the subsequent ride through the city, were supposedly forebodings of misfortune. No similar prophecies seem to have occurred at the first coronations of the Age of Liberty. Gustaf Bonde, province governor of Östergötland and later Councillor of the Realm, who was an eager supporter of the rule of the Estates from the very beginning and who was present at the coronations of both Ulrika Eleonora and Frederick, merely commented that they had been performed 'according to ancient custom and with the usual ceremonies'.[50] At a later point in the Age of Liberty, a

---

50 Gustaf Bonde, *Sverige, under Ulrica Eleonora och Fredric I, eller ifrån 1718 till 1751: Efter den, af framledne hans exellens, riks-rådet herr grefve*

level-headed spectator described the connection between power
and symbolism during Antiquity, and his concluding characterisation was just as much directed at his own contemporaries:

As soon as the king had been elected and tribute had been paid to
him, he acceded to government without any intervening coronation.
No reminder is necessary that the highness belonging to Swedish
kings is in no way diminished thereby; for everyone knows in
advance that the coronation neither increases nor reduces the value
of the ruler.[51]

In other words, there is reason not to overinterpret the implications of the visual elements of the coronation. Certain ceremonial
elements might be significant to the expression of social conditions. Quite a few other elements instead depended on traditional
customs: people at the time often spoke of 'that which is old
and ancient' in order to impart legitimacy and weight to legal
provisions.[52] The same preservation of tradition is likely to have
played a role in the royal rituals. It is true that the public ceremony
might give expression to a changed relationship between the king
and the Council; but it could also illustrate the relationship between
the Magistracy – here understood as the king in Council – and
the subjects at large. The Instruments of Government of the Age
of Liberty had transferred the greater part of the executive power
to the Council of the Realm, but the king was a prerequisite for
its functioning: without a king, there could be no Council of the
Realm. Making the curbing of the royal authority visible might

---

*Gustaf Bonde författade handskrift med ett Tillägg om fredsunderhand-
lingarna i Åbo 1741–1742, af r.r. herr gr. H. Cedercreutz; Ett bihang till
skriften: Tessin och Tessiniana* (Stockholm: Ecksteinska tryckeriet, 1821),
p. 15 ('efter gammal plägesed och med vanliga ceremonier'), see also
pp. 29–30.

51 Johan B. Busser, *Utkast til beskrifning om Upsala*, 2 vols (Uppsala:
Johan Edman, 1769–73), I: *Om Upsala stad, dess äldre och nyare öden,
samt förnämsta märkvärdigheter* (1773), p. 84 ('Så snart Kungen var
vald och hyllad tillträdde han Regeringen utan någon mellankommande
Kröning. Man behöfver ej påminna, att härigenom afgår ingen ting af den
höghet, som Svenska Konungarne tillkommer; ty någor hvar vet förut, att
Kröningen hvarken ökar eller minskar de Regerandes värde'). This opinion
is stated already in [Busser], *Historisk berättelse*, pp. 6–7, where he argues
that reverence for the king comes from the laws of God and Nature.

52 See, e.g., Fritz Kern, *Kingship and Law in the Middle Ages*, trans. by
S. B. Chrimes (Oxford: Basil Blackwell, 1956), pp. 149–51.

not only provoke the opposition that worked for its restoration; it would also undermine the Council's own power. 'The Magistracy' (*överheten*) was the common term for the highest executive power in society. In a restricted and basic sense, it referred to the king only. The Council of the Realm appealed to the Magistracy as well, never describing itself as a part of it. In a real and constitutional sense, however, the Magistracy or government authority was the same as the king in the Council in session – that which was referred to as 'His Royal Majesty' (*Kungl. Maj:t*) until the 1974 Instrument of Government.

Within the four walls of the Council chamber, the actual power relations – that is, the fact that the king lacked the power to make decisions without his Councillors – were of great importance. With respect to the general public, though, this relationship was mainly constitutional sophistry: His Royal Majesty ruled the country, and his subjects had an unconditional duty of obedience towards all Magistracy. This authority was religiously sanctioned and was inculcated through fundamental Lutheran discipline. Somewhere between the legal force of the sworn commitments and the visual expression of the power of the Magistracy in the coronation ceremony were the coronation sermons. Admittedly, they involved no legal obligation; but they could be perceived as an exhortation or a memento from the higher power to which all people were subordinated. Nor do the coronation sermons of 1719 and 1720 leave any doubt as to their political messages.

Kings by the grace of God

Since the beginning of the Middle Ages, the kings of Europe had ascribed to themselves a divine sanction for their offices. The expression *Dei gratia*, 'by the grace of God', was used as early as late Antiquity by Christian bishops. From at least the eighth century onwards, the formula was used by princes – initially, it seems, by the Frankish kings. The significance of this claim was subjected to various interpretations. In its original form, it was an expression of humble submission before God; it was a formula of submission or devotion which confirmed that God accepted rather than appointed the holder of an office. With this expression, Pepin the Short supposedly referred to the special divine providence that had placed him on the Frankish throne because of circumstances, and not because of any right of inheritance confirmed by an election. Divine sanction became especially vital precisely when princes pursued a

confirmation of their claims of inheritance; and in the medieval
power struggles between the Church and the Crown, bishops might
offer this in exchange for personal advantages.[53]
This validation of the claims of individual princes, originally
personal and singular, was sublimated during the Middle Ages
into a divine foundation of official power as such. Arguments were
taken from Paul's epistle to the Romans (Romans 13. 1–2), where it
was said that all Magistracy was of God, and from the fourth com-
mandment (Exodus 20. 12). Against this background, the formula
might be used in order to inculcate a duty of obedience in princes
even if they were imperfect, but it was more common to claim that
divine authority came from a prince's ability to promote justice and
piety. This ability was associated with the infallibility of the king,
a capacity that was attached to the office rather than to the person.
In some countries, such as France and England, the divinity of the
king was understood to be all but literal, while in other countries,
e.g. in the Habsburg states and the Scandinavian kingdoms, the
connection was more symbolic.

Regardless of the theoretical significance given to the phrase,
'by the grace of God' soon developed into a standard expression
for independent princes, and it was used as such in titles and forms
of address. In Sweden, the formula was demonstrably used by
King Knut Eriksson at the end of the twelfth century, and even
at this early point in time it seems to have been a fixed element in
the Swedish royal title. From the reign of Albert, King of Sweden
('Albrecht of Mecklenburg'), the formula *Dei Gratia Rex Sveciae* or

---

53 See, in general, Kern, chapter I:1, 'The Divine Right of Kings', esp.
pp. 42–43, 51–53, 64; *Kulturhistoriskt lexikon för nordisk medeltid*,
III: *Datering–Epiphania* (1958), s.v. 'Dei gratia'; *ibid.*, XIV: *Regnebræt–
Samgäld* (1969), s.v. 'Rex iustus och iniustus'; Horst Dreitzel,
*Monarchiebegriffe in der Fürstengesellschaft: Semantik und Theorie der
Einherrschaft in Deutschland von der Reformation bis zum Vormärz*,
2 vols (Cologne, Weimar and Vienna: Böhlau, 1991), II: *Theorie der
Monarchie*, pp. 515–28; Nicholas Henshall, *The Myth of Absolutism:
Change and Continuity in Early Modern European Monarchy* (London
and New York: Longman, 1992), pp. 141–43; Paul Kléber Monod, *The
Power of Kings: Monarchy and Religion in Europe 1589–1715* (New
Haven and London: Yale University Press, 1999), pp. 42–54; Sergio
Bertelli, *The King's Body: Sacred Rituals of Power in Medieval and Early
Modern Europe* (University Park: Pennsylvania State University Press,
2001), Chapter 1, 'His Majesty'.

the abbreviation D.G.R.S. can invariably be found on coins minted by the Swedish Crown.[54]

In the religious forms of legitimation that gradually grew more forceful, only to finally culminate during the Age of Absolutism, the formula was thoroughly natural. It was still used during the Age of Liberty, though, and at that time it was occasionally a cause of perplexity. For common subjects, who formed their picture of the world in accordance with Martin Luther's Table of Duties and Sunday sermons, it was not entirely easy to internalise the deeper theoretical implications in a way that corresponded to accepted doctrine. The analogy of 'one God, one king' was close at hand; and when the Catechism was taught, the words of Paul were quoted: 'there is no power but of God: the powers that be are ordained of God' ('then Öfwerhet som är, hon är skickad af Gudi', Romans 13. 1). A typical application of these words can be found in an anonymous laudatory verse from the beginning of the Age of Liberty: 'ULRICA anointed by God to wear the royal crown, [...] ULRICA anointed by God to govern the people and the land.'[55] The idea that God tangibly appointed princes, and that the kings of the world had an immediate mandate from the King of Heaven, easily wormed its way into popular conceptions. After all, that notion was what the constitutional theorists of the absolute monarchy had taught and transmitted through the Church; and because of the inertia of an ingrained way of thinking, some people continued to proclaim it at the beginning of the Age of Liberty.[56]

Conversely, the authors of the Constitution of the Age of Liberty advocated the idea of a contract under natural law, according to which God merely indirectly appointed and deposed kings. This view was promoted as early as 1719 in the manifesto of David Silvius. Regardless of the theoretical foundation, it was the common people and the Estates who in actual fact had power

54 Cf. [Nehrman], 'Inledning till Thet Swenska Jus Publicum', B 762, KB, 2:VI, fols 70–79.

55 *Underdånig lyck-önskan til Hennes Kongl. Maj:t Sweriges Göthes och Wändes stormächtigste drottning Ulrica Eleonora då huldnings-acten blef firat i Stockholm den 7 april åhr 1719* (Stockholm: Kungl. tryckeriet, 1719) ('ULRICA Smord af Gud, at Konglig Cronan bära, [...] ULRICA, Smord af Gud at Styra Folck och Land').

56 Normann, pp. 34–47, 69, 73–74, 92–93. See also Ekedahl, pp. 82–86, 113; Nilsén, *Att 'stoppa munnen till på bespottare'*, pp. 74–75, 77–78; Ihalainen, pp. 154–56.

over and control of the situation at the 1719 and 1720 sessions of the Riksdag. However, by the following assembly of the Estates in 1723 the royalist opposition had already awakened in earnest. The Peasant Estate collectively supported a petition saying that King Frederick should be allowed to enjoy 'the royal power and authority wielded by the ancient erstwhile kings of Sweden'. This petition created dismay in the other Estates, and it was suspected that external forces tried to influence the peasants. Investigations eventually led to a notary, Abraham Dahlén, who was arrested together with several accomplices. In Dahlén's possession were found several petitions in which he expressed his ideas. Referring to the impartiality of the royal authority, he argued that the primary intention behind his suggestion was to give the king the authority to prohibit, abolish and suppress iniquity, violence and injustice. The wording was taken from the Instrument of Government, and Dahlén's intention was, according to his own account, to invest real power in the function and status of the king.[57]

An Estate commission court (ständerkommission) was given the task of judging the matter, and the judgement it pronounced contained a theoretical exposition on the foundation of the prevailing form of government that came to serve as guidance throughout the Age of Liberty. In one of his petitions, Dahlén maintained that 'the king, being in God's stead, should, next to God, have in his highest authority complete and unimpeded power'. Here kings were still portrayed as gods on earth. Because the words of Paul were still current through the Lutheran Catechism, their correct interpretation required a little exposition by the commission court. It therefore emphasised that even though

---

57 Carl Gustaf Malmström, Sveriges politiska historia från konung Karl XII:s död till statshvälfningen 1772, 2nd edn, 6 vols (Stockholm: Norstedts, 1893–1901), I, pp. 367–70, 379–83. The petition of the Peasants has been published in Sveriges ridderskaps och adels riksdags-protokoll, II:1: 1723 (1876), p. 82 ('den Kongl. Mackt och myndighet, som Sveriges forna framfarne Konungar haft hafva'). The original documents in this case, including Dahlén's petitions, can be found in Protokoll och handlingar i saken över kommissarien Osthof/Minutes and documents regarding the case of Commissioner Osthof, vol. 1, R 5614, RA. Dahlén felt that the king should have authority in accordance with chapters 2 and 4 of the Royal Code of the Law of the Realm, and §§ 2 and 4 of the Instrument of Government.

the temporal Magistracy is and should be treated as a dispensation
from God, the Magistracy nevertheless received its power indirectly
through those who have assigned to him the power and authority
to rule and reign over them; because God has not prescribed any
particular form of government, but left it to the discretion of a free
people to themselves choose not only their Magistracy, but also their
legitimate form of government, which they according to the situation
of the time and the nature of the people itself would find most secure
and advantageous for themselves, whereafter the Magistracy, which
also for this reason in the sacred words of God is called a human
order, receives its power and authority to govern and rule in an either
less or more limited fashion[.][58]

Here the idea of a contract under natural law recurred, and the
interpretation of the commission became a kind of official doctrine
that was referred to in many contexts during the Age of Liberty.[59]

---

58 The judgement of the commission of the Estates of the Realm concerning Abraham Dahlén, Anders Prange, Johan Friedrich Osthof and Lars
Wigström, 23 July 1723, in Protokoll och handlingar i saken över kommissarien Osthof/Minutes and documents regarding the case of Commissioner
Osthof, vol. 2, R 5615, RA ('Konungen, såsom i Guds stad och ställe,
bör, näst Gud, äga uti dess högsta wälde fullkomlig oförkränkt macht';
'den werldzliga Öfwerheten är och bör hållas för en Guds skickelse, så
hade dock Öfwerheten dess wälde medelbart genom dem, som honom
updragit macht och wäld öfwer sig at råda och regera; aldenstund Gud
icke föreskrifwit något wist Regeringssätt, utan lämnat uti ett fritt folks
egit godtfinnande, at icke allenast sielf wällia sig Öfwerhet, utan ock hwad
lofligit Regeringssätt, de efter tidernas beskaffenhet och sielfwa folkeslagets
art worde för sig säkrast och nyttigast finnandes, hwarefter Öfwerheten,
som ock derföre uti Guds heliga ord kallas en mennisklig ordning, undfår
sin macht och myndighet at styra och regera antingen mindre eller mera
inskränkt').
59 See, e.g., [Nehrman], 'Inledning till Thet Swenska Jus Publicum', B 762, KB,
2:V, § 15, fols 68–69; En Ärlig Swensk (Stockholm: Historiographi regni,
1755), pp. 365–66; [Isac Faggot], Swea rikes styrelse efter grund-lagarne
(Stockholm: Johan Georg Lange, 1768), p. 7; [Johan Funck], Genwäg
til kundskap och utöfning af swensk lagfarenhet (Stockholm: Kungl. tryckeriet, 1761), p. 52. This view was also emphasised in an anonymous
poem on the death of King Frederick (Klagan jämte tröst, då den i lifstiden
stormäcktigste herre Svea, Götha och Wendes konung, konung Friedrich
den förste, med skjäl kallad den Milde, Svea barns hulldaste fader, odödelig,
til dess dödeliga del i konunga-grafwen jämte de odödeliga Carlar bisattes
den 11. april. 1751 [n.p.]: B.V., [n.d.]):

When we then your demise bewail,
Gracious FREDRICH, Great FREDRICH

The devotional formula 'by the grace of God' continued to exist emptied of its concrete content; but it reflected the fundamental ideology of the confessional state, it expressed an inherited authority in the administration of justice, and in accordance with diplomatic tradition it signalled an independent majesty. In all these cases, the phrase also expressed the fact that the kingdom belonged to a wider Christian community. Even so, the formula was used sparingly, virtually only on coins and as a preamble in the official letters of the king and Crown. Eventually, Adolf Frederick also accepted the official interpretation. When the climate was at its frostiest between him on the one hand and the Council and the Hat party on the other, the King wrote an open letter to the Estates in which he said he would rather return the sceptre 'which God and the free election of the Estates of the Realm had entrusted me with, than to wield the same in trepidation and without royal dignity'. At the beginning of the letter, he wrote of 'all-wise Providence' ('allwisa försynen') which had guided the unexpected choice of the Estates as if by a supernatural hand.[60]

We nevertheless take comfort
    That the well-being and rudder of the realm
Has now been left in the hands of ADOLPH FREDRICH
By GOD and the Estates.

(När wi då Tin bortgång klage,
    FREDRICH Milde, FREDRICH Stor,
Wi likwäl til hugnad tage,
    At nu Rikets Wäl och Ror
Uti ADOLPH FREDRICHS händer
Lämnadt är af GUD och Ständer.)

See also Erik Fahlbeck, 'Studier öfver frihetstidens politiska idéer', part 1, *Statsvetenskaplig tidskrift för politik, statistik, ekonomi*, 18 (1915), 325–45 (p. 336); Per Nilsén, 'Die problematische königliche Alleinherrschaft und die verständnislosen Ausländer: Über die Bedeutung Jacob Wildes (1679–1755) für die Entwicklung des schwedischen Staatsrechts bis 1772', in *Geschichte und Perspektiven des Rechts im Ostseeraum: Erster Rechtshistorikertag im Ostseeraum 8.–12. März 2000*, ed. by Jörn Eckert and Kjell Å. Modéer, Rechtshistorische Reihe, 251 (Frankfurt am Main: Peter Lang, 2002), pp. 45–58 (pp. 48–49). Similar lines of reasoning could be found in Great Britain as well during the eighteenth century; see Linda Colley, *Britons: Forging the Nation 1707–1837* (London: Pimlico, 1994), pp. 48, 232.

60 Adolf Frederick's open letter to the Estates of the Realm of 6 November 1755, copy in D 182, Politiske skrifter/Political writings, KB ('den Gud och Riksens Ständers fria wal mig anförtrott, än at densamma föra med

Naturally, the Hat party's journal *En Ärlig Swensk* had a good deal to say in this matter. To be sure, the authors perceived God's concrete intervention in Swedish politics; but not in the sense that God appointed kings. On the contrary, in this context liberty itself was a beam of divine light and was manifested in concrete terms in the Instrument of Government. *En Ärlig Swensk* saw how 'the finger of the Lord' ('Herrans finger') had intervened at the demise of absolutism. It was pointed out that there had been a large number of hereditary princes who could have succeeded Charles XI during the Age of Absolutism, but that all of them had died in infancy. Only the Crown Prince, the future Charles XII, had reached adulthood, but he was taken from the royal throne in his prime without leaving any heirs and without having arranged for the succession. In this way the kingdom had, contrary to all expectations, been given full sovereignty to control the form of government on its own. 'Has not the Supreme Being then in such a visible manner Himself provided most graciously for our blessed liberty?'[61]

Isac Faggot was even less unambiguous on this issue. According to him, it was the private affair of the citizens of a society to decide for themselves about their form of government. 'Surely there is according to natural law no absolute necessity to have a king', he argued boldly, and it went against all natural freedom to make this king an absolute monarch. Even the best of kings may die, he declared, but wise laws and constitutions are immortal.[62]

Kings were perfectly ordinary individuals with perfectly ordinary qualities, Faggot maintained, and no transcendental qualities elevated them above other people. At least that is how one must understand his characterisation of absolute monarchs. With reference to logical conclusions, Faggot showed that absolutism was an offence against the laws of both God and Nature. If sovereignty was not derived from either of these sources, it must therefore be a self-assumed power that had some kind of purpose for the individual ruler. This purpose could not be to promote the highness, ambitions or pleasure of the ruler, because through such dominion he would make himself despised by the wiser world.

ängslan och utan konungslig wärdighet'). For the background of this letter, see Malmström, *Sveriges politiska historia*, IV, pp. 146–59.

61 *En Ärlig Swensk*, p. 269 ('Har icke då den Högsta på et så synbart sätt sjelf dragit nådig försorg för wår sälla frihet?').

62 [Faggot], quotation on p. 7 ('Af Naturens Lag följer wäl icke någon absolut nödwändighet, at hafwa Konung'); see also pp. 14, 30–31.

Instead he must believe that he could benefit other people, and for this reason he must know in advance everything that was to happen, feel everything that was currently going on and have precise knowledge about everything in the world around him. 'Such things can rightly be requested of those who wish to be absolute rulers; for a person who aspires to the one should be able to achieve the other.'[63] But such an ability did not exist in any human being, not even a king.

Over the course of the century, other currents of ideas manifested themselves that made direct references to the intervening hand of God in political circumstances increasingly obsolete. This development can be discerned in the mottoes of the kings: Ulrika Eleonora and Frederick, 'God is my hope'; Adolf Frederick, 'The public weal is my weal'; Gustav III, 'The fatherland'.[64] The basis of legitimation proceeded from one abstract magnitude to another – from God to the People. (To be on the safe side, the anachronistic Gustav IV Adolf referred to both: 'God and the people'.) When Gustav III reintroduced the effective royal power, its legitimacy nevertheless continued to rest on the same popular contractual basis as it had in the Age of Liberty. In his inaugural address as the new king at the 1771 session of the Riksdag, he emphasised that his 'greatest good fortune is to be Swedish, and the greatest honour is to be the first citizen among a free people', and this same kind of rhetoric continued throughout his entire reign.[65] Even as a Crown Prince,

---

63 *Ibid.*, pp. 32–33 ('Sådant kan med rätta äskas af den, som wil wara absolute Regerande; Ty den som affecterar det ena, bör kunna præstera det andra').

64 'Gud mitt hopp'; 'Allmänt väl, mitt väl'; 'Fäderneslandet'. This change has been observed in similar contexts by Normann, pp. 2–3. Cf. Monod, pp. 311–15.

65 The speech of Gustav III to the Estates of 25 June 1771, reproduced in, e.g., *Utdrag utur alle ifrån den 7. decemb. 1718.[–1794] utkomne publique handlingar, placater, förordningar, resolutioner och publicationer*, ed. by Reinhold Gustaf Modée, 15 vols (Stockholm: Lorentz Ludwig Grefing; Kungl. tryckeriet, 1742–1829), IX (1801), pp. 739–41 ('största lycka at wara Swensk, och den största ära, at wara den förste Medborgaren ibland et fritt folk'). The wording lived on in the renewed Accession Charter agreed to by Gustav III on 21 August 1772 after the coup d'état and the 'eternal' Accession Charter that was established during the 1778–79 session of the Riksdag; *Sveriges regeringsformer 1634–1809 samt konungaförsäkringar 1611–1800*, ed. by Emil Hildebrand (Stockholm: Norstedts, 1891), pp. 266–68. See also Mikael Alm, *Kungsord i elfte timmen: Språk*

he had literally been forced to learn this lesson. The educational programme that had been drawn up for him by the Riksdag's Secret Committee emphasised such principles as 'Royals are not created better than other people', that 'the choice of the people is the basis for the highness of royals' and that 'in free governments there is less a need for a king than a human being on the throne'.[66] Here, the ideas that Chief Judge Christian König had presented a few years earlier were officially applied for the first time:

> First a young prince should learn, from his youth, that he is a human being, the same as the meanest of his subjects; consequently he has several inseparable natural commitments to GOD, himself, and others, which obligations he cannot discharge, unless he can hear and can tolerate the truth, and then act accordingly.[67]

This thoroughly desacralised image of the office of the king was shared by various political camps. In a pamphlet critical of the government, the philosopher Peter Forsskål maintained that 'an excessive belief in the holiness of the crowned goes a long way to protect even the most unjust of sovereigns'. Birger Frondin also rejected the divinity of the royal authority. Only Israel had had kings who were appointed by God, he pointed out. Those who 'had defended like a tenet the highest authority being instilled by Heaven, have thereby had the commendable intention of fortifying the thrones of the rulers'. But, he maintained, the authority retained its eminent status to an equal degree and was as unimpaired even when 'the people's own measures are the most immediate source

---

och självbild i det gustavianska enväldets legitimitetskamp 1772–1809 (Stockholm: Atlantis, 2002), chapter 4. Cf. also Ihalainen, pp. 170–73, 361–66, 531–34.

66 Excerpt from the minutes of the Secret Committee of 14 February 1756: Anders Johan von Höpken's introduction to the instruction for Crown Prince Gustav, quoted in Utdrag utur, VI (1761) pp. 3887–88 ('Kongl. Personer icke äro af finare slag skapade än andra menniskor'; 'folkets wal är grunden til deras höghet'; and 'Uti fria Regeringar behöfwes mindre en Konung, än en Menniska på Thronen']).

67 Christian König, Lärdoms öfning; sjunde tomen, om stats-kunskapen, Swerges rikes ungdom, til tjenst (Stockholm: Lars Salvius, 1748), p. 132 ('Först bör en unger Prints ifrån ungdommen lära, at han är människa, äfwen som den ringaste ibland hans undersåtare, följakteligen står han i många ouplöseliga naturliga förbindelser emot GUD, sig sjelf, och androm, hwilka förpliktelser, han ej kan fullgöra, så framt han icke hörer, och tol sanningen, och sedan gör derefter').

from which this same authority flows'. In other words, the social contract had the same standing and binding power as a divine ordination.[68]

The death of Frederick and the accession of Adolf Frederick

The last public ordinance that bore the name of Frederick I was issued on 20 March 1751. Less than a week later, a proclamation announced that the King, 'in life the most gracious father of our country' ('Wår i lifstiden huldaste Landsens Fader'), had departed this earthly existence after a long illness. His subjects, it was said, nevertheless had reason to thank God, who had given the King a long life and a happy reign.

May he also console, during their present grief, with his divine comfort and strength from on high, His Majesty our present reigning most gracious King, Her Majesty the Queen, the Crown Prince and the other hereditary princes, as well as the other kin of the royal family, and all our kingdom.[69]

It was essential to claim that there was continuity in the nation's government, and in the first few days following the death of the King a large number of proclamations were issued describing the death of the old King and the accession of the new King: Adolf Frederick's affirmation in the Council chamber against absolutism (not to be confused with the Accession Charter, which the King agreed to in

---

68 [Peter Forsskål], *Tankar om borgerliga friheten* (Stockholm: Lars Salvius, 1759) § 6; ('En förlångt drifwen tanke om kröntas helighet, skyddar mer än mycket äfwen de mest orättwisa Förstar'); cf. Peter Forsskål, *Thoughts on Civil Liberty: Translation of the Original Manuscript with Background*, ed. by David Goldberg, trans. by Gunilla Jonsson (Stockholm: Atlantis, 2009), pp. 14–15; [Birger Frondin], *Riksdags-manna rätt: Til dess grund och beskaffenhet förestäld* (Stockholm: Lars Salvius, 1747), pp. 18–19 ('tros-artikel försvarat, at den Högstrådande Magten af Himmelen ingjutes, hafva dermed haft et berömeligit afseende, at starkare befästa de Regerandes throner'; 'människornas egit åtgörande är närmaste orsaken, hvadan den samma härflutit').
69 *Tacksäjelse efter högstsal. Hans Kongl. Maj:t* ([Stockholm]: Kungl. tryck-eriet, 1751) (official proclamation, annual print series) ('Han hugswale ock, under närwarande sorg, med sin gudomeliga tröst och styrcko af högdene Hans Maj:t Wår nu regerande Allernådigste Konung, Hennes Maj:t Drottningen, Cron-Printsen med de öfrige Arf-Printsarne, samt thet Kongl. Husets höga Anförwandter och hela Wårt Rike').

connection with the coronation), the speech of Chancery President
Carl Gustaf Tessin on the same occasion, the King's response to this
speech, a general prayer to be used in sermons around the country,
a renewed form of oath for officials of the Crown and an order for
the citizens of the capital to wear mourning and cancel all plays and
all musical entertainments.[70]

After a few more days came the doctors' narrative about the
King's illness and final days, followed later by the pathologists'
protocol from the postmortem examination. No physical defects
were kept from the public, and any subjects who happened to
believe that royals escaped bodily decay were deprived of their
illusions. The purpose of these careful anatomical accounts, which
had a long tradition, will surely have been to scotch any rumours
that might arise of foul play with regard to the death. At the same
time, they bear witness to a time when the natural functions of
the body had not yet been relegated to a more private sphere.
Consequently, speculations on the causes of 'the many and often
recurring bouts of flatulence, of which His late Royal Majesty
so often complained during his lifetime' were not considered too
private to be announced in churches all over the country. Even if
it was not the primary intention, the careful descriptions of the
King's many war wounds may also have contributed to inspiring
the respect of the audience.[71]

---

70 *Kongl. Maj:ts försäkran, gifwen Stockholm i råd-cammaren then 26. martii
    1751* (Stockholm: Kungl. tryckeriet, [n.d.]; *Underdånigst tal til Hans Kongl.
    Maj:t, hållit uti råds-salen wid öpna dörar then 26. martii 1751. af […]
    grefwe Carl Gustaf Tessin* (Stockholm: Kungl. tryckeriet, [n.d]); *Kongl.
    Maj:ts nådiga swar uppå thet, af herr riks-rådet och cancellie-præsidenten,
    uti samtelige rådets namn, håldne talet. Then 26. martii 1751* (Stockholm:
    Kungl. tryckeriet, [n.d.]); *Allmänelig bön efter predikan och bönestunder,
    at brukas i församlingarne; utgången then 26. martii 1751* ([Stockholm]:
    Kungl. tryckeriet, [n.d.]); *Tro- och Huldhets ed* [26 March 1751] ([n.p.]:
    [n. pub.], [n.d.]); *Publication angående sorgedrägts anläggande efter högst-
    sal. Hans Kongl. Maj:t. Stockholm af kongl. slotts-cancelliet then 27. martii
    1751* ([Stockholm]: Kungl. tryckeriet, [n.d]) (all official proclamations,
    annual print series).
71 *Berättelse om högst sahlig Hans Kongl. Maj:ts konung Friedrich then
    förstes sidsta sjukdom och högstbeklageliga dödsfall* ([Stockholm]: Kungl.
    tryckeriet, 1751) (official proclamations, annual print series). Quotation
    from *Berättelse om thet, som observerades uppå högstsalig Hans Kongl.
    Maj:t konung Friedrich then förste, tå thess andelösa lekamen blef öpnad
    och balsamerad af lif-chirurgis assessorerne Ribe och Schützer, i närwaro*

Some time after these announcements came rules of procedure concerning the late King's burial in Stockholm, and the proclamation of a general day of mourning that would be held throughout the entire realm. Not until 27 September 1751, four days after the opening of the Riksdag and six months after the death of King Frederick, did the funeral take place in the Riddarholmen Church in Stockholm. Funeral sermons were ordered to be held, and the bells were to be rung in every church in the kingdom.[72] The coronations of Adolf Frederick and Louisa Ulrika took place two months later, on 26 November. That the need for symbolic representation increases as the king's power decreases is an assumption that is supported by this event, which may well have been the most lavish royal ceremony in Swedish history. At the same time, it was the first double coronation to have been held in Sweden, where the King and the Queen were both crowned on the same occasion, something which of course increased both the costs and the solemnity of the ceremony. The programme had been drawn up by the architect Carl Hårleman, a disciple of Tessin, and the general arrangement was approximately the same as for the most recent previous occasions.[73] Consequently, there is no reason to once again review the ceremonial in detail; but certain circumstances that were significantly different should be highlighted. In addition, there are grounds for drawing attention to the spoken word at royal ceremonies in general.

---

af archiatrerne Ribe och Rosén, lif-medicis Bäck och Réef, stads-physico assessoren Strandberg, samt chirurgis Boltenhagen och Acrel, som hade then nåden, i högstsalig Hans Kongl. Maj:ts lifstid thess höga person at betjena och upwackta [30 March 1751] ([Stockholm]: Kungl. tryckeriet, [n.d.]) (official proclamations, annual print series) ('the många och ofta återkommande wäderspänningar, hwaröfwer Högstsalig Hans Kongl. Maj:t så ofta i lifstiden klagade').

72 *Kungjörelse, uppå Kongl. Maj:ts nådigste befallning, angående högstsalig Hans Kongl. Maj:ts begrafning, med mera. Stockholm, af kongl. slottscancelliet then 3. sept. 1751* (Stockholm: Kungl. tryckeriet, [n.d.]); *Wid hög-salig Hans Kongl. Maj:ts konung Friedrich then förstes begrafning, som sker uti Riddarholms kyrkan, then 27. septembr. 1751. kommer följande at i akt tagas* ([Stockholm]: Kungl. tryckeriet, [n.d.]) (both official proclamations, annual print series).

73 Åke Stavenow, *Carl Hårleman: En studie i frihetstidens arkitekturhistoria* (Uppsala: Almqvist & Wiksell, 1927), p. 301.

The speeches from the throne at the sessions of the Riksdag

During the Age of Liberty, it had become the established custom for the king's public speeches to be delivered by the Chancery President. It has been intimated that the reason for this was King Frederick's poor knowledge of Swedish, but that interpretation does not seem entirely convincing. It has been shown that Frederick understood Swedish, and his spoken Swedish should not have been so bad that he would not have been able to read a written text out loud if necessary. Also, the King always seems to have personally answered the brief congratulatory addresses that the Speakers of the Estates commonly recited at the opening of a Riksdag session.[74] If anything, the custom should rather have been a reflection of the form of government; but this interpretation should not be pushed too far. The speech from the throne was an account of the activities of the Council since the previous Riksdag, and it was not a given that the delivery of this long document must be made by the King.

---

74 On Frederick's poor Swedish, see, e.g., Lagerroth, *Frihetstidens makt-ägande ständer*, I, p. 29. During the 1746 session of the Riksdag, when Crown Prince Adolf Frederick and his wife Louisa Ulrika participated at the opening of the Riksdag, the Estates expressed their congratulations to them as well. The fact that Her Royal Highness's answer was 'given in Swedish' ('Gifwit på Swenska') was explicitly emphasised on the printed title pages; *Hennes Kongl. Höghets nådiga swar, gifwit på swenska til [ridderskapet och adelens/preste-ståndets/borgare-ståndets/bonde-ståndets] deputerade, tå the aflade theras underdåniga hälsning then 23. september 1746.* (Stockholm: Kungl. tryckeriet, [n.d.]) (official proclamation, annual print series). See also the detailed description of the ceremonial in *Borgarståndets riksdagsprotokoll från frihetstidens början*, ed. by Nils Staf and others, 12 vols (Uppsala: Almqvist & Wiksell; Stockholm: Riksdagsförvaltningen, 1945–), IX:1: *1746–1747* (2003), pp. 74–75. Both the Crown Prince and the Crown Princess learned Swedish early; and in a private letter to the Chancery President, Louisa Ulrika promised that she intended to use the language: 'I thank you for your letter and give you my word I will speak Swedish' ('Jag tackar för ert bref och Jag lofwar ehr att tahla Swänska'), Louisa Ulrika to C. G. Tessin, Uppsala 6 June 1746, in Tessinska samlingen/ Tessin Collection], vol. 17 (E 5731), Brev till Carl Gustaf Tessin/Letters to Carl Gustaf Tessin], RA. Cf. *Ceremonial, som wid riksdagens början år 1751. kommer at i akt tagas* ([Stockholm]: Kungl. tryckeriet, [n.d.]); *Ceremonial, wid riksdagens början 1755* ([Stockholm]: Kungl. tryckeriet, [n.d.]); *Ceremonial wid riksdagens början 1760* ([Stockholm]: Kungl. tryckeriet, [n.d.]); *Ceremonial wid riksdagens början 1765* ([Stockholm]: Kungl. tryckeriet, [n.d.]) (all official proclamations, annual print series).

Nor was he the subject of the text, but he was spoken of in the third person. At least since the reign of Charles XI (1672–1697), the king's speech was usually read by a proxy, who at that time was the Chancellor of the Realm and later the Chancery President. Nor can anything be said for certain about the impression it made that someone else spoke in the King's stead. It may just as well have been an expression of exaltedness as of distance. Nevertheless, it should be recalled that the speech from the throne was the only context in which the Constitution of the Age of Liberty allowed the king to personally address the Estates or be involved in their deliberations. A monarch who wished to make the most of his potential to influence public opinion in the political centre of the kingdom was therefore wise to make good use of these occasions.[75]

The fact that Gustav III, being the last of the monarchs of the Age of Liberty, spoke in person before the Estates in 1771 has been said to be remarkable and has been seen as a factor that contributed to his popularity.[76] In analogy with what was said earlier about changes in the coronation ceremonial, I would argue that the changes to the king's speech from the throne should not be invested with too great symbolic significance. The openings of the sessions of the Riksdag, unlike the coronations, were frequently occurring

75 All of the king's government bills to the Estates were to be handed in in writing and countersigned by the Council; see the 1723 Riksdag Act, § 13; Accession Charter 1751, § 8. The latter paragraph amounted to a specification, or tightening-up, compared with the corresponding § 9 in the 1720 Accession Charter. Cf. Malmström, *Sveriges politiska historia*, VI, pp. 261–64. On the speeches from the throne in earlier times, see Grauers, *Riksdagen under den karolinska tiden*, Sveriges riksdag, I:4 (Stockholm: Victor Pettersons, 1932), pp. 153–54.

76 See *Hans Kongl. Maj:ts tal, til riksens ständer uppå riks-salen wid riksdagens början den 25 junii 1771* (Stockholm: Grefingska, 1771) (official proclamation, annual print series). Unlike the earlier speeches from the throne, this statement was written in the first-person singular. Fredrik Axel von Fersen mentions the campaign of Gustav III to increase his popularity among the common people, saying in connection with this that the Estates were moved to tears by hearing the King's voice: Fredrik Axel von Fersen, *Historiska skrifter*, ed. by R. M. Klinckowström, 2nd edn, 8 vols (Stockholm: Norstedts, 1867–72), III (1869), pp. 65–66. See also *Riksdags-Tidningar*, no. 1 (16 October 1771); Malmström, *Sveriges politiska historia*, VI, pp. 223–24; Marie-Christine Skuncke, *Gustaf III – Det offentliga barnet: En prins retoriska och politiska fostran* (Stockholm: Atlantis, 1993), pp. 267–70, cf. pp. 120–22; Alm, pp. 66–67.

ceremonial occasions where many spectators could make comparisons with previous established customs.[77] Many eyewitness reports recount the noteworthiness of Gustav III, in a departure from the prepared programme, speaking in person; but that need not signal greater authority, or that he had now assumed command of national policy. It is more likely that it was the unorthodox procedure in itself that attracted attention – and, it would seem, astounded admiration. To 'hear the speech of a great and gracious King from the throne', maintained the Lord Marshal, was 'a privilege which no Swedish man has been accorded in over a century'.[78] The newspaper *Dagligt Allehanda* spoke of a 'for the Estates and the entire kingdom all the more gratifying and encouraging occasion, in that it will hardly have happened that a Swedish King has spoken to the Estates since the time of the great King Gustaf [II] Adolph'. The newspaper therefore also wanted to satisfy the demands of the public for 'a little review' ('en liten recension') of the lofty ideas that had been expressed in this address. The speech also inspired the poet Anders Nicander to compose a long poem in hexameter verse, and the poet and songwriter Carl Michael Bellman enthusiastically wrote, 'You Solomon of this age, Come speak more from your throne.'[79]

---

77 Cf. Carl Tersmeden, *Amiral Carl Tersmedens memoarer*, ed. by Nils Sjöberg and Nils Erdmann, 6 vols (Stockholm: Wahlström & Widstrand, 1912–19), [V]: *Gustaf III och flottan* (1918), p. 18; Daniel Tilas, *Anteckningar från riksdagen 1769–1770*, ed. by Olof Jägerskiöld (Stockholm: Kungl. Samfundet för utgivande av handskrifter rörande Skandinaviens historia, 1977), pp. 6–7. Ralph E. Giesey has made a similar observation regarding the *entrées* and *lits de justice* of the French kings, which, unlike coronations and funerals, were recurring manifestations before the people; see Ralph E. Giesey, 'The King Imagined', in *The Political Culture of the Old Regime*, ed. by Keith Michael Baker, The French Revolution and the Creation of Modern Political Culture, 1 (Oxford: Pergamon Press, 1987), pp. 41–59 (pp. 42–43).

78 *Sveriges ridderskaps och adels riksdags-protokoll*, XXIX:1: 1771–1772 (1969), p. 30 ('höra en stor och nådig Konungs tal ifrån Thronen, [var] en förmon som på mer än et seculum icke någon svensk man fått äga'). In the ceremonial the Chancery President had, in the customary manner, been assigned the task of speaking in the king's stead; *Utdrag utur*, IX (1801), p. 738.

79 *Dagligt Allehanda*, no. 139 (27 June 1771) ('för Ständer och hela Riket så mycket mera glädjande och upmuntrande tilfälle, som det knapt lärer hafwa händt at någon Swensk Konung talat til Ständerna, sedan den Store Konung Gustaf Adolphs tid'); Anders Nicander, *Guds staf i Gustafs hand*

Almost immediately, concerned dissatisfaction was voiced regarding this new practice that was being established. At the tribute of the Estates in July 1772, two days after the coronation of Gustav III, the King again spoke to the people. According to protocol, the Chancery President was supposed to have spoken as usual, and a departure from this practice would have been made at the King's own initiative.[80] The field marshal and politician Fredrik Axel von Fersen presented a critical description of this occasion in his historical writings:

> The King gave a very elegant speech to the Estates and to the people, which nevertheless did not have the effect the King expected; the charm of novelty had worn off, and the following day the Caps discussed how to return the King to the previous custom of not allowing himself be heard in public, but instead letting the Chancery President speak on his behalf. The public distrust in the King had increased to such a degree that the most noble sentiments, spoken with all the embellishments of a pleasing eloquence, lost their strength and their appeal.[81]

Fersen's memoirs are permeated by a markedly critical attitude to Gustav III, and little weight can be attached to his evaluation of the state of public opinion.[82] Three decades later the poet Gustaf

---

skal hägna Svea land (Stockholm: Henric Fougt, 1771); Carl Michael Bellman, Öfwer Hans Kongl. Maj:ts tal på Riks-salen d. 25 jun. 1771: Författat den 26 jun. följ (Stockholm: Carlbohm, Kungl. finska boktryckeriet, 1771) ('Du Salomon i dessa Tider, Kom tala mera från Din Thron').

80 Cf. Ceremonial, wid Hans Kongl. Maj:ts wår allernådigste konungs konung Gustaf den III:s hyllnings-act, som sker then 1:sta junii 1772 (Stockholm: Henric Fougt, 1772) (official proclamation, annual print series). See also Gustaf Fredrik Gyllenborg, Mitt lefverne, 1731–1775: Själfbiografiska anteckningar, ed. by Gudmund Frunck (Stockholm: Seligmann, 1885), pp. 94–96.

81 Fersen, III (1869), p. 83 ('Konungen höll ett mycket skönt tal till Ständerna och till folket, som likväl ej gjorde den effekt Konungen väntat sig deraf; nyhetens behag var förbi, och Mössorna öfverlade följande dagen derom, huru man skulle återföra Konungen till det bruk, som förr var gällande, att ej låta höra sig offentligt, utan låta kansli-presidenten tala å sina vägnar. Misstroendet mot Konungen hade så tilltagit hos allmänheten, att de mest ädla känslor, sagde med alla prydnader af en skön vältalighet, förlorade deras styrka och deras behag').

82 Carl Gustaf Malmström, 'Axel Fersen såsom memoarförfattare', in Smärre skrifter rörande sjuttonhundratalets historia (Stockholm: Norstedts, 1889), pp. 209–40 (pp. 231–36).

Fredrik Gyllenborg, a wholehearted admirer of the King, remembered a completely different atmosphere on the same occasion:

At previous tributes, it was common for the President of the Chancery to speak on the king's behalf. Gustav III spoke in person, with a clear and pleasant voice, the sound of which rang out over all of the vast stage. A person had to have been sold body and soul to a foreign power not to be moved by this voice, and I am also convinced that even his bitterest enemies, for one moment at least, were captivated. From this moment the general public were enraptured, and retained such a feeling for evermore.[83]

At all events, it seems reasonable to assume that the King's speech was perceived as a potential instrument of power that worried the Council. His public appearance influenced the view of the person of the King and, by extension, the perception of the office of the king. Gustav III worked purposefully to strengthen his reputation before the revolution in the late summer of that year.

Regardless of how to interpret the fact that the Chancery President spoke in the King's stead during the Age of Liberty, the custom was expedient in every way; and there is no doubt that it was the opinions of the Council that were presented rather than those of the King. That he held a trusteeship with limited powers was emphasised in Adolf Frederick's speech from the throne at the opening of the session of the Riksdag on 23 September 1751, when he stood before the Estates as their king for the first time.

Early on there had been rumours about the new royal couple's ambition for power, and that dimension was expressed in the 1751 speech. However, as was customary, criticism that concerned members of the royal family was directed at people in their immediate surroundings, or was described as malicious slander. The King's speech from the throne therefore foregrounded the 'unfounded rumours and demeaning invectives which have been spread about' his alleged wish to abuse the love of the people as

---

83 Gyllenborg, pp. 95–96 ('Vid förra hyllningar var vanligt, att presidenten i kansliet förde ordet på konungens vägnar. Gustaf den tredje talade själf med en klar och behaglig stämma, hvaraf ljudet utbreddes kring hela den vidsträckta skådebanan. Man skulle vara såld till kropp och själ åt en främmande makt för att icke röras af denna stämma, också är jag öfvertygad, att äfven hans bittraste ovänner för ett ögonblick åtminstone blefvo intagne. Allmänheten blef det med hänryckning från denna stund och bevarade känslan deraf för evärdiga tider').

a means towards 'the adoption of more extensive power'. Such rumours, the King maintained via the Chancery President, were highly offensive to a Majesty whose only ambition was 'to rule over a free and happy people within the limits prescribed'.[84]

Even though he himself was portrayed as innocent, such reminders were a warning to the King. After he was elected as successor in 1743, the formula that God appointed kings with the people (the Riksdag) as intermediaries began to be applied in concrete terms (Figure 13). Adolf Frederick confirmed this relationship once more when he met the delegates of the Estates as king:

> The Estates of the Realm may always be convinced of my love for a country whose government has been entrusted to me by GOD, through the voluntary and unanimous election of the Estates of the Realm.[85]

The King thus had a double mandate – from God and from the people – and in accordance with the mediating functions of the royal authority, it was important to emphasise the unanimity of the election. The stated formula was a theoretical justification for the reintroduced elective monarchy which, albeit under some measure of duress, maintained a foundation of theological principles. It is impossible to escape the impression that this religious justification was a concession to tradition and a customary symbolic language, and not really necessary to provide the requisite power for the royal authority. In his Accession Charter Adolf Frederick also confirmed that it was the Estates that had 'entrusted to us royal power and authority'.[86] It will be apparent from a later context that

---

84 *På Kongl. Maj:ts wägnar, [...] högwälborne grefwe Carl Gustav Tessins tal, hållit upp Riks-salen wid riksdagens början then 23. september 1751: Tryckt uppå Hans Kongl. Maj:ts befallning, och samtelige riksens ständers begäran* (Stockholm: Kungl. tryckeriet, [n.d.]) (official proclamation, annual print series) ('ogrundade rykten och förklenliga tilmälen, hwilka utspridde blifwit'; 'et widare sträckt wäldes wedertagande'; and 'at, innom the utstakade gräntzor, Regera öfwer ett fritt och lyckligt folck').

85 *Hans Kongl. Maj:ts nådige swar, gifwit samtelige riksens ständers deputerade, then 12. october 1751* (Stockholm: Kungl. tryckeriet, [n.d.]) (official proclamation, annual print series) ('Riksens Ständer kunna altid wara öfwertygade om Min ömhet för et Land, hwilkets Regering GUD, genom Riksens Ständers friwilliga och enhälliga wahl Mig anförtrodt').

86 Accession Charter 25 November 1751, preamble, quoted in *Frihetstidens grundlagar*, p. 72 ('updragit oss konungamagt och myndighet').

Figure 13 The election of Adolf Frederick as successor to the Swedish throne in the Great Hall of the temporary royal palace on 23 June 1743. This joint assembly of all four Estates was led by the Speaker of the Nobility. King Frederick, pictured sitting on the throne with the regalia beside him, was not in fact present on this occasion. However, the Council of the Realm was in attendance. Kettledrummers and trumpeters announce the decision through the windows. Representatives of the four Estates are seen in the hall, with some clergymen and a peasant in the foreground. The King's Guard ensures good order. Engraving by an unknown artist. Photo: Björn Green, KB.

when the two mandates were pitted against each other, the elective principle was undoubtedly the one that had precedence: it was real, whereas the theological one was metaphorical and formal. It was a monarchy in the service of the realm, and the people alone had the power to set the limits of its extent.

As Mikael Alm has shown, Gustav III employed the rhetoric of the Age of Liberty to a high degree. It was a conscious tactic of his to emphasise political continuity as far as possible, in order to disarm the opposition and placate foreign powers. It was certainly with reference to the earlier formula that he maintained that his royal power came from 'God and the inhabitants of the realm'.[87] Nevertheless, there is no doubt that Gustav III, faced

---

87 Alm, p. 166 ('Gud och Riksens Inbyggare'); on the adherence to the rhetoric of the Age of Liberty, see, e.g., *ibid.*, pp. 234–35.

with a hypothetical choice, would only have been able to legitimise his position with reference to a popular mandate. Jakob Johan Anckarström, who later murdered the same king, also confessed to harbouring ideas that were far older than the impulses provided by the French Revolution: 'A king is in himself merely a sinful human being like all others', he maintained in his letter of confession, but the monarch has been 'entrusted by the nation with the task of safeguarding law, liberty, and security, and thus with making sure that everything is done in the proper manner, when the nation [the Riksdag] is not itself assembled.'[88]

A national coronation ceremony

The texts that were read at the joint coronation of Adolf Frederick and Louisa Ulrika made it clear that the theological justification was primarily intended to set prudential limits for the King himself. On the King's arrival at the church, the Bishop of Skara, Daniel Juslenius, read the following prayer:

> O LORD GOD Heavenly Father, thou who knowest that no man is of his own power capable of permanence, grant the grace that this thy servant, whom thou hast placed over thy people as their ruler, through thy divine aid be fortified, to the comfort and joy of all who are subject to his rule, through thy Son Our LORD Jesus Christ.[89]

This prayer had already been used at the coronation of Frederick; but this time the Bishop of Linköping, Andreas Rhyzelius, added a short sermon on I Kings 10. 9 that dealt with the same theme, i.e. that God will provide strength to the king to rule wisely

---

88 Anckarström's confession, signed 3 April 1792, quoted in *Biografiskt lexikon öfver namnkunnige svenska män*, 2nd rev. edn, 10 vols (Stockholm: Beijers, 1874–76), I (1874), p. 187 ('en kung är i sig sjelf blott en syndig menniska som alla andra' and 'fått nationens förtroende att vårda lag, frihet och säkerhet, och således tillse att allt går rätt till, då nation [riksdagen] ej sjelf är tillsamman').

89 *Wid theras Kongl. Majestäters … kröning* (official proclamation, annual print series) ('O HERre GUD Himmelske Fader, Tu som west, at ingen Menniska förmår af sin egen kraft blifwa wäl bestående, gif Nådena at Thenne Tin Tienare, hwilken Tu öfwer Tit folk til en Regent satt hafwer, må igenom Tin Guddomeliga hjelp styrckt warda, allom til tröst och hugnad, som Thess Regemente undergifne äro, genom Tin Son Wår HERRA JESUM Christum').

over the people of Israel. In other words, this is a variation on the provision found in the opening section of the Instrument of Government, which said that kings are subject to the same religious commandments as any other subject. The King was the servant of the realm, and religion was his guide. Here was a pronounced difference from the message that had been conveyed during the act of anointment of Charles XII. On that occasion the Bishop of Åbo (Turku), Johan Gezelius, had instead turned to the congregation exhorting its members to thank God who had provided them with such a mild and Christian Magistracy. While Frederick and Adolf Frederick were subject to religion and had been placed on the throne by the people, Charles XII had been chosen by an act of God and Providence to rule over land and people and interpret the religious commandments as he saw fit. During the Age of Liberty, by contrast, the office of the king was there for the realm and the religion was there for the person of the King, not the other way round.

The coronation of 1751 also became a manifestation of national unity in the sense that, at the request of the commoners, delegates from all four Estates were allowed to escort the King in the coronation procession. This was an honour that had previously been granted to the Nobility only; but the argument of the commoners was that each of the Estates was equally powerful and that they should therefore all be accorded a place close to the head of the realm. Within the Nobility, it was claimed that although the Estates were *pares potestate* they were not *pares dignitate* – they were equals in power but not in dignity – and that on previous occasions they themselves had not escorted the king as the Estate of the Nobility but as individual noblemen. Against a united front of Clergy, Burghers and Peasantry, and in order to maintain peace and unity among the Estates, the Nobility was obliged to give in on condition that they were given the places closest to the King in the procession.[90]

---

90 *Sveriges ridderskaps och adels riksdags-protokoll*, XVIII:1: *1751–1752* (1911), pp. 194–96, 199–202, 206, 222–23; *Bondeståndets riksdags-protokoll*, VII: *1751–1756* (1963), pp. 67–74, 78–80. Anders Claréus, 'På offensiven: Bondeståndet under slutet av frihetstiden', in *Riksdag, kaffehus och predikstol: Frihetstidens politiska kultur 1766–1772*, ed. by Marie-Christine Skuncke and Henrika Tandefelt (Stockholm: Atlantis, 2003), pp. 95–103.

Early on, the King had ordered the participants to avoid sartorial ostentation. This wish was in line with the intention of the sumptuary laws; but there was also a symbolic aspect that could be underscored. The King believed that it would be most becoming for the ceremony if 'Swedish men are dressed in Swedish clothes manufactured within the kingdom, without any addition of foreign showiness and finery.' Military officers were urged to wear nothing but their uniforms.[91]
The national tenor was also reflected in the symbolic language that was used. Since at least the time of the introduction of the hereditary kingdom, the coronation – in addition to elevating the kings – had been a way to consolidate the dynasty in question. Consequently, the coat of arms of the royal dynasty had been given a prominent, sometimes dominant, place next to the national coat of arms. At the coronation ceremony of 1751, however, the coat of arms of the new Holstein-Gottorp dynasty was entirely excluded. Instead, all iconography was focused on the national coat of arms, the three crowns. The ground upon which the royal couple walked outside the royal residence and the coronation church was covered in blue cloth adorned with yellow crowns. This decoration also recurred on the interior walls of the church and on individual objects that were carried in the procession. The most striking novelty was the change of the royal standard, which always had a prominent place close to the King during these ceremonies. The crowned greater national coat of arms lacked an inescutcheon and bore only the coats of arms of the kingdoms of the Swedes and the Goths. The tip of the pole of the standard was reused from earlier occasions; but in the location where Frederick's monogram had been, there were three crowns instead. Similarly, the coat of arms with the three crowns had been inserted on the crowning shield of the silver throne as a substitution for the monarch's monograms that had always adorned this location before. The two thrones made especially for this occasion by the architect Jean Eric Rehn also lacked dynastic markings. In fact, the Holstein-Gottorp coat of arms does not seem to have appeared on any ceremonial item

---

91 *Kongl. Maj:ts nådiga wilja och förklaring, huru med klädedrägter wid thess höga kongl. kröning förhållas må. Stockholm i Råd-cammaren then 14. maji 1751* (Stockholm: Kungl. tryckeriet, [n.d.]) (official proclamation, annual print series) ('Swenske Män äro klädde uti Swenska innom Riket tilwerkade Kläder, utan all tilsats af utländskt Prål och Grannlåt').

except for the modernised and repainted coronation coach. Adolf
Frederick himself was on horseback, though, and the caparison of
his horse was adorned only by the lesser national coat of arms.[92]
Whether this iconographic change was obvious to spectators
cannot be determined, but at any rate it was a symbolic statement:
the King had been reduced to an official in the service of the realm.
The king was whoever held the office at the time in question and
at the discretion of the people, but it was the office and not the
person that was essential. The art historian Merit Laine has stressed
the role of the royal family as a unifying national symbol during
the Age of Liberty. The politically and culturally dominant noble
elite could not represent the kingdom on their own: for this they
lacked both legitimacy and means. During the seventeenth century,
the aristocracy had competed with a strong monarchy in building
palaces and promoting the arts, which can be seen as a form of
assertion of strength among competing interest groups. The bureau-
cratised administrative nobility of the eighteenth century lacked the
means and the ambition for such a contest – a symptom of the
professionalisation and bureaucratisation process not only among
the nobility, but also in society as a whole. The nobles no longer
figured as independent magnates but as officials of the state, that is,
as the Crown's officials. The magnificence and cultural flourishing
that were important to showcase in order to maintain the prestige
of the kingdom abroad were increasingly focused on the royal
authority, the official representative of the realm. Academies and
learned societies confirmed their status through royal privileges, the
artistic maturity of the nation was manifested in the construction

---

92 Åke Setterwall, Stig Fogelmarck and Lennart af Petersens, *Stockholms slott
och dess konstskatter* (Stockholm: Bonniers, 1950), pp. 40–42; Cederström,
pp. 255–62. Ulrika Eleonora's and Frederick's royal standards have not
been preserved, but their design with dynastic coats of arms is clear from
the watercolour miniatures of Johan Henrik Schildte (see Figures 8 and 11).
Cf. Gudrun Ekstrand, *Kröningsdräkter i Sverige* (Stockholm: Carlssons,
1991), pp. 63–85; *Solen och Nordstjärnan: Frankrike och Sverige på
1700-talet*, Nationalmusei utställningskatalog, 568 (Höganäs: Bra Böcker,
Wiken; Stockholm: Nationalmuseum, 1993), pp. 108–17; Astrid Tydén-
Jordan, *Kröningsvagnen: Konstverk och riksklenod; En studie i barockens
karossbyggnadskonst* (Stockholm: Livrustkammaren, 1985), pp. 137–60.
David Nehrman attributed the national coat of arms only to constitutional
law, while the kings' dynastic coats of arms 'rather belong to History',
i.e., to volatile private law; [Nehrman], 'Inledning till Thet Swenska Jus
Publicum', B 762, KB, 2:VI, § 14, fol. 74.

of the new Royal Palace in Stockholm, and royal ceremonies gave official Sweden an opportunity to present itself to its subjects and to the surrounding world. The coronations of Adolf Frederick and Louisa Ulrika constituted the culmination of these rites.

Laine sums up the cultural duties of the royal family in three points: to be the focus of public art and the display of magnificence; to act as patrons of art and science; and to consume the luxury goods that allowed the mercantile industries of the kingdom to prosper. 'These tasks were at bottom impersonal and passive, while an active, independent participation was rather a disadvantage to the elite in power who were joint actors with Adolf Frederick and Louisa Ulrika on the Swedish art scene', Laine summarises.[93] The king and his queen had been reduced from subjects to objects, and as such they symbolised the greatness of the kingdom.

Of course, republics also managed to hold their own on the international stage, and the absence of a king was hardly detrimental to the United Provinces of the Netherlands as far as prestige was concerned. On the contrary, that country's economic, cultural and scientific prosperity was associated with its free republican form of government even by eighteenth-century contemporaries. The free form of government in Sweden also aroused admiration in certain places abroad, and there may well have been philosophers who thought that abolishing the monarchy would have perfected it, even if this was hardly ever put into words. Heinrich Ludwig von Hess believed that the Swedish solution, where the king exercised his sovereignty within the framework of the law and through the Council, was a model solution.[94] If the cultural link to the royal

---

93 Merit Laine, *'En Minerva för vår Nord'*: *Lovisa Ulrika som samlare, uppdragsgivare och byggherre* (Stockholm: M. Laine, 1998), pp. 197–201, quotation on p. 200 ('Dessa uppgifter var i grund och botten opersonliga och passiva, medan ett aktivt, självständigt deltagande snarast utgjorde en nackdel för den maktägande elit som var Adolf Fredriks och Lovisa Ulrikas medagerande på den svenska konstscenen'). See also Merit Laine, 'Kungliga slott som nationella byggnader under frihetstiden', in *Nationalism och nationell identitet i 1700-talets Sverige*, ed. by Åsa Karlsson and Bo Lindberg, Opuscula Historica Upsaliensia, 27 (Uppsala: Historiska institutionen, 2002), pp. 101–12 (pp. 110–12); Merit Laine, 'En drottning med "manna-wett"', in *Drottning Lovisa Ulrika och Vitterhetsakademien*, ed. by Sten Åke Nilsson (Stockholm: Vitterhetsakademien, 2003), pp. 17–39 (pp. 26–28).

94 Ere Nokkala, 'Rewriting Eighteenth-Century Swedish Republican Political Thought: Heinrich Ludwig von Hess's *Der Republikaner* (1754)', *History of European Ideas*, 42 (2016), 502–15 (p. 509).

family mentioned above is understood as a conscious choice among several possible alternatives, it can thus partly be regarded as a misjudgement; the same prestige would have been possible to achieve even without a king. In reality, though, the abolition or continuation of the monarchy was not something that any single or collective actor could control. The monarchy bore with it a continuous legitimacy and tradition that could be discontinued only through revolutionary upheaval – from above or from below. In addition, the form of government during the Age of Liberty had come into existence in a historical situation where the kingdom faced a perceived threat of total annihilation, and in that situation it was not possible to further undermine the permanence of the state authority by robbing it of its symbolic foundation. The national prestige was to a great extent tied to the representative dignity of the monarchy, and its being a cultural rallying point therefore became an additional function that may be added to the ethos of the royal authority, along with its political elements. For this reason, it may be worth looking at the costs associated with the royal family during the Age of Liberty.

The costs of the royal family

Measured in absolute numbers, the cost of maintaining the court followed a consistently rising curve throughout the Age of Liberty (Diagram 1).[95] A study of the trend line shows that the size of the court budget increased fivefold over the course of this period. Each of the peak years that interrupt the curve line has a specific

---

95 All numbers and descriptive facts on government expenditure have been obtained from Karl Åmark, *Sveriges statsfinanser 1719–1809* (Stockholm: Norstedts, 1961), chapter 7. The so-called Estimates (*riksstaten*) show current government expenditures, but are a budget rather than an actual profit and loss statement. This is relatively unimportant in the present context, where we are interested in economic priorities and relative trends. Figures for the Estimates are absent prior to 1722; but here the trend is followed until 1777, when a coin reform makes further comparisons more difficult. How the Estimates were regulated during the Age of Liberty has been investigated in Lagerroth, *Frihetstidens maktägande ständer*, II, pp. 265–311. For a detailed discussion of methodological problems in reading the Estimates, see Gunnar Artéus, *Krigsmakt och samhälle i frihetstidens Sverige*, Militärhistoriska studier utgivna av Militärhistoriska avdelningen vid Militärhögskolan, 6 (Stockholm: Militärhistoriska förlaget, 1982), pp. 89–99, cf. also pp. 108–17.

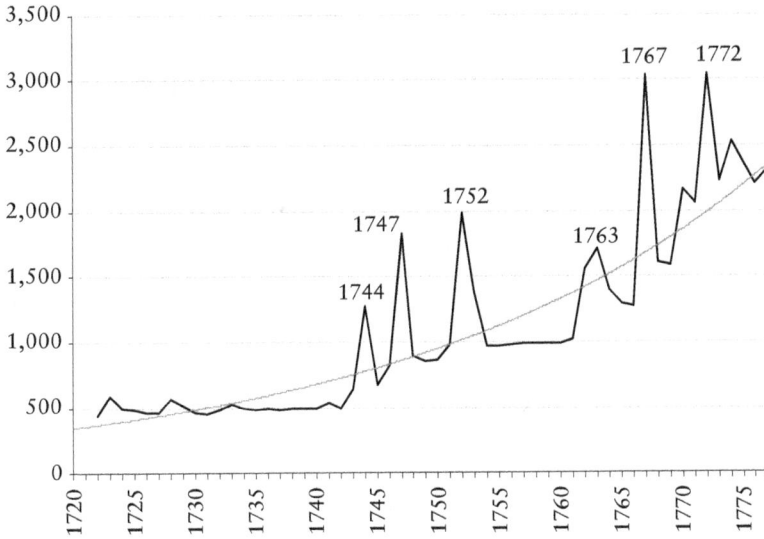

Diagram 1 The size of the court budget, 1722–1777, in thousands of silver *daler*

Source: Karl Åmark, *Sveriges statsfinanser 1719–1809* (Stockholm: Norstedts, 1961), tables 16–17, pp. 314–17, 321–24.

Note: The diagram shows only the Estates' ordinary grant for the court budget, excluding certain items, among others the budget for the royal palaces (*slottsbyggnadsstaten*) and the grants for the king's Drabant Corps and Life Guard regiment (see Åmark, p. 320). With the arrival in Sweden in 1744 of the successor to the throne and his wife, double court budgets were kept until the death of Frederick. Crown Prince Gustav and the other royal children also had their own special budgets, which grew as the years passed. The ordinary court budget was often complemented with funds for additional expenses. These are not shown in the diagram.

explanation: the year 1744 includes extra expenses for the nuptials of the successor to the throne and his betrothed; in 1747 extra funds were added in order to restructure the Crown Prince's debts, which had accumulated among other things as a result of the birth of Prince Gustav; in 1752 coronation costs and expenses for the King's trip to Finland were added; in 1763 a lump sum was paid for settling the accumulated debts of the court; 1767 brought with it heavy expenses for the marriage of the Crown Prince to Sophia Magdalena; and in 1772 there were new coronation costs.

The fluctuations are therefore easy to explain, but the image of a rising trend is misleading because of inflation. If one instead studies the court budget's percentage share of the national budget, one obtains a crude but fair image of the priority of maintaining the court. With such a curve, the same peak years appear as in the previous diagram, while the trend line lies at around 9 per cent, with only a minor increase over time (Diagram 2). The patent reduction seen at the end of the 1750s and in the low year of 1760, when the court budget made up only about 4.5 per cent of the national budget, is explained by the increase in public expenditure caused by the Pomeranian War, with an increased budget deficit as a consequence. When Diagram 2 is compared with Diagram 1, it

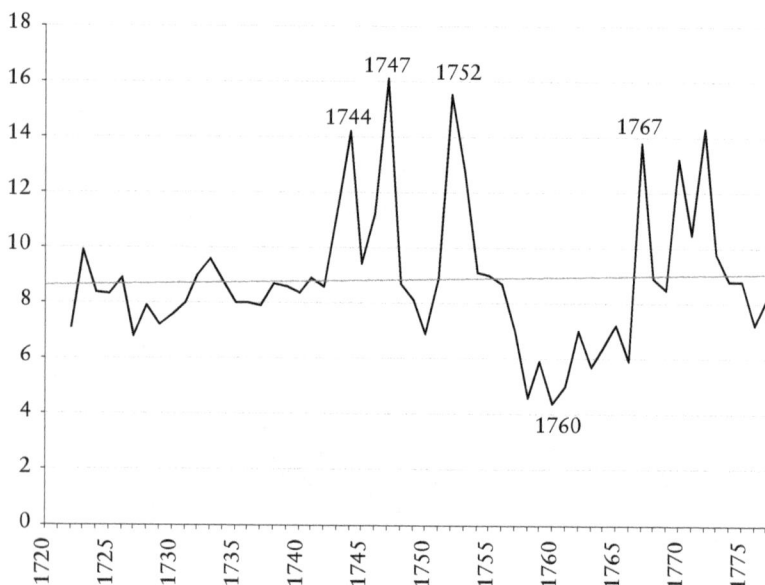

Diagram 2 The court budget's share of the Estimates, 1722–1777, expressed in percentages

Source: Karl Åmark, *Sveriges statsfinanser 1719–1809* (Stockholm: Norstedts, 1961), table 16, pp. 314–17.

Note: The diagram shows only the Estates' ordinary grant for the court budget, excluding certain items, among others the budget for the royal palaces (*slottsbyggnadsstaten*) and the grants for the king's Drabant Corps and Life Guard regiment (see Åmark, p. 320). With the arrival in Sweden in 1744 of the successor to the throne and his wife, double court budgets were kept until the death of Frederick. Crown Prince Gustav and the other royal children also had their own special budgets, which grew as the years passed. The ordinary court budget was often complemented with funds for additional expenses. These are not shown in the diagram.

transpires that the size of the court budget was in fact unchanged over the same period.

To summarise these simple calculations, it is clear that the royal family accounted for around 10 per cent or more of government expenditure during the Age of Liberty. These expenses were approximately of the same magnitude as they had been during the latter part of the seventeenth century. By international standards, the figure was fairly normal, or indeed somewhat on the low side. With the exception of certain peak years, the costs of the court of the Holy Roman Empire during the first two thirds of the seventeenth century amounted to around 15 per cent of government expenditure, decreasing slightly thereafter. The French royal household, which included multiple courts, usually consumed between 15 and 30 per cent of the national budget during the second half of the seventeenth century. At the beginning of the 1780s, these expenses remained at around 14 per cent; but owing to various reforms they were reduced to around 5.7 per cent by the outbreak of the French Revolution. In absolute numbers, the French court cost many times more than the court of the Holy Roman Empire; but for both governments the court was consistently the third largest item of state expenditure, military expenses and the national debt being the two largest ones. Converted into silver, the costs of the English court during the 1680s were almost three times as large as those of the Swedish court, while the size of the English court was only double that of the Swedish one. All these countries, one must remember, had significantly larger state coffers to draw upon than did the Swedish state. In certain German princedoms, which were smaller and poorer than Sweden, the court might consume over half of government expenditure. In both France and the Habsburg countries, the earlier levels were maintained throughout the eighteenth century; they possibly decreased slightly, relatively speaking, because of expanding economies. Through reforms and budget cuts, the court's share of the national budget decreased significantly in both France and the Habsburg countries during the 1780s.[96]

---

96 Fabian Persson, *Servants of Fortune: The Swedish Court between 1598 and 1721* (Lund: Department of History, 1999), pp. 68–70; Jeroen Duindam, *Vienna and Versailles: The Courts of Europe's Dynastic Rivals, 1550–1780* (Cambridge: Cambridge University Press, 2003), pp. 124–28; William R. Newton, *La petite cour: Service et serviteurs à la cour de Versailles au XVIIIe siècle* (Paris: Fayard, 2006), p. 391.

The costs of the Swedish court were actually higher than those presented in Diagrams 1 and 2, because several related expenses – for His Majesty's Life Guards, upkeep of the royal palaces, etc. – were distributed among other budget items. In other words, the maintenance of the court consumed comparatively large sums. Roughly it would have made up around a third of civilian government expenditure, which in total oscillated between 30 and 40 per cent of the budget over the entire period. It can also be noted that the fluctuations in the political standing of the king do not seem to have led to corresponding fluctuations in the allocation of funds by the Estates. To some extent this had to do with each item of expenditure having a fixed so-called allocation budget (*anordningsstat*) that made the national budget slow to change; but it may also be explained by the fact that it was the King in person who challenged the political system, while it was to the office of the king, and by extension the realm, that government funds were allocated.

The coronations of Gustav III and Sophia Magdalena as a nationwide celebration

The coronation of Gustav III in 1772 took place in a tense political situation. 'The King pledged allegiance to an Instrument of Government which he had already resolved to abolish; the Estates swore to respect the King's rights, which they daily trod under their feet', as Malmström somewhat pointedly summarises the situation.[97] The coronation, which was originally planned for September 1771, had long been postponed because of practical problems and an inflamed battle over the Accession Charter, in which important principles for the right of commoners to hold higher offices were finally established. Even if politically initiated people were in the process of planning a royalist coup d'état, or, alternatively, suspected that something was afoot, this was not permitted to disturb the solemn celebration.

---

97 Malmström, *Sveriges politiska historia*, VI, p. 293 ('Konungen besvor den regeringsform, hvilken han redan föresatt sig att omintetgöra; ständerna svuro att akta konungens rättigheter, hvilka de dagligen trampade under fötterna'). See also Clas Theodor Odhner, *Sveriges politiska historia under konung Gustaf III:s regering*, 2 vols (Stockholm: Norstedts, 1885–96), I: *1771–1778* (1885), pp. 95–96.

The coronation was a double act this time as well – Gustav III
and Sophia Magdalena were both crowned on Friday, 29 May in
St Nicholas in Stockholm. The ceremonial had been thoroughly
vetted by the King himself, and was more detailed than the one
that had been followed in 1751. A large number of objects could
be reused from previous coronations, though, and it was a pronounced ambition that anything that had to be manufactured from
scratch should, as far as possible, be produced within the country.
It was emphasised that the economic situation, with a financial
crisis and crop failure, ought to curb any over-ostentatious expenditure; but there were no indications of the difficult situation in the
celebration.[98]

The ceremonial elements of the coronations of 1719, 1720
and 1751 have been examined in some detail above, and no
similar scrutiny is necessary here. Instead, our eyes may be turned
towards the dissemination effects of the ceremonies. Insofar as
these manifestations of royal elevation are considered to have had
any political significance at the national level, their contents must
have been communicated outside the limited circle of spectators
who had an opportunity to witness the proceedings personally.
Such communication must be said to have been well developed
by the end of the eighteenth century, and not many subjects in
the kingdom would have failed to take notice of the coronation in
Stockholm.

Celebratory speeches and tributary verses dedicated to the royal
family were a flourishing genre during the Age of Liberty. The
number of booklets and pamphlets produced is almost impossible
to measure, and a very large percentage of these must have remained
unpublished. Apart from the major events – coronations, deaths,
royal tours of the country (*eriksgator*) and so on – even the royal
birthdays and name days were commemorated through various
kinds of celebrations around the country; such tributes from the
subjects will be discussed in greater detail in the following chapter.

---

98 On the coronations of Gustav III and Sophia Magdalena, see *Ceremonial
wid Hans Kongl. Maj:ts höga kröning* (Stockholm: Henric Fougt, 1772)
(official proclamation, annual print series); Ekstrand, pp. 86–102; Lena
Rangström, *Kläder för tid och evighet: Gustaf III sedd genom sina dräkter*
(Stockholm: Livrustkammaren, 1997), pp. 103–23. For the conflict over
the Accession Charter, see Niklas Tengberg, *Konung Gustaf III:s första
regeringstid till och med 1772 års statshvälfning: Fragment av Gustaf III:s
historia*, ed. by Clas Theodor Odhner (Lund: Gleerups, 1871), pp. 49–83.

From the coronations of Gustav III and Sophia Magdalena alone I have traced over ninety tributary publications from all parts of the kingdom and the provinces.[99] Before the coronation day, people could purchase the sheet music for the compositions that would be performed in advance, as well as copper-engraved plans of the procession and the seating in the church. In addition, a number of odes and verses by more or less well-known authors were sold.[100] Plans of the procession had already been produced for the coronation of 1751; but this time they were compiled, complemented with additional engravings and plates, in a magnificent illustrated book that had to be ordered by subscription.[101] Among the 406 subscribers, there were approximately as many nobles as burghers, mayors as well as smallware dealers, intermixed with the occasional clergyman and a handful of noblewomen. The list of subscribers provides a picture of a diverse upper- and middle-class stratum. Olof Beckman, delegate to the Riksdag for the Peasant Estate, and Johan Göthe, palace stonemason, who otherwise stand out because of their titles, would also have been included in this middle-class tier. Even though the illustrated work of Pehr Floding was more lavish than other publications from the coronation, the list of subscribers nevertheless provides an interesting indication of the group of consumers at which this type of publication was aimed. It was to a large extent the same noble groups that had traditionally been

99 See Appendix 1 to the Swedish edition of this study: Jonas Nordin, *Frihetstidens monarki: Konungamakt och offentlighet i 1700-talets Sverige* (Stockholm: Atlantis, 2009).
100 See advertisements in *Stockholms Post-Tidningar*, nos 41–42 (25–28 May 1772). It is also made clear by information in some of the publications that they had been produced in advance.
101 Pehr Floding, *Solemnités, qvi se sont passées à Stockholm, capitale du royau.me de Svede, dans les années 1771 et 1772, consistantes en des décorations, emblems, inscriptions, plans, élevations et processions, tant à l'enterrement de feu Sa Majesté le roi Adolphe Frederic à l'Église de Riddarholmen, qu'au sacre de Leurs Majestées regnantes le roi Gustave III. et la reine Sophie Magdelaine à l'Église de S:t Nicolas, avec l'acte de l'hommage. On y a joint le discours de Sa Majesté le roi, lors de la nouvelle forme du gouvernement récuë et jurée par les états dy royaume; avec le plan de la Salle des États à cette occasion, &c:a* (Stockholm: [n. pub.],1772). This work also has a Swedish parallel title. 'The coronation march' of 1751, engraved in copper and printed on imperial-size paper, was sold in the royal printing shop for 18 *daler* in copper; see the advertisement in *Stockholms Post Tidningar*, no. 98 (16 December 1751).

thought to be in opposition to the royal family. Even those who were the political opponents of the king saw usefulness and value in the monarchy as an institution.

The coronation celebration in Norrköping

All across the kingdom, celebrations took place in parallel with the coronation. How such festivities were organised locally may be exemplified by the city of Norrköping, where the local administration carried out extensive tributary ceremonies which, according to the organisers themselves, attracted several thousand delighted residents.[102] As early as five o'clock on the morning of the coronation, the city's inhabitants were awakened by the sound of thirty-two cannon shots, the first of many such salutes over the course of the day, which was a Friday. The military troops of the city paraded and conducted drills, after which the city commandant and mayor gave a speech on the virtues of the native King and the excellence of the form of government. He expressed the hope that the new King would be able to restore unity, mutual trust and the Swedish liberty and security which had for so long being trodden underfoot by arbitrariness and envy. In addition, he repeatedly emphasised that the King ruled with the assistance of the Council of the Realm and the greatly revered Estates of Sweden. The speech concluded with several salutes and three cheers from the many thousand spectators.

To the celebration was attached a purpose aimed at the common good in that twenty-two boys, between four and twelve years old, from the newly instituted so-called Gustavian orphanage presented themselves to the public. The orphanage had been established with the aid of money collected from the city administration as well as from burghers and persons of rank in the city, and it had

---

102 The following description is based on an eight-page octavo pamphlet with the title and date *Norrköping den 3. junii 1772* (Norrköping: Johan Benjamin Blume, [n.d.]); the text begins 'Then on the 29th of May last, occurred the general day of joy for the whole of the kingdom of Sweden' ('Då, uppå den 29. sidstledne Maji, inföll hela Sweriges Rikes allmänna Glädje-dag'). This entire story was also printed together with other similar accounts in an extra appendix to *Inrikes Tidningar: Continuation til Inrikes Tidningen n:o 46 af d. 15 junii 1772*. Such reports were received in large numbers from all over the realm and continued to be published in the newspaper during the rest of the year.

obtained royal patronage in the previous year, when Gustav III had stopped in the city on his way home from Paris. Now the children were presented to the public before they were taken to be fed by the city's merchants. The leading circles of the city dined elsewhere, whereupon both groups assembled in the city hall. More salutes and speeches followed before the evening's ball began, an activity that continued until six o'clock the following morning.

The following Saturday was spent in tranquillity; but at the Sunday morning service reason was once again found to 'praise the Almighty, who has given our country such a wise, benevolent, just, and gracious King, and in addition described the duty of the subjects to their gracious King'.[103] Psalms were sung and two cannon salutes of sixty-four shots each were fired. The festivities continued on the Monday, when the tributary oaths of the Estates were sworn in Stockholm, and went on until the Thursday, when the city administration and officials swore their tributary oaths before the representative of the province governor. Everywhere in the streets during these days children were heard shouting, 'Long live King Gustav and Queen Sophia Magdalena! ('Leve konung Gustav och drottning Sofia Magdalena!').

Reports of similar celebrations exist from all over the kingdom and from the entire Age of Liberty. The official concerns of the royal family were manifested in various ways around the country; and even if the printed descriptions are often extreme in their professions of joy, there is no reason to doubt the sincerity of the tributes. The subjects became involved in all the important private and political affairs of the royal family, and this happened with a parallelism that reinforced a sense of community in the kingdom. The Irish sociologist Benedict Anderson has emphasised the simultaneity created by the printing press and the emergence of the newspaper as perhaps the most important prerequisite for creating an imagined community that formed the basis of the nationalism of later ages. This was a long-term effect of 'print-capitalism'; and even though Anderson places the great breakthrough in the nineteenth century, there is no doubt that the forms of communication were already sufficiently developed to fulfil this function

---

103 ('prisa Den Alsmägtige, som gifwit wårt Land en så wis, öm, rättwis och nådig Konung, samt tillika förestält Undersåtares pligt emot deras nådige Konung'). See note 102 above.

in the eighteenth century.[104] The ways in which this creation of community was manifested, as well as the ways in which the images of the royal family were conveyed through the mass media during the Age of Liberty, make up the joint subject of the next chapter.

---

104 Benedict Anderson, *Imagined Communities: Reflections on the Origin and Spread of Nationalism* (London and New York: Verso, 1991), esp. chapter 3, 'The Origins of National Consciousness'.

3

Communication of the king's image

The Constitution regulated the position of the king in government life, and through public ceremonies he appeared in all his majesty. In different ways both were important for regularising the monarchy, but they had a limited sphere of influence. In reality, few subjects would actually have read or acquainted themselves with the details of the Instrument of Government, and the ceremonies as such reached only the people present. A sense of involvement was conveyed through the parallel celebrations organised in town halls, schools and parish halls around the country in connection with the royal feast days. These tributes from the subjects were, strictly speaking, not mandatory; but they were widespread, and they evoked a sense of community among the subjects of the Swedish Crown. In this way, the royal family contributed to creating a sense of national solidarity in the extensive kingdom. As will be shown below, this type of event was not limited to major feast days, coronations and the like; all across the country subjects also observed the name days and birthdays of the royal family. In addition to ecclesiastical feast days, these functioned as secular feast days that strengthened national unity. The king also functioned as a unifying institution in more everyday contexts, and the knowledge that all Swedish subjects obeyed the same laws and were subject to the same monarch was drummed into the population through various channels. In spite of the comparatively rudimentary forms of mass communication at the time, this message cannot have escaped a single subject.

The most effective means of communication with the subjects that the central power had at its disposal was undoubtedly the so-called proclamation system. In their extant printed form, these proclamations can be studied in the annual print series (*årstrycket*), which was above all a collection of statutes presenting new laws and ordinances. But the annual print series also contained many other things that the Magistracy wished to communicate to its subjects, sometimes on the basis of unclear principles of selection: prayers, propaganda pamphlets, narratives about important events in the kingdom, advice on how to cure disease and many other things. These decrees and messages were read out from pulpits all over the kingdom – at the beginning of the 1770s, the normal print run for generally disseminated proclamations was around 5,000 copies – and the actual printed documents were intended to be kept at the local vicar's residence, properly bound and provided with a table of contents, for future reference.[1] For a long time, the annual print series was a series of sources that escaped systematic study; but recently several thorough investigations of its contents and effects have been published.[2] Many of the aspects that are focused on here can hence be reconstructed on the basis of this literature. With the aid of recent scholarship, a few brief comments will therefore be presented about how the royal authority was manifested in public proclamations. An independent investigation will then be undertaken of another medium of mass communication, albeit one that was less widely disseminated: the newspaper.

---

1 On the annual print series and its contents, see Kurt Winberg, 'Årstrycket och dess förteckningar: Projekt till en bibliografi', *Nordisk tidskrift för bok- och biblioteksväsen*, 62–63:4 (1975–1976), 113–26; Kurt Winberg, 'Årstrycket: En avslutad historia', *Tal över blandade ämnen*, Collegium curiosorum novum, yearbook 1984–86 (Uppsala: Carmina, 1988), 223–40. On the procedures for reading out the proclamations, see Carin Bergström, *Lantprästen: Prästens funktion i det agrara samhället 1720–1800; Oland-Frösåkers kontrakt av ärkestiftet*, Nordiska museets handlingar, 110 (Stockholm: Nordiska museet, 1991), pp. 117–24.

2 Jonas Nordin, *Ett fattigt men fritt folk: Nationell och politisk självbild i Sverige från sen stormaktstid till slutet av frihetstiden* (Eslöv: Symposion, 2000), chapter 3; Elisabeth Reuterswärd, *Ett massmedium för folket: Studier i de allmänna kungörelsernas funktion i 1700-talets samhälle*, Studia historica Lundensia, 2 (Lund: Historiska institutionen, 2001); Peter Ericsson, *Stora nordiska kriget förklarat: Karl XII och det ideologiska tilltalet*, Studia historica Upsaliensia, 202 (Uppsala: Historiska institutionen, 2002); Anna Maria Forssberg, *Att hålla folket på gott humör: Informationsspridning, krigspropaganda och mobilisering i Sverige 1655–1680*, Stockholm Studies in History, 80 (Stockholm: Almqvist & Wiksell, 2005); Joachim Östlund, *Lyckolandet: Maktens legitimering i officiell retorik från stormaktstid till demokratins genombrott* (Lund: Sekel, 2007).

148 Monarchy in the Age of Liberty

The presentation of the royal authority in public proclamations

In a study of the intercession-day announcements that were the first proclamations each year, the historian Göran Malmstedt has argued that during the Age of Liberty the subjects of the kingdom would hardly have been able to identify any limitations on the royal exercise of power on the basis of the information conveyed in these proclamations. On the contrary, kings appeared 'before the people as powerful leaders with patriarchal and almost theocratic traits'.[3] Malmstedt's observation is equally valid for public proclamations in general. In the preambles through which the audience was addressed it was consistently 'We, N.N., by the Grace of God King of Sweden, the Goths and the Wends' ('Vi N.N. med Guds nåde Sveriges, Götes och Vendes Konung') who issued all new laws and ordinances. This formula remained fixed throughout the entire Age of Liberty, from Ulrika Eleonora to Gustav III.

The historian Elisabeth Reuterswärd has investigated the image of the Magistracy that emerged from the proclamations, asking what perceptions of central contexts in the kingdom were communicated through them. She summarises as follows:

> They [the subjects] had excellent access to information about what the men of power had decided, what laws they had made, and what they had decreed. The subjects knew that they had a king, a government, and administrative boards, as well as province governors and lower officials. They were well acquainted with the names of the king and the province governor, the crown bailiff, and the provincial sheriff; but most of the real holders of power at a central level were completely anonymous. The names of the lords of the Council of the Realm were not made official.[4]

3 Göran Malmstedt, 'Frihetstidens karismatiska kungar', in *Maktens skiftande skepnader: Studier i makt, legitimitet och inflytande i det tidig-moderna Sverige*, ed. by Börje Harnesk (Umeå: Institutionen för historiska studier, 2003), pp. 75–89 (p. 88) ('inför folket som kraftfulla ledare med patriarkala och närmast teokratiska drag').
4 Reuterswärd, p. 293 ('De hade en ypperlig tillgång till information om vad maktens män beslutat, lagstiftat och förordnat. De visste att de hade en kung, en regering, kollegier, samt landshövdingar och lägre tjänstemän. De var väl förtrogna med namnet på konungen och landshövdingen, krono-fogden och länsman men de flesta verkliga makthavare på central nivå var helt anonyma. Namnen på herrarna i riksrådet kungjordes inte').

In this context it is important to note that the entire hierarchy
of power, from the king at the top to the provincial sheriff at the
bottom, was presented through the proclamations, but in a limited
manner. The name of the province governor and other lower
officials might therefore be well known to local communities, while
on the other hand the lords in the Council were rarely mentioned by
name: at the head of the kingdom, as far as the proclamations were
concerned, was the king alone.

In other words, it was a powerful but at the same time rather
featureless monarch who was presented through the proclamations.
This officially sanctioned and also legally important dissemination
of information concerned only the political activities of the king,
the exercise of his official duties. Very little was conveyed about
the private affairs of the royal family. The exception consisted
of major ceremonies, such as the opening session of the Riksdag,
marriages and deaths, where the Queen, too, could be glimpsed at
the side of the King in the narratives. Still, such occasions could be
considered to constitute public obligations, albeit often of a family-
law nature, and did not really concern the private lives of the royal
family. For a long period they were of a similar kind, although the
newspaper articles were shorter and dry as dust, but the two media
increasingly diverged, and the private activities of the royal family
were given more and more space in the newspapers.

The royal family in the newspapers

During the greater part of the Age of Liberty, the domestic newspapers were relatively underdeveloped. Among the newspapers the
semi-official *Posttidningar*, published on Mondays and Thursdays
each week, was alone for a long time. It is estimated that the print
run was somewhere between 1,500 and 2,000 copies, but the
influence of the newspaper was far greater than these seemingly
modest figures suggest. The emphasis was placed on foreign events,
although the space for domestic news grew over time.[5] From the

5 On *Posttidningar* during the Age of Liberty, see esp. Otto Sylwan,
  Svenska pressens historia till statshvälfningen 1772 (Lund: Gleerups,
  1896), pp. 80–109. See also *Den svenska pressens historia*, ed. by Karl
  Erik Gustafsson and Per Rydén, 5 vols (Stockholm: Ekerlids, 2000–03), I: *I
  begynnelsen (tiden före 1830)* (2000), pp. 118–29, and *Världens äldsta: Post-
  och Inrikes Tidningar under 1600-, 1700-, 1800-, 1900- och 2000-talen*,

autumn of 1760, *Inrikes Tidningar* began to be published as an appendix to *Posttidningar*, which in spite of this new publication continued to print news about the royals for the rest of that year. However, at the beginning of 1761 *Posttidningar* almost entirely ceased its domestic reporting, and with respect to royal news only information about appointments remained. This information was published exclusively in the form of notices, forming a recurring element included in virtually every issue. Such information could also be found in *Inrikes Tidningar*, as can be seen in Diagram 3; but how the announcements of both newspapers were otherwise related to each other after 1760 has not been investigated.

News about the royals was regularly included in both *Posttidningar* and *Inrikes Tidningar*. The literary historian Otto Sylwan has found that royal notices claimed significant space in both these newspapers, but that they rarely contained anything of direct political value. 'The more the political powerlessness of the king increased and the more the conflicts between the royal couple on the one hand and the leadership in the Council and the Riksdag on the other intensified, the more breathlessly subservient became the tone in these narratives', writes a later researcher.[6] The comment is more witty than correct, at least if one wishes to see a simple causal connection between the observed phenomena. It is doubtful whether the increasing reporting can be seen as a means of obscuring the political weakness of the King, and whether the conflicts between the King and the Council were the reason for the servile tone of voice. This deferential tone was the result of greater attention rather than a changed political situation. Internal affairs in general were initially given little space, and because the doings of the royal family were not described at all, there was no place for a submissive humility in the tone of voice. The increase in the number of royal notices happened in parallel with a heightened interest in internal affairs in general, and this

ed. by Karl Erik Gustafsson and Per Rydén (Stockholm: Atlantis, 2005), pp. 120–92. The two latter works partly follow Sylwan's account. *Posttidningar* is here used as an aggregate name; at the beginning of the century the newspaper was actually called *Stockholmiske Post-Tijdender*, which was changed in 1722 to *Stockholmske Post Tidningar*. From 1735 it was called *Stockholms Post-Tidningar*, a name that, with or without a hyphen, was retained until 1820.

6 Ingemar Oscarsson in *Den svenska pressens historia*, I, p. 122 ('Ju mer kungens politiska maktlöshet tilltog och ju mer motsättningarna skärptes mellan kungaparet och de styrande i råd och riksdag, desto mer andlöst underdånig blev tonen i dessa berättelser'); Sylwan, pp. 89, 92–96, 99–100.

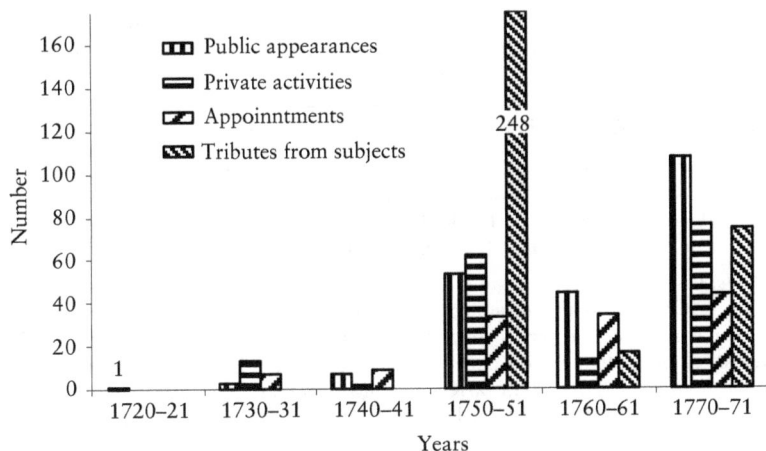

Diagram 3 Royal notices in *Posttidningar* and *Inrikes Tidningar*,
1720–1771

Source: Posttidningar, 1720–21, 1730–31, 1740–41, 1750–51, 1760;
Inrikes Tidningar, 1760–61, 1770–71.

should be seen as a sociological rather than a political phenomenon which was connected to a growing public sphere, to borrow a term familiar from research.[7] Regardless of whether it was cause or effect, the number of domestic news items in the newspaper increased in general. Even if these were not instances of direct political moralising, they contributed to creating a sense of patriotic solidarity in the kingdom. In this the royal family was an important ingredient, and a great change occurred in the mid-1740s.

A statistical summary shows powerful quantitative growth in the number of royal notices. We can see that from a single notice in 1720, the number had increased to 152, or around three per week, by 1771. Between these two years appears the peak year of 1751, with a total of 228 notices mentioning the royals (Table 1).

These statistics must be read with a degree of caution. Royal deaths occurred in both 1751 and 1771, and the reporting surrounding these events partially explains the large numbers.

---

7 For a balanced discussion of the concept of the public sphere during the Age of Liberty, see Karin Sennefelt, 'Mellan hemligt och offentligt: Sven Hofman vid riksdagen 1765–66', in *Riksdag, kaffehus och predikstol: Frihetstidens politiska kultur 1766–1772*, ed. by Marie-Christine Skuncke and Henrika Tandefelt (Stockholm: Atlantis, 2003), pp. 209–27 (pp. 210–17).

Table 1 Numbers of news items concerning the Swedish royal family
in *Posttidningar* and *Inrikes Tidningar*, selected years in the period
1720–1771

1720	1721	1730	1731	1740	1741	1750	1751	1760	1761	1770	1771
1	0	7	16	4	14	168	228	39	70	150	152

Source: *Posttidningar*, 1720–21, 1730–31, 1740–41, 1750–51, 1760;
Inrikes Tidningar, 1760–61, 1770–71.

Note: Until 1736 *Posttidningar* published one issue per week, and thereafter two.
The statistics up to and including 1731 are thus normally based on 52 issues per
year, while after that year there were between 100 and 102 issues per year. The
year 1721 of *Posttidningar* is poorly preserved, and only 14 issues remain in public
collections. The year 1760 of *Inrikes Tidningar* contained a mere 5 issues, and the
subsequent year had 97 issues, while the years 1770 and 1771 contained 102 and
101 issues, respectively.

The number of notices skyrocketed in 1750 as well, which may be
explained by this being the year of Prince Frederick Adolf's birth.
In contradistinction, there was a death in the royal family in 1741,
that of Queen Ulrika Eleonora, without this amounting to anything
other than a marginal increase in the number of notices published.
Dividing the statistics into categories also reinforces the impression
of a general increase in interest in the royals.

In the present chapter, the notices regarding the royal family are
divided into four categories: (1) public appearances; (2) private
activities; (3) appointments; and (4) tributes from subjects.

The first category consists of the royal exercise of official duties,
primarily by the King himself but sometimes also by other members
of the royal family. This category includes reports on decisions
made or other interventions, as well as accounts of public appearances and ceremonies, for instance at audiences for ambassadors
and the opening session of the Riksdag. Sometimes the newspapers
would announce that royal proclamations and the like had been
published. Such notices have not been included in the data summarised here unless they indicated royal activity in some other way.[8]

---

8 Of the years investigated, this type of news item was most common in
1740, a year which otherwise contained few reports about the royal family.
It is true that references to royal ordinances were one way of spreading
knowledge about measures taken by the government, and the fact that
these have not been included in the statistics may distort impressions to
some extent. His Royal Majesty was mentioned at least indirectly in such

Included in private activities are reports on the doings of the royal family outside their official duties. Often both the King and the Queen, as well as the royal children, figured in these contexts. The notices might describe important occasions for the royals, their journeys between their out-of-town residences, their putting on mourning for deaths in foreign princely houses and tributes by subjects in the presence of the royal family. Appointments announced in newspapers were matters that almost exclusively concerned the King, but one of the princes might be involved as well. A newspaper would often begin with such notices, and through them readers were provided with brief accounts about appointments, awarded orders, new ennoblements, dismissals with a pension and other matters that had been decided by the King. Only posts and appointments that were explicitly said to have been dealt with by the King or by some other member of the royal family have been included in the data. Finally, the category of tributes from subjects includes royalist marks of honour that took place without a royal presence. These include the many ceremonies and expressions of appreciation that were arranged all around the kingdom in connection with royal deaths, coronations and the like. The exceptional number of royal notices in 1751 can primarily be explained by reports about such events having been received in large numbers from all across the realm. If these notices are excluded, the oscillations of the curves become less dramatic. It may be added that the information under a single newspaper heading – indicated by location and date – has been counted only once in the data even if a member of the royal family has been noted under this heading for several subsequent interventions assigned to the same category. Conversely, these items have been counted as two or more when they belong to different categories and are separated from one another by the beginning of a new paragraph. Finally, it should be noted that information from advertising material, which might take up as much as a quarter of the pages in a newspaper, has not been included in the data.

Although these statistics are fraught with problems regarding the drawing of boundaries, and even though the royal notices were unusually numerous during several of the studied years because of

---

notices during this year as well. On the other hand, *Posttidningar* provided no information of this kind that had not already been conveyed through the usual proclamations.

exceptional events, the trend should be clear: attention surrounding the royals increased steadily over time in *Posttidningar* and its
complementary successor *Inrikes Tidningar*. (The seeming decline
in 1760–1761 can to a great extent be explained by the fact that the
new domestic newspaper had not yet found its form and its content.
After an initial lack of interest, reports about the royals increased
significantly during the second half of 1761.) In order to illustrate
this change more clearly, though, a rather more detailed investigation of the contents of the reports is required.

Lack of interest in the royals in *Posttidningar*, 1720–1721

Strictly speaking, *Posttidningar* did not contain any news at all of
the royals in 1720. In the first issue, the aim of this newspaper was
stated as reporting on 'what takes place abroad' ('som utomlands
sig tildrager'). This intention was not so closely adhered to in
practice, as isolated domestic news items found their way into the
paper among the regular lists of ships that had passed through the
strait of Öresund or arrived at Dalarö, the customs station located
at the shipping lane to Stockholm. The only notice concerning royal
activities appears in the last issue of the year, and only in some
copies. It was then reported from Stockholm, on 1 January (!), that
His Royal Majesty's minister resident in Vienna, Georg Vilhelm
von Höpken, had returned to Sweden against orders. 'His Royal
Majesty, as a consequence of the conduct of this aforesaid resident
minister, hence finds himself under the obligation of ordering his
arrest under civil law, until the matter can be duly settled at a later
date by means of legal scrutiny and judgement.'[9] In this single royal
notice, the King was thus the agent.

When notices were lacking, subscribers could nevertheless obtain
an idea of what happened centrally in the kingdom through the
royal ordinances that were still disseminated via *Posttidningar*
at the beginning of the Age of Liberty. On 12 January, a list was
thus appended of all ordinances and decisions 'that have been
published by the printing office, from Her Royal Majesty our most
gracious Queen Ulrica Eleonora's accession to government on
7 December 1718 to the end of 1719'. David Silvius's manifesto

---

9 *Stockholmiske Post-Tidender*, no. 53 (31 December 1720) ('Altså är Hans
   Kongl. Maj:t igenom en sådan bemelte Residentens Conduite worden
   föranlåten, at låta antyda honom en Civil Arrest, til dess saken frambättre
   medelst laga ransakning och Domb behörigen kan blifwa afgiord').

against absolutism – which was not a royal ordinance, but rather the new rulers' adopted interpretation of the Constitution – was, as noted earlier, appended to the newspaper on 26 January. On 7 May, Frederick's Accession Charter, the election agreement of the Estates (*ständernas valförening*) and the ceremonial for the coronation were distributed. Three weeks later the new Instrument of Government was disseminated.[10] The readers of *Posttidningar* could thus stay abreast of changes in the form of government; but they were not yet given any detailed information about the activities of the royal family.

A slow increase in the interest in royalty: the 1730s and 1740s

A decade later, in 1731, the situation had changed somewhat. Almost all reporting about the King's doings from 1731 dealt with his journey to his hereditary country of Hesse. It was said that wherever Frederick went, he was met with tributes and receptions. The letters quoted in *Posttidningar* were often foreign messages that were published without being edited. Following the King's arrival in the capital of Kassel, an impressive number of visiting dignitaries were named. The newspaper could report that 'the number of princes, counts, and other men of quality in attendance is uncommonly great'. On a later occasion, it was reported that the Free City of Frankfurt had sent three representatives to congratulate the King and that Frederick had 'treated them with an extraordinary degree of royal grace and forbearance'.[11] These enthusiastic bulletins, which figured in the columns of the paper for a couple of months, probably filled Swedish subjects with patriotic pride; and at the beginning of November, 'the joyous tidings' that His Royal Majesty had returned to his kingdom and landed at Karlshamn were finally reported. The story ended on the fifteenth of the same month with a detailed account of Frederick's return to the capital, where he

---

10 *Stockholmiske Post-Tidender*, 1720: no. 2 (12 January) ('som ifrån Hennes Kongl. May:ts wår Allernådigste Drottnings Ulricæ Eleonoræ anträde til Regementet den 7 Decemb. 1718. in til slutet af 1719. igenom trycket äre utgångne'); no. 4 (26 January); no. 19 (7 May); no. 22 (28 May).

11 *Stockholmske Post Tidningar*, no. 36 (6 September 1731) ('antalet på de härwarande Furstar, Grefwar och andre förnäme Herrar är ogement stort'); no. 41 (11 October 1731) ('bemött dem med särdeles hög Kongl. nåd och mildhet').

Figure 14 Illuminations on King Frederick's return to Stockholm in 1731. Engraving by Georg Biurman. On the left, Mercury announces, 'Rejoice Sweden God has speeded our King's happy return'. The German text reads, in a free translation, *Welcome Frederick! Thus speaks every man today. Yes, everyone must rejoice, and so do I. Welcome Frederick!* On the right, the King and Queen's monogram is displayed, as well as a burning heart bearing the words 'Long live Sweden's father and mother'. The inscription on the plinth reads, in translation, *Long, long live the King of Sweden, who has returned home!* The verse in Swedish connects patriotism to that loyalty to the king which was regarded as a special characteristic of Swedes. Photo: Björn Green, KB.

was received by the Council of the Realm, generals, persons of rank and the city administration, along with large crowds of delighted subjects. It was reported that Stockholm had been adorned with triumphal arches, that beautiful music was played from several of the church towers and that fires and illuminations were lit in the evenings (Figure 14).[12] This fairly detailed reporting was something new. After all, in 1730 Frederick I himself had still pressured *Posttidningar* to publish the congratulatory letters he had received when he assumed control of his hereditary country of Hesse.[13]

Another decade later, two dramatic episodes stood out among the news: the attack on Russia, and the death of Ulrika Eleonora.

---

12 *Stockholmske Post Tidningar*, no. 45 (8 November 1731) ('de hugnelige tidender'); no. 46 (15 November 1731).

13 Sylwan, p. 93.

On 30 July 1741, the newspaper reported that royal heralds had proclaimed the declaration of war in the streets of the capital two days earlier, and that the same proclamation, comprising the reasons 'that obliged His Royal Majesty to declare war on the Tsar of Russia', were available for purchase. The demise of the Queen was reported on 26 November with an expression of regret, two days after her death, but without any follow-up in later columns.[14]

After a tentative beginning, interest in the royals increased somewhat towards the middle of the century. The focus remained entirely on the public affairs of the King and Queen. Those who knew nothing about the country's true form of government could not intuit the actual power relations from reading *Posttidningar*. The newspaper distinguished as little between the King's personal decision-making and the collective decision-making of the Council as did the royal ordinances. Indeed, the King's proclaimed declaration of war against the Tsar would eventually be used against him, as we shall see in a later context.

Otto Sylwan has dated the breakthrough for royal news in *Posttidningar* to the period following the Russo-Swedish War of 1741–1743 ('the War of the Hats') and the arrival of Adolf Frederick and Louisa Ulrika in the kingdom, and his impression is confirmed by the present investigation. The change occurred in parallel with an increased interest in domestic news in general. From previously having been made up entirely of scattered notices, domestic news took up on average a little over a tenth of the space in the newspaper for the rest of the 1740s and throughout the entire 1750s. The royal family had a prominent place in this material. Curiosity about the young and charming Crown Prince couple, and above all the enthusiasm surrounding the births of the royal children, contributed to increasing the attention paid to the royals.[15] Even though most of the interest focused on the Crown Prince couple and their family, readers were also treated to occasional news items about the activities of the King. Usually those items had to do with appointments and ceremonial appearances,

---

14 On the start of the war: *Stockholms Post-Tidningar*, no. 59 (30 July 1741) ('som föranlåta Kongl. May:t at förklara Krig emot Czaren af Ryssland'); cf. also no. 65 (20 September 1741). On the death of the Queen: *Stockholms Post-Tidningar*, no. 93 (26 November 1741).

15 Sylwan, p. 93. See also Ingemar Oscarsson, 'Från statstidning till akademitidning 1734–1809', in *Världens äldsta*, pp. 131–236 (pp. 142–44).

but some dealt with his leisure activities, as in the following notice
from the late summer of 1750:

> When His Majesty on Saturday morning last rode in his carriage
> in Karlberg's hunting grounds, his Majesty without support shot a
> passing deer from the carriage, and in the afternoon a few partridges
> in the nearby fields.[16]

The notice may seem wholly anecdotal, but the primary aim was
presumably to emphasise that the ageing King was in good health.
Posttidningar had earlier reported on his various attacks of illness
and how these had been overcome, among other things by taking
the waters.

The new royal couple: the 1750s

The real upswing in writing about the royals came with the succession of Adolf Frederick to the throne in 1751. On the death of
Frederick I and the elevation of Adolf Frederick, a long report of
a little over a full page in length was published in *Posttidningar*
(Figure 15). This notice recounts Frederick's last moments in life
and Adolf Frederick's elevation on the following day. The oath
against autocracy, which he swore on this same occasion, was
published in its entirety. The narrative continued with an account
of thanksgiving services held in the churches of the capital, the
condolences of foreign emissaries and the tributes of government offices and subjects. Finally, a special account was supplied
about the first action taken by the new king, a pledge to carefully
observe section 20 in the Instrument of Government when making
future appointments in the Cabinet. During Frederick's long last
illness, this section had been suspended – probably meaning that
a number of appointments had been left unfilled – and according
to the account in the newspaper, the Council of the Realm consequently received this message with the deepest reverence and
humble obedience. They therefore joyfully renewed the oath they
had sworn, 'that is, on all occasions to desire to organise their
humble consultation according to that which is to an equal degree
demanded and required by the [...] Instrument of Government,

---

16 *Stockholms Post-Tidningar*, no. 64 (16 August 1750) ('Då Hans Maj:t
   sidstledne lördag förmiddagen åkte uti Carlbergs Diurgård skiöt Hans Maj:t
   på fri hand utur wagnen en förbi strykande Hiort, och om eftermiddagen
   någre stycken Raphöns uppå de deromkring belägne fälten').

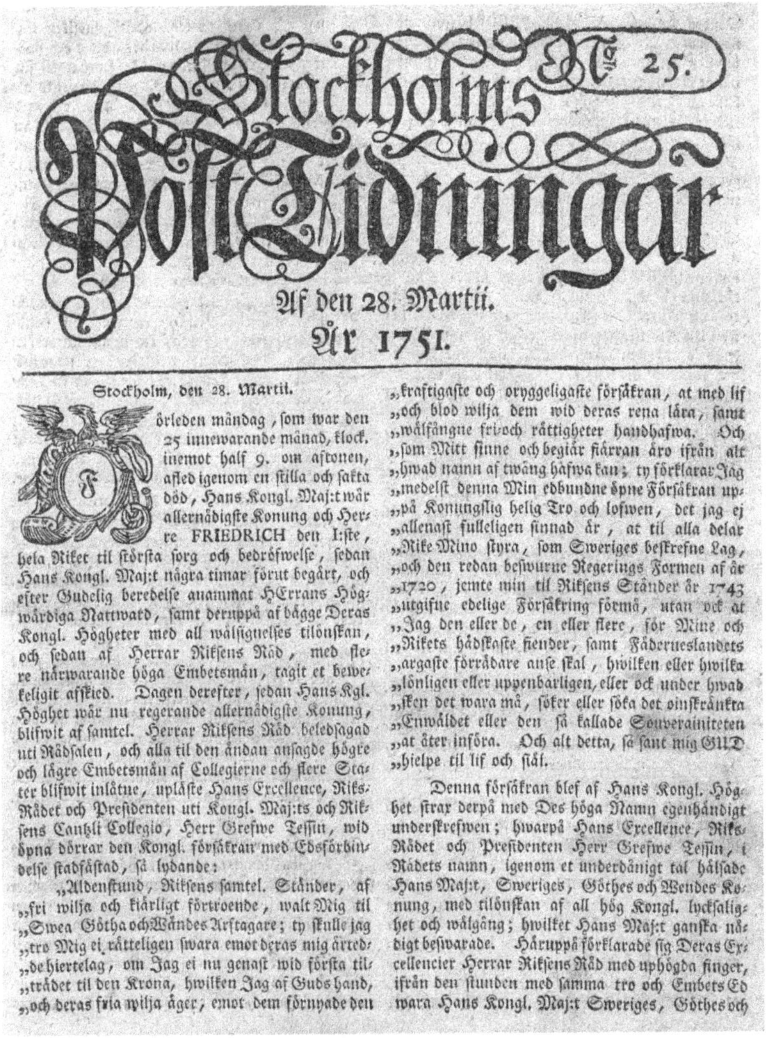

Stockholms Post-Tidningar N:o 25.

Af den 28. Martii. År 1751.

Stockholm, den 28. Martii.

Förleden måndag, som war den 25 innewarande månad, klock. inemot half 9. om aftonen, afled igenom en stilla och sakta död, Hans Kongl. Maj:t wår allernådigste Konung och Herre FRIEDRICH den I:ste, hela Riket til största sorg och bedröfwelse, sedan Hans Kongl. Maj:t några timar förut begärt, och efter Gudelig beredelse anammat HErrans Högwärdiga Nattwatd, samt deruppå af bägge Deras Kongl. Högheter med all wälsignelses tilönskan, och sedan af Herrar Riksens Råd, med flere närwarande höga Embetsmän, tagit et bewekeligit afskied. Dagen derefter, sedan Hans Kgl. Höghet wår nu regerande allernådigste Konung, blifwit af samtel. Herrar Riksens Råd beledsagad uti Rådsalen, och alla til den ändan ansagde högre och lägre Embetsmän af Collegierne och flere Stater blifwit inlåtne, upläste Hans Excellence, Riks-Rådet och Presidenten uti Kongl. Maj:ts och Riksens Cantzli Collegio, Herr Grefwe Tessin, wid öpna dörrar den Kongl. försäkran med Edsförbindelse stadfästad, så lydande:

„Aldenstund, Riksens samtel. Ständer, af „fri wilja och kiärligt förtroende, walt Mig til „Swea Götha och Wändes Arfstagare; ty skulle jag „tro Mig ei rätteligen swara emot deras mig ärtedde hiertelag, om Jag ei nu genast wid första tilträdet til den Krona, hwilken Jag af Guds hand, „och deras fria wilja äger, emot dem förnyade den „kraftigaste och oryggeligaste försäkran, at med lif „och blod wilja dem wid deras rena lära, samt „wälfängne fri- och rättigheter handhafwa. Och „som Mitt sinne och begiär fiärran äro ifrån alt „hwad namn af twång häfwa kan; ty förklarar Jag „medelst denna Min edbundne öpne Försäkran uppå Konungslig helig Tro och lofwen, det jag ej „allenast fulleligen sinnad är, at til alla delar „Rike Mino styra, som Sweriges beskrefne Lag, „och den redan beswurne Regerings Formen af år „1720, jemte min til Riksens Ständer år 1743 „utgifne edelige Försäkring förmå, utan ock at „Jag den eller de, en eller flere, för Mine och „Rikets hädskaste fiender, samt Fäderneslandets „argaste förrådare anse skal, hwilken eller hwilka „lönligen eller uppenbarligen, eller ock under hwad „sken det wara må, söker eller söka det oinskränkta „Enwåldet eller den så kallade Souverainiteten „at åter införa. Och alt detta, så sant mig GUD „hielpe til lif och siäl.

Denna försäkran blef af Hans Kongl. Höghet strax derpå med Des höga Namn egenhändigt underskrefwen; hwarpå Hans Excellence, Riks-Rådet och Presidenten Herr Grefwe Tessin, i Rådets namn, igenom et underdånigt tal hälsade Hans Maj:t, Sweriges, Göthes och Wendes Konung, med tilönskan af all hög Kongl. lycksalighet och wälgång; hwilket Hans Maj:t ganska nådigt beswarade. Häruppå förklarade sig Deras Excellencier Herrar Riksens Råd med uphögda finger, ifrån den stunden med samma tro och Embets Ed wara Hans Kongl. Maj:t Sweriges, Göthes och

Figure 15 The newspaper *Stockholms Post-Tidningar* of 28 March 1751, containing accounts of the death of Frederick I and the accession of Adolf Frederick. Photo: Jens Gustafsson, KB.

Your Royal Majesty's highness and authority, and the freedoms and rights of the Estates of the Realm'.[17] The account in *Posttidningar* was unusually detailed, but because of a rather prosaic reporting style the description did not stray far from that provided in the general proclamations. However, the newspaper's readers received added value during the following weeks. In a couple of issues, accounts of the public display of the royal corpse appeared, and the general public was informed of the opportunity to view the open coffin and the crown regalia in the temporary royal palace. The funeral procession was also described in a comprehensive account, the disposition of which corresponded to the official report but complemented it with certain details.[18] In subsequent issues, the decorations in the church were described with a level of detail that was lacking in the proclamations, so it is obvious that the newspaper had a reporter on site.[19] Over the

17 *Stockholms Post Tidningar*, no. 25 (28 March 1751) ('at neml. wid alla tilfällen wilja inrätta Deras underdåniga Rådslag efter det, som likmätigt samma Regerings-Form, Eders Kongl. Maj:ts Höghet och Myndighet, samt Riksens Ständers fri- och rättigheter kräfja och erfordra'). Cf. Carl Gustaf Malmström, *Sveriges politiska historia från konung Karl XII:s död till statshvälfningen 1772*, 2nd edn, 6 vols (Stockholm: Norstedts, 1893–1901), IV (1899), pp. 7–9. During Frederick's last illness the Council had often given in to the King's whims when it came to appointments. It was hardly the joy of now being able to stop this indulgence that the Council expressed publicly in this manner.
18 *Stockholms Post Tidningar*, nos 26–27, 29 (4, 8, 15 April 1751). Cf. *Reglemente, som wid högstsalig Hans Kongl. Maj:ts konung Friedrich then förstes, bisättnings-process ifrån Konungshuset til Ridderholms Kyrckan, som sker then [11] April. 1751. bör i akt tagas och eferföljas* ([Stockholm]: Kungl. tryckeriet, [n.d.]) (official proclamation, annual print series).
19 *Stockholms Post Tidningar*, no. 30 (18 April 1751). The rest of this issue described Adolf Frederick's first chapter meeting of the three royal orders and described the speech delivered at that same time by Chancery President Carl Gustaf Tessin, which was later circulated as a proclamation: *Tal hållit uppå ordens-dagen, then 17. april 1751. af [...] högwälborne Carl Gustaf Tessin* (Stockholm: Kungl. tryckeriet, [n.d.]) (official proclamation, annual print series). The usual praxis seems to have been that the descriptions of ceremonies in *Posttidningar* were based on public proclamations complemented by eyewitness descriptions. Cf., e.g., the description in the newspaper of the opening session of the Riksdag in 1751 with the proclaimed ceremonial: *Stockholms Post Tidningar*, no. 74 (23 September 1751); *Ceremonial, som wid riksdagens början år 1751. kommer at i akt tagas* ([Stockholm]: Kungl. tryckeriet, [n.d.]) (official proclamation, annual print series).

following weeks, a large number of descriptions of tributary ceremonies and the taking of oaths from all over the country were published. Many of these ceremonies had been planned for 17 April or 3 May, which were the birthdays, according to the Julian calendar, of the old and the new King, respectively. In the autumn, a detailed description of Frederick's funeral was published – a ceremony which had, according to the account in the newspaper over the following weeks, been commemorated in towns all across the realm.[20] The newspaper reported on memorial services and ceremonies in Uppsala, Gothenburg, Västerås, Karlskrona, Kalmar, Malmö, Växjö, Vänersborg, Vadstena, Linköping, Västervik, Ystad, Visby, Örebro, Nystad, Skara, Strängnäs, Härnösand, Sala, Ulricehamn, and Gränna, as well as on the island of Visingsö and in the church at Rimstad outside Norrköping.

However, the news that received the most attention in that year was the coronations on 26 November, the delineation of which filled two entire issues and crowded out all other news and most of the advertising material. The account of the ritual itself adhered closely to the printed ceremonial; but with respect to that evening's public meal in the Hall of State, *Rikssalen*, readers were given some additional information about decorations and procedures. This time, too, subsequent issues of the newspaper described a large number of tributes from subjects all over the kingdom. The sheer number of these tokens of respect even occasioned the extraordinary measure of several subsequent issues of the newspaper being printed with an extra sheet in order to accommodate them all.[21] Similar stories of tributes were reported from more than a hundred locations all over the realm, both towns and country parishes, from the markets of Jokkmokk and Kautokeino in the north to Ystad in the south, and from Gothenburg in the west to Jokkas at Lake Saimaa in present-day Finland in the east. Bulletins of this kind continued to be reported from distant ends of the country far into the new year.

---

20 On the funeral: *Stockholms Post Tidningar*, no. 76 (30 September 1751). As previously, this description corresponds with the printed ceremonial but is complemented with details. Cf. *Wid hög-salig Hans Kongl. Maj:ts konung Friedrich then förstes begrafning, som sker uti Riddarholms kyrkan, then 27. septembr. 1751. kommer följande at i akt tagas* ([Stockholm]: Kungl. tryckeriet, [n.d.]) (official proclamation, annual print series).

21 *Stockholms Post Tidningar*, nos 93–94, 97–98, 100–01 (28 November and 2, 12, 16, 23, 30 December 1751).

The royal family as a unifying factor

The name days and birthdays of the royals were usually celebrated by their subjects in both private and public contexts. A large number of occasional verses, festive speeches and songs from such celebrations have been preserved from the entire period. The verses and the speeches could be of high literary quality or complete rubbish; the authors might be anyone from a Councillor of the Realm or a bishop to a student or a peasant miner; and the celebrations took place in the capital and in the small towns, as well as in the countryside. In most cases the verses were written in Swedish, but they could also be written in another language, usually Latin, French or German. Many of the simpler verses were printed in several editions and as small duodecimos; preserved examples are often well thumbed. Taken together, these things indicate that the latter books were aimed primarily at, and actually found buyers among, a popular audience.[22] Descriptions of these popular feasts of celebration were randomly reported to *Posttidningar* and printed in its columns. In addition to the ecclesiastical feast days, these celebrations became a kind of national secular feast days which while not celebrated by decree were nevertheless common. The assistant vicar of Torneå, Carl Brunius, called Gustav Day on 6 July 'one of the happiest of the entire year', when the subjects were reminded of the achievements of both Gustav I and Gustav II Adolf for their fatherland and their religion.[23]

To an even greater extent the observance of more exceptional events, such as royal deaths and coronations, would have instilled a sense of national unity and common destiny. Thanks to the simultaneous and nationwide ceremonies, these occasions were transformed into national rites of passage that converted a public manifestation into an internalised passion within the

---

22 In and for this study, the entirety of the collection of such prints at the National Library of Sweden has been reviewed. This collection consists of hundreds of miscellaneous items collected under the classifying designations 'Svenska samlingen, 1700–1829'/'Vitterhet Sverige'/'Verser kungliga'/'Broschyrer' ('Swedish collection, 1700–1829'/'Belles-lettres, Sweden'/'Verse, royal'/'Brochures'). This material has been assembled in chronological order according to the reigns of the individual monarchs. Even though no systematic compilation of the material has been made for the present text, several references herein were produced by this review.
23 *Inrikes Tidningar*, no. 65 (22 August 1771) ('en af de gladaste i hela året').

individual subject. Through the coronation a new *pater patriae* was inaugurated, and the subjects vied with one another in displaying their expressions of joy and their deferential tributes. Forms varied; but common elements were petitionary prayers, cannon and rifle salutes, and balls and receptions with musical entertainment and frequent toasting, as well as orations and recitations of poorly written poems of their own making. For instance, in Gamla Karleby in the eastern part of the kingdom (present-day Karleby or Kokkola in Finland), the young Anders Chydenius, who was then still a student but later became a priest and a well-known writer on political economy, delivered 'a Swedish speech in prose on *The Prosperity of Finns under a Swedish Crown* on behalf of his countrymen, [and] testified to the pure passion that inspired each and every one to surpass one another in the most humble reverence and confidence in the King and Crown of Sweden'.[24]

A common measure of the sincerity of the tributes seems to have been that the festivities continued until early the next morning. A typical such lengthy celebration among many others was reported from Nederkalix in the far north, and the account published in *Inrikes Tidningar* in 1771. (The tribute had in fact taken place the previous summer, but because of the slow postal services the reporting of it had been delayed. In spite of almost eight months having passed, the editor felt that the notice still had news value.) The conclusion of the yearly company rally of the Kalix Company had coincided with the name day of the King (as Adolf) on 23 June. This event was celebrated with a two-hour drill before an audience of both sexes, followed by a mock assault on a redoubt. Next came a parade march with salutes, followed by 'a rather fine speech' given by the vicar and suitable for this lofty occasion. Regimental prayers were said, and the newspaper reported that the military rally was concluded with hymn-singing. In the evening there was a meal in the vicarage for soldiers and people of rank. The illuminated monograms of the royal couple brightened the gathering, toasts were drunk, salutes were fired, and there was dancing until early the next morning.[25]

---

24 *Stockholms Post Tidningar*, no. 3 (9 January 1752) ('et obundit Swenskt tal om *Finnars flor under Swensk Krona* å sina Landsmäns wägnar [och] betygade den rena eld, som en och hwar upmuntrade, at öwerträffa hwarandra uti underdånigaste wördnad och förtroende för Swea Konung och Krona').

25 *Inrikes Tidningar*, no. 16 (25 February 1771) ('et ganska wackert Tal').

Furthest up in the northernmost regions of the realm the image of a national community was maintained in this way, held together by a shared head of state and a well-trained military force. With the toasting in descending order, from the royals down to the lower officers, a chain of command was also made visible where His Majesty himself was only a few handshakes away. Many other examples of information about similar celebrations can be provided, and these filled many issues of the newspapers.

The king was in no way superfluous or meaningless during the Age of Liberty. How the royal authority was perceived by the common people will be discussed in later chapters, but regardless of the political functions of the king, he played an important socio-logical role. The king was an important unifying force in society, and his subjects organised their lives on the basis of royal feast days and arranged the reckoning of their time according to the reigns of their kings. In this respect the king's actual political influence lacked relevance; knowledge of the doings of the royal family mattered more. It is thus possible to argue that the king's sociological signifi-cance increased over time and in parallel with the development of communication media, and that, for instance, Adolf Frederick was more present in the everyday perceptions of the common people than Charles XI in his day, no matter how absolute a monarch the latter may have been. Formally, the nationwide swearing of oaths that was frequently reported in the papers also constituted an important bond of union. In the absence of actual citizenship (the first citizenship law in Sweden came in 1858) the oath of allegiance was the bond that tied a subject to the Crown and the state from a legal point of view. Crimes against the state were also long defined as crimes of lese-majesty, as subsequent chapters will show.

The King's family in focus

A change that happened over time and because of specific circum-stances was that the royal *family* were accorded ever greater space in newspaper columns. During the last decade of Frederick's govern-ment, the kingdom had had no Queen; nor were there any princes and princesses to write about. However, immediately following the arrival of Adolf Frederick and Louisa Ulrika in the kingdom, the phrase 'Their Royal Highnesses' began to appear in news reports; and in the descriptions of public ceremonies and private affairs, the three princes and the princess – born between 1746 and 1753 – quickly became a frequently recurring feature in the notices while they were still children. Crown Prince Gustav was the first royal child born in the kingdom since the 1680s, and newspapers and public tributes rarely neglected to point out the fact that Sweden now had a *native* successor to the throne. When George III, born in 1738 and a contemporary of Gustav III, succeeded to the throne of Great Britain in 1760, this event was hailed in a similar manner as a much-longed-for 'accession of a British King', and he was the first of the Hanoverian dynasty to gain general popularity.[26]

The travels of the royal family and the places in which they stayed were frequently reported, as in the following typical notice from July 1771:

> On Thursday last His Majesty the King, together with Their Royal Highnesses the hereditary princes, travelled to Svartsjö Palace to visit Her Majesty the Queen Dowager; from where His Majesty and the royal hereditary princes returned yesterday evening at 11 o'clock to the royal residence.[27]

Usually the reporting was limited to information about the location where the royal family was staying, normally the residence in Stockholm or the royal out-of-town residences of Drottningholm and Ulriksdal. Sometimes, though, when the reports dealt with travels around the country, the notices were supplemented with more detailed accounts of receptions and official duties, among other things. At times the planned route along which the royals would travel might be announced in advance, probably to give curious people the opportunity to see them in person. It was doubtless also prudent to notify stages and innkeepers when the royals were on the way. When the Queen Dowager and the Princess journeyed to Berlin in the autumn of 1771, the route along which they travelled was announced in good time beforehand. Eleven overnight stays, including a day of rest, were planned along the

---

26 J. G. A. Pocock, 'Monarchy in the Name of Britain: The Case of George III', in *Monarchisms in the Age of Enlightenment: Liberty, Patriotism and the Common Good*, ed. by Hans Blom, John Christian Laursen and Luisa Simonutti (Toronto, Buffalo and London: Toronto University Press, 2007), pp. 285–302 (p. 288). See also Edward Gibbon, *Memoirs of my Life*, ed. by Georges A. Bonnard (London: Nelson, 1966), pp. 110–11.

27 *Inrikes Tidningar*, no. 56 (22 July 1771) ('Förl. Torsdag begaf sig Hans Maj:t Konungen tillika med Deras Kongl. Högheter Arf-Prinsarne, til Swartsjö, at göra besök hos Hennes Maj:t Enke-Drottningen; hwarifrån Hans Maj:t och Kongl. Arf-Prinsarne i går aftons kl. 11 återkommo hit til Kongl. Residencet').

road between Stockholm and Ystad. That *'Her Royal Majesty* had graciously forbidden all otherwise common marks of honour' in the towns they passed through only seems to have been heeded to a limited extent.[28] The royal ladies brought along fifty-eight people as their servants. The more high-ranking attendants in their turn had their own servants, an additional twenty-four people. In total, the retinue consisted of eighty-four people, as well as horses that would have to be fed and housed at night. When the royal family with their entourage travelled to Loka Spa in 1761, they needed 280 coach horses. The visit, which was a success, was repeated the following summer, and then 400 horses were required to transport the royal retinue (Figure 16). At Sophia Magdalena's arrival in Sweden as the new Crown Princess in 1766, it took fifty horses merely to transport her wardrobe. Stories from the age of Gustav III reveal that the royal journeys could drive the peasants who supplied new horses to the brink of despair.[29]

With respect to regularity, the only competitors of travel notices in the newspapers were reports of the court going into mourning. As a part of the diplomatic etiquette vis-a-vis foreign countries, due manifestations of mourning were always observed when deaths occurred among the dynasties of Europe. The degree of respect varied with the distinction of the princely house in question as well as with its degree of affinity with the Swedish royal family. For instance, in November of 1760 the following was announced in *Posttidningar*:

> Yesterday the Royal Court went into three months' mourning for His Majesty the King of England. The women wear silk, with black

---

28 Quoted in *Inrikes Tidningar*, no. 88 (11 November 1771) (*'Hennes Kongl. Maj:t i Nåder hade förbudit all eljes wanlig Ärebetygelse'*); see also reports on the progress of the journey in several subsequent numbers. The itinerary and the composition of the retinue of the royals had been announced in *ibid.*, no. 84 (28 October 1771).

29 Loka: Elisabeth Mansén, *Ett paradis på jorden: Om den svenska kurorts-kulturen 1680–1880* (Stockholm: Atlantis, 2001), pp. 380–82; Iréne Sjögren, *Nils Rosén von Rosenstein: Mannen som förlängde människolivet. En trilogi* (Stockholm: Carlssons, 2006), pp. 87–91. On the wardrobe of Sophia Magdalena: Henning Stålhane, *Gustaf III:s bosättning, brudfärd och biläger: Kulturhistorisk studie* (Stockholm: Nordisk Rotogravyr, 1946), p. 52. On despairing peasants who supplied fresh horses: Beth Hennings, 'Gustav III:s hovliv på Gripsholm', in *Fyra gustavianska studier* (Stockholm: Norstedts, 1967), pp. 95–127 (pp. 100–01).

Figure 16 'His Royal Majesty's arrival at Loka on 2 July 1762.' The carriages of King Adolf Frederick and Queen Louisa Ulrika are just passing by the marble monument which the Queen caused to be erected beside the entrance to the spa area, in memory of the King's miraculously cured headache during their stay the year before. The advance riders have reached the courtyard, and plenty of activity is going on in preparation for welcoming the royal party. On a hill in the background, a salute battery with 11 guns is in position. Engraving by Jacob Gillberg after a template by Augustin Ehrensvärd. Photo: Björn Green, KB.

fans and gloves, and a pink hem; the gentlemen wear black shoe buckles and swords as well as smoothly turned-up cuffs.[30]

Whether this merely served as general information or as instructions for those who intended to visit the court is not clear. The reporting was not completely consistent: sometimes it was announced that court mourning had been abolished without its

---

30 *Stockholms Post-Tidningar*, no. 92 (24 November 1760) ('J går anlades wid Kongl. Håfwet Sorgen på 3 Månader efter Hans Maj:t Konungen af England. Fruntimren bära Sidentyg, swarta Solfjädrar och Wantar samt skär fåll; Cavaillererne swarta Skospännen och Wärjor samt slätt fållade manchetter').

preceding imposition having been announced. Such inconsistencies were, generally speaking, fairly common in the newspapers of the time; consequently, they are an imperfect source for evaluating the routines of the royal court.

It should also be mentioned that the content in the newspapers' accounts from abroad was, by and large, the same: there were proclamation-like notices about state matters, and there was sporadic information about the private affairs and public ceremonies of the princely houses. In these cases, the reporting was of course even more idiosyncratic.

The reporting on royalty in *Dagligt Allehanda*

A look at the competitors of *Posttidningar* can be of interest by way of comparison. It was only towards the end of the Age of Liberty that more serious challengers to the dominance of *Posttidningar* appeared. The most important among these was *Dagligt Allehanda* from the printer Peter Momma, which began publication in 1767, first as a supplement to *Stockholms Wekoblad* but soon thereafter as a regular newspaper on weekdays. Thus was born the first daily newspaper in the country, and it soon became the largest newspaper in the kingdom. In the beginning it mainly contained notices of a proclamatory nature, but soon it also published longer reports that might be of public interest. *Dagligt Allehanda* had a bad reputation because of its many scandalous and libellous texts; but at the same time these, together with frequent criticism of the authorities, contributed to its popularity.[31] However, the affairs of the royal family only appeared sporadically in its columns. Once or twice a month, scattered notices would be published presenting the schedules and the official duties of the royals, as in the following notice:

> On 8 November Sunday next, there will be an assembly at the Royal Court, in the evening at 7 o'clock with Their Royal Majesties, at 6:30 with Her Royal Highness the Princess, and at 5:45 with Their Royal Highnesses the Princes; these will henceforth take place every Sunday, until further notice is given.[32]

---

31 Sylwan, pp. 428–37; *Den svenska pressens historia*, I, pp. 145–47.
32 *Allehanda: Hörande til Stockholms Wekoblad*, no. 44 (6 November 1767) ('Nästa Söndag den 8 Nov. blifwer wid Kongl. Hofwet Cour, om afton Klockan sju hos Deras Kongl. Majestäter, Kl. half sju hos Hennes Kongl. Höghet Prinsessan, samt Tre fierdedelar til Sex hos Deras Kongl. Högheter Prinsarne; hwilket härefter wara alla Söndagar, tills det warder afsagdt').

The reporting about the royals was fairly similar to that provided in *Inrikes Tidningar*, and among the events related in this manner were, for instance, chapter meetings of the royal orders, the assumption of court mourning, travels to the out-of-town residences, etc. It is not possible to discern any particular principle used in the selection of notices, but in exceptional cases they might also have a political content. For example, it was reported in some detail when Adolf Frederick laid down his work in December 1768.[33]

On 11 March 1769, *Dagligt Allehanda* reported that all four royal children had been inoculated against smallpox a few days earlier. Their states of health when a light fever set in became a serial story over the subsequent weeks. 'The pustules of Their Royal Highnesses', it was finally announced on 25 March, 'have now dried up, and the scabs should soon fall off. Their Highnesses are all doing well in other respects.'[34] The inoculation against smallpox was the great medical breakthrough of the time, but because a certain suspicion against the method could be discerned among the broader population, educated and prominent people all around Europe acted as models by, as it was called, variolating themselves and their children. Here the Swedish royal family thus appeared as role models in the private sphere.

Persons of distinction in the capital used this joyous occasion as an excuse to arrange a magnificent feast in connection with the King's birthday on 14 May. The celebrations were concentrated around the House of Nobility and the nearby islet Strömsborg, and they included a hunting regatta, fireworks, cannon salutes and trumpet fanfares, as well as a public concert at the House of Nobility under the direction of Ferdinand Zellbell, Royal Court Kapellmeister. The law clerk Carl J. Hallman gave a speech suitable for this solemn occasion. The royal family themselves were in Norrköping for the concurrent session of the Riksdag, but had announced their gracious approval of the solemnities.[35]

In comparison to *Inrikes Tidningar*, people from the bourgeois public sphere were far more visible than the royal family in *Dagligt*

---

33 *Dagligt Allehanda*, nos 227–29 (20–22 December 1768).
34 *Dagligt Allehanda*, nos 59–68 (11–25 March 1769) ('Kopporna äro nu torkade på deras Kongl. Högheter och lära rukorna snart falla. Deras Högheter må för öfrigit alla wäl'). On 7 April Prince Charles's fever and vesicles returned and confined him to his bed for yet another few days. See also Sjögren, pp. 99–103, 265–67.
35 *Dagligt Allehanda*, no. 109 (19 May 1769).

Allehanda. The royal notices were after all rather few in number, whereas the work of the Riksdag, for example, received a good deal of coverage in comparison. Not even the death of Adolf Frederick and the accession to the throne of Gustav III, which was given so much space in *Inrikes Tidningar*, came in for particular attention in *Dagligt Allehanda.*

To a great extent, *Dagligt Allehanda* based its reporting on material that had been sent to the editorial office. This was precisely why the newspaper was a genuine expression of an emerging public sphere. The writers paid to see their contributions published, which was therefore also considered a right.[36] A large percentage of the texts were morality pieces in verse or prose. The epistolary form was popular, too. Some time after the death of Adolf Frederick, but before the return of Gustav from Paris, where he had received the news of his father's death, the pseudonymous Pileus's 'Swar til en Wän på Landet' ('Reply to a Friend in the Countryside') was published as an appendix. Pileus wanted to comfort his friend, who was worried about the future following the death of the King. Be at ease, urged Pileus, for surely Sweden has never been in a more fortunate situation following a royal death. The kingdom is at peace with its neighbours, he consoled his friend, and it has an uncontested order of succession and a mature and capable successor to the throne. 'What do you have to fear? Was it the party system that frightened you?', he proceeded to ask. After this followed an interesting exposition, which illustrates the mature turn the political system had taken, but also the indispensable role played by the king in this context:

> My dear friend! Be not concerned at these phantoms [the parties]: they are inseparable from all free states; yes, they are even useful when they are kept in balance. Under a strict supervision of liberty, both of them work to promote the security and the betterment of the fatherland. They may argue about the means: but precisely through this, the righteous are discovered to the ruler; and you may be sure of this, that our Gustaf both understands and wants to promote the best; for he is convinced of this truth, that a Swedish king can never become great and illustrious in any other way.[37]

---

36 Sylwan, p. 432.
37 Pileus [pseud.], 'Swar til en Wän på Landet', appendix to *Dagligt Allehanda*, no. 53 (5 March 1771) ('Hwad har du då att frukta?' and 'Käre min wän! oroa dig icke öfwer dessa spöken: de äro oskiljaktiga ifrån alla fria Stater, ja, äfwen nyttiga, då de hållas i jämnwigt. Under en sträng upsikt öfwer

Here, in fact, a parliamentary idea was expressed where parties were presented as the very life of a free state and where even the king, as the sole executive power, was guided by the will of the people. In the carefully considered wording, the power of the Council – which was in reality under parliamentary control – was not mentioned. But that intermediary stage was not necessary, because the king himself, according to Pileus, was under pressure from public opinion to do what was right. About a year earlier, the same thought had been expressed in verse form in the same forum. It was then said about Adolf Frederick that 'Where a clear law does not exist, He follows the supreme law.' This was a reference to his motto – *Salus publica, salus mea*, 'The public weal is my weal' – which in its turn paraphrased the well-known maxim *Salus populi, suprema lex esto*, 'The welfare of the people shall be the supreme law'.[38]

Ideas about the royal authority as guided by public opinion and as the executor of the will of the people became widespread in eighteenth-century Europe, and this happened under a number of different forms of government. In an influential article, the Norwegian historian Jens Arup Seip has written about the Danish absolute monarchy as being governed by public opinion, arguing that the gaps between absolute and constitutional forms of government were not so great.[39] Parliamentarianism in Great Britain was a

---

friheten, arbeta de bägge på Fäderneslandets säkerhet och förkofring. De twista wäl om medlen: men just derigenom updagas de sanskyldiga för Regenten; och war säker derpå, at wår Gustaf både förstår och wil befordra de bästa; ty Han är öfwertygad om den sanningen, at en Swänsk Konung aldrig på annat sätt kan blifwa Stor och Lysande').

38 *Dagligt Allehanda*, no. 117 (30 May 1769) ('Där tydlig Lag ej fins, Han Högsta Lagen följer').

39 Jens Arup Seip, 'Teorien om det opinionsstyrte enevelde', *Historisk tidsskrift* (Norway), 38 (1958), 397–463. See also Edvard Holm, *Om det Syn paa Kongemagt, Folk og borgerlig Frihed, der udviklede sig i den dansk-norske Stat i Midten af 18de Aarhundrede (1746–1770)* (Copenhagen: J. H. Schultz, 1883); Edward Holm, *Den offentlige Mening og Statsmagten i den dansk-norske Stat i Slutningen af det 18de Aarhundrede (1784–1799)*, Indbydelsesskrift til Kjøbenhavns Universitets Fest i Anledning af Hans Majestæt Kong Christian IX.'s Regeringsjubilæum, den 15. November 1888 (Copenhagen: J. H. Schultz, 1888); Michael Bregnsbo, *Samfundsorden og statsmagt set fra prædikstolen: Danske præsters deltagelse i den offentlige opinionsdannelse vedrørende samfundsordenen og statsmagten 1750–1848, belyst ved trykte prædikener; En politisk-idéhistorisk undersøgelse* (Copenhagen: Museum Tusculanum Forlag, 1997), pp. 243–68.

model for Europe as a whole, not least because it combined liberty with order, things that were otherwise often seen as opposites. It is true that public opinion was not referred to as a legitimising factor in politics until the 1780s, but no eighteenth-century contemporary questioned the idea that both Parliament and the executive power acted for the common good. For instance, the philosophers of law Montesquieu and Jean Louis De Lolme felt that the strength of the British form of government was that the different state authorities counterbalanced rather than repressed one another, as was – in their opinion – the case in Sweden.[40] Immanuel Kant defended absolute monarchy as a means but not as a principle, and said about the monarch that 'his lawgiving authority rests on his uniting the general public will in his own'.[41] In France the idea of a popular monarchy also found favour, even though developments there did not follow a given trend. For example, the attempts of Minister of Finance Jacques Necker to create a more transparent and deliberative government machinery were unsuccessful; and in its own way France became the exception that proved the rule: in the end, an inability to broaden political participation, if only in theory, made revolution the only option.[42] The development of Swedish

---

40 John Louis De Lolme, *A Parallel between the English Constitution and the Former Government of Sweden; Containing Some Observations on the Late Revolution in that Kingdom; and an Examination of the Causes that Secure us against Both Aristocracy, and Absolute Monarchy* (London: Almon, 1772); Linda Colley, *Britons: Forging the Nation 1707–1837* (London: Pimlico, 1994), pp. 195–236; T. C. W. Blanning, *The Culture of Power and the Power of Culture: Old Regime Europe 1660–1789* (Oxford: Oxford University Press, 2002), pp. 353–56.

41 Immanuel Kant, 'What is Enlightenment?' (1784), in *Foundations of the Metaphysics of Morals and What is Enlightenment?*, trans. and ed. by Lewis White Beck, Library of Liberal Arts, 113, 2nd edn (Upper Saddle River: Prentice-Hall, 1997), pp. 83–90 (p. 88). See also Simone Zurbuchen, 'Theorizing Enlightened Absolutism: The Swiss Republican Origins of Prussian Monarchism', in *Monarchisms in the Age of Enlightenment*, ed. by Blom, Laursen and Simonutti, pp. 240–66 (pp. 249–50).

42 J. M. J. Rogister, 'The Crisis of 1753–4 in France and the Debate on the Nature of the Monarchy and of the Fundamental Laws', in *Herrschafts-verträge, Wahlkapitulationen, Fundamentalgesetze*, ed. by Rudolf Vierhaus, Veröffentlichungen des Max-Planck-Instituts für Geschichte, 56 (Göttingen: Vandenhoeck & Ruprecht, 1977), pp. 105–20; Keith Michael Baker, 'Politique et opinion publique sous l'Ancien Régime', *Annales: Economies, sociétés, civilisations*, 42 (1987), 41–71; Mona Ozouf, 'L'opinion publique', in *The Political Culture of the Old Regime*, ed. by Keith Michael

parliamentarianism was thus in line with the general European development of ideas that paved the way for the liberal break-through in the nineteenth century. In its actual practice, however, the Swedish form of government was unusually consistent, because even the inviolable executive power was in fact made subject to popular representation according to a republican model.

The image of the royal authority that was conveyed in the news-papers left no room for its essential limitations. On the contrary, the royal family were the object of continually increased interest, and this was true with respect to both their official duties and their private affairs. Those who followed politics only through this source were therefore given the impression that the king had a key role in the government of the realm. Nevertheless, the most balanced summary of the situation is surely that the semi-official dissemination of news did not draw attention to the true distribu-tion of power in the kingdom, but nor did it make any serious attempt to conceal it. Precisely this latter fact suggests that one should be careful not to dismiss the public image of the king as merely cynical and propagandistic. Even in his limited role, the king had an important function to fill in public life. In both his political and sociological roles, the king was indispensable and irreplace-able, and the value attributed to him was taken seriously.

In summary, the king's subjects ought to have had a relatively good idea of what the monarch was doing, or what he believed he was doing. The newspapers did not primarily have a popular consumer base; but the content of the articles that concerned the royal authority did not contradict the ideas that were conveyed in the general proclamations, the real mass medium of the age. What visual impressions the subjects had of their head of state is another question, which will be investigated in the next chapter.

Baker, The French Revolution and the Creation of Modern Political Culture, 1 (Oxford: Pergamon Press, 1987), pp. 419–34 (p. 423); Franco Venturi, *The End of the Old Regime in Europe, 1776–1789*, 2 vols (Princeton: Princeton University Press, 1991), I: *The Great States of the West*, pp. 325–53; John Hardman, *Louis XVI* (New Haven and London: Yale University Press, 1993), pp. 67–68; Blanning, pp. 357–427.

4

Visualisation of royalty

The popular image of the king that was conveyed during the Age of Liberty was not visual to any great extent. Neither sculpture, nor painting, nor printed images were media that were visible in the public space, even if printed images had a certain potential to achieve wider dissemination. Woodcuts had been distributed as leaflets, and copper engravings and etchings had been used to spread propaganda ever since the sixteenth century. In their simpler and cheaper forms, they were for a long time produced outside Sweden only, and as a rule they treated religious subjects or dealt with spectacular events: natural disasters, astronomical phenomena, executions and so on. It has been said that the half-length portrait of Charles XII in a fur-trimmed uniform jacket in the 1703 edition of the Bible was the first portrait the Swedish people saw of their monarch. Consequently, access to a generally disseminated template may, along with the special aura of the King, explain the popularity of the topic among peasant artists far into the nineteenth century. As late as 1824, the folk painter Hans Wikström produced a full-length portrait of the hero king on the basis of this image from the Bible and with the text 'King CHARLES XII in his usual war UNIFORM'.[1]

---

1 On folk portraiture: Maj Nodermann, *Från Altranstädt till Delsbo: Bildtryck och bonader med Carl XII* (Stockholm: Nordiska Museet, 1984), p. 11, cf. plates 18, 25–27. See also *Signums svenska konsthistoria: Frihetstidens konst* (Lund: Signum, 1997), image 564. On Wikström's portrait: mural from Bärby, Östervåla, now at Disagården in Old Uppsala, the open-air museum of Upplandsmuseet. Nodermann reproduces a similar painting by Wikström from 1823 and the province of Gästrikland: (*Från Altranstädt till Delsbo*, plate 25). It should be added that what was noteworthy about the widely distributed image of Charles XII was that it was a full-face and not a profile portrait.

The Swedish production of so-called popular prints (*kistebrev*) –
coloured single-sheet woodcuts – did not have a particularly
long tradition in the eighteenth century. The name *kistebrev*
(literally 'trunk prints') comes from the fact that they have usually
been preserved papered on the insides of the wooden trunks
of farmhands and maids; but they were also pasted up, singly
or joined together, as wall decorations or wallpapers. Written
testimony attests to their use both in private homes and in taverns,
inns and other public settings. The study of popular printed images
is encumbered by many problems of a source-critical nature.
Questions regarding production and reception are always difficult
to investigate with respect to older prints, but here they are even
more tangible. We rarely know exactly when a print was produced,
the sheets are unevenly preserved, and we have little knowledge
concerning the size of print runs and distribution. What we do
know for certain is that the subjects treated and the total print runs
were considerably more numerous than evinced by the examples
that have been preserved until the present time. The ethnologist
Nils-Arvid Bringéus, who has studied Swedish popular prints in
detail, maintains that 1,000 copies was a fairly common print run,
but that the number of editions of any given work is more difficult
to determine.[2]

In Denmark popular prints began to be produced at the
beginning of the eighteenth century, and they were also disseminated in southern Sweden. Domestic production started somewhat
later, and the oldest known Swedish example was issued in
Stockholm in 1718. Petter Lorens Hoffbro's printing office in the
capital, which made woodcuts from at least 1744, and the Berling
office (*Berlingska boktyckeriet*) in Lund, whose oldest known print

---

2 Good surveys of and introductions to popular printed images are V. E.
Clausen, *Folkelig grafik i Skandinavien* (Copenhagen: Berg, 1973); V. E.
Clausen, *Det folkelige danske træsnit i etbladstryk 1565–1884*, Danmarks
folkeminder, 85 (Copenhagen: Foreningen Danmarks Folkeminder, 1985),
pp. 9–50; Nils-Arvid Bringéus, *Skånska kistebrev: Berlingska Boktryckeriet,
N. P. Lundbergs Boktryckeri och F. F. Cedergréens Boktryckeri* (Stockholm:
Carlssons, 1995), pp. 9–103. Bringéus discusses a number of source-critical
issues in the introduction to *Popular Prints and Imagery: Proceedings of
an International Conference in Lund 5–7 October 2000*, ed. by Nils-Arvid
Bringéus and Sten Åke Nilsson, Kungl. Vitterhets Historie och Antikvitets
Akademien, Konferenser, 53 (Stockholm: Almqvist & Wiksell, 2003); on
the numbers of copies printed, see *ibid.*, p. 11.

has been dated to 1759, were active during the Age of Liberty. In addition, there were Johann Ernst Kallmeyer and Johan Georg Lange in Gothenburg, as well as the father and son Eric and Carl Hasselrot, who worked in Nyköping.[3] The art historian Sten Åke Nilsson has called Petter Lorens Hoffbro the first major maker of popular printed images in Sweden. He was active at least between the years 1744 and 1759, and he aimed at a clientele from the lower social orders, who had had very limited access to printed images thus far.[4] Distribution was, at least in part, handled by Hoffbro himself; and at a seizure by the customs authorities at Lindesberg in 1745, it is registered that he had brought a supply consisting of 1,139 sheets. There are several contemporary statements regarding the distribution of his works among the peasantry; and in a speech on the abominable nature of satire, the poet Johan Henric Kellgren mentioned the belief that 'each and every *Hoffbro* could paint like *Raphael*'. In addition, the troubadour Carl Michael Bellman sang of cherubs as being 'lovely samples of *Hoffbro*'s art'. The printing office retained his name after his death, and 'in the manner of Hoffbro' was a designation still used in the nineteenth century. The references to Hoffbro may thus, as they do several times in Bellman's texts, refer more accurately to a school or type; but this does suggest that the dissemination and influence of his prints were significant. In spite of a relatively long period of activity and the demonstrably great impact of its prints,

---

3 Clausen, *Folkelig grafik*, p. 89; Bringéus, *Skånska kistebrev*, pp. 22–23; Sten Åke Nilsson, 'Populärkonst som "kistebrev": De första exemplen i Sydsverige', *Rig: Tidskrift utgiven av Föreningen för svensk kulturhistoria i samarbete med Nordiska museet och Folklivsarkivet i Lund*, 60 (1977), 35–46; Nils-Arvid Bringéus, 'Massmedium i miniformat: En översikt över den svenska kistebrevsproduktionen', *Rig: Kulturhistorisk tidskrift*, 91 (2008), 129–39; Jonas Nordin, 'Mediating Images of Monarchy from Castle to Cottage in Eighteenth-Century Sweden', in *Media and Mediation in the Eighteenth Century*, ed. by Penelope Corfield and Jonas Nordin (Lund: Swedish Society for Eighteenth Century Studies/Division of Book History, Lund University, 2023), pp. 25–71 (pp. 59–67).

4 Sten Åke Nilsson, 'Petter Lorens Hoffbro och frihetstidens bildmanipula-tioner', *Vetenskapssocieteten i Lund årsbok 1976* (Lund: Gleerups, 1976), 5–34 (p. 25). See also Sten Åke Nilsson, 'On Heroes and Traitors: The First Popular Prints in Sweden', in *Popular Prints and Imagery*, pp. 169–80, and Gunnar W. Lundberg, 'Formskärar Hoffbro', in *Bellmansfigurer: Kulturhistoriska tidsbilder och personhistoriska anteckningar till Fredmans-dikten* (Stockholm: Gebers, 1927), pp. 99–117.

only some ten images from his office have been identified with any certainty.

Hoffbro's series of monarchs

One early print from the Hoffbro printing house portrays the ruling Frederick I and his predecessors on the Swedish throne, from Gustav I onwards (Figure 17).[5] King Frederick is depicted in a wig; and like the other monarchs, he is arrayed in royal purple and a dark blue mantle. Primarily, however, the crown is what signals his royal status. The print will have been produced around the mid-1740s. These images do not resemble the subject as a portrait would do, but it is possible to discern an attempt at historical accuracy: the oldest monarchs have beards, and Charles X Gustav and Charles XI have long hair or wigs, whereas Charles XII wears his own short hair. All the male rulers are accompanied by the abbreviation 'S.G.V.R.', for 'King of the Swedes, the Goths and the Wends'. In contradistinction, Christina is merely given the title of ruleress (*regentinna*) of Sweden, while Ulrika Eleonora has been left out; it is possible that her brief reign was perceived only as a prelude to that of Frederick. At the bottom of the print there is a prayer to God to preserve the political government of the kingdom: the father of the country, Frederick, 'our gracious King, our protection and our safeguard', and in addition the Councillors of the Realm, and all the Estates. The frame is filled with acanthus and cherubs in the baroque style. The title of the print is *Svenska konungars åminnelse, samt deras födelse, ålder och år* ('Commemoration of the Kings of Sweden, along with their Births, Ages and Reigns'). Such reference-book-like information presumably increased the usefulness of the image; but the promise has not been fulfilled, as the biographical dates have been added in only a few cases.

As far as is known, this was Hoffbro's first attempt at collective royal portraits. His inspiration came from religious imagery. In an earlier print, Hoffbro had copied a print by the German woodcutter Albrecht Schmid showing Christ on the Cross surrounded by apostles and evangelists. In view of the large number of them in the preserved material, it is obvious that religious topics found buyers; but Hoffbro must have been tempted to boost demand by

---

5 Kistebrev/popular print 43:2, KB. Cf. Nilsson, 'Petter Lorens Hoffbro', pp. 6–8, and Nilsson, 'On Heroes and Traitors', p. 172.

Figure 17 'In Remembrance of Swedish Kings'. Woodcut by Petter
Lorens Hoffbro, after 1744. Photo: Björn Green, KB.

broadening the circle of topics to include royals as well. In *Svenska
konungars åminnelse*, the ruling king assumed the place of Christ,
with previous rulers replacing the apostles.[6]

---

6 See the plates in Maj Nodermann, 'Kistan från Forssa', *Fataburen:
Nordiska museets och Skansens årsbok* (1994), 145–58 (p. 150); Jonas
Nordin, 'Brevmålaren Petter Lorens Hoffbros regentlängder och deras
förlagor', *Biblis: Kvartalstidskrift för bokvänner*, 43 (2008), 30–41 (p. 32);
Nordin, 'Mediating Images of Monarchy', pp. 41–50.

Later, Hoffbro further developed the style, execution and pedagogic elements in a considerably more elaborate series, also based on German models and preserved in at least three different variants. The oldest bears the title (with lacunae), *Kort Beskrifning öfwer alla Swea och Götha Konungars Regemente i en [serie från Magog] som regerade 88. åhr efter syndafloden, til wår allernådigste K[onung] FREDRICH I* ('A short Description of All the Reigns of the Kings of the Swedes and the Goths in a [series from Magog,] who Ruled 88 Years after the Flood, until our Most Gracious K[ing] Frederick I') (Figure 18). This large print measures around 61 cm in height and 50 cm in breadth. Here Hoffbro completed his pedagogic endeavour and delivered a series of representations of all 152 (!) monarchs of Sweden since Magog, the grandson of Noah. This was thus the legendary list of kings that had been established by the Swedish bishop Johannes Magnus in his posthumously published work *De omnibvs Gothorvm Sveonvmqve regibvs* (1554), which had great influence as an instrument of patriotic propaganda during Sweden's Age of Greatness.[7] In Hoffbro's sequence, the long and proud line of princes led up to the elected successor to the Swedish throne, Adolf Frederick. To each image was added a brief text, usually with the years of the King's birth and death or the years of his reign, along with a brief character sketch of a sentence or two.[8]

Another inspiration was the type of list of kings that has been preserved at least since the age of Charles XI. These lists supplied concise information about the previous rulers of Sweden in precisely the same way as in Hoffbro's print, but without any portraits. Hoffbro even borrowed the heading from one such *Tabula Chronologica*, which reproduced a concentrated version of Johannes Magnus's history of kings.[9] These collective portraits

7 Regarding this, see Bernd Roling, *Odins Imperium: Der Rudbeckianismus als Paradigma an den skandinavischen Universitäten (1680–1860)*, Mittellateinische Studien und Texte, 54, 2 vols (Leiden: Brill, 2020).

8 Petter Lorens Hoffbro, *Kort Beskrifning öfwer alla Swea och Götha Konungars Regemente i en [...] som regerade 88. åhr efter syndafloden, til wår allernådigste K[...] Fredrich I* (Stockholm: Petter Lorens Hoffbro, [n.d.]).

9 *Tabula Chronologica eller Kort beskrifning öfwer alla Swea och Götha konungars regemente, i en wiss ordning, ifrå Magog, som regerade 88 åhr efter syndafloden, till wår allernådigste regerande konung, k. Carl den XII. utdragen af de trowärdigste scribenters chrönicor* ([n.p.]: [n. pub.], [n.d.]), one full sheet. See Carl Gustaf Warmholtz, *Bibliotheca historica*

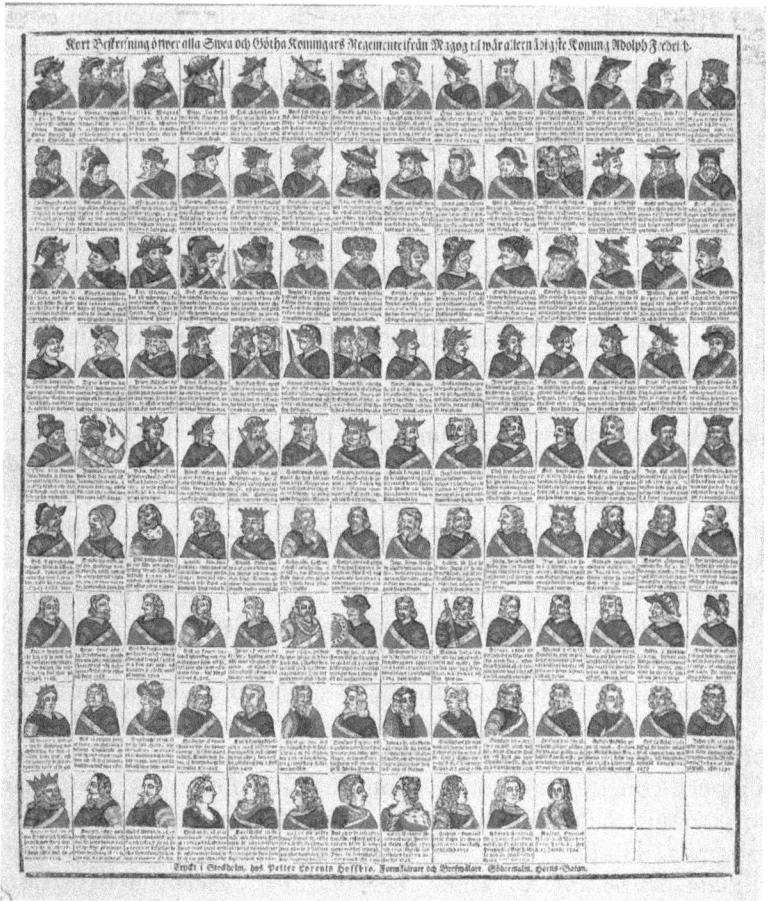

Figure 18 Chart of Swedish Kings from Magog to Crown Prince Gustav.
Woodcut by Petter Lorens Hoffbro, 1750s. Second edition, with newly
cut images and portraits reduced by 30 to 123. See also Figure 21.
Photo: Jens Gustafsson, KB.

*Sveo-Gothica; eller Förtekning uppå så väl tryckte, som handskrifne
böcker, tractater och skrifter, hvilka handla om svenska historien, eller
därutinnan kunna gifva ljus; med critiska och historiska anmärkningar,*
15 vols (Stockholm: Anders Jacob Nordström and Uppsala: Zeipel &
Palmblad, 1782–1817), V (1790), no. 2479.

also reveal a relationship with a kind of informative 'tables' of countries and monarchs that were printed in poster format in the seventeenth century.[10] These edifying charts were presumably not primarily intended for the common people, but neither were they aimed at the top social tiers, where access to more advanced sources of information was available. The direct model for Hoffbro's work was in any event an illustrated chart of kings in full sheet format, printed in Nuremberg. In this model his images can be found in a technically more advanced form, produced with copper engraving instead of woodcut, and with the texts placed separately in the lower half of the plate (Figure 19).[11]

As prices were kept low, it is easy to imagine that Hoffbro's prints became a great success. This first variant was probably published at the end of Frederick's reign, and within a few years another two updated editions were published (Figures 20–22).[12] The most recent variant ends with Crown Prince Gustav, his year of birth given erroneously as 1744 instead of 1746. Later editions were completely new works in relation to the oldest print. Although the chart of monarchs had now been extended to include the folk hero Engelbrekt, the number of portraits had been reduced from 153 to 123. Several mythical kings had vanished, and as a consequence those who wished to construct a correctly numbered lchar of monarchs could no longer do so, because a number of Charleses and Erics had been removed. By way of compensation, the second king of the realm, Sveno, had been endowed with a brother, Götar: 'Sveno, the eldest son of Magog, King of the Swedes, and Götar, King of the kingdom of the Goths, from these two rulers the inhabitants of the kingdoms of the Swedes and the Goths are descended.'[13]

---

10 See, e.g., *Florerande general Europæ land- och regente-spegel som korttydeligen wisar och repræsenterar de i dag, d. 1 januarii, 1740, warande förnämsta europæiska* (Stockholm: Lorentz Ludwig Grefing, 1740), one full sheet.

11 *Verzeichnüß und Conterfeÿen aller Könige in Schweden wie solche Ordentlich nacheinander gefolget von den Ersten biß auf den jetzt Regierenden* ([n.p.]: [n. pub.], [n.d.]), one full sheet. Warmholtz, V, no. 2478.

12 The title and publishing information are identical: *Kort Beskrifning öfwer alla Swea och Götha Konungars Regemente ifrån Magog til wår allernådigste Konung Adolph Fredrich* (Stockholm: Petter Lorens Hoffbro, [n.d.]).

13 'Sweno. magogs äldste son kon. öfwer swea, och Giöthar, k öfwer götha rike, af desse twenne regenter härstamma Swea och Götha rikens Jnbyggare.'

Figure 19 *Verzeichnüß und Conterfeÿen aller Könige in Schweden wie solche Ordentlich nacheinander gefolget von den Ersten biß auf den jetzt Regierenden.* Undated (after 1720), engraving by Johann Georg Puschner, published by Christian Sigmund Froberg, Nuremberg. Detail. Photo: Björn Green, KB.

Figure 20 Chart of Swedish Kings from Magog to successor to the throne Adolf Frederick. Woodcut by Petter Lorens Hoffbro after Puschner and Froberg, before 1751. Detail. Photo: Jens Gustafsson, KB.

Figure 21 Chart of Swedish Kings from Magog to Crown Prince Gustav. Woodcut by Petter Lorens Hoffbro, 1750s. Detail of Figure18. Photo: Jens Gustafsson, KB.

This genealogical connection is interesting: not only had both of these co-rulers given their names to parts of the kingdom, but all Swedes were descended from them. Here the close links between the kings and the people were given a tangible illustration.

Even if the oldest monarchs were, naturally enough, described in a rather impersonal fashion, the later prints represented a significant step forward when it came to resemblance to the original subjects. All monarchs from the seventeenth and eighteenth centuries can be identified without help from the text. Hoffbro will have used portraits on coins as his models; by tradition, coins were always adorned with portraits in profile (Figure 23).[14] (For ordinary people, portraits on coins would be the most reliable portraits available. These will therefore be discussed in greater detail below.)

14 Coins and medals as sources for portraits are discussed by Francis Haskell, *History and its Images: Art and the Interpretation of the Past* (New Haven and London: Yale University Press, 1993), pp. 36–41.

Figure 22 Chart of Swedish Kings from Magog to Crown Prince Gustav.
Woodcut by Petter Lorens Hoffbro, 1750s. Later variant, with an
updated portrait of Adolf Frederick. Detail. Photo: Jens Gustafsson, KB.

The pedagogical value of the prints under discussion was
obvious: in a decorative and easily understandable way, they
helped spread knowledge about the monarchs of the realm. That
the history of Sweden was the history of its kings was made clear
in no uncertain terms, and in this respect prints of this kind were
no different from, for instance, Olof von Dalin's official Swedish
history commissioned by the Riksdag or Charlotta Frölich's tales of
Christian kings for 'the peasantry of Sweden' ('Sweriges almoge').[15]
But the people were meant to feel involved in the history, and not
least the wars, of their monarchs, which were therefore described in

15 Olof [von] Dalin, *Svea rikes historia ifrån dess begynnelse til wåra tider*,
    3 vols (Stockholm: Lars Salvius, 1747–62); [Charlotta Frölich], *Swea
    och Götha christna konungars sagor, sammanfattade til underrättelse för
    Sweriges almoge och menige man, som af dem kunna lära, huru deras k.
    fädernesland ifrån flera hundrade år tilbakars blifwit regerat, samt se, huru
    på gudsfruktan, laglydnad, dygd och enighet altid följt Guds wälsignelse;
    men deremot synd, lagens och eders öfwerträdelse, samt oenighet, haft til
    påföljder swåra landsplågor, blodsutgiutelser, förödelser m. m.* (Uppsala:
    Kongl. Akademiska tryckeriet, 1759).

Figure 23 Swedish sovereigns from Gustav II Adolf to Frederick I. From Johann Carl Hedlinger's medals of sovereigns. Engraving by Chretien de Mechel, 1786. Photo: Björn Green, KB.

a concentrated form. Among other things, it was said that Gustav II Adolf had 'in Denmark, Poland and Germany earned a splendid reputation for himself and his nation'.[16]

---

16 'Gustaf Adolph, kr. 1617 han har i dannemarck, pohlen och tyskland sig och sin nation et dråpeligit beröm förwärwat.' See Figure 18.

The genre retained its popularity. From the Gustavian era (1772–1818), there are at least three variants of a print showing 'the royal Gustavian dynasty' ('Kongeliga Gustawianska Ätten'), where the portraits had been modelled on well-known original works (Figure 24). The woodcuts were included in a small popular booklet with brief biographical data on the kings of Sweden, but the portraits were also sold separately.[17] The sequence begins with Gustav I and ends with Gustav III, in later editions with Gustav IV Adolf. The heading referred to the dynastic continuity with the Vasa kings that Gustav III was eager to showcase, but which had been emphasised already when Adolf Frederick was elected successor to the Swedish throne.[18] The price of the prints is given as two shillings (skillingar), or as much as the price of a couple of lemons. This cost may be compared to Jacob Gillberg's engraved half-length portrait of Gustav III, which in 1773 cost 18 daler in copper, i.e. as much as a year's subscription to Dagligt Allehanda or one and a half barrels of imported Mediterranean salt.[19]

17 Kort historia, om den kongl. gustavianska familien, ifrån glorwyrdigst i åminnelse konung Gustaf den förste, intil wår nu regerande allernådigste konung Gustaf III: Jämte de höga kongl. personernas portraiter (Stockholm: J. C. Holmberg, 1786); Kort historia om den kongl. gustavianska familien, ifrån glorwördigst i åminnelse konung Gustaf den förste, intil wår nu regerande allernådigste konung Gustaf IV Adolph: Jämte de höga kongl. personernes portraiter, 2nd edn (Stockholm: J. C. Holmberg, 1797).
18 See, e.g., Jonas Bång, Hans Kongl. Höghets af Swerige Adolphi Friederici ättartal (Stockholm: Peter Momma, 1743), one broadside tracing the genealogy of the successor back to the eleventh-century King Stenkil. See also [Andreas Hesselius, Americanus], Swea- och Götha-rikens underdånige fägne-ljud, hördt wid Hans Kongl. Höghets, Sweriges rikes arf-furstes hertig Adolph Fredrichs högstönskelige intog, uti kongl. residence-staden Stockholm, then 14 octobris åhr 1743 (various edns from Linköping, Stockholm and Strängnäs, 1743); Hertig Adolph Friedrichs intog til Sweriget och hufwud staden Stockholm beskrifwen på gammalt sätt i en wisa helt ny: År 1743 ([n.p.]: [n. pub.], [n.d.]); Öfwer Hans Kongl. Höghets hertig Adolph Fredrichs lyckeliga ankomst til Stockholm, den 14. octobris 1743 (Stockholm: Peter Jöransson Nyström, [n.d.]).
19 Kistebrev 63:5–7, KB; Johan Fischerström, En gustaviansk dagbok: Johan Fischerströms anteckningar för året 1773, ed. by Gustaf Näsström (Stockholm: Bröderna Lagerström, 1951), pp. 124, 127.

Figure 24 'The Royal Gustavian Dynasty'. Chart of sovereigns geared to maintaining the notion of an unbroken domestic dynasty since the national hero Gustav I. The images, good likenesses, were derived from prestigious and well-known originals, and they were sold both separately and in a brief booklet containing a history of the kings of Sweden. Photo: Björn Green, KB.

The royals in the popular prints

Otherwise, remarkably few royal portraits of the popular-print type have been preserved from the Age of Liberty. The collection in the National Library of Sweden, which may be the largest in the country, does not contain more than a handful. With the addition of those known from other collections, the total number does not exceed a dozen. If one adds to this the partially anachronistic comment that several of these are copies treating the same topic, the sample becomes even more limited. The number of images from the Gustavian era containing royals is considerably greater. Whether this has to do with an actual increase of production or with a greater degree of preservation is uncertain. In any event, the amount of lost material will have been considerable.

In Denmark many more images of the royal family have been preserved from the entire century, something which may have

several explanations. The Danish printing offices also produced
portraits of Swedish monarchs. They may certainly have been
intended for domestic consumption, in the same way as Hoffbro
and Berling produced images of Frederick the Great of Prussia
and other contemporary and historical celebrities. The importing
of foreign popular prints into Sweden was prohibited in 1749,
and the Danish prints had demonstrably reached the market in
southern Sweden as well.[20] In some cases the Danish prints were
also used as models for Swedish copies. A print from Copenhagen
from the 1740s thus portrays the Swedish heir to the throne, Adolf
Frederick, and his wife Louisa Ulrika (Figure 25). A reversed
version of the same image with an updated text was printed in 1758
at the Berling printing office in Lund (and in some other versions).[21]
In a later example, Christian VII and Caroline Matilda of Denmark
were transformed into Gustav III and Sophia Magdalena merely by
changing the national coat of arms in the image (Figures 26–27).[22]
A German engraving portraying Adolf Frederick was copied by
Johan Rudolph Thiele to represent not only this monarch, but later
also Gustav III and Gustav IV Adolf (Figures 28–29).

It was common for Danish popular prints to reflect events in
the royal family – acts of tribute, marriages, deaths and similar
events. Such references to topical events are lacking in the Swedish
material that has been preserved from the Age of Liberty. There are
a few examples from the Gustavian era, though. Several popular
prints were also published with verses that paid tribute to the
virtues of Gustav III and compared his qualities to those of the
two Gustavs who preceded him (i.e. Gustav I 'Vasa' and Gustav
II Adolf).[23] Sometimes the images were provided with verses that
were easy to memorise. One of the pithier ones ran as follows

20 'Kongl. Slotts-Cantzliets Publication, angående Förbud emot målade
Pappers införsel', 16 May 1749, in Utdrag utur alle ifrån den 7. decemb.
1718.[–1794] utkomne publique handlingar, placater, förordningar, resolutioner och publicationer, ed. by Reinhold Gustaf Modée, 15 vols
(Stockholm: Lorentz Ludwig Grefing; Kungl. Tryckeriet, 1742–1829), IV
(1754), p. 2867.
21 Kistebrev 61:4, KB; Bringéus, Skånska kistebrev, pp. 167–69. V. E. Clausen
catalogues two Danish portraits of Charles XII, one of Ulrika Eleonora,
four double portraits of Adolf Frederick and Louisa Ulrika, two of Gustav
III and two of Sophia Magdalena as a Swedish queen; Clausen, Det
folkelige, pp. 113–14, 116, 136–38, 143–44, 147.
22 Bringéus, Skånska kistebrev, pp. 60–61, 170–71.
23 E.g. Kistebrev 62:7, 62:9, 62:12, 63:16, KB.

ADOLPH FRIDERICH,
Udvaldt Thronfolger og Cron-Printz udi
Sverrig, x. x.
KJOBENHAVN, hafuel Jthult i Skinker Galen ligt ret for ber Faru-Tole.

LOVISA ULRICA,
Cron-Printzeffe udi Sverrig, fod Kongel. Printzeffe
til Preuffen, x. x.
KJOBENHAVN, hafuel uftuld i Skinker Galen ligt ret for ber Faru-Tole.

Figure 25 Crown Prince Adolf Frederick and Crown Princess Louisa Ulrika. Woodcut by Johan Jørgen Høppfner, Copenhagen, before 1751. Photo: Björn Green, KB.

(rhyming in Swedish): 'All virtues unite / In SOPHIA MAGDALENA' (Figure 30).[24] A childhood portrait of Prince Gustav referred to the new dynasty's – in reality distant – kinship ties to the Vasa family: 'You, Prince, who delight everyone's hearts / In virtue you are like your ancestors' (Figure 31). In these cases the verses struck a royalist chord that was obviously to the regime's liking. Still, while official campaigns surely played a part, it is at least as likely that the images proceeded from a perceived demand.

After the restoration of royal power, though, the popular woodcuts were enlisted in the service of political propaganda in ways that were more than merely generally royalist. One image shows a mounted Gustav III before a naïve rendering of the Stockholm Royal Palace (Figure 32). The King is wearing a cordon and carrying a marshal's baton, and the accompanying verse pays

---

24 Kistebrev 43:18, KB ('Alla Dygder sig förena / Hos SOPHIA MAGDALENA'). This image is identical to that of 43:13, which has a longer verse of fourteen lines.

Figure 26 Gustav III. Woodcut printed by Eric Hasselrot of Nyköping, 1770s. Photo: Björn Green, KB.

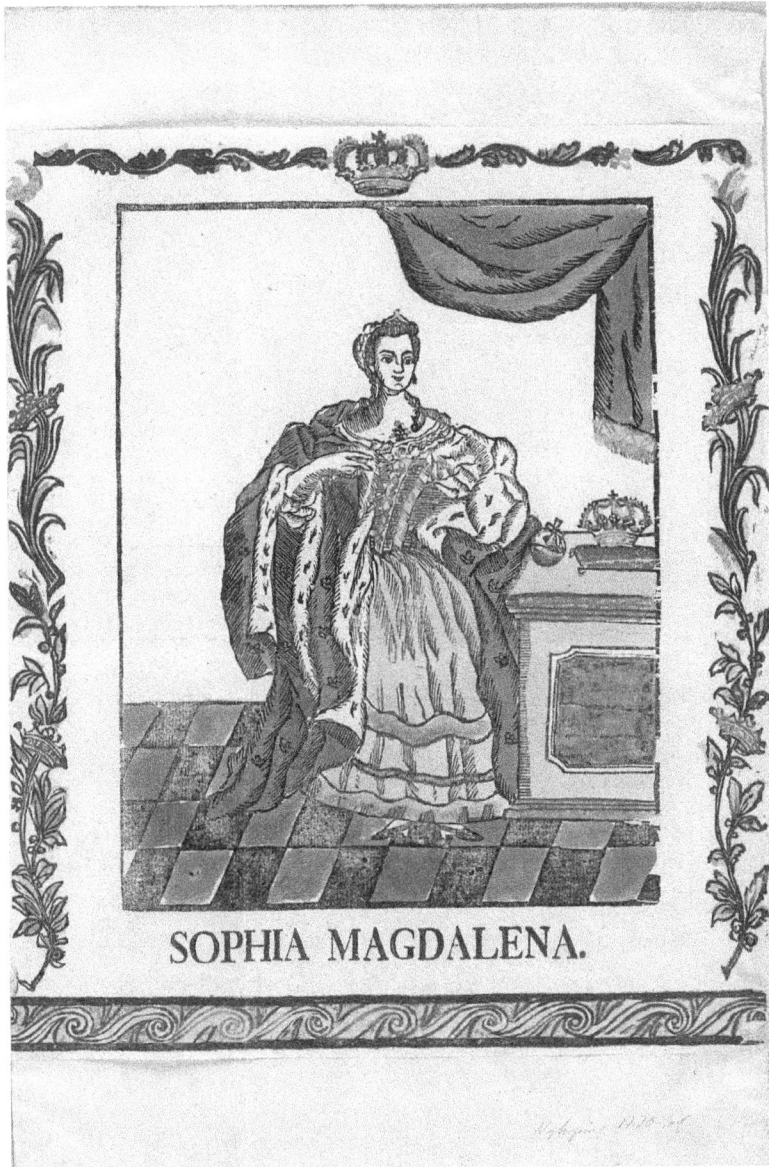

Figure 27 Sophia Magdalena. Woodcut printed by Eric Hasselrot of Nyköping, 1770s. Counterpart of Figure 26. Photo: Björn Green, KB.

Figure 28 'Adolf Frederick, King of the Swedes, Goths, and Wends. The promising prince has reinvigorated Sweden, in that God and Justice and Election have elevated him to the throne.' The text accompanying the representation anticipates the course of events, having promoted the newly elected Crown Prince to king. Compare Figure 29. Engraving by Christian Gottlob Liebe the Elder, Halle, 1744. Photo: Björn Green, KB.

Guftafus den Tredie.

Konge til Sverrig, de Wenders og Gothers, Hertug til Sleswig, Holsteen, Holsteen Gottorp, Stormarn og Ditmarsken, Greve til Oldenborg og Delmenhorst, 2c. 2c. Fodt d. 24. Jan. 1749. Formælet d. 8. Nov. 1766. Kom til Regieringen d. 12. Jan. 1771.

Den Svenske Kong Gustaf i alt tilsyne lader,
At Han regiere vil som Landets, Folkets Fader.
Ubundne Hænder Han med Folkets Frihed fik,
Da Han Regieringen gav en forbedret Stik.

Kiobenhavn, tryki og findes tilkiobs hos Joh. Rud. Thiele, boende i store Helliggeiststrade.

Figure 29 Gustav III. Woodcut by Johan Rudolph Thiele, Copenhagen, after 1772. Thiele had previously used the same block when portraying Adolf Frederick, and it was subsequently reused for an image of Gustav IV Adolf; there are counterpart portraits of the Queen on a horse in Danish collections. The original of this image is a German equestrian portrait representing Adolf Frederick; see Figure 28. Photo: Björn Green, KB.

Figure 30 Sophia Magdalena. Woodcut, probably printed
by Eric Hasselrot, Nyköping. Photo: Björn Green, KB.

Figure 31 Hereditary Prince Gustav (III). Woodcut based on a painting
by Gustaf Lundberg, 1746. Photo: Jens Gustafsson, KB.

tribute to the coup d'état in August 1772 and the end of party
divisions. The print was produced in the same year as the royal
takeover, but it is also known from later variants. An undated half-
length portrait of the Queen, executed somewhat in the same spirit,
also exists (Figure 33).

GUSTAF III.

Sweriges Göthes och Wendes Konung ꝛc. ꝛc. ꝛc.
Född d. 24. Januarii 1746.
Deß anträde til Regeringen 1771.
Krönt d. 29. Maji 1772.

Figure 32 Gustav III in front of the Royal Palace of Stockholm.
Woodcut produced by Eric Hasselrot in Nyköping in 1772.
Photo: Björn Green, KB.

Another well-documented example from the beginning of the reign of Gustav III shows the King receiving representatives from the four Estates (Figure 34). Originally Danish, the print was copied by Berling in 1773 and is known in versions with various accompanying texts. The image shows the four Estates approving the new Instrument of Government that ended the Age of Liberty. Gustav III sits under a canopy, wearing the crown regalia. Under the orb lies an open book, probably the book of statutes. The representatives

Figure 33 Sophia Magdalena. Woodcut printed in Nyköping, 1770s?
Photo: Björn Green, KB.

Figure 34 'The King of Sweden allows the Estates of the Realm to kiss his hand.' Woodcut by Johan Rudolph Thiele, Copenhagen, probably 1772. Photo: Uppsala University Library.

of the four Estates are easily identifiable: the nobleman genuflects and kisses the King's hand, the clergyman awaits his turn, and the burgher seems to have just signed a document (the Instrument of Government?), while the peasant stands at the end of the table pointing to a letter (in view of the origin of the model it could be a supplication, which was the normal medium for the Danish peasantry to communicate with their king). Above the entire scene shines the national coat of arms with the Holstein-Gottorp inescutcheon. In the Danish version, the content of the new Instrument of Government is summarised in a long text. According to this text, the previous constitution was extreme, affording His Majesty so little influence and so little say that the royal title was almost the sole thing that remained. Now, on the other hand, it was only the name that differentiated the form of government from 'being a complete and well-organised autocracy and absolutism'.

In fact, the change of constitution caused a good deal of alarm in the Danish government because it was perceived to entail an increased military threat. Conversely, with respect to the subjects there was surely no drawback in portraying the absolutist form of government as such as desirable. Berling's more concise Swedish text announced that the Constitution had been adopted in full agreement and that the Estates would be summoned for a session after six years. In four short verses, the Estates expressed favourable opinions about the King, about the salvation of the kingdom and about the Instrument of Government. Additional variants without any text are also known to exist.[25]

What images of the royal family did the popular prints convey? First and foremost it must be emphasised that popular prints portraying royals seem to have made up a very small part of the image production during the eighteenth century; religious topics were by far the most common. The common people were thus hardly given any strong visual impressions of the monarch through this type of medium.

The prints often have strikingly vivid colours. The bright 'illumination' will frequently have been as important as the topic. The words of the architect Carl Fredrik Adelcrantz, intended for a completely different line of reasoning about the art of painting, come to mind:

> The agreeableness and liveliness of the colours, the many different things that are simultaneously depicted and that make the painting

25 Variant prints and texts can be found in Bringéus, *Skånska kistebrev*, p. 193. On Denmark and RF 1772 see Knud J. V. Jespersen and Ole Feldbæk, *Revanche og neutralitet 1648–1814*, Dansk udenrigspolitiks historie, 2 (Copenhagen: Danmarks Nationalleksikon, 2002), pp. 339–41, 352–54.

rich, divide the attention of spectators, flatter their eyes, and prevent them from becoming aware of small flaws in the drawing[.][26]

The more expensive copper engravings and etchings, which were aimed at a wealthier clientele, were produced by skilful artists and collected in portfolios as often as they were framed to adorn drawing-room walls. The popular prints, on the other hand, were meant to be decorative as images while being able to function as a substitute for wallpapers. In some prints, as in Hoffbro's first collective image of kings, the bright colours also seem to have served as a substitute for a frame.[27]

Certain types of royal portraits seem to have dominated. In view of the scarcity of the material, popular prints from both the Age of Liberty and the Gustavian era, showing both Swedish and foreign rulers, will be discussed here. The images can be divided into three categories: equestrian portraits, full-length portraits and half-length portraits. The first two types seem to have been the most common ones. Almost without exception, the preserved prints are grouped into pairs containing a man and a woman. Normally the King and Queen were represented, but from the Gustavian era there are double portraits containing the King's siblings: either the Dukes Charles and Frederick Adolf (Figures 35–37), or the latter together with their sister, Sophia Albertina. Frederick II of Prussia was also illustrated together with his brother, Prince Augustus William.[28]

In the equestrian portraits, royal status seems to have been considered sufficiently emphasised by placing the person in question on horseback. To this is added a baton in the King's hand and an implied richness of fabric in the Queen's clothes. The background is usually made up of a view of a distant city. In the full-length portraits, on the other hand, there is almost always some form of attribute: royal regalia, a coat of arms or a monogram. These do not merely signal royal status: because the resemblance to the original subject is usually slight, it is only through the attributes

---

26 Carl Fredrik Adelcrantz, *Tal om de fria konsters värde och nytta; hållit för Kongl. Vetenskaps Academien vid præsidii nedläggande, den 23 julii, år 1757* (Stockholm: Lars Salvius, 1757), p. 24.

27 Cf. Bringéus, *Skånska kistebrev*, pp. 47–53.

28 Bringéus, *Skånska kistebrev*, pp. 170–71, 186. My typologisation is based primarily on a survey of the collection of Kistebrev at KB, series 37–38, 43, 61–63. A similar analysis can be made of the twenty-three popular prints with royal topics from the Berling printing office that have been compiled by Bringéus, *Skånska kistebrev*, pp. 167–93.

Figure 35 Prince Frederick Adolf, youngest brother of Gustav III.
Woodcut, origins unknown. The ribbons belonging to all Swedish orders
of knighthood are worn from the right to the left, and the image is in all
likelihood based on some foreign model.

that the person in question can be identified. When these markers
are lacking, identification becomes all but impossible.[29]

The half-length portraits, finally, make up the smallest group.
Bringéus reproduces only one such Berling print, representing
Frederick V of Denmark and his queen, Juliana Maria. With a

---

29 *Ibid.*, pp. 67–68.

Figure 36 Prince Frederick Adolf, youngest brother of Gustav III. Woodcut, origins unknown. The image is undoubtedly reused from some different topic. The price quoted on the sheet, three shillings, shows that the image was created after the coinage reform in 1776. Photo: Björn Green, KB.

different text, the image of the Queen was also used as a portrait of the King's first wife, Queen Louise.[30] The portraits have oval frames and are placed on pedestals with explanatory texts. Both the King and the Queen have been draped in mantles, and in the foreground

---

30 Ibid., pp. 178–80.

Figure 37 'Prince CARLES, Duke of Södermanland'. Woodcut, origins unknown. Photo: Björn Green, KB.

curtains have been opened to expose the images to view. The National Library of Sweden has a couple of similar prints showing Gustav III and Sophia Magdalena. The image of the King in a cuirass and mantle harks back to an original painting by Alexander Roslin, which was engraved by several artists and was probably fairly widely distributed. It can be found, for example, as a frontispiece in Johan B. Busser's description of Uppsala. The woodcuts are skilfully executed, and the resemblance to the original subjects is strong.[31]

---

31 Kistebrev 63:10 (Gustav III), 63:14 (Sofia Magdalena), KB. Gunnar W. Lundberg, *Roslin: Liv och verk*, 3 vols (Malmö: Allhem, 1957), III:

In these examples the royal couple were represented in companion pieces, thus bringing to mind contemporary engravings or painted portraits in privileged social settings. Lists of monarchs in the form of miniatures, either as a sequence of independent portraits or painted on a common foundation, were also produced for a more distinguished clientele.[32] Equestrian portraits on the other hand were a form of royal portrait that all but vanished from representational art during the Age of Liberty. The relatively obscure Jean David Kock (1675–1744), mainly known as a copyist, painted an equestrian portrait of Frederick I in a gold-embroidered full-dress uniform with a cuirass. This is not a state portrait but a small painting, 81 cm by 72 cm in size. It is possibly a copy of a painting by Georg Desmarées.[33] Apart from a couple of minor Gustavian exceptions, which rather belong to the category of historical paintings, the genre would not return in earnest until the reign

---

Katalog och bilagor, catalogue no. 319; Nordin, 'Mediating Images of Monarchy', pp. 59–67. Francis Haskell has pointed out that educated readers at the end of the seventeenth century began to display a more critical attitude to bad depictions with a poor resemblance to the original subjects; see Haskell, pp. 74–79.

32 Eva-Lena Karlsson, 'Regentserier', in *Ulrica Fredrica Pasch och hennes samtid*, ed. by Eva-Lena Bengtsson (Stockholm: Konstakademien, 1996), pp. 21–25. See the examples by Niclas Lafrensen the Elder and Ulrica Fredrica Pasch in Gunnar W. Lundberg, *Svenskt och franskt 1700-tal i Institut Tessins samlingar* (Malmö: Allhems, 1972), p. 107, and *Catherine the Great & Gustav III*, Nationalmuseum Exhibition Catalogue, 610 (Stockholm: Nationalmuseum, 1998), p. 368. K. K. Meinander catalogues five examples from Finland. They all begin with Gustav I; one ends with Charles XII and two with Frederick I and Gustav III, respectively; see Meinander, *Porträtt i Finland före 1840-talet* (Helsinki: Söderström, 1931), p. 265. On sequences of portraits from Gustav I up to and including Frederick I, see 1920:1089, 1924:1916, 1926:436, 1937:870, 1957:2365, 1958:56, 1982:91, Svenska Porträttarkivet/Swedish Portrait Archive (SPA). On miniatures on glass with a list of monarchs from Gustav I up to and including Adolf Frederick, see Nordiska museet, inv. 54.670–74; see also *Gustav Vasa tur & retur: Guide till svenska folkets kungaminnen* (Stockholm: Livrustkammaren, 2003), pp. 47–48.

33 SPA, 1937:1409, 1937:1933. *Katalog över statens porträttsamling på Gripsholm*, 2 vols (Stockholm: Victor Pettersons, 1951–92), I: *Porträtt före 1809* (1951), Grh 2308. During his years as a crown prince, preliminary work was carried out for an equestrian portrait of Adolf Frederick, but this remained at the project stage; Carolina Brown and Merit Laine, *Gustaf Lundberg 1695–1786: En porträttmålare och hans tid*, Nationalmusei skriftserie, n.s., 19 (Stockholm: Nationalmuseum, 2006), pp. 121–23.

of Charles XIV John (1818–1844).[34] In popular art, on the other hand, with its old-fashioned characteristics, the equestrian portrait remained the very epitome of royalty.

In addition to the producers of popular prints copying one another, the originals on which their prints were based consisted to a large extent of more extravagant engravings. It is therefore difficult to express an opinion about any special meanings in the popular broadside prints as a genre. Rather than conveying and popularising messages from above, the illuminators of prints used the expectations of the group of prospective buyers as their starting point. The decorative function was in that respect the most important one. After all, royal persons were people who meant something (or at least were familiar) to the general public. Otherwise contemporary personalities were portrayed only if they had achieved something spectacular: the discredited Baron von Goertz, Major Malcolm Sinclair who was murdered by Russian agents during a diplomatic mission, the executed royalist perpetrators of the coup of 1756, well-known generals, and so on. If customers requested portraits of a more permanent value, the royal couple will have been the best investment.

In most cases, resemblance to the original subjects was not striking, so the images did not provide a very good idea of the visual appearance of the monarch. Often the person in question could only be identified with aid of the text and various attributes. Others were quite impersonal, and there are, as was stated above, several examples of how a woodblock was reused with a new text that provided a different identification. The images also functioned more as types than as direct portrayals. They were images of *royalty* rather than images of a specific king. Even the Roslin painting of Gustav III mentioned above was thus the model for an anonymous woodcut rendering of 'K. ADOLPH FRIEDRICH' (Figure 38). An equestrian portrait of 'Gustaf II Adolph' from the mid-1700s is perhaps an even clearer example. The rider, fashionably dressed

---

34 The exceptions are Hugues Taraval's unfinished allegory of the political revolution of Gustav III and Niclas Lafrensen the Younger's historicising portrait of Gustav IV Adolf from 1800. See depictions in *Catherine the Great & Gustav III*, catalogue no. 55, p. 123, and Bo G. Wennberg, *Niclas Lafrensen den yngre* (Malmö: Allhems, 1947), image 102. To this can be added Pehr Hilleström the Elder's many portraits of Gustav III during carousels and in the field. However, all the images mentioned are historical paintings rather than portraits.

S. ADOLPH FRIEDRICH.

Figure 38 'K. ADOLPH FRIEDRICH'. Woodcut printed by Eric Hasselrot, Nyköping. The model was Alexander Roslin's portrait of Gustav III, painted in Paris in 1771. Photo: Björn Green, KB.

in a *justaucorps* with a wig and a tricorn, does not in any way resemble the historical figure (Figure 39). Similarly, a portrait of Ulrika Eleonora the Younger (1688–1741) has been used as a model for a popular print that is said to show Princess Sophia Albertina (1753–1829). The woodcutter has also incorrectly copied the closed crown, which was otherwise not worn by royalty below the throne (Figure 40; cf. Figure 1).[35]

Similar techniques can be identified in the more exclusive images. For instance, even in the established art of portraiture royals continued to be depicted in cuirasses long after these were no longer in military use. Martial armour had become a royal attribute even for princes who had never actually gone into the field. Even so, conservatism was still stronger in popular art, which generally had an archaic appearance. For example, popular prints and other folk art often continued to depict eighteenth-century costume well into the nineteenth century. The intimate and informal royal portraits that became common during the latter part of the eighteenth century lacked an equivalent in popular art, which continued to imitate official state portraits. During the Age of Liberty and the Gustavian era, no state portraits of the king on horseback were painted, as was mentioned above; but the way of depicting the monarch continued to be common in popular prints, a circumstance that had its own particular reasons. If the popular images had been deprived of their solemn dignity, they would have been emptied of content and become fairly uninteresting since resemblance to the original subject was negligible. On the other hand, likeness to the original subject was not so important for the clientele, because it usually could not be verified. Buyers 'knew' that the king was on horseback or wore a mantle and a crown, but they could not know whether his facial features were accurately rendered.

Sculpture

In Sweden, the erection of public statues was in all essentials a nineteenth-century phenomenon. During the Age of Greatness, on the other hand, several sculptures were planned of Swedish kings on horseback. The architect Simon de la Vallée had drawn an equestrian

---

35 The same model was later also used to portray Princess Hedvig Elisabeth Charlotta in 1801: Nordin, 'Mediating Images of Monarchy', figure 2:4, p. 39.

Figure 39 'Gustav II Adolph'. Woodcut, origins unknown. The equestrian representation, which does not bear the slightest resemblance to the seventeenth-century monarch, forms part of the same series as Figure 35. Photo: Björn Green, KB.

SOPHIA ALBERTINA.
Swea Rikes Arf-Prinseßa, född den 8 October 1753.
Coadjutrici af Stifter Qvedlingburg 1767.

Figure 40 Princess Sophia Albertina, younger sister of Gustav III.
Woodcut, origins unknown, probably after 1776. Based on an engraving
representing Queen Ulrika Eleonora the Younger; see Figure 1.
Photo: Björn Green, KB.

image, probably depicting Gustav II Adolf, for the courtyard of the House of Nobility, which had originally been planned as an enclosed space. His son and successor Jean de la Vallée wanted to see Charles X Gustav in the saddle in front of the rebuilt western façade he had drawn for the royal castle in Stockholm. Nicodemus Tessin the Younger designed several equestrian statues of Swedish hero kings. The most far-reaching among them were the plans for a monument of Charles XI, which was intended for the courtyard of the new Royal Palace in Stockholm. Several sketches and a *bozzetto* of the statue have been preserved. The project is said to have been terminated at the planning stage by Charles XII. A projected arsenal on the opposite side of the water, facing the Royal Palace, was to be adorned with equestrian bronzes of the four heroes of the Age of Greatness: Gustav II Adolf, Charles X Gustav, Charles XI and Charles XII. These, like the spectacular project for the arsenal in its entirety, remained on the drawing board.[36]

The first Swedish sculpture of a king to be exhibited in public represented Frederick I (Figure 41). Throughout the eighteenth century, the King's Garden (*Kungsträdgården*) in Stockholm was open to the public at certain times and under certain conditions. A marble bust of King Frederick was moved there from the out-of-town royal residence of Karlberg and exhibited in summertime. The plinth bore a Latin inscription where the King was designated as the protector of peace, justice and liberty, and which bombastically exclaimed, 'In marble the features, in the features a king, in the King a hero'. Exactly when the bust was exhibited is unclear, but it was probably long after the King's death: various years between 1765 and 1772 have been suggested. In any event, it was not in place for more than a few years, and it had been removed by April 1774 at the latest.[37]

36 Andreas Lindblom, 'Karolinska ryttarmonument i Stockholm', in Andreas Lindblom, *Fransk barock- och rokokoskulptur i Sverige: Studier* (Uppsala: Almqvist & Wiksell, 1923), pp. 13–26; Martin Olin, *Det karolinska porträttet: Ideologi, ikonografi, identitet* (Stockholm: Raster, 2000), pp. 128–32.
37 The inscribed plinth is kept at the Historiska Museet/Swedish History Museum, inv. no. 23439 ('In marmore vultus. In vultu Rex. In Rege heros'). The bust is probably a German work from before Frederick's reign; he is adorned with the Prussian Order of the Black Eagle, which he was awarded in 1703. Axel Reuterholm, *Axel Reuterholms dagboksanteckningar under riksdagen i Stockholm 1738–39*, ed. by Göran Nilzén (Stockholm: Kungl.

Figure 41 Frederick I. Marble, artist unknown, after 1703. In the 1760s, the bust was located in the King's Garden (*Kungsträdgården*) in Stockholm. Photo: Alexis Daflos, Royal Collection Department. © Kungl. Hovstaterna.

Samfundet för utgivande av handskrifter rörande Skandinaviens historia, 2006), p. 65; [Carl Christoffer Gjörwell], 'Anteckningar af Carl Christopher Gjörwell om sig sjelf, samtida personer och händelser 1731–1757', in *Samlingar utgifna för De skånska landskapens historiska och arkeologiska förening*, ed. by Martin Weibull, 9 vols (Lund: Berlings, 1874–80), III: *1875* (1874), pp. 31–142 (p. 84); Carl Christoffer Gjörwell, *En Stockholmskrönika ur C. C. Gjörwells brev, 1757–1778*, ed. by Otto Sylwan (Stockholm: Bonniers, 1920), p. 105; Johan Elers, *Stockholm*, 4 vols (Stockholm: H. Nordström junior, 1800–01), I (1800), pp. 178–79; see also *ibid.*, II (1800), pp. 250–51; Nils G. Wollin, 'Kungsträdgården i Stockholm. II', *Samfundet S:t Eriks årsbok 1924* (1924), 93–121 (pp. 103–10).

This concludes the discussion of projects that were realised. The public royal statues of the Age of Liberty were hence few in number, but several monuments that were completed much later were planned during the period. Consequently, the considerations behind their conception tell us something about ambitions of the era. The idea of adorning public places with memorials for great men was many centuries old, and in the eighteenth century more didactic justifications were added to it. As a result, the potential gallery of subjects was expanded to include people from below the circle of royal persons, and suggestions were made for various types of memorials to the authors of the Instrument of Government, Per Ribbing and Carl Gustaf Gyllencreutz, to Thomas Plomgren, Speaker of the Burgher Estate for many years, and to the industrialist Jonas Alströmer.[38]

In the mid-1750s, both State Councillor Carl Fredrik Scheffer and the architect Carl Fredrik Adelcrantz spoke of the usefulness of public monuments in their inaugural lectures before the Royal Swedish Academy of Sciences (*Kungl. Vetenskapsakademien*). Scheffer described how science, belles-lettres and the arts had recently begun to flourish in Sweden, but claimed that the country completely lacked the 'splendid statues in marble and bronze' that kept the memory of great men alive in other countries. Even though Scheffer saw possible examples among statesmen, scientists and men of business, it was primarily the kings who were to be memorialised; and, he argued, 'there are few countries in the world that can enumerate rulers as great as ours'. He furthermore noted that the times of war had passed in Sweden and that the kingdom now, 'under the sceptre of our benevolent King', instead built its glory on combining political wisdom with science and art. The speech was fashioned as a quiet plea for this monarch's deserving such a memorial, rather than his warlike predecessors. In the following year, Superintendent of the King's Buildings Carl Johan Cronstedt

---

38 About these statue projects, see, e.g., Johan Cederlund, *Skulptören Pierre Hubert L'Archevêque 1721–1778*, Nationalmusei skriftserie, n.s., 18 (Stockholm: Nationalmuseum, 2003), pp. 153–67. In September 1774 Carl Christoffer Gjörwell wrote that the intention was for Ribbing's bust, 'according to the Estates' decision of 1756, to be erected along with the bust of Chief Judge Gyllencreutz, who dared speak at the House of Nobility against the introduction of absolutism by King Charles XI, in the great hall of the House of Nobility as being *numina libertatis* [spirits of liberty)'; Gjörwell, *En Stockholmskrönika*, pp. 126–27.

duly submitted a petition to the Council (dated 24 March 1756) requesting that the reign of Adolf Frederick be commemorated through monuments in public places in the kingdom. The petition preceded the attempted royalist coup by only a few months and therefore never had any effect.[39] In July 1757, Adelcrantz delivered an oft-quoted speech to the Academy of Sciences in which he foregrounded the general usefulness of art for the welfare of the kingdom as well as the didactic usefulness of public sculpture:

> What can be a more decent adornment in a city than to erect, in its public places, the statues of great kings, whose memory is blessed by native men and venerated by foreigners? What can better encourage virtue, bravery, industry, than seeing the images of great heroes, wise men, and useful citizens, adorning the prominent places that a grateful posterity, to their well-deserved honour, have dedicated to them?[40]

Adelcrantz emphasised that Stockholm was almost the only European capital 'in which no statue had been erected, in memory of its renowned kings'.[41] He thus cautiously emphasised that *posterity* should erect monuments to a person's *memory*, or when closing the accounts of the activities of the person portrayed. The idea that the reigning monarch should be honoured with a memorial was certainly dead; but Adelcrantz at least ventured to assert that 'on the throne of Sweden sits a KING who no less should be called the father of the ARTS than the FATHER OF THE COUNTRY'

---

39 Carl Fredrik Scheffer, *Tal, hållit för Kongl. Vetenskaps academien, vid præsidii afläggande, den 2 augusti, år 1755* (Stockholm: Lars Salvius, 1755), pp. 9–14 ('de präktige Stoder i Marmor och Bronze'; 'få Länder i verlden finnas, som kunna upräkna så stora Regenter som vi'; and 'under vår milda Konungs Spira'); Ragnar Josephson, 'Larchevêque och svenskarna', in *Septentrionalia et orientalia: Studia Bernhardo Karlgren dedicata*, Kungl. Vitterhets Historie och Antikvitets Akademiens handlingar, 91 (Stockholm: Almqvist & Wiksell, 1959), pp. 236–51 (pp. 238–42); Cederlund, pp. 114–15.
40 Adelcrantz, pp. 23–24 ('Hvad kan vara en Stad til anständigare prydnad, än at på dess allmänna Platser hafva stora Konungars Stoder upreste, hvilkas Åminnelse af infödde Män välsignas, af Utlänningar vördas? Hvad kan mera upmuntra til dygd, til tapperhet, til idoghet, än at se store Hjältars, vise Mäns, nyttiga Medborgares Bilder, pryda de utmärkte ställen, som en tacksam efterverld dem til välförtjänt heder invigt?').
41 *Ibid.*, pp. 24–25 ('hvarest ingen Stod blifvit uprest, dess namnkunnoge Konungar til åminnelse').

(Figure 42). In his reply, the Secretary of the Academy, Pehr Wargentin, added the hope that handicraft, arts and sciences rather than wars and conquests would cause the name of Adolf Frederick to be remembered by posterity.[42] This speech was, ironically enough, given less than two months before Sweden's declaration of war on Prussia was delivered to the Imperial Diet in Regensburg in Adolf Frederick's name.

Meanwhile Scheffer had not abandoned his idea, and he could now promote his updated views through his father-in-law, Johan Christopher von Düring, the governor of Stockholm. Among all the deserving Swedish monarchs, the latter suggested in a petition to the Council that Gustav II Adolf should be especially commemorated with a statue in the capital. No doubt Scheffer was behind this suggestion. After the attempted coup and against the will of the royal couple, Scheffer had been elevated to the post of tutor to the Crown Prince. He knew that Gustav II Adolf was as highly admired by Louisa Ulrika as he was by her brother Frederick II of Prussia, against whom Sweden had just started a war. In addition to the main goal of beautifying the capital, an apotheosis of the victorious hero of the Protestants could therefore serve the double purpose of satisfying the royal family and maintaining the dignity of the monarchy, even though the plans for a monument to Adolf Frederick had been consigned to oblivion.[43]

The conciliatory plan that seemed capable of satisfying all parties was nevertheless disapproved of by another actor, Fredrik Axel von Fersen, leader of the Hat party. Through various shenanigans in the State Deputation (statsdeputationen), the Deputation on the Construction of the Royal Palace (slottsbyggnadsdeputationen), the Directorate of the House of Nobility (riddarhusdirektionen) and the Riksdag's Secret Committee, he managed to bring the Gustav II Adolf project to a halt. The French sculptor Pierre-Hubert L'Archevêque had already designed a proposal that had been approved by the Council. Fersen instead made sure that L'Archevêque and the material that had already been set aside for the casting were made available for the topic he himself had suggested, namely a statue of Gustav I. In this way, public funds were transferred to an Estate-affiliated corporation in order to be

42 Ibid., p. 43 ('På Sveriges Thron sitter en KONUNG, som ej mindre bör kallas KONSTERNAS, än LANDSENS FADER'), and Wargentin's reply, p. 47.
43 Josephson, 'Larchevêque och svenskarna', pp. 237, 242–45. See also Cederlund, p. 115.

Figure 42 Adolf Frederick as patron of the arts. Engraving by Pehr
Floding, 1761, on the basis of an idea by Carl Reinhold Berch and a
drawing by Charles Nicolas Cochin. The addition, in Swedish, to the
legend – 'That the Fine Arts in Sweden are regarded with benevolence
by a Gracious King, and supported by the Distinguished Estates of the
Realm' – was included at the insistence of Floding, 'for peasants know
no Latin'. A connection to the Vasa dynasty is implied by the bust on
the left. Photo: Björn Green, KB.

used for propaganda directed against the royal authority – for it
was the nobility that was formally behind Fersen's suggestion, using
the justification that 'Gustav Vasa' (stressing his ancestral name)
had been one of them, a nobleman. On an earlier occasion, Fersen
had made sure that the Vasa coat of arms was placed above the seat
of the Lord Marshal in the great hall of the House of Nobility, in
memory of a brilliant example from the nobility's own circle.

Gustav II Adolf was certainly considered an excellent ruler, but
he was felt to be too warlike and to have autocratic tendencies. The
thrifty Gustav (I) Vasa was thought to be a better model: an elected
native king originating in an aristocracy that had always, according
to Hat-party mythology, been the primary defenders of Swedish
liberty. His statue would be placed in the middle of the square
outside the House of Nobility. At the time, people interpreted the
composition of the sculpture as meaning that the King was on his
way *from* the House of Nobility, looking *towards* the Royal Palace.
The pedestal was in place as early as 1765, but the casting of
the statue itself met with several mishaps. In the summer of 1772,
the Directorate of the House of Nobility attempted to expedite the
work so that it would at least be finished for the 250-year jubilee
of the King's accession to the throne.[44] That schedule could not
be kept; and besides, Gustav III had executed his coup d'état before
the day of commemoration.

The attempt by the nobility to expropriate the national hero
was answered by the re-energised holder of power, Gustav III. The
King's tactics can primarily be described as a counteroffensive to
recapture the Vasa name. It was a recurring feature in his rhetoric
to refer to his alleged Swedish ancestors on the throne, particularly
both of the Gustavs. Therefore, his vision was to make the unveiling
of the statue into a ceremony that illustrated the union between
king and people. The statue was finally erected in December 1773,
but the King wished to delay the unveiling until Midsummer Eve
the following year. It was, as all contemporaries were careful to
point out, both the anniversary of Gustav (I) Vasa's entry into
Stockholm and the date of the election of Adolf Frederick as

---

44 Josephson, 'Larchevêque och svenskarna', pp. 245–47; Cederlund,
  pp. 141–51; Gunnar Mascoll Silfverstolpe in *Sveriges riddarhus: Ridderskapet och adeln och dess riddarhus*, ed. by Carl Hallendorf (Stockholm:
  Historiska Förlaget, 1926), pp. 167, 174–83; Elers, I, pp. 105, 167–69;
  Gjörwell, *En Stockholmskrönika*, pp. 74, 82–83; Fischerström, pp. 92, 95,
  106, 109, 117, 122–23.

successor to the Swedish throne – and what is more, it was the day
that had been elevated to a national feast day in celebration of the
foiled royal coup of 1756. In connection with his own coup d'état,
the King had already neutralised the medal issued in memory of his
parents' failed revolt by reusing the same topic with the Goddess of
Liberty in a medal of his own. The earlier text about the preservation of liberty was replaced by the inscription *Proscripta licentia*,
the banning of licence, which was of course directed against the
Estates and the party system. The reverse bore the declaration 'on
21 August 1772 Gustav III […] regained from the Estates of the
Realm the Instrument of Government that had traditionally been in
force', which was a barefaced historical lie.[45] In fact it had been the
first time an Instrument of Government was submitted from above
to the Estates for approval. The members of the Riksdag had been
summoned by force, all party leaders were locked up, and the acclamation had been voiced under military guard. Previous Instruments
of Government had always been drawn up on the initiative of the
Estates, and it had been the kings who had been called upon to
consent to the contract.

The stage-managed popular feast that Gustav III fantasised
about at the unveiling of the statue was meant to illustrate the
bond between the new and the old dynasty and the union between
king and people. Only certain elements of the achievements of
Gustav I as king were to be foregrounded: the revolt against foreign
influence, the unity within the country and the national rallying
around the King, symbol of the fatherland.[46] The element of liberty
thus involved only liberation from foreign oppression, and there
were no visual traces of Axel von Fersen's economical national
householder. The unveiling did take place on the designated day,
but it was done without any ceremony. Nevertheless, some of the
intended effects were achieved. Among other things, the troubadour

---

45 Bror Emil Hildebrand, *Sveriges och svenska konungahusets minnespenningar,
    praktmynt och belöningsmedaljer*, 2 vols (Stockholm: Vitterhetsakademien,
    1874–75), II (1875), pp. 154–55 ('Den 21 augusti år 1772 återfick Gustav
    III […] av rikets ständer den regeringsform, som av gammalt varit gällande');
    Nordin, 'Mediating Images of Monarchy', pp. 56–59, figures 2:13–14.
46 The King provided a detailed description of the project in a letter to Carl
    Fredrik Scheffer of 18 October 1773, in *Gustave III par ses lettres*, ed.
    by Gunnar von Proschwitz (Stockholm: Norstedts; Paris: Jean Touzot,
    1986), pp. 145–49. See also Sven Delblanc's detailed analysis in *Ära och
    minne: Studier kring ett motivkomplex i 1700-talets litteratur* (Stockholm:
    Bonniers, 1965), pp. 155–66, see also pp. 113–14.

Bellman, upon first sight of the monument over Gustav I, composed a royalist poem: 'Swedish chronicles give testimony to / the noble-mindedness of that king. The same virtues are revived / in the blood of the third Gustav.'[47]

The 'great and world-renowned *hero of liberty* GUSTAV ERICSON VASA' was such an uncontested national hero that his memory could apparently express a variety of political standpoints.[48] The characteristic qualities of the Swedish people were generally felt to include a love of freedom handed down from one generation to the next and a traditional royalism.[49] Gustav (I) Vasa functioned as a unifying symbol for both of these, sometimes conflicting, perspectives. As has already been demonstrated, he could be used by the noble opposition as well as by the royal authority during the transition from the Age of Liberty to the Gustavian era. There are other examples: the printer Lars Wennberg was responsible for the publication of some of the more radical texts relating to the conflict between the Estates at the end of the Age of Liberty. After the coup d'état, several of his offensive publications were either banned or led to his being prosecuted. On the day before Gustav III limited the freedom of the press in 1774, Wennberg was even sentenced to fourteen days in prison. This did not silence him, and later he also began to produce popular prints. In 1782, Wennberg – 'at his own expense' – published a leaflet picturing the monument to Gustav I (Figure 43).[50] According to the leaflet's heading, the King's monument had been erected 'in memory of his great deeds for the

---

47 Quoted in *Sveriges riddarhus*, p. 180 ('Svenska häfder vittnen gifva/ om den kungens ädelmod./ Samma dygder sig upplifva/ i den tredje Gustafs blod'). See also Carl Gyllenborg's verse on the same occasion in Delblanc, p. 165.

48 Quoted in *Inrikes Tidningar*, no. 28 (11 April 1771) ('Store och Werlds-kände *Frihets-Hjelten* GUSTAV ERICSON VASA').

49 See Jonas Nordin, *Ett fattigt men fritt folk: Nationell och politisk självbild i Sverige från sen stormaktstid till slutet av frihetstiden* (Eslöv: Symposion, 2000), esp. chapter 4.

50 Kistebrev 43:16, KB ('på egen Bekostnad'). Bengt Åhlén, *Ord mot ordningen: Farliga skrifter, bokbål och kättarprocesser i svensk censurhistoria*, ed. by Agneta Åhlén, Lillemor Widgren Matlack and Christer Hellmark (Stockholm: Ordfront, 1986), pp. 112, 118; Thomas von Vegesack, *Smak för frihet: Opinionsbildningen i Sverige 1755–1830* (Stockholm: Natur och kultur, 1995), pp. 77–79; Bengt Åhlén and Agneta Åhlén, *Censur och tryckfrihet: Farliga skrifter i Sverige 1522–1954* (Södertälje: Fingraf, 2002), nos 17.254, 17.256, 17.258, 17.261, 17.264, 17.266.

Figure 43 Gustav I, memorial statue on the square in front of the House of Nobility. Woodcut by Lars Wennberg, 1782. Photo: Björn Green, KB.

fatherland'. That the House of Nobility funded the statue was not
mentioned anywhere; by contrast, the text emphasised how the
nobility had wavered when the freedom fighter had sought their
aid in throwing off the Danish yoke. Instead it was the common
Dalecarlians who, after some initial hesitation and 'without a
leader' ('utan Anförare'), had beaten the Danish army and thereafter successfully completed the work of liberation. The popular
print contains cautious but unambiguous criticism of the nobility.
It thus became a counter-image that captured the nobility's original
rhetorical figure and reversed it. In order to reinforce this tendency,
Wennberg also fabricated a completely new maxim for King Gustav
I: 'His motto was 'GOD and the peasantry of Sweden'. In actual
fact, the motto of Gustav I, like all earlier royal mottoes, had had
an exclusively religious content.[51]

The statue of Gustav (I) Vasa is an excellent illustration of the
impartiality and elevation of the royal authority. Anyone could
utilise the favourable connotations encompassed in the renown of
King Gustav I. The nobility saw him as a defender of liberty originating in their own circles; Gustav III wished to connect his own
royal achievements to those of Gustav I; and in Wennberg's print,
Gustav I became a symbol of the resistance of the people and the
lethargy of the nobility. The actual freestanding bronze sculpture
itself must have been perceived as a wonderful thing when it was
finally erected. In the speech quoted earlier, Carl Fredrik Adelcrantz
emphasised the pedagogic value of the visual arts:

> The orator and the poet are understood by only a few, the artist by
> all. Infants reach for his works before they can speak: the ignorant
> peasant is as captivated by them as a king. Briefly put: The language
> of the artist is understood by every country, every age, every Estate.[52]

The statue of Gustav (I) Vasa seems to have made precisely such an
impression. A few days after its unveiling Gustav III made a detour
with his life guards in order to salute the statue, and the commoners

---

51 ('Hans Wahlspråk war, GUD och Sweriges Allmoge'.) A total of four
   variants of Gustav's maxims are known; see Bertel Tingström, Svensk
   numismatisk uppslagsbok: Mynt i ord och bild 1521–1972, 3rd rev. edn
   (Stockholm: Numismatiska bokförlaget, 1972), p. 67.
52 Adelcrantz, p. 13 ('Oratoren och Poëten begripas allenast af få, Konstnären
   af alla. Späda barn räcka efter dess arbeten sina händer innan de kunna
   tala: den okunnige Bonden är däraf så betagen, som en Konung. Med et
   ord: Konstnärens tal förstås af alla land, af alla åldrar, af alla stånd').

were overwhelmed, if the publicist Carl Christoffer Gjörwell is to
be credited:

> Every day of the week peasants from all over the country still stand
> gaping at Gustav I. He does look respectable, though.

In the same breath Gjörwell noted that the bronze bust of Per
Ribbing, 'he who was Lord Marshal in 1719 and restored liberty to
us', had been put away in an out-of-the-way room in the House of
Nobility.[53]

The year after the unveiling of the statue of Gustav (I) Vasa,
Gustav III acquired funds for the completion of the equestrian
statue of Gustav II Adolf. He also selected the place opposite the
Royal Palace where it should be erected. In spite of royal support,
the work was encumbered by all manner of delays and difficulties. The statue was cast in 1779 and put in place in 1791; but it
was not unveiled until 1796, four years after the death of Gustav
III and almost forty years after the suggestion had originally been
presented.[54]

Peter Burke has described the 'statue campaign' of Louis XIV,
during which freestanding sculptures of the King were erected in
Paris and in fifteen provincial towns, as an important method for
manifesting his absolute power.[55] Nicodemus Tessin was impressed
by this enterprise; and in view of the dominant position of French
culture at this time, it is natural that these examples would have
been influential all across Europe. Few countries, however, had
as plentiful resources as did France, which continued to put up
public monuments during the reign of Louis XV as well.[56] One
might imagine that the Danish absolute monarchy had the same
need to manifest itself as that of France. Even so, the erection of
monuments in Denmark was, on the whole, no more impressive

---

53 Gjörwell, *En Stockholmskrönika*, pp. 126–27 ('Alla dagar står ännu den
   ifrån landet inkommande allmogen och gapar på Gustaf I. Han ser ock
   respectable ut' and 'han som var landtmarskalk 1719 och återgaf oss
   friheten').

54 Andreas Lindblom, 'Gustav II Adolfs monument i Stockholm', in Lindblom,
   Fransk barock- och rokokoskulptur i Sverige, pp. 77–123; Josephson,
   'Larchevêque och svenskarna', pp. 248–49; Cederlund, pp. 115–39.

55 Peter Burke, *The Fabrication of Louis XIV* (New Haven and London: Yale
   University Press, 1992), pp. 92–97.

56 Andreas Lindblom, 'Pierre-Hubert L'Archevêques ryttarbild av Gustav
   Adolf: Några blad ur dess tillkomsthistoria', *Nationalmusei årsbok*, 5
   (Stockholm: Gunnar Tisells Tekniska Förlag, 1923), 31–54 (pp. 31–32).

than it was in Sweden. The Danish capital had acquired its first public sculpture of a king in the 1680s. That is when the equestrian statue of Christian V (r. 1670–1699), which was criticised by Tessin, was placed in the square of Kongens Nytorv. After that it was not until 1752 that the Frenchman Jacques-François-Joseph Saly was commissioned to make an equestrian statue of Frederick V (r. 1746–1766). A model was completed by 1755; the statue itself was erected in 1768, but was not unveiled until three years later; and it was not until 1774 that the entire monument was finished.[57] It has almost been taken for granted that it was the 'party spirit' that delayed the execution of the Swedish monuments,[58] but the obstacles thus do not appear to have been significantly fewer in the absolute monarchy of Denmark.

Frederick V is represented in the same strict Classical style as Gustav II Adolf in Stockholm. Both Frederick V and Christian V are dressed in Roman costume, while the Swedish kings are shown in contemporary, if idealised, outfits: Gustav I in a Burgundian suit, Gustav II Adolf in armour; the second half of the eighteenth century was a transitional period between a classicist and a historicising artistic ideal. The most important difference, however, is that both of the Danish sculptures were planned as monuments to living monarchs, while the Swedish ones were memorials over heroic kings long since dead. That the first public statue of a king in Sweden happened to portray Frederick I was mostly coincidental. The fountains in the King's Garden had been filled in, and a leftover bust was available at Karlberg. The bust was put in place at least a decade after the death of the King; and although he lived on in memory as 'the gracious and beneficial King of Sweden', he did not achieve the same status as the rulers who would later be honoured with planned memorials: Gustav I, Gustav II Adolf and Gustav III.[59]

---

57 Birgitte Bøggild Johannsen and Hugo Johannsen, *Kungens kunst*, Ny dansk kunsthistorie, 2 (Copenhagen: Fogtdal, 1993), pp. 190–96; Ragnar Josephson, *Tessin i Danmark* (Stockholm: Bonniers, 1924), p. 17; Emma Salling, 'Frederiks plads: J. F. J. Salys ryttarmonument for Frederik V', *Architectura*, 21 (Copenhagen: Selskabet for Arkitekturhistorie, 1999), 49–76.

58 Lindblom, 'Pierre-Hubert L'Archevêques ryttarbild', p. 43; Josephson, 'Larchevêque och svenskarna', p. 245.

59 On the assessment of Frederick see Elers, I, p. 178 ('Sveriges milde och nyttige Konung').

Coinage in Sweden

Coins as a popular source of images have already been mentioned in passing, and they were without doubt the likenesses of a monarch that had the greatest dissemination during the eighteenth century. That does not mean that they were abundantly circulated, though. During the Age of Liberty, the use of coins declined significantly. From 1726 onwards, taxes could be paid in banknotes, and these increasingly became the legal tender in circulation. The value of money was gradually undermined; and during the second half of the Age of Liberty, Sweden had, in practice, a paper-based fiat currency. Only the higher denominations of coins bore the king's image. During the Age of Liberty, such coins were minted in three types: ducats, *riksdaler* and the so-called caroline (mark). The first of these was a gold coin and the latter two were silver coins. The minting of mark coins was discontinued in 1755, and neither the ducat nor the *riksdaler* was part of the national monetary system but both were used in foreign trade. In other words, neither coin type circulated to any significant degree.[60]

All gold and silver coins were minted in Stockholm, while copper coins were usually minted close to where the metal was mined, primarily in Avesta. The plates and the copper coins could be stamped with the coat of arms bearing the three crowns of the national coat of arms or with the king's monogram, but never with the king's portrait. Local mints also existed in the foreign provinces of Sweden, but the ensuing discussion mainly deals with coins that were minted within the realm.

---

60 Tuukka Talvio, 'Sedlarnas århundrade: Mynt och pappersmynt från 1724 till 1818', in *Myntningen i Sverige 995–1995*, Numismatiska meddelanden, 40 (Stockholm: Svenska numismatiska föreningen, 1995), pp. 201–18; Lars O. Lagerqvist and others, *Sveriges och dess forna besittningars guldmynt och riksdaler från Gustav I till Carl XVI Gustaf: Samling Julius Hagander/Goldmünzen und Reichstaler Schwedens und seiner früheren Besitzungen von Gustav I. bis Carl XVI. Gustaf; Sammlung Julius Hagander* (Stockholm: Svenska numismatiska föreningen; Bern: Verlag Stämpfli + Cie, 1996), pp. 321–32. A complete description of the corpus of coins of the Age of Liberty can be found in Torgny Lindgren, *Sveriges mynt 1719–1776* (Stockholm: Kungl. Myntkabinettet, 1953), and most recently in *Den svenska mynthistorien: Frihetstiden och den gustavianska perioden 1719–1818* (Stockholm: Kungl. Myntkabinettet and Svenska numismatiska föreningen, 2007).

The respective number of the various kinds of coins can be determined with a fair degree of accuracy. During the entire Age of Liberty, just over 2,400,000 portrait coins were minted. More than 1,500,000, or about 60 per cent, of these consisted of various denominations of ducats and *riksdaler*. The rest were carolines (mark coins).[61] The total coinage of these kinds of coins during the Age of Liberty as a whole corresponded roughly to the population of the kingdom at the middle of the century. Although the number of coins in circulation was not negligible, it was nevertheless at no time sufficient to supply all the subjects in the realm with one portrait coin each.

Consequently, coins bearing the king's portrait were not something that people handled on an everyday basis. For instance, we know that Frederick I distributed *riksdaler* coins during his travels, and to members of the Riksdag from the Peasant Estate. In those cases the coins functioned rather like medals and would probably have been kept. Nor does it seem too far-fetched to imagine that most subjects would have seen coins bearing the king's portrait at least at some point during their lives, but they were not an everyday source of images for the people.[62]

Portrait coins

The ducats used in foreign trade bore the monarch's profile portrait on the obverse and, from the minority of Charles XI, 1660–1672, onwards, the crowned monogram of the king instead of the national coat of arms on the reverse. During the early years of the reigns of Ulrika Eleonora and Frederick, the great national coat of arms with the dynasty inescutcheon returned in exceptional cases; but from 1734 ducats were given a basic design that was retained throughout the eighteenth century: the obverse bore the bust or head of the King in a right profile, whereas the reverse bore the

---

61 In rounded figures: just over 280,000 double, half- and quarter- ducats (1719–1771); just over 930,000 *riksdaler* (1719–1769); just over 315,000 half-, quarter- and eighth-*riksdaler* (1723–1768); almost 890,000 eight-, four-, two- and one-mark coins (1719–1755). These values have been calculated on the basis of tables in Tingström, pp. 265–67, 281–82, 287.

62 *Den svenska mynthistorien* contains a complete catalogue of pictures of all types of coins from the Age of Liberty. See also Lagerqvist and others.

minor national coat of arms and the King's motto, for a long time in Latin but from 1771 onwards in Swedish.[63]

The Swedish-minted *riksdaler* was also relatively uniform. In the same way as that of the ducat, the obverse of the *riksdaler* bore a profile portrait of the monarch, while the reverse was adorned with the national coat of arms. Except for the coinage from 1748, the great national coat of arms was represented with the coat of arms of the Holstein-Gottorp dynasty in the inescutcheon. A number of memorial coins were also minted during the reign of Frederick. For instance, in the jubilee year of 1721 a coin was issued with portraits of Gustav I and Gustav II Adolf on the obverse in memory of the defence of liberty and religion; the juxtaposition with Frederick's image marked the continuity of the essential values of the realm. In connection with the 1727 session of the Riksdag and Frederick's journey to his hereditary land of Hesse in 1731, memorial coins were minted with the profiles of both the King and the Queen. This design accentuated the dynastic union along with the possibility of the Queen being reinstated as ruler (Figure 44).[64]

It is worth pointing out that during the reign of Ulrika Eleonora and throughout the entire reign of Frederick, the *riksdaler* (unlike the ducats) bore the King's motto in Swedish: 'God is my hope'. A return to Latin occurred during the reign of Adolf Frederick: *Salus publica, salus mea*, 'The public weal is my weal'.

As mentioned, the year 1748 stands out as the only year during Frederick's reign when the *riksdaler* was minted with the lesser national coat of arms. In the same year, the Royal Order of the Seraphim was created (or reinstated, as was said at the time); and the lesser national coat of arms was therefore encircled by the collar of the order.[65] From 1751 and for the rest of the century this usage was followed without exception, on both ducats and *riksdaler* coins. What this meant in practice – and this was certainly not an undesirable consequence for the rulers of the realm – was that

---

63 *Den svenska mynthistorien*, catalogue nos 4:1–2, 5:1–21; Lagerqvist and others, catalogue nos 341–43, 345–86, 432–59, 484.

64 *Den svenska mynthistorien*, catalogue nos 5:1–2, 4, 23–24, 27–28, 31; Lagerqvist and others, pp. 171–72, catalogue nos 390–91; Eva Wiséhn, *Mynt till ära och mine: Svenska jubileums- och minnesmynt* (Stockholm: Sveriges riksbank, 2005), pp. 10–11.

65 *Den svenska mynthistorien*, catalogue no. 5:33; Lagerqvist and others, catalogue no. 427.

Figure 44 Medal struck for the Reformation Jubilee in 1721 (top). Double *riksdaler* struck to commemorate Frederick's journey to Hesse in 1731 (bottom). The double *riksdaler* was struck with two different reverses. One bore a text in Latin (translation: 'Their glory shines around the world'); the other had the same ornamentation as the ordinary *riksdaler*, but bore the King's motto expressed in the plural. All three types of coins were struck by Johann Carl Hedlinger and were brought along to be distributed on Frederick's journeys. Engraving by Chretien de Mechel, 1786. Photo: Björn Green, KB.

the coat of arms of the royal family disappeared from the coins. The King was hence no longer portrayed as the representative of a dynasty but as a symbol of the entire kingdom. As was pointed out above, the same significant heraldic change was made at the coronations of Adolf Frederick and Louisa Ulrika. The dynastic inescutcheon would return during the reign of Charles XIV John, then as the unifying link in the coat of arms of the union between Sweden and Norway from 1814.

The coins of high denominations minted in the Baltic dependencies during the seventeenth-century had had the same obverse containing the king's portrait as the Swedish coins. In the German provinces, which were part of the Holy Roman Empire, the imperial double-headed eagle along with the emperor's name still appeared on the coins during the eighteenth century. The reverse was in all cases adorned with the relevant city's or province's coat of arms. For the disparate Swedish state formation of the seventeenth and eighteenth centuries, the king (feudal lord) was often the sole common denominator, while the provinces were in other respects governed according to their local privileges. During the greater part of the Age of Liberty, dependency coins were minted only in Wismar. Some minting was carried out in Stralsund during the Seven Years War. In this context it is worth noting that after Frederick's succession to the landgraviate of Hesse-Kassel in 1730, a special *Taler* was minted that was almost identical to the Swedish *riksdaler* and adorned with the great Swedish national coat of arms. Frederick was styled *D. G. REX SUECIAE*, but on the reverse his royal motto had been replaced by the text *HASSIÆ LANDGR.*[66] The royal title was personal and associated with great prestige, even when the prince did not rule as a king.

A special type of portrait coins intended directly for the people was the so-called largesse coins. These were tossed out to the people in connection with royal coronations and funerals as an expression of the wealth and generosity of the king. The largesse riders were usually carefully instructed to toss the coins in different directions in order to avoid creating turmoil. On these same occasions, medals were distributed to people of the higher orders. The largesse coins were minted in silver, and they had the monarch's portrait on one side and a Latin device on the other. Not until the coronation of Adolf Frederick was a king portrayed on a largesse coin wearing his crown and coronation costume. During the Age of Liberty, only two types of symbols occurred on the reverse: the North Star and a king's crown. To judge by the wear on these coins, largesse coins also circulated as a means of payment.[67]

About the portraits on the coins, it may be stated that they were of high quality and created by skilful craftsmen. Several coins were engraved by the Swiss Johann Carl Hedlinger, who was active in Sweden between 1718 and 1745 and who also completed several

---

66 Lagerqvist and others, pp. 174–75, 186–88, catalogue nos 430–31, 481–83. See also Wolfgang Böhm, 'Die hessischen Münzen des Landgrafen Friedrich (1730–1751): Eine Betrachtung über das Münzewesen in jener Zeit', in *Friedrich, König von Schweden, Landgraf von Hessen-Kassel: Studien zu Leben und Wirken eines umstrittenen Fürsten (1676–1751)*, ed. by Helmut Burmeister (Hofgeismar: Verein für hessische Geschichte und Landeskunde, 2003), pp. 309–42.

67 Tingström, pp. 224, 227–28. Instructions for the largesse riders can be found in the coronation rituals of Ulrika Eleonora and Frederick.

Swedish commissions after this period.[68] The baroque style characteristic of, for instance, the coins of Frederick I was employed
in the fashioning of typical royal portraits that had their origins
in Antiquity. The bust portraits of the King afford glimpses of
the classical attributes of rulers, the mantle and the antique suit
of armour. The coins of Adolf Frederick and Gustav III were
all adorned by bust portraits that were of course also based on
models from Antiquity. The exchange value represented by the
coins was ultimately guaranteed by the ruler: the right of minting
was a regality. The gold and silver coins, all of which bore the
King's image and had fixed denominations, presumably represented this purchasing power better than the banknotes and copper
coins that only had symbolic value. It would have been natural
to assume that the need for symbolic representation would have
increased as the difference grew between the value of the metal and
the nominal value of the currency. However, it would seem to have
been considered insulting to lend the king's countenance to the
smaller-denomination coins.

That the king's portrait or symbolic representation on the
coins could arouse emotions is clear from a couple of court cases
from the Age of Liberty. In 1731 Jonas Norlin, a tailor in Växjö,
refused to accept 'the King's coins' because he was annoyed with
Frederick's debauchery and bad qualities as a ruler. 'He said, to the
Devil with the King's money', and that although it was true that
he lacked money, he did not lack *his* (the King's) money.[69] In 1757
Johan Petter Råbock, a parish blacksmith, behaved in a similar
way but in the opposite direction. Paid in plate money embossed
with the monogram of Adolf Frederick in the corners, he kissed the
plate and said, with reference to the King, 'God bless you, for you
have many persecutors.'[70] To both Norlin and Råbock, the king's
coins immediately evoked associations with the head of state in
Stockholm.

---

68 Gunnar W. Lundberg, 'Medaljgravören Johann Carl Hedlinger', in
   Lundberg, *Svenskt och franskt*, pp. 72–79.
69 Justitierevisionen/Judicial Review Division, Besvärs- och ansökningsmål
   (utslagshandlingar)/Cases of appeal and application (adjudication documents), 27 April 1731, no. 44, RA ('Konungens Mynt' and 'Han sade att
   han gifer Konungens penningar fanen').
70 Justitierevisionen, Besvärs- och ansökningsmål, 20 July 1757, no. 37, RA
   ('Gud wälsigne dig, du har ock många förföljare').

Painted portraits

Reproductions of portrait engravings and popular prints have already been discussed. Another, more exclusive source of images was painted portraits. That these were not in the possession of common people does not mean that they were completely excluded from being seen by them. For example, the well-preserved town hall of Sigtuna, inaugurated in 1744, has painted portraits of Charles X Gustav, Charles XI, Charles XII, Frederick I and Hedvig Eleonora, all hung there in the time of Mayor Eric Kihlman, or by 1759. At the beginning of the nineteenth century, the collection was supplemented with portraits of Gustav I, Charles IX and Gustav II Adolf.[71] There are sure to have been similar examples in other places. Churches have also had royal portraits among their fixtures and furnishings. To give some random examples, the pulpit in the church of Åre is adorned with no fewer than four images of Charles XII;[72] and in the Ulrika Eleonora Church in Stockholm there is a magnificent portrait of Gustav II Adolf, copied from a work by Jacob Elbfas, which has been there at least since 1754. It would be possible to obtain a clearer idea of the existence and dissemination of painted portraits in older parish churches through catalogues and inventories; but the work would be time-consuming, and the results would still be uncertain. To sum up, portraits in churches or other public spaces – like the other types of images discussed here – do not seem to have been entirely uncommon, but neither were they the norm.

The painted portraits that figured in the above-mentioned official or semi-official contexts were all state portraits of a conventional kind, and in this respect they were no different from those hanging in palaces and manor houses. For this reason, their various types will be discussed in the section 'Images in polite society' below.

Reception

How, then, were these different images perceived? Because of the nature of the source material, the historian is rarely able to conduct generally valid reception analyses. A researcher is mostly restricted to using individual statements taken out of context, and

---

71 Gunnar Redelius, *Sigtuna rådshus: Byggnadsminne i Stockholms län* (Stockholm: Länsstyrelsen, 1997), pp. 11–12.
72 See image in Nodermann, *Från Altranstädt till Delsbo*, p. 31.

such statements are occasionally of a normative kind. When, in the speech quoted several times above, Carl Fredrik Adelcrantz emphasised the power of art over minds, he was of course pleading his own case. That does not necessarily mean that his perception was false. At best, differing statements can be verified in comparison to each other and thus lend greater weight to an utterance. In order to conduct a reasonably complete art-sociological reception analysis, one must consider the intentions of the sender, the dissemination and impact of the medium, and the perceptions and interpretations of the receiving target groups. This final element is usually the one that is most difficult to investigate; but if the two former components can be determined one may hope to come closer to a solution to the equation. In this context, no comprehensive analysis can be made of the circumstances, so I will only add a few marginal comments.

Of the visual media discussed above, some had an inherently limited capacity for dissemination while others could potentially reach large groups of people. Being unable to seek out their viewers, sculptures belonged to the former category, whereas coins belonged to the latter. That a possible capacity for dissemination was not the same as an actual one has already been discussed. However, it can be argued that media reserved for the few also helped reinforce more general perceptions. For instance, the impression made by a statue in Stockholm on the occasional visitor could arguably be conveyed orally and become part of a wider narrative about a king's character, against which ideas taken from other sources would be balanced. The American historian Theodore K. Rabb has maintained that the prestige of Louis XIV was scarcely increased by the allegorical imagery in all the fountains in the park at Versailles. But the mere fact that he had the resources to construct more fountains than any other ruler impressed people, and the magnificence of Versailles was easy to recount even though few subjects had seen its splendours with their own eyes.[73] The demonstrative

---

73 Thedore K. Rabb, 'Politics and the Arts in the Age of Christina', in *Politics and Culture in the Age of Christina: Acta from a Conference Held at the Wenner-Gren Center in Stockholm, 4–6 May 1995*, ed. by Marie-Louise Rodén, Suecoromana, 4 (Stockholm: Swedish Institute in Rome, 1997), pp. 9–22 (pp. 14–15). For a similar line of reasoning, see also Gérard Sabatier, 'Beneath the Ceilings of Versailles: Towards an Archaeology and Anthropology of the Use of the King's Signs during the Absolute Monarchy', in *Iconography, Propaganda, and Legitimation*, ed. by Allan Ellenius (Oxford: Clarendon Press, 1998), pp. 217–42.

opulence – that which is usually called conspicuous consumption – was more effective than the iconographic content. If this line of reasoning is accepted, it leads to the idea that it is not the impact of the individual medium that is decisive but the overall impression. The book historian Robert Darnton follows a similar line of reasoning about the forming of opinions. He rejects linear connections and direct explanations of causes; instead he sees the communications circuit as a network of intersecting and reciprocally operating circles. In ways that are difficult to specify, this network, taken altogether, creates something that may be called the spirit of the age (Darnton speaks of 'discourses').[74]

Although it cannot be proved that any particular medium shaped the popular image of the king, there is nevertheless reason to assume that most of his subjects had some form of visual conception of their monarch. However, one may assume that this was not always necessarily an image of the ruling King, and that it was frequently an image of royalty rather than of a royal subject. In the same way, an image of the good king as an ideal figure probably created a conception of the benevolent ruler (as a person), and vice versa. The memory of the great Gustav II Adolf or the heroic Charles XII might give rise to expectations of Frederick I.

In a survey of the estate inventories of 160 clergymen and clergymen's widows from a total of 114 parishes in the province of Västergötland between 1692 and 1760, one can see that royal portraits were not entirely uncommon in the property left by the deceased. While this survey cannot be used for statistical calculations, it nevertheless affords some idea of the existence of images. Kings and queens appear to have been among the most common topics; but there were also religious images, depictions of battles and portraits of particular individuals. It frequently transpires that the pictures were paintings; but sometimes one must assume that they were engravings. If a picture was framed, that fact was pointed out, because this circumstance considerably increased its value. The portraits were usually companion pieces showing both a king and a queen. The royals mentioned in the estate inventories are Charles X Gustav, Charles XI, Ulrika Eleonora the Elder, Charles XII, Ulrika Eleonora the Younger, Frederick I, Adolf

---

74 Robert Darnton, *The Forbidden Best-Sellers of Pre-Revolutionary France* (New York and London: Norton, [1995]), chapters 6–7.

Frederick and Louisa Ulrika. To this was added a 'Tabula cronologica or the reigns of the kings of Sweden', a list of rulers without
any images but with short biographical data on the monarchs of
Sweden from time immemorial and onwards.[75] Its value is given
as four *öre*, an insignificant sum. Simpler images, such as popular
prints, are not otherwise included in these inventories. One of the
larger collections of portraits was left after a death in Odensåker
in 1759:

> Half-length portraits of Their Royal Majesties our most gracious
> King and Queen with gilded frames – eight *daler*, one cabinet piece
> with our late King Frederick I and Queen Ulrika Eleonora – three
> *daler*, one ditto with our late King Charles XII. The Royal Gustavian
> family in plaster set off with silver work, black with glass in the
> form. The childhood of Prince Gustav, copper engraving covered
> with glass[.][76]

It is interesting to note that coins left in someone's estate were
specified. Thanks to the inclusion of this information, it can be
established that ducats and silver *riksdaler* coins seem to have been
of interest to collectors. An example is found in an estate inventory
from 1765, which lists a coin from 1638 that bore the image of
Queen Christina. Görtzian coins appeared in the collections as
well. This was a series of what were known as emergency coins
(*nödmynt*) in copper, issued between 1715 and 1719, which functioned as bonds without interest. The value of their metal content
was negligible, but the historical narrative they carried with them
made them interesting to collectors. Quite a few coronation and
funeral coins, some of them rather old, were also preserved.[77]

---

75 'Tabula cronologica eller Swea konungars regemente'; see image in Nordin,
   'Brevmålaren', p. 35.
76 Carl-Martin Bergstrand, *Ur västgötaprästers bouppteckningar från tiden
   före 1761* (Skövde: Skövde antikvariat, 1977), pp. 141–42, 172–75 ('Deras
   kungl. majestäters vår allernådigste konungs och drottningens bröstbilder
   med förgylte ramar – 8 daler, ett cabinetts stycke med högsalig konung
   Friedrich den förstes och drottning Ulrica Eleonoras – 3 daler, ett dito
   med högsalig konung Carl XII. Den kongelige Gustafiske familien i
   gips [avsatt] med silvererat arbete, svart med glas i formen. Prins Gustafs
   barndom, kopparstick med glas över'). Apart from three exceptions, all
   estate inventories are from the Age of Liberty.
77 *Ibid.*, pp. 74–77; Carl-Martin Bergstrand, *Ur västgötaprästers bouppteckningar från tiden 1761–1800* (Skövde: Skövde antikvariat, 1978), pp. 75–79.

It has already been mentioned that Frederick I liked to distribute silver coins as tokens of favour and when he stayed overnight in vicarages. These gift coins functioned almost as a kind of medal. One might also suspect that clergymen, through the collection box and the church treasury, had particular access to a good flow of coins that could be exchanged for regular coins and then preserved. For different reasons, the peasantry often had access to their local vicarage; and even though this assumption is founded on mere speculation, it is not unlikely that a country parson's displaying his little collection of coins and portraits was something that helped maintain his prestige in the local parish.

Some of the lines of reasoning above suggest that the images owned and displayed by the elite may also be worth analysing. In addition to the impressions given to their direct circle of consumers, these pictures conveyed mediated images to the common people. The portraits that hung in churches, in town halls and in other public environments, often simply executed and in a naïve style, were often created by some local master on the basis of a distinguished model.

Images in polite society

That the popular single-sheet prints reflected state portraiture has already been established. During the entire eighteenth century, however, these prints retained a static design while the art owned by the elite developed as fashions changed. Full- and half-length portraits retained forms that were similar to those of the previous century, while the most exalted image of the ruler, the *rex et imperator* of the equestrian portraits, disappeared from Swedish pictorial art during the Age of Liberty. At the same time, one can begin to discern a new type of portrait with a previously unprecedented intimacy. On the whole, however, this development, which adhered to international currents, belonged to the final decades of the eighteenth century and had its main impact during the Gustavian era. The royal portraits from the Age of Liberty continued a tradition rather than pointing forward.

The full-length images retained their representative character. Normally the kings, and more rarely the queens, were depicted in full royal splendour in this type of image – if not in their coronation costumes, then at any rate with royal attributes or with the subject posing in a symbolic context. A combination of the latter can be seen in the portrait of five-year-old Crown Prince Gustav (III),

Figure 45 Crown Prince Gustav (III) around 1751. The portrait, several copies of which exist, was painted to be displayed to the court of Denmark in connection with the Crown Prince's engagement to the Danish princess Sophia Magdalena. Oil painting by Gustaf Lundberg, his studio. Nationalmuseum, Stockholm (NMDrh 156).

Figure 46 Crown Prince Gustav (III) aged seven. Jacques Philippe
Bouchardon, statuette in polychrome terracotta, 1753. Photo: Erik
Cornelius, Nationalmuseum, Stockholm (NMSk 1625).

which was possibly a collaboration between Martin Scheffel and
Gustaf Lundberg (Figure 45).[78] In this portrait the prince wears the
same type of clothes as those he wore for a terracotta figurine by
Jacques Philippe Bouchardon a few years later. In the figurine, the
seven-year-old Prince has a fashionably unbuttoned waistcoat and
assumes a relaxed *contraposto* with his hat in one hand and the
other hand in his pocket (Figure 46). The statuette was produced
as a prop for a theatrical performance at court, and the royal
lineage of the little boy is indicated by his cuffs being trimmed with
ermine and his wearing the blue ribbon of the Royal Order of the
Seraphim. In the painted portrait, though, the status of the boy

---

78 Brown and Laine, pp. 123–24, 202.

could be indicated through other attributes. He is standing in front of a double column with a marshal's baton in one hand and the other hand pointing nonchalantly at the Temple of Glory. On the chair behind him hangs an ermine-trimmed mantle, and a globe and maps indicate predestined fame, possibly won through the martial virtues suggested by a cuirass lying on the floor. In an engraving with a similar composition, the Crown Prince seems to be about a year older. The attributes here are the same as in the painted portrait: a marshal's baton, pieces of armour, surveying instruments and an open book on fortifications (Figure 47). In this portrait of

Figure 47 Crown Prince Gustav (III). Engraving by Christian Fritsch after Johan Henrik Scheffel. Photo: Jens Gustafsson, KB.

Figure 48 'Le Prélude de la Gloire'. Queen Louisa Ulrika and the royal children: Crown Prince Gustav, Prince Frederick Adolf, and Prince Charles. Oil painting by Johan Pasch and Gustaf Lundberg, 1752. Photo: Hans Thorwid, Nationalmuseum, Stockholm (NMDrh 500).

a child, all the means used by baroque artists were employed to represent royalty in allegorical form.

Johan Pasch and Gustaf Lundberg's roughly contemporary painting of the Crown Prince together with the Queen and both of his younger brothers appears completely different, at least initially. At first sight, this painting appears to show a relaxed family scene with a mother supervising her three sons playing (Figure 48). On closer inspection, however, the references from more traditional representative pictorial art become obvious. Crown Prince Gustav is holding a firework in his hand like a baton while Prince Charles is posing with one arm in a classic field commander's pose with the other resting on a sheet of paper that could be a commander's map. Merit Laine has pointed out that the blue coats are a reference to Swedish army uniforms and were part of a well-established tradition at that time. The infant Frederick Adolf is too young to participate in the game in earnest, and he is instead made to function as a putto with his eyes and one of his hands directed towards Heaven in the time-honoured manner. The allegorical language in the depiction is enhanced by the statuesque pose of the Queen, which makes her appear as a bust rather than a person. Anyone who might happen to miss the allusions had them explained in more or less plain text in an accompanying verse entitled 'Le Prélude de la Gloire', or a prelude to glory.[79] Though this more informal picture contains poorly concealed symbolic information, it differs from an older type of royal family portrait in one essential respect: it lacks patent dynastic references (the succession to the throne followed the male line, and the King is absent in the picture). During the reign of Charles XI, David Klöcker Ehrenstrahl painted a series of royal family portraits in a tradition that was internationally well known but lacked domestic precursors. In part this can be explained in purely practical terms: because of the irregular Swedish line of monarchs, it had, since the Vasa era, rarely been possible to display a royal family that included several generations at one time. Nor had the succession to the throne, from the time of Eric XIV to that of Charles XI (or for exactly a century), been undisputedly handed down from father to son. Besides, Charles X Gustav had been the first of his dynasty, and he had met his son only once, just before his death, when the boy was a mere four years old. Consequently, there had not been a good foundation for painting dynastic family portraits.

This state of affairs changed with Charles XI and Ulrika Eleonora the Elder. Three of their seven children reached adulthood, and here were several consecutive generations that could be portrayed on one and the same occasion. In perhaps the best-known group portrait, from 1683, the picture is focused on Crown Prince Charles (XII), who is surrounded by his parents, the royal couple; his sister Hedvig Sophia; his grandmother Hedvig Eleonora; and the latter's sister-in-law Maria Euphrosyne (Figure 49). The originator of the dynasty, Charles X Gustav, watches over these figures from a painted portrait on the wall. Later, Ehrenstrahl also produced other similar pictures as the royal children grew older. Even more common were group portraits with only the royal children, their dead siblings hovering in the air as angels.[80]

79 Marie-Christine Skuncke, *Gustaf III – Det offentliga barnet: En prins retoriska och politiska fostran* (Stockholm: Atlantis, 1993), p. 106; *Catherine the Great & Gustav III*, catalogue no. 20; Brown and Laine, pp. 116–20.
80 Allan Ellenius, *Karolinska bildidéer*, Ars Suetica, I (Uppsala: Almqvist & Wiksell, 1966), esp. pp. 90–111.

Figure 49 Three generations of the Palatinate dynasty: the dynasty founder
Charles X Gustav in the portrait oval; Charles XI standing; and Crown
Prince Charles (XII) at the centre between his mother, paternal grand-
mother, elder sister, and paternal aunt. Oil painting by David Klöcker
Ehrenstrahl, 1683. Nationalmuseum, Stockholm (NMGrh 1365).

Because the domestic situation at the beginning of the 1750s
was similar to that of the 1680s, with the succession again secured
through native-born heirs, one might imagine that this aspect would
be emphasised in the pictorial art; after all, the succession to the
throne was of as great interest to the royal family as to their subjects.[81]

---

81 After half a century with childless monarchs the throne had been con-
solidated above all expectation and almost in excess of the wishes of the

But at the middle of the eighteenth century, this simple demonstration of continuity across generations had begun to matter less. At this time, royal portraiture was shifting in the same direction all across Europe. Persons of standing were increasingly often portrayed in relaxed, informal and casual poses. This was especially true of family portraits. While the official full- or half-length state portraits did remain, royal family portraits were painted almost exclusively in an intimate style. The historian Simon Schama has spoken of 'the domestication of majesty'.[82] This style was not fully developed in Sweden until the Gustavian era; well-known examples of different kinds and varying degrees of intimacy are the interior piece *Konversation på Drottningholm* ('Conversation at Drottningholm') by Pehr Hilleström the Elder, the line etching of the royal family in the Pillared Hall (*Pelarsalen*) at Stockholm Palace by Johan Fredrik Martin (Figure 50) and the portrait of Gustav (IV) Adolf on a rocking horse by Carl Fredrik von Breda.[83]

It is almost impossible to make a comprehensive inventory of royal portrait paintings intended for public environments and upper-class circles. However, the collections of the Swedish Portrait Archive provide a good idea of the types of images that were common at the time.[84] On the basis of these collections, the regular

---

subjects, the young student John Jennings declared in a celebratory speech. They now had 'as many princes to put on the throne as we count crowns in the ancient coat of arms of the realm'; John Jennings, *Undersåtelig fägnad, wid Hans Kongl. Maj:ts Friederich, 1. Swea, Göthes och Wendes konungs &c. &c. &c. födelse-dag betygad wid kongl. academien i Upsala den 17. april MDCCXLIX* (Stockholm: Lars Salvius, 1749), p. 5.

82 Simon Schama, 'The Domestication of Majesty: Royal Family Portraiture, 1500–1850', *Journal of Interdisciplinary History*, 17 (1986), 155–83.

83 *Solen och Nordstjärnan: Frankrike och Sverige på 1700-talet*, Nationalmusei utställningskatalog, 568 (Höganäs: Bra Böcker, Wiken; Stockholm: Nationalmuseum, 1993), catalogue no. 625; *Catherine the Great & Gustav III*, p. 252, catalogue no. 224.

84 The observations below are based on a survey of the collections of the Svenska porträttarkivet/Swedish Portrait Archive (SPA) in the Nationalmuseum, regarding Ulrika Eleonora the Elder and Frederick I, Adolf Frederick and Louisa Ulrika, Gustav III and Sophia Magdalena, and the royal children Charles, Frederick Adolf and Sophia Albertina. This means that a total of c. 1,400 pictures has been studied. Among these many are of course doubles, copies and variants of the same topic, and no attempt has been made to quantify the images or classify them according to type. However, the inventory provides a good picture of the production of royal portraits overall during the period in question.

Figure 50 The royal family in the Pillared Hall in the Royal Palace, Stockholm. An example of the increasingly informal pictures of royal persons that are particularly connected to the Gustavian era. Line etching by Johan Fredrik Martin. Photo: Jens Gustafsson, KB.

portraits of kings and queens may be divided into double and single portraits, full- and half-length portraits, and busts and heads. The royals could be depicted in civilian or military clothes, historical dress or coronation attire. Though the material does not allow for an analysis of representativeness and dissemination, some general reflections on the development of the genre may be supplied.

The full-length portraits were reserved for state paintings where the king or queen was depicted in full royal splendour and with the crown regalia present. The ermine-trimmed royal mantle was always in evidence. The queens were dressed in expensive garments, preferably their coronation clothes, while the kings could wear their coronation costume, a military uniform, or armour. In a category below the full-length state portraits were the half-length and three-quarter-length portraits (depicting the sitter down to his or her knees, hips or waist). Sitters were often depicted in their official positions in their coronation attire, uniforms or armour. After 1748, they might also be shown in the dress of an order. However, the regalia were not always present in these pictures, even though this was a common occurrence. The kings were often depicted holding a commander's baton. Finally there were the head-and-shoulders portraits. It was more common for these to depict kings rather than queens, and in spite of the limited space the status of the sitter was indicated by the glimpse of a cuirass and perhaps the tip of a mantle. There were also portrait medallions showing the king in profile, wearing antique armour. These were closely related to the images on coins.

During the time of Frederick I and Ulrika Eleonora, all royal portraits were executed in a fairly formal style. Since they had no children, there were no family portraits; but one preserved painting borders on this genre. The King is depicted standing between the Queen and his sister Sophie Charlotte, Princess of Hesse. The picture was painted by David Kock around 1727 and is known to exist in two versions, one full-length portrait and one three-quarters portrait (Figure 51). This particular painting is a relatively

Figure 51 King Frederick I with his sister Sophia Charlotta Karolina on his left and Queen Ulrika Eleonora the Younger on his right. Oil painting by David Kock, 1727, copy after Georg Engelhardt Schröder. Nationalmuseum, Stockholm (NMGrh 1395).

relaxed depiction which does not display any symbols of rulership, but the ermine trimming of the ladies' mantles and the King's coat nevertheless reveals their exalted birth.

Generally speaking, there were no great changes in portraiture during the reign of Adolf Frederick and Louisa Ulrika. The portraits can be divided into the same types as before. One addition was that the King was almost without exception depicted with the insignia of the Royal Order of the Seraphim. In the full-length portraits with the King in his coronation robes, he wore the great collar of the order; in the half-length pictures, dressed in uniform or civilian clothes, he instead wore the blue silk ribbon, sometimes also the badge of the order. On a single occasion, the Queen figured in a previously unknown type of portrait of a more informal character. This is the half-length portrait of Louisa Ulrika by Antoine Pesne, where she holds a masquerade mask in her right hand, which she at the same time rests on the back of an armchair. It is impossible to mistake this for anything other than a portrait of a noble lady, but there is nothing in the painting that reveals her royal birth. This anomaly is accounted for by the fact that Pesne was a Prussian court painter, and that the picture was painted before Louisa Ulrika became the Swedish Crown Princess. Even so, it has been disseminated in several replicas in Sweden, too, and for this reason it has contributed to the visual representation of the monarchs of the Age of Liberty. To avoid misunderstandings, however, a crown placed on a cushion has been added in the background of these copies (Figure 52).

Another famous type of portrait was completed in 1745 by François-Adrien Grasognon de Latinville, representing the future queen as Aurora. This painting was commissioned by Carl Gustaf Tessin in Paris and is known through several copies and engravings (Figure 53). Even though Louisa Ulrika wears rather casual attire of a classical style, her mantle adorned with crowns reveals her status. The mythological style belongs to an international tradition, and Merit Laine has compared this portrait to the princely apotheoses of the baroque age.[85] The future queen's relaxed posture also demonstrates a kinship with the more informal eighteenth-century royal portraits in a form that was used primarily to depict women of royal birth. Allusions to the many portraits of the daughters

---

85 Merit Laine, 'En Minerva för vår Nord': Lovisa Ulrika som samlare, uppdragsgivare och byggherre (Stockholm: M. Laine, 1998), pp. 18–19.

Figure 52 Louisa Ulrika as a Prussian princess. The copy was executed after her arrival in Sweden, as is seen from the added presence of the crown in the background. Oil painting by Antoine Pesne, his studio. Nationalmuseum, Stockholm (NMGrh 658).

Figure 53 Crown Princess Louisa Ulrika as Aurora, goddess of the dawn. Engraving by René Gaillard after a painting by François-Adrien Grasognon de Latinville. Photo: Jens Gustafsson, KB.

of Louis XV by Jean-Marc Nattier come readily to mind. An additional type of image that stands out from the multitude was produced by Gustaf Lundberg and copied by several other masters. It is a head-and-shoulders portrait where the Queen is depicted in full profile, something that was usually reserved for coins and medals, and was uncommon in portraits in oil or pastel.[86]

During the latter part of the Age of Liberty, there were princes and a princess to portray for the first time in half a century. With the exception of the successor to the throne, they were never depicted in full-length portraits. In rare cases, these portraits lacked all royal attributes. This was particularly the case with respect to Princess Sophia Albertina, and Her Royal Highness could not be distinguished from a regular upper-class person. In addition, there is a childhood portrait where a perhaps three-year-old Crown Prince Gustav has been depicted completely informally together with a lambkin.[87] Apart from this picture (in which the identification of the sitter is not entirely certain), all pictures of the Crown Prince contain at least some attribute to indicate his status.

During the reign of Gustav III, there was much greater variety among the royal portraits. From his time there are different types of genre and background pieces, state portraits and informal depictions in highly varying forms. Backgrounds may be anything from battlefields to drawing-rooms and theatre stages. However, this variety of images is a phenomenon seen only after the coup d'état of 1772; it therefore falls outside the scope of the present investigation. At the same time, it must be emphasised that even if the range of types had increased, the King continued to be portrayed as elevated above the people around him in these new image categories as well. No room for doubt was left regarding who was the main character of the representation; nor can this ever be the intention with a royal picture, in which the presence of the monarch is what creates the occasion and lends distinction even to the most insignificant event.

In summary, the royal portraits of the Age of Liberty may be said to have been of an exclusively representative character. The style could vary from the regular full-length state portraits

---

86 E.g. Grh 2305, Drh 52, SPA 1937:861. There is also a naïve portrait of
    Gustav III in profile done in oil by Jonas Åkerström of the province of
    Hälsingland in 1779; SPA 1997:345–46.
87 SPA 1920:2152.

with the regalia to head-and-shoulders images which nevertheless signalled royal eminence thanks to their details. At first sight it may seem as though the queens were often portrayed in a more informal style than the kings. On closer inspection, however, there is a natural explanation for this perceived dissimilarity. With respect to a ruling person, be they king or queen, no room for doubt was left regarding the sitter's royal status. For non-ruling queens, and even more so for princes and princesses, the royal attributes could to some extent be pushed into the background. Even in these cases, though, it was rare for them to be completely absent; the exceptions are primarily Sophia Albertina, and in some cases the Dukes Charles and Frederick Adolf. Although the secluded and intimate life at court was embraced as an ideal by rulers contemporaneous with Adolf Frederick and Louisa Ulrika, this development had no impact on royal portraiture in Sweden. This state of things was entirely in line with the symbolic role played by the royal family, where representativeness was the main issue. As the executive royal authority became ever more redundant, its symbolic functions appeared to be all the more important.

5

Public opinion on politics

In March 1745, at the very middle of the Age of Liberty, a comprehensive hearing was held at the Svea Court of Appeal regarding a sensitive crime of lese-majesty. His Royal Majesty had ordered the Court of Appeal to 'hear and pass judgement on this case with the utmost speed, and handle it in the greatest secrecy'.[1] The in-camera hearing at the Court of Appeal therefore only took place in the presence of the secretary, the attorney counsel (*advokatfiskal*) and the recording clerk. This case demonstrates the dilemma that crimes of lese-majesty often involved for the people governing the kingdom: on the one hand, the criminal had to be duly reprimanded; on the other, the authorities wanted at all costs to avoid giving publicity to the crime itself. In order to retain secrecy, the accused – who did not know the charges in advance – was taken from the place of detention in the town-hall guard-house to the more secure city guard-house in Castenhof at Norrmalmstorg, and was prohibited from receiving visitors.

The case concerned Johan Åman, Finnish master of the wine transporters' guild in Stockholm, who had hurled vicious assertions in Finnish against the King and the successor to the throne. According to the translation in the minutes of the Court of Appeal, Åman had made the following, highly injurious statement:

> Things will never go well as long as Germans are kings of Sweden; German dogs have come here to eat the Swedish Crown; surely there

---

1 His Royal Majesty, 14 February 1745, quoted in the extract from the minutes of Svea Court of Appeal of 12 March 1745, in Justitierevisionen/ Judicial Review Division, Besvärs- och ansökningsmål (utslagshandlingar)/ Cases of appeal and application (adjudication documents), March 1745, nos 41–45, RA ('skyndsammast ransaka och döma, samt thenna sak med all tysthet handtera').

is someone under the Crown of Sweden who can give them a bullet in the side.[2]

According to the investigation, the most immediate reason for Åman's outburst had been the fact that the son of a burghership-holding citizen had been recruited to the royal life guards, in violation of the city's privileges. The pronouncement had been made in the afternoon and in a state of sobriety, and three unanimous witnesses, all of whom were Finnish speakers, made the presentation of evidence rather simple. Åman had incited his listeners to murder of the king and the successor to the throne, and for this crime the death penalty was prescribed, according to chapter 5, section 1 of the Misdeeds Code (*Missgärningsbalken*):

> Anyone who injuriously speaks, or writes, anything against the King, or the Queen, or the person who has been declared the Successor to the Government; shall be beheaded.[3]

Because the negotiations were held in camera, Åman's request for a lawyer was rejected. Even so, Åman tried to defend himself during the trial by denying the alleged utterance. According to his own story, his words had referred to a German journeyman tobacco-spinner and not the 'German government' ('Tyska Regeringen'). Furthermore, Åman claimed that the witnesses were prejudiced, and in addition he lodged, together with his wife, a counter-complaint against the informer, one Lieutenant Paul Silvius. Åman's wife could report that on an earlier occasion, Silvius himself had made dubious statements about the judicial system and the government. He had cursed his service under the Crown and, a newly sharpened sword in hand, claimed that he wanted to administer his own justice. This narrative did not receive wholehearted support from the witnesses that were produced, but on the other hand Silvius did not dare to deny the accusation under oath.

---

2 Extract from the minutes of Svea Court of Appeal of 12 March 1745, in Justitierevisionen, Besvärs- och ansökningsmål (utslagshandlingar), March 1745, nos 41–45, RA ('Thet går aldrig wäl, så länge Tyskar är Konungar i Swerige; Tyska hundar hafwa kommit hit at äta Swenska Kronan; det finnes wäl någon under Sweriges Krona, som kan gifwa dem en Kula i sidan').

3 *Sveriges rikes lag gillad och antagen på riksdagen år 1734*, reprint of the 1780 edn, Rättshistoriskt bibliotek, I:37 (Stockholm: Institutet för rättsh-istorisk forskning, 1984), p. 130 ('Hvar som lasteliga talar, eller skrifver, något emot Konungen, eller Drottningen, eller then, som til Efterträdare i Regementet förklarad är; varde halshuggen').

In Åman's case the evidence was overwhelming. It is worth observing that the Court of Appeal in its assessment took the position and the intent of the accused into account. The Court of Appeal evaluated not merely the injurious words, but also the degree of seriousness behind them. In addition, it was an aggravating circumstance that Åman had uttered opinions about a royal command. In other words, he had interfered in the affairs of the Magistracy; and in reality, all negative opinions on government matters were considered inappropriate. In theory, the decisions of the Magistracy were infallible, and consequently the critical opinion of an individual subject must have been caused by a lack of knowledge of the actual state of affairs. But the fact that something had been done through ignorance was also, as in Åman's case, a mitigating circumstance. In addition, the Court of Appeal assumed that Åman had had no real intention to commit murder. Since there had been no intent, he was able to escape the death penalty. For this reason it was only the opprobrious content that had to be assessed, but then again, this was also especially grave. It was so grave that the Court of Appeal wished to expunge the words from the actual records, so that the rest of the world and posterity would not learn of them.

In other words, the seriousness of this matter was not that it concerned a plot against the King's person, but that the King had been verbally disparaged. In this respect, the wider the dissemination of the utterance, the more heinous the crime. It was considered a mitigating circumstance that the insults had been spoken in private, and now the greater risk was that the judicial decision would provide publicity for the content. Several of the members of the Court of Appeal returned to this aspect when the possible punishment was discussed. The most exhaustive opinion came from Associate Judge David Hollsten, who, among other things, felt that

> from the actual *ordine imperandi et parendi* [order between commander and subordinate], on which a well-functioning government depends, and the associated *sanctitate imperii civilis* [inviolability of the civil government], follows the incontrovertible obligation that the subjects should have an unadulterated respect and reverence for their exalted Magistracy, and that any insult to this, in word or in deed, should be severely punished.[4]

---

4 Extract from the minutes of Svea Court of Appeal, 27 February 1745, in Justitierevisionen, Besvärs- och ansökningsmål (utslagshandlingar), March 1745, nos 41–45, RA ('af sielfwa ordine imperandi et parendi, hwarpå ett

Utterances of the kind Åman had made thus threatened to overthrow the entire social order, and the crime was unquestionably so serious that it warranted severe corporal punishment, the court reasoned. The problem for the Court of Appeal was that corporal punishment was in equal measure a punishment and a general deterrent, and in the latter case the nature of the deed had to be made public. Nor was it possible to keep the judgement secret, because so many witnesses were familiar with Åman's pronouncements. The assistant judge Johan August Grevesmöhlen had misgivings about a 'public punishment, through which the general public might be induced to make a curious enquiry about such a serious crime, which for good reason one might wish to conceal'.[5]

His Royal Majesty and the Judicial Review Division realised the predicament, and decided instead to impose a sentence of three weeks' imprisonment on bread and water followed by hard labour for an indefinite period. The directions of the Judicial Review Division regarding the records and other documents in the case are also interesting. These were to be kept under the seal of the president and all the members of the Court of Appeal, with the instruction that it might be opened only on the gracious command of His Royal Majesty.[6]

Lieutenant Silvius was also considered to be obviously guilty of his reprehensible acts, but at the same time he was the one who had reported Åman's serious crime. Because he had demonstrated civic zeal by so doing, it might seem too dishonourable to mention him together with a person sentenced to capital punishment

wälbestält Regemente beror, samt then thermed förknippade sanctitate imperii civilis then skyldigheten owedersäjeligen följer, at Undersåtare böra hafwa för sin höga Öfwerhet en oförkränkt wördnad och högaktning, samt at alt förolämpande, som theremot skier med ord eller giärning, alfwarsamt straffas bör'). In British case law, written insults were judged more harshly than oral ones, while the opposite was true in Russia, where literacy was low; Angela Rustemeyer, *Dissens und Ehre: Majestätsverbrechen in Russland (1600–1800)*, Forschungen zur osteuropäischen Geschichte, 69 (Wiesbaden: Harrasowitz, 2006), p. 98.

5 Extract from the minutes of Svea Court of Appeal, 27 February 1745, in Justitierevisionen, Besvärs- och ansökningsmål (utslagshandlingar), March 1745, nos 41–45, RA ('publiqvt straff, hwarigenom menigheten torde upwäckas til någon nyfiken efterfrågan om ett så groft brott, som man med skiäl önskade måtte kunna förtigas').

6 Registry of the Judicial Review Division, 17 April 1745, fols 124ᵛ–127ʳ, RA.

(the original judicial decision was always announced before any possible reprieve). For this reason the Court of Appeal recommended that separate judicial decisions be issued, and that Silvius should be declared exempt from punishment because of mitigating circumstances. This was approved by His Royal Majesty.[7]

The Åman case was in no way unique. On the contrary, it exhibits several typical characteristics of what crimes of lese-majesty looked like and how they were handled judicially. Åman had been provoked by a Magistracy decision he had perceived as unjust. This had occasioned a grave and sweeping accusation against the one perceived to be responsible, namely the King. A large part of the judicial proceedings was taken up by the attempts of the accused to invalidate the testimonies with a kind of whataboutism. The Court of Appeal also reasoned in a typical fashion. The crime was serious, the punishment had to be severe, and secrecy must necessarily be maintained. The mitigating circumstances eliminated the death penalty, though, and instead Åman was sentenced to three weeks of starvation followed by hard labour for an indefinite time. The punishment on this occasion turned out to be ten months, and after his wife's application for mercy Åman was able to return to her and their five children in February 1746.[8]

In spite of, or perhaps because of, the case being a conventional one in several ways, it raises questions about what ordinary people felt, thought and said about the royal authority. How was this kind of crude utterance perceived, and was it common for people to ascribe political responsibility to the King even for minor matters? In addition, it raises questions about the view that the people in power had of the royal authority. Why was an at bottom imprudent tirade considered a serious crime by the courts? In this chapter, the crimes of lese-majesty against which legal proceedings were conducted during the Age of Liberty will provide the basis of the analysis. Even so, the focus is not on the crimes or the judicial proceedings in themselves, but on the attitudes and popular ideas about the royal authority that can be deduced from the frequently detailed records of the hearings.

---

7 Svea Court of Appeal to His Royal Majesty, 3 April 1745, in the Justitierevisionen, Besvärs- och ansökningsmål (utslagshandlingar), March 1745, nos 41–45, RA; Registry of the Judicial Review Division, 17 April 1745, fols 124^v–127^r, RA.

8 Registry of the Judicial Review Division, 13 February 1746, fols 121^v–122^v, RA.

Court documents as a source of popular attitudes

The people's loyalty to the king in earlier times is something that is regularly taken for granted by scholars. For the peasantry, a strong royal authority was their primary safeguard against the power of the lords, which was seen as a threatening alternative; and the alliance between king and people was important during the two constitutional revolutions that bestowed absolute power on Charles XI and Gustav III, respectively. 'Rather one master than a hundred' is believed to have been the pithy constitutional principle that guided the peasantry in the early modern age. The invocation was not new; it can be traced through the history of Europe all the way back to Homer:

> No good thing is a multitude of lords; let there be one lord, one king, to whom the son of crooked-counseling Cronos has given the scepter and judgments, so that he may take counsel for his people.[9]

The idea of the people's profound loyalty to the king is axiomatic in Swedish historical research – axiomatic, reasonable and uncon-firmed. Few studies of popular opinion have been conducted other than at a general level. There is no reason to question the basic perception; but from a scholarly point of view, it is unsatisfactory to base central conclusions on unfounded assump-tions. An in-depth investigation of the attitudes of the common people to politics, ideology and the royal authority may also reveal nuances that enrich our understanding of the past. All too often the peasantry is described as a homogeneous group with a uniform conception the world. But there were varying percep-tions within this group as well, from people who were unfamiliar with or indifferent to political affairs to those who took an active

---

9 *The Iliad*, 2:202–05, in A. T. Murray's revised translation from 1924: Homer, *Iliad, Books 1–12*, trans. by A. T. Murray, rev. by William F. Wyatt, Loeb Classical Library, 170 (Cambridge, MA: Harvard University Press, 1999), p. 77. The son of Cronos was Zeus. With respect to the other things discussed in this paragraph, see Karin Sennefelt, *Den politiska sjukan: Dalupproret 1743 och frihetstida politisk kultur* (Hedemora: Gidlunds, 2001), pp. 54–55, 60–63. Cf. David Martin Luebke, *His Majesty's Rebels: Communities, Factions, and Rural Revolt in the Black Forest, 1725–1745* (Ithaca and London: Cornell University Press, 1997), pp. 163–67, by which Sennefelt, too, was inspired.

interest in politics and who possessed considered and well-informed points of view.[10]

In this chapter, attention will be focused on popular attitudes towards and sentiments concerning the royal authority. What ideas about and expectations of the king did the subjects have? It was against the background of these perceptions and dispositions that the rulers were obliged to shape the formation of public opinion that was tested in manifestations, propaganda and proclamations. As we have seen, the official rhetoric maintained the chimera of an executive royal authority. The question is whether this description had any real impact. In the relationship between the royal authority and the power of the lords, two issues in particular are crucial: (1) whether responsibility for policy was ascribed to the King or whether others (the lords) were believed to govern the kingdom in his stead, and (2) whether, supposing that the latter case applied, people believed that policy would be pursued better or worse with a strengthened royal authority.

His Royal Majesty was considered to be a power resource that the Council was compelled to control: without royal sanction, its decisions lacked the required legitimacy. Besides, all political decrees were issued in the name of the king. The issue of how successfully this was conveyed is therefore of central importance to the analysis presented in this book. Did the King appear as a ruler to his subjects, and was the Council successful in maintaining the illusion of the King as the actual ruler of the kingdom?

These problems have not been thoroughly analysed in research. To some extent, this is due to a difficult situation with respect to the source material; but lack of interest is a significant factor, too. Even though there is a dearth of sources in which the voices of the common people can be heard, such investigations may still be productive. In her doctoral thesis Den politiska sjukan ('A Political Affliction'), Karin Sennefelt has reconstructed the peasants' political world of ideas by studying material from the legal commission set up following the great Dalecarlian rebellion of 1743. A systematic study of the material that the Peasant Estate produced during their work in the Riksdag would almost certainly also be very fruitful. In the present study, however, the supporting documents have been

10 Cf. Linda Oja and Karin Sennefelt, 'En ny historia varifrån? Om perspektivvalet i forskning om tidigmodern tid', Historisk tidskrift, 126 (2006), 803–10.

limited to another, in this context disregarded, series of sources: court proceedings concerning crimes of lese-majesty.

Among social historians, court documents have long been used to study everyday circumstances in the past. In spite of the fact that the situation in court may be exceptional in itself, the detailed hearings in many cases provide a great amount of information about ideas, notions and circumstances that historians cannot access in any other way. Because this information is often secondary to the main issue that was being tried legally, it is usually deemed to constitute reliable source material. The hearings for crimes of lese-majesty have turned out to be an exceptional source for identifying ideas about and expectations towards the royal authority harboured by broad groups in the population whose voices are not heard in other sources. The material has the advantage of including all social classes, from nobles and high officials to peasants and journeymen. What is most interesting is hearing the voices of those whom I have indeterminately called 'common people', among whom are included peasants and soldiers, maids and farmhands, apprentices, innkeepers and wives – in short, many of the people who were excluded from the political transactions and whose voices were not normally heard in any other way. Though the material that the analysis draws on includes an unusual wealth of statements from such ordinary people, it does not allow for statistical pronouncements or an in-depth study of opinions on the basis of class. The investigation will, however, provide a sample of attitudes and ideas that were prevalent among the masses. In this way I will show that ordinary subjects were in no way a homogeneous mass with uniform attitudes on political issues. On the other hand, certain ideas will recur so often that they must be said to have been generally prevalent.

Even though the social range in the material is wide, there are other reasons why the crime of lese-majesty may cause difficulties from the point of view of representativeness. The circumstances are not necessarily commonplace, and critical voices may be expected to be overrepresented. However, my assessment is that these problems are relatively minor in this context. First of all, the nature of the around 250 investigated cases is extremely varied, and they provide both recurring and trivial cases as well as singular and highly exceptional ones. There are certain clear patterns in the material, something that also makes the deviations stand out. The detailed hearings often allowed opposite views to be heard in the same case; after all, informers and witnesses tended to have different opinions regarding the circumstances of the crime from those of the accused. In addition, crimes of lese-majesty were intrinsically equivocal at this time. With support from international research, it has been pointed out that the 'naïve monarchism' of the peasantry was in many cases a well-thought-through strategy for putting forward oppositional ideas with a reduced risk of suffering any consequences.[11] Under the guise of simplicity, common people might refer to the officially expressed will of the king, which did not always correspond with the actual policies of the state authority. With reference to the ignorance of the peasantry, confidence could thus be placed in the prince without this being perceived as culpable; even if power was shared, it nevertheless officially lay in the hands of the king even during the Age of Liberty. In theory, this view is correct; and several examples in the following investigation seem to support it. It should be pointed out that the constitutional situation during the Age of Liberty meant that crimes of lese-majesty could equally well be crimes *for* the majesty as *against* it. On many occasions, the accused persons must be described as royalists rather than as opponents of the royal authority. Still, the fear of absolutism meant that a pleading of ignorance was hardly accepted for actions that could be perceived as plots against the Instrument of Government.

The gaps in the material constitute a greater problem. Because the crime of lese-majesty was a crime against the state with potentially sensitive consequences, it required tactful handling. The hearings often took place in camera, and even at the time these parts of the court records were weeded out in order to minimise the risk of the improprieties becoming public knowledge. As a result, the published reasons for the judicial decisions contained only a general reference to the crime without stating its nature in detail; it is therefore frequently impossible to reconstruct individual offences. Nevertheless, enough records have been preserved for it to be possible to form a good picture of the nature of this type of felony and how it was dealt with during the period. No wholly consistent systematic method can be discerned in the principles for weeding out material from the records. The sentences give no indication of whether it was only particularly severe crimes that were deleted from the court documentation. On the contrary, the records regarding serious misdeeds have sometimes been preserved

---

11 Sennefelt, *Den politiska sjukan*, p. 60.

precisely because the Judicial Review Division expected appeals or other continued processing of such cases.

The focus in this chapter is on popular ideas of the royal authority, not on the crimes of lese-majesty in themselves. The court documents are the means, not the end. My ambition is to shine a light on the attitudes that appear in the material with respect to certain themes. The judicial processing is thus not the primary issue in the analysis, although it will be discernible in many places. The relationship between the defendant and the officers of the court expresses the dynamics between the defenders of the system and its critics in its own way, and this relationship can therefore in many cases be seen as an exponent of various ideas about the form of government. However, the crime of lese-majesty as such will be given some attention at the end of the next chapter. After all, the judicial authorities' assessments of lese-majesty crimes also say something about the significance and nature of the royal authority in the society of the time. Court documents form the systematic basis as source material for this analysis, but wherever possible, or where it has been deemed appropriate, the investigation will be complemented with other suitable material.

My ambition has been to access the mentality and opinions of the common people as far as possible. One cannot expect to find a consistent and uniform popular attitude: no such uniform world view existed. Instead, we will see a variety of different thoughts, perceptions and ideas which, taken together, supply a range of ordinary people's political perceptions. Which of these dominated and which were peripheral is impossible to determine on the basis of the present investigation.

The German historian Reinhart Koselleck has emphasised that while sources cannot tell the researcher what to say, they prevent us from saying certain things. Koselleck speaks of the sources' power of veto. What makes history history cannot be found in the sources alone: a theory is required to make the sources speak at all.[12] The study of monarchy on the basis of content, mediation and opinions has been an attempt to organise the impressions gained from the investigations underpinning this book. In reality, people's thoughts do not exist on different levels, and thought patterns do

---

12 Reinhart Koselleck, 'Standortbindung und Zeitlichkeit: Ein Beitrag zur historiographischen Erschließung der geschichtlichen Welt', in *Vergangene Zukunft* (Frankfurt am Main: Suhrkamp, 1979), pp. 176–207 (p. 206).

not fit themselves into different layers: they form a wholeness which
is made consistent by each individual through continual dynamic
re-examination. The ensuing section focuses on the emotions and
attitudes that existed regarding the royal authority. I will not
present a uniform picture, and for completely natural reasons there
will be many variations and contradictions. Even so, the opinions
should correspond to the ethos that has been elucidated in previous
sections. After all, this ethos has been defined as a form of master
ideology, so it should be possible to accommodate various attitudes
and differences of opinion within its framework (alternatively, we
are witnessing a revolutionary change of opinion, a paradigm shift).

A historical investigation like this one is never written in a rec-
tilinear fashion, but in a dynamic dialogue between section and
chapter. Questions and answers are formulated and reformulated,
and what eventually (one hopes) becomes a convincing or at least
plausible narrative has been subjected to examination and re-
examination. This has been the case when the images of the royal
authority's ethos and popular perceptions of it have been fused:
they have had to be adjusted now and then in order to correspond
with one another. My understanding of the monarchism of the
common people will emerge in the following pages.

King and people

The royal family was evidently a recurring point of reference that
was present in the everyday lives of the people. The yeoman Jon
Jönsson averred that he harboured a great and humble love and
reverence for the exalted Magistracy, which he included every
day in his prayers.[13] Drinking the King's toast was also common

---

13 Case of appeal and application, 1750.XII.12/A10. Because of the large
number of documents cited, the cases of appeal and application and the
adjudication documents of the Judicial Review Division, RA, are cited with
only the date (in the form: year.month.day) followed by the case number for
the month in question. The reference in this footnote should in other words
be read as Case of appeal and application, 12 December 1750, no. A10,
Justitierevisionen/Judicial Review Division, RA. Military offences were
reported to His Royal Majesty (the Judicial Review Division) by way of
the Judge Advocate General (*generalauditören*). These cases normally have
no case numbers and are here referred to with 'GA' after the date. In most
cases reference is made only to the case file as a whole. The comprehensive
examination of the material means that it has not been practicable to state

at everyday gatherings. For Maria Meisner, a burgher wife in the Södermalm district of Stockholm, it seems to have been habitual behaviour to say a blessing for the King and the recently widowed Queen Dowager when opening her windows to a view over Stockholm and the Royal Palace.[14] Such daily intercessions and formulaic blessings appear to have been natural, and they were said without deeper reflection. They were part of an internalised cultural pattern where a respect for God and the Magistracy was a basic constituent.

People could also experience great joy at seeing the King or the royal couple in real life. When the Crown Prince left Karlskrona following an inspection tour in 1749, a woman called Smed-Maja ('Smithy-Maja') called down God's blessing on him and was seconded by the people around her. In 1751 Sergeant Johan Ljunggren told his friends that he had just seen the King ride across Riddarhustorget, and described the delight he felt every time he had the good fortune to see His Royal Majesty.[15] The tradesman Carl Arvedson from Nyköping had been so moved when seeing the royal couple in connection with the coronation that same year that he had burst into a flood of tears and been obliged to take to his bed and be medicated with drops. For the inhabitants of the capital, it was not an uncommon occurrence to see the royal family among the crowds in the street; but Faste Ekeborn, a former provision-dealer in Stockholm, was glad that this had not happened to him for a while. He was tormented by obsessive thoughts, and in spite of his 'wishing the Magistracy nothing but the best', he feared that he might attack the King if he met him in the street. He thanked God that this had not happened during one of his periods of confusion.[16]

A provision-dealer's assistant who had recently moved to Stockholm from the province of Ångermanland became so enthusiastic after having seen the King that he wrote a little ditty about his encounters. The lyrics of the song were written to fit a well-known

the type of document to which each reference refers – petition from the Court of Appeal, judicial investigation documents, appendices to letters or other items. As far as is possible and has been considered justified, I have instead tried to specify this in the running text.

14 On the king's toast: 1730.XII.09/15. On Meisner: 1774.II.04/9; see also 1773.XI.17/52.
15 On Smed-Maja: 1749.IX.20/GA. On Ljunggren: 1752.I.10/8.
16 On Arvedson: 1752.VII.01/6–7. On Ekeborn: 1760.II.07/3 ('önskar Öwerheten alt godt').

tune and form a small popular propaganda piece about the coup
d'état of Gustav III; but in its naïve tone of voice the song is a
reminder of encounters between commoners and the monarch
described in other places:

A heart-felt joy has befallen me,
Who just arrived in the city,
A gracious King I have beheld,
Who is steadfastly mild and pious:
My joy did now burst into song,
Especially since it was the first time
That I saw my King.

His retinue then captivated me so deeply,
Whenever he rode past me;
My simplicity cannot enough
All this correctly disseminate:
And this was all the more so,
Because I seven times in three days
Was able to look upon his face.[17]

---

17 Peter Sellstedt, *En ung drängs glädje-sång öfwer Hans Kongl. Maj:t kong
Gustaf den tredje, när han, år 1772 den 19 augusti, hade den nåden, at
första gången se Hans Kongl. Maj:t, hwilket upwäckte en owanlig och
besynnerlig stor glädje i honom, at han däröfwer sammanskref följande,
under melodie*: Hwar man må nu wäl glädja sig, &c. (Stockholm:
Wennberg & Nordström, 1772):

En hiertans glädie är mig skedt,
Som nyss til Staden kommer,
En nådig Konung jag fått sett,
Som är fast mild och frommer:
Min Glädje nu utbrast i Sång,
Hälst som det war den första gång,
Som jag min Konung skådat.

Dess Swit då mig så djupt intog,
När Han förbi mån' rida;
Min enfaldighet kan ej nog
Alt detta rätt utsprida:
Och det så mycket mera war,
Som jag sju gånger på Tre dar
Hans Ansigt fick beskåda.

The song has eight stanzas. There is a later variant of the song in which
the words 'His retinue then' in the second stanza have been changed to
'The sight of him'. This corresponded more closely to the popular image
Gustav III was so fond of cultivating.

Most examples of such personal encounters with the King that are mentioned in the sources are, for natural reasons, from the capital. During the second half of the eighteenth century, the population of Stockholm remained fairly stable at around 60,000 inhabitants. Although the built-up areas reached up into the surrounding larger islands and mainland, trade in the city was centred in the cramped medieval core, which was dominated by the Royal Palace.[18] The members of the royal family often moved around in this urban environment accompanied by an escort, made excursions to nearby parks and hunting grounds and travelled between their residence in the city and the rural residences of Karlberg, Ulriksdal and Drottningholm. Anyone who was well dressed could gain access to the masquerades at the Royal Palace. Those who could not afford to pay the small entrance fee instead had the opportunity to see the King during the performance of his official duties, when he drilled his troops or when he simply moved through the city.[19]

The inhabitants of the capital had fairly regular opportunities to see the King and the Queen. Being seen by and freely moving among the people contributed to the popularity of the royal family. A curious expression of this popularity was the King's efforts when there was a fire in the city. At larger fires, he always personally helped with the firefighting. When the Town Hall in Stockholm caught fire in 1753, *Posttidningarna* acknowledged 'the aid of the Supreme Being and the esteemed presence of His Royal Majesty' for the fire not having spread further.[20] Such royal rescue work was not an isolated Swedish phenomenon. During the Great Fire of London in 1666, Charles II – in spite of the opposition of his councillors – dashed around in the streets and urged on the firefighting, and a foreign observer described the eagerness of Peter the Great to participate in firefighting as something approaching

---

18 *Staden på vattnet*, ed. by Lars Nilsson, Monografier utgivna av Stockholms stad, 159:1 (Stockholm: Stockholmia, 2002), I: *1252–1850*, pp. 189, 201.
19 Cf. Carl Christoffer Gjörwell, *En Stockholmskrönika ur C. C. Gjörwells brev, 1757–1778*, ed. by Otto Sylwan (Stockholm: Bonniers, 1920), pp. 14, 30, 35–37.
20 *Posttidningarna*, 20 December 1753, quoted in Otto Sylwan, *Svenska pressens historia till statshvälfningen 1772* (Lund: Gleerups, 1896), p. 94 ('den Högstas bistånd och Hans Kongl. Maj:ts höga närwaro'). Similar interventions were already being reported during his time as a Crown Prince; see *Stockholms Post-Tidningar*, no. 48 (21 June 1750).

a passion.[21] Wars, crop failures, epidemics and fires were the national scourges that threatened people and kingdoms, and on such occasions it was the king's duty to protect his subjects. As the Swedish warrior kings of the Age of Greatness showed by example, this role of protector could be perceived literally, not just symbolically and administratively. After the great city fire of Stockholm in 1751, *Posttidningar* described Adolf Frederick's heroic efforts for the salvation of the capital. The fire might have had even more dangerous consequences, said the newspaper, 'if His Royal Majesty in person had not been everywhere present and taken both fatherly and necessary measures'. The King had participated in the firefighting until three o'clock in the morning, and the fire would no doubt have 'caused even greater damage, if the measures taken by His Majesty, who was everywhere present, had not fortunately prevented such a development'.[22]

The royal family themselves tried to capitalise on their popular support; and in 1756, when the conflict with the Council was at its most intense, Adolf Frederick went for a propagandistic ride through the city as a demonstration of strength against the Hat party and in order to, in the Queen's words, 'keep them within some limits of respect'.[23] Those who did not reside in Stockholm

21 Mark Kishlansky, *A Monarchy Transformed: Britain 1603–1714* (London: Allen Lane, Penguin Press, 1996), p. 214; Lindsey Hughes, *Russia in the Age of Peter the Great* (New Haven and London: Yale University Press, 1998), p. 367.

22 *Stockholm Post Tidningar*, no. 44 (10 June 1751) ('om icke Hans Kongl. Maj:t i egen hög person warit å alla ställen tilstädes och giordt så wäl faderliga, som nödige anstalter' and 'förorsakat än större skada, om icke genom de af Hans Maj:t, som öfwer alt war tilstädes, tagne mått sådant lyckeligen förekommit'). See also *Stockholm Post Tidningar*, no. 45 (13 June 1751); cf. Carl Gustaf Malmström, *Sveriges politiska historia från konung Karl XII:s död till statshvälfningen 1772*, 2nd edn, 6 vols (Stockholm: Norstedts, 1893–1901), IV (1899), p. 220; Elise M. Dermineur, *Gender and Politics in Eighteenth-Century Sweden: Queen Louisa Ulrika (1720–1782)* (London and New York: Routledge, 2017), pp. 101–02, 143.

23 'Utdrag ur Drottning Lovisa Ulrikas journal för åren 1755 och 1756', in Fredrik Axel von Fersen, *Historiska skrifter*, ed. by R. M. Klinckowström, 2nd edn, 8 vols (Stockholm: Norstedts, 1867–72), II (1868), p. 240 ('hålla dem inom vissa gränser av respect'). See also [Carl Christopher Gjörwell], 'Anteckningar af Carl Christopher Gjörwell om sig sjelf, samtida personer och händelser 1731–1757', in *Samlingar utgifna för De skånska landskapens historiska och arkeologiska förening*, ed. by Martin Weibull, 9 vols (Lund: Berlings, 1874–80), III: *1875* (1874), pp. 31–142 (pp. 95–96).

had the opportunity to see the King and Queen in real life during the royal couple's private and official travels, which were often undertaken with a large escort and a good deal of pageantry. In addition, Frederick I and Adolf Frederick made major royal tours of the country (*eriksgator*): Frederick I in Svealand and Götaland in 1722, and Adolf Frederick in Finland in 1752, in Scania in 1754 and in Dalecarlia in 1755. As a Crown Prince, Adolf Frederick had undertaken a journey around the country during the autumn of 1743, as well as a trip that attracted a lot of attention in 1744 to the recently rebellious province of Dalecarlia, and he visited the silver mine at Sala in 1750. In 1768, Crown Prince Gustav travelled to Bergslagen as part of a deliberate political campaign. The King ordered him to behave modestly and unpretentiously in order to awaken the sympathy of the general public. This means of gaining popular support had otherwise been limited following the attempted coup in 1756. The Estates had then decided that any travel beyond visits to the out-of-town royal residences around the capital had to be approved by the Council; the King was not himself allowed to choose his travelling companions among the Councillors; and his useof travel grants was restricted.[24]

The subjects who came into visual contact with their King and Queen were often greatly impressed by the grandeur, and their loyalty towards their royal majesties was strengthened. Carl Linnaeus described the journey of the young successor to the throne and his wife through Mariestad during the summer of 1746. According to him, it was above all the Crown Princess who aroused admiration:

> The people from both the town and the countryside around it thronged to see such a splendid princess. They saw, they loved, and venerated her beauty, wisdom and gentleness.[25]

---

24 Henrika Tandefelt, 'Prins Gustafs resa i Bergslagen år 1768: Kronprinsen som politisk aktör under frihetstidens slut', in *Riksdag, kaffehus och predikstol: Frihetstidens politiska kultur 1766–1772*, ed. by Marie-Christine Skuncke and Henrika Tandefelt (Stockholm: Atlantis, 2003), pp. 229–52 (p. 239 and *passim*); Malmström, *Sveriges politiska historia*, IV, pp. 240–41.
25 Carl Linnaeus, *Wästgöta-resa, på riksens högloflige ständers befallning förrättad år 1746: Med anmärkningar uti oeconomien, naturkunnogheten, antiquiteter, jnwånarnes seder och lefnads-sätt, med tilhörige figurer* (Stockholm: Lars Salvius, 1746), p. 18 ('Folket så ifrån staden, som från landet deromkring trängdes at få åskåda en så förträffelig Princessa. De sågo, de älskade och wördade Hennes skönhet, wishet och mildhet').

Twenty years later, Chamberlain Adolf Ludvig Hamilton described in greater detail how Crown Prince Gustav was received when travelling through the country. With some derision, he also noted the unabashed gawping of the common people, while persons of rank satisfied their curiosity from a dignified distance:

> The Magistracy [the King and Queen] followed him [the Crown Prince] in sloops from Drottningholm to Fittja, and all the way to Scania an extensive but poor country dressed in their best finery. Almost every Swedish mile there was a change of horses, and at every change of horses there were curious people, peasants, French hoods [i.e., servant-girls], jackets [i.e., commoners] closer to the coaches, gowns [i.e., people of quality] on the hills, spruce twigs on the gates and overridden horses along the road, shooting, tottering burgher cavalry, speeches, ill-made, hardly listened to at the town gates, tallow-candle illuminations, good intentions everywhere.[26]

Emanuel Geijer, an ironworks proprietor from the province of Värmland later ennobled as Emanuel af Geijerstam, described with enthusiasm his meetings with a mild and omniscient Gustav III at the beginning of 1772. Geijer was sixteen years older than the young King, educated and fairly widely travelled; but he was carried away by unconditional admiration for His Majesty:

> I had the favour, both in Stockholm and then at Loka, of several times speaking with the King, and given leave to present the affairs of the country. [...] I, who am unaccustomed to speaking with a crowned head, was anxious, but the Master told me [not] to worry, speak the frank truth, and this I did, too, and so graciously [did he] respond that I was ordered to *eat at his own illustrious table*, a favour highly unusual for a commoner and a mere ironworks owner. [...] I have in all my life [never] had such joyous days as these at Loka, to be allowed to see and speak with a great King about the means of helping the country. [...]. The King departed,

26 Adolf Ludvig Hamilton, *Anekdoter till svenska historien under Gustaf III:s regering*, ed. by Oscar Levertin, Svenska memoarer och bref, 4 (Stockholm: Bonniers, 1901), pp. 22–23 ('Öfverheten följde honom på slupar från Drottningholm till Fittja, och på hela vägen till Skåne satte sig ett vidsträckt men fattigt land i gala. Merändels vid hvar mil var skjutsombyte, vid hvart ombyte nyfiket folk, bönder, bindmössor, koftor närmre vagnarna, rober på höjderna, granris på grindarna och förkörda hästar längs vägen, skjutning, vacklande borgare-kavalleri, tal, illa utförda, knappast påhörda vid stadsportarna, talgljusilluminationer, välmening öfverallt'). One Swedish mile at this time equalled approximately 10 km (10.69 km).

the people wept tears of joy, he was blessed by the people, and on 19 August brought about the true and blessed revolution, which reunited fractured minds, drove away discord and dissension and made us a united people.[27]

Apart from praising the virtues of the King, Geijer was seduced by the aura of majesty that was nourished by the King's ceremonial elevation. It was not simply the content of the conversation at dinner that filled Geijer with admiration, but to an equal degree the honour of being invited into the inner circle of the King (the emphasis in the quotation is Geijer's own). The notes were written down or edited after the coup d'état, and they are wholly in keeping with the propaganda picture Gustav III himself wished to convey. He was skilful at exploiting both a latent royalism and the well-promoted image of the king as a unifying force elevated above party factions. The mood Geijer put into words was therefore a prerequisite for rather than a product of the coup d'état.

How the public image appealed to the subjects is clear from the journey Crown Prince Gustav made through the country in 1766. That year it was finally time for Crown Prince Gustav to enter into the marriage with the Danish Princess Sophia Magdalena that had been decided as early as 1750, when the parties were four years old. The wedding ceremony itself was performed by proxy in Copenhagen – the Swedish ambassador standing in for the Crown Prince – and when Gustav travelled to meet the Princess at her landing in Helsingborg, he was thus already married to the woman on whom he then laid eyes for the first time. For the reputation of the kingdom, a grandiose reception was essential, and the journey of the married couple through the country developed into a celebratory

---

27 Emanuel af Geijerstam, *Emanuel af Geijerstams levernesbeskrivning* (Stockholm: Norstedts, 1954), p. 80 ('Jag hade den Nåden, så i Stokholm, som sedan wid Loka, at få flera gånger tala med Konungen, och få föreställa landets angelägenheter. [...] Jag som owan, at tala med Ett Krönt Hufwud war bekymrad, men Herren bad mig [ej] oroas, tala franco sanning det iag ock giorde, och så nådigt uptog, at iag blef befalt *spisa wid des Egit Höga Bord*, en Nåd, som war högst owanlig för en ofrälse och blott BruksPatron. [...] Jag har i all min lefnad [aldrig] hafft så glada dagar, som dessa wid Loka, at få se och tala med En Stor Konung om Landets hielp [...]. Konungen reste, folket utgiöt glädietårar, wälsignades af folket, och utförde den 19 augusti den rätta och wälsignade revolutionen, som åter förenade söndrade Sinnen, bortdref split och osämja, och giorde oss til ett förenat folk').

royal tour with frequent stops to listen to the ovations of the people. This bridal procession has been described in detail by Henning Stålhane in a study closely based on contemporary sources. To judge from the many and long congratulatory calls that were paid on the Crown Prince couple, veneration for the royal family was undiminished among the inhabitants of the kingdom. Each town or village they passed through taxed its resources to the full in coming up with suitable tokens of respect. Their abilities did not always live up to their ambition, but the sincerity was therefore all the more apparent. The disappointment was also great in the towns and villages that the exalted company had to pass by without stopping because of a lack of time. The city of Malmö, which was passed over for this reason because the Crown Prince chose to spend the night in nearby Lund, nevertheless wanted to display its loyal veneration and sent a delegation consisting of the mayor of justice, two city aldermen and several officers from the burgher cavalry and infantry. Because their request for a visit from the Prince was regretfully rejected, the whole burgher troop resolutely marched to Lund on the following day in order to parade at his departure. Stålhane repeatedly emphasises how the Council and the Estates obstructed the princely propaganda tour, but the subjects' reverence for Their Royal Highnesses does not seem to have been diminished either by the political conflicts or by the impotence of the royal authority (Figure 54).[28]

In the same way as the splendour surrounding the royal family was intended to maintain the status of the kingdom in relation to foreign countries, the tributes of the various towns were also part of a competition among them. Such an opportunity to show off their industriousness and emphasise their loyalty as subjects must not be squandered. In other places as well, the subjects made use of some ostensibly rather far-fetched stratagems in order to attract a visit by the royals. In the church of a distant rural parish outside Umeå in northern Sweden, a royal seat was thus constructed 'in the humble hope that, in due course and according to God's gracious dispensation, we may delight in the highly desired and exceedingly gratifying arrival here of Your Royal Majesties'.[29]

28 Henning Stålhane, *Gustaf III:s bosättning, brudfärd och biläger: Kulturhistorisk studie* (Stockholm: Nordisk rotogravyr, 1946); on Malmö: p. 90.
29 *Stockholms Post Tidningar*, no. 90 (18 November 1751) ('i den underdåniga förhoppning, at i sinom tid, och efter Guds nådiga skickelse, få glädia sig af Deras Kongl. Majestäters högtönskade och ganska hugneliga hitkomst').

Figure 54 'Ceremony conducted at the entry of Her Royal Highness our present Crown Princess into the Royal Residence City of Stockholm on 4 November 1766.' The procession started out from the royal out-of-town residence of Karlberg, whose towers can be glimpsed at the far end of the avenue. The Crown Prince's empty carriage can be seen on the top row in the middle of the image; the Crown Princess' carriage follows it. Engraving by an unknown artist, printed at Johan Georg Lange's in 1768. Photo: Jens Östman, KB.

The popular royalist expressions of emotion were often slogan-like and conventional, which did not prevent their being sincere. Still, they were frequently perceived as ridiculous or even provocative by people who overheard them. Expressions of loyalty to the king were sometimes perceived as naïve or hypocritical. Statements of that kind might be met with the objection that the king was unlikely to devote any attention to an individual human subject, and royalist credulousness could provoke disparaging statements. When the Crown Prince was expected in Borås in 1754, the yeoman Olof Assarsson declared that he would seek the Crown Prince's support in a conflict with Jacob Esaiasson, a former Riksdag delegate. The latter scornfully replied about the Crown Prince that 'he doesn't have much sense'. This crime, which to modern ears sounds like a petty offence, was perceived as very serious because it called into question the intellectual gifts of the Crown Prince. Sergeant Ljunggren, who had expressed his joy at having seen Adolf Frederick at Riddarhustorget, was met by the artillerist Lars

Wijnbladh with the scornful statement that 'I can't stand him, nor could I ever stand him.' Similarly, the blessings of Mrs Meisner of Södermalm on the King and the Queen Dowager were answered by the journeyman miller Johan Bromberg, who felt that 'Her Royal Majesty the Queen Dowager would deserve to – – –'. The injurious statement, censored by the court, had been followed by an explanatory comment about how the state coffers were drained because of the Dowager Queen's construction work at Drottningholm and Svartsjö, that the wages of labourers were paid to foreign craftsmen and were thus taken out of the kingdom, and that the foreign comedy actors she had summoned were all scoundrels.[30]

The Queen's alleged mismanagement of the kingdom's funds was also commented on by Captain Gustaf Bagge at a tavern in Skara. He could even specify that she had wasted all of seventy barrels of gold on operas and comedies. The city court felt that such a story of economic irresponsibility was intended to disparage the gracious clemency harboured by the Queen for the kingdom and its inhabitants. Bagge did not deny the statement as such, but argued that it had been uttered in a conversation about the advantageous circumstances the kingdom was in both domestically and abroad because of its fortunate form of government. The splendour of the court and its honourable ways of life contributed to the high regard in which the kingdom was held abroad, he said in his defence. The Court of Appeal could not find it proved that Bagge had had malicious intent, but felt that it was a crime in itself to speak of the Queen in such a way that it could inspire evil thoughts, even though this had not been the intention.[31] That it had happened while the Riksdag was in session and on public premises aggravated the misconduct.

Both the journeyman Forsman and Captain Bagge would appear to have held carefully considered ideas about the state of affairs at court. Bagge's excuse is perhaps not completely convincing, and from other cases it can be understood that rumours about the

---

30 On Jacob Esaiasson: 1754.VII.10/19 ('Det är intet stort beskied med honom'). On Wijnbladh: 1752.I.10/8 ('jag tål honom intet, och har ej [h]eller någonsin tålt honom'). On Meisner: 1774.II.04/9 ('Hennes Kongl. Maij:t Enke Drottningen woro wärd att – – –').

31 1759.VII.04/2. Seventy barrels of gold were officially the equivalent of seven million silver *daler*. This can be compared to His Royal Majesty's court budget in total, which had been just over 9.2 million silver *daler* during the years 1751–1758; Karl Åmark, *Sveriges statsfinanser 1719–1809* (Stockholm: Norstedts, 1961), table 17, pp. 322–23.

extravagances at court was a well-liked feature of tavern gossip at the time. Swearing that powerful people and the king and queen had neither honour nor integrity was no doubt also part of a general popular culture of protest, of which we will see further examples below.

The authority of the king

Because the king guaranteed the impartiality of public power during the Age of Liberty as well as before it, both the questioning of public ordinances and disrespectful behaviour towards state officials could be considered crimes of lese-majesty. All ordinances were issued in the name of the king, and he also formally appointed all officials. In the eyes of the public, the king was thus involved even in the smallest decisions. Many cases of lese-majesty therefore concerned not the office or the person of the king but the public exercise of power as such.[32]

The reason for the vigilance of the authorities and the strict execution by the courts in these cases was the importance of the unconditional obligation of obedience in the hierarchical social thinking of the time. The curator of the armouries, Staff Sergeant (*rustmästare*) Torsten Rydberg, had refused to drink to the King's health because he did not feel he had been remunerated according to his merits for his service to the Crown. Associate Judge Bastian Bering of Göta Court of Appeal then compared the subject's relationship to the king with a servant's relationship to his or her master. Both God's law and secular law established that the servant is always worth his wages, he explained. Among private individuals, it was considered dishonourable if a servant claimed to be underpaid by his or her master. It was therefore even more inappropriate when someone claimed to be poorly paid by the Magistracy.[33]

There were two elements in this emphasis on submission. On the one hand, the exercise of power by the lords had to be obscured as far as possible, and this reason was specific to the form of government with a limited royal authority. On the other hand, all exercise of public authority rested on supremacy and submission,

---

32 Cf. the discussion on the crime of lese-majesty and the subjects' duty of obedience in *En Ärlig Swensk* (Stockholm: Historiographi regni, 1755), pp. 133–35, 537–38, 978–79.
33 1730.XII.09/15.

and this foundation was the same irrespective of whether the royal authority was strong or weak. In actual fact, the need to maintain the reverence for His Majesty was greater during the Age of Liberty than, for instance, during the strong rule of Gustav III. This apparent paradox was due to the discrepancy between the function (ethos) of the royal authority and the image conveyed of it. Public power during the Age of Liberty ultimately rested on a foundation that was a fiction. The Council had a position of power without independent rationality or power of justification. Its institutional authority was based on the legitimacy of another state organ; or, otherwise expressed, the Council had the power, but the king had the authority. The autocratic monarchy of Gustav III, on the other hand, accumulated all of the state's resources in the King's hands, and for this reason he could accentuate his position of power using real means of coercion. This is precisely why he could also relax the rigorous principle of maintaining the symbolic strength of the royal authority. Harsh and strict upholding of the law was therefore not necessary for Gustav III; on the contrary, he was happy to forgive his enemies. Because the threat of a strict execution was the same as before, mercy, good will and clemency became a more efficient method of asserting the authority of the king. Gustav III's dislike of capital punishment was probably genuine, and during his government it was implemented only in three cases involving crimes against the state, all during the Russo-Swedish War of 1788–1790.[34]

At the beginning of the Age of Liberty, royal authority was questioned in several ways in an interesting case from Färs Hundred in the province of Malmöhus. On the same day as the new billeting order (*kvartersordning*) had been read out in church, Helge Höjman, previously convicted and punished as a thief, let his horse out to graze. The farmers who owned the meadow protested, referring to the recently proclaimed ordinance: 'Did you not hear

---

34 In 1778 Gustav III reinstated the so-called institute of reference (*underställ-ningsinstitutet*), which meant that all death sentences issued by the courts of appeal would be reviewed by the King. That the implementation was actually mitigated by the King's reforms is shown in a crude but clear way by the statistics. In 1772–1778, an average of 24.6 people were executed each year. During 1779–1792, this figure was reduced to 9.8. As a comparison, it can be noted that in 1760–1771 the yearly average was a little over 32 people executed. These figures have been calculated on the basis of Knut Olivecrona, *Om dödsstraffet*, 2nd rev. edn (Uppsala: W. Schultz, 1891), table IV, pp. 110–45.

the order of His Royal Majesty being read out today, that no one
should presume to let their horses out into the farmer's best grass?'
This was in the summer of 1719, during the brief reign of Ulrika
Eleonora. According to the witness statements, Höjman answered,
'The order of the King, we have no king.' The farmers objected that
they instead had a queen, to which Höjman replied that he 'didn't
give a damn'.[35]
  The incident may certainly be interpreted as though Höjman
merely acted in a spirit of general insubordination. The statement
'we have no king' may have been spur-of-the-moment sophistry
thought up in order to annoy his antagonists and need not have
been a genuine rejection of the Queen's authority. The underlying intentions were uninteresting as far as the judicial authorities
were concerned, though, and for them it was a serious matter
that the royal majesty could be questioned at all on the basis of
personal qualities, in this case the female sex of the holder of the
title. Besides, the royal authority, unlike the person of the King or
Queen, was permanent. During the Age of Liberty, a person could
also be prosecuted for having, for instance, questioned the ordinances of Charles XI, or for having spoken in disparaging terms
about Charles XII.[36] It was the nature of the offence rather than
its content that made it a crime. That fact is brought out in, for
example, the previously mentioned case of the prothonotary Johan
Jacob Pfeif, who had raised objections regarding an appointment.
The crime in this case consisted of having already questioned a
decision that had been made, which was considered a rejection of
royal mandate as such.[37] Even in the matter of a minor appointment, the king was the decision-maker with all the appurtenant
power and authority.
  Questioning appointments to offices was a rather common
reason for being reported, and the crime had two dimensions.
First, it questioned the authority of the person whose job it was
to implement the orders of the Magistracy; second, it questioned
the judgement of the person who was responsible for the appointments, i.e. the king. In both cases it tarnished the honour of His

---

35 1724.II.19/42 ('hörde du icke Kongl. Maij:ts ordning läsas i dag, at dhe
    intet skulle så understå sig släppa sina hästar i Bondens bästa grääs';
    'Konungens ordres, wij hafwa ingen Konung' and 'skitter i dett').
36 1725.VII.01/1; 1731.IV.30/62.
37 1725.V.26/58.

Royal Majesty. These two dimensions could be discerned when the assistant vicar Henrik Voigt from Savolax in Finland had censured the local vicar with the statement that he sat like a scoundrel with his letter of commission. The words had been uttered in Finnish and could also be interpreted to mean that he sat with a letter of commission issued by a scoundrel. It was impossible to clarify what had been intended, but both statements were considered injurious by the court.[38] In some cases, an examination was made as to whether the injurious statement had referred to the king himself or merely to the decisions and servants of the king, in which case the crime could be seen as less serious.[39]

On many occasions, subjects presumed the King's involvement in issues where he could not reasonably have had any influence. Sigrid Lisa Holst of Linköping saw his intervention even in individual court cases. When she had heard the judicial decision regarding herself being read out in some minor criminal case, she held the King directly responsible for the unfair decision. Before the court in session, she embarked on a sulphurous tirade:

> May God curse such a King and such a verdict; may the Devil strike the head of such a King, he is a worse bloodsucker than the old one was. May God curse him, the Queen, and the princes.[40]

In this case, the offensive injurious statement was the main issue. That decisions over which he had no actual influence were attributed to the King in person was in no way a problem, since this merely reinforced the power of the royal authority. It was worse when the King's ability to govern was questioned on constitutional grounds: then the state system itself was shaken to its foundations. The student Thomas Collander argued that the ordinances of the powerless Frederick barely had any legal effect. 'I have no esteem for the ordinances of King Frederick, we have the [...] ordinances of our old Kings, according to which we should direct our lives.' When the people around him reprimanded him for these words, he had added that 'King Frederick is not sovereign; today he lives, tomorrow he is dead, which may God in his grace

---

38 1736.XII.09/34.
39 1726.II.11/24; 1751.VI.28/47; 1752.V.20/43.
40 1751.X.18/45 ('Gud förbanne en sådan Kong och sådan dom; fan fare i hufwudet på en sådan Kong, han är wärre blodsugare han, än den gamle war. Gud förbanne honom, drottningen och Printzarne').

delay.'[41] Collander respected the King's person but felt that a ruler who was not an absolute monarch lacked the necessary authority and was therefore superfluous.

A little over thirty years later, the boatswain Mårten Lax was somewhat more ambiguous. At a tax-collection meeting in Sollefteå he became involved in an altercation with the local sheriff (*länsman*) and shouted, 'I don't give a damn about you nor about the King either. I have served other Kings, I have; I have no respect or esteem for him in comparison to the Kings I have served [...] I have no more esteem for the King than I do for my old shoes.' Lax was a sixty-eight-year-old soldier who had fought in Finland in both the 1710s and the 1740s. For many people, the military exploits of Charles XII had an air of romance about them, and one can easily imagine that the dead King had greater authority than Adolf Frederick among martially orientated subjects. Even though this circumstance may have been a factor affecting his statement, it is doubtful that Lax should be taken at his word, and the incident should not be overinterpreted. In this case the statement was rather about Lax himself, not about the King. Referring backwards in the list of rulers was a way for him of saying, 'You can't beat experience and I have been around a long time.' Even understood along these lines, the incident shows that previous and present kings were active points of reference in the subjects' world view.[42]

In 1743 there was a widespread peasant revolt in Dalecarlia, a province to the north-west of Stockholm. A large number of armed peasants reinforced by conscripted soldiers (*indelta soldater*), in total around 5,000 men, marched on the capital to protest against

41 1727.XII.06/24 ('Jag estimerar intet Konung Friedrichs Förordningar, Wij hafwa wåra gambla Kongars [...] Förordningar, som wij bör lefwa efter' and 'Konung Friedrich är intet souverain, i dag lefwer han i morgon är han död, det Gud nådeligen fördröije').
42 1761.XII.02/3 ('jag skiter i dig och Konungen den med. Jag har tiendt andra Konungar jag, jag aktar eller estimerar honom intet emot the Konungar jag har tient [...] jag aktar intet Konungen mer än mina gamla skor'). Notices about people who had reached a remarkably advanced age were common in the newspapers, and the stories were often centred on how many kings the old person had lived under, or recounted memorable incidents from their reigns. For instance, in no. 86 of *Inrikes Tidningar* (1 November 1770), one could read about the widow Agneta Hane, who had died at the age of 107. According to the notice she could still, in her twilight years, 'in great detail tell the story about the coronation of King Charles XI' ('noga berätta om Konung Carl den Elloftes Kröning').

the war and the politics pursued by the Council and the Riksdag. In addition to detailed economic reforms, the rebels wanted those responsible for the unfortunate war against Russia to be punished, a strengthening of the royal authority and the election of the Danish Crown Prince as successor to the Swedish throne. The rebel army was defeated by force of arms when it reached the capital. Between forty and fifty people were killed, around ninety were wounded, and six of the leaders were executed. In order to strengthen the Crown's preferential right of interpretation, the clergy's responsibility for general proclamations was regulated in greater detail following this event. Information about the rebellion was suppressed by the authorities, but it spread by way of rumour, and in subsequent years the Dalecarlian rebellion constituted a background for much speculation and political reflection all across the kingdom.[43]

The thirty-one-year-old yeoman Anders Nilsson of Färnebo parish in the province of Värmland did not respect either the King's person or his authority. Anders Nilsson, who was prosecuted in 1744, shortly after the Dalecarlian rebellion, had a carefully considered, comprehensive view of the state of affairs that included the law, the royal authority and foreign trade. The old law – which he called the law of Charles XI, but which referred both to the doctrine of sovereignty and the medieval Law of the Realm, replaced eight years earlier – had corresponded with Danish law and provided for an absolute monarchy and an election of the successor to the throne by the assembled peasantry of the realm at the Stone of Mora, where kings had been appointed during the Middle Ages. Following the abolishment of the law of Charles XI, prices in the country had risen, partly through 'the mad factories' ('the galna Fabriquer') that destroyed foreign trade, and partly through a prohibition against grain imports, which allowed the nobility, clergy and ironworks owners to raise prices and thus run the peasants into debt. The important trade with Denmark, particular, was now impermissible, Anders Nilsson pointed out. For this reason 'he wanted to have another king and the old privileges and the previous

43 The Dalecarlian rebellion has been thoroughly discussed by Bjarne Beckman, *Dalupproret 1743 och andra samtida rörelser inom allmogen och bondeståndet* (Gothenburg: Elanders, 1930) and Sennefelt, *Den politiska sjukan*. On the change of the proclamations: Carin Bergström, *Lantprästen: Prästens funktion i det agrara samhället 1720–1800; Oland-Frösåkers kontrakt av ärkestiftet*, Nordiska museets handlingar, 110 (Stockholm: Nordiska museet, 1991), pp. 122–23.

ordinances back'. All the difficulties taken together had one solution: the election of the Danish Crown Prince as successor to the Swedish throne. In this way trade with Denmark would open up again and absolutism would be reinstated, to the relief of the peasantry.

Because the Crown Prince of Denmark was in Anders Nilsson's opinion the true Magistracy of the realm, he refused to stand trial while Frederick reigned. He rejected the election of Adolf Frederick as the Crown Prince because it had been done through the intermediacy of the Council and the Estates and 'not by the assembled peasantry' ('eij af samtel. Allmogen') directly, as was prescribed by the old law. This illegal election had been the cause of the uprising of the Dalecarlian peasantry in the previous year, he claimed.

Anders Nilsson maintained that his ideas had general support in his home parish. Fifteen of his comrades were therefore summoned for questioning, but even though some of these men had marched together with the Dalecarlian peasants, they all protested that they in no way shared Anders Nilsson's opinions. Quite the opposite; 'they were all happy with our gracious Magistracy, His Royal Highness, our elected hereditary prince, our adopted law and government, which some had confirmed with tears and prayers for the welfare of the Magistracy'.[44]

---

44 1744.IX.20/30 ('wore the alla nögde med wår Nådiga Öfwerhet, Hans Kongl. Höghet, wår utkorade Arffurste, wår antagne Lag och regering, hwilket en del med tårar och böner för Öfwerhetens wälgång bekräftadt'). Demands for a return to 'the salutary ordinances of Charles XI' ('Carl den XI:s hälsosamma förordningar') had also been made by the rebellious Dalecarlian peasants; 'Dalekarlarnas Postulata vid allmänna Landztinget 1742', § 1, in *Handlingar rörande Skandinaviens historia*, ed. by Kungl. Samfundet för utgifvande af handskrifter rörande Skandinaviens historia, 60 vols (Stockholm: Elmén & Granberg and others, 1816–60), III (1817), p. 220. Many of Anders Nilsson's ideas could be found in a similar form in an anonymous pamphlet printed in Denmark in 1743, in which an argument was made for increased royal power, for an end to party strife, for the choice of the successor to the throne being made by the people of Sweden and not by foreign ministers, for the choice falling on the Danish Prince Frederick, for the Scandinavian kingdoms entering into a political union and many other things; see *En redlig swänsk patriots politiska tros bekiännelse* ([n.p.]: [n. pub.], [1743]). Several of these survived more than a decade later; see the pamphlet 'Svea rikes tillstånd', in Ingemar Carlsson, *Frihetstidens handskrivna politiska litteratur: En bibliografi*, Acta bibliothecae universitatis Gothoburgensis, 9 (Gothenburg: Göteborgs universitetsbibliotek, 1967), no. 631; transcripts: D 158:1, 'Assessor Höppeners samlingar rörande Sweriges stats hwälfningar ifrån 1719 til

Anders Nilsson's world view is exciting because it was based on a long succession of misunderstandings about the actual circumstances, but in spite of that it was consistent and well thought through. The court tried to reason with him, attempting to persuade him that his reflections were unreasonable; but Anders Nilsson had well-considered answers to most things. His sententious notions were based in equal parts on hearsay, his own experiences, and mediated knowledge about law and justice, as well as on what appears to be an inherited tradition and deeply rooted conflicts among the Estates. He painted an idealised picture of the imagined law of Charles XI that suggested a contented past when society had been in harmony and the king had been on the side of the common people against the lords and the clergy. The key to this happy state of affairs was a strong royal authority.

Anders Nilsson's idea of society had been cobbled together in a way that seems to have been common within the peasantry, though their conclusions need not always have been the same. The proclamations announced by the local clergyman were mixed with rumours floating around, personal political experiences in the independent government of the parish, and stories from the representatives of the hundred about work in the Riksdag. Regardless of the validity of the underlying information, the resulting view of the world was as firmly rooted as that of any university scholar ever was. How politics were actually implemented was not as important as how they were interpreted.

Anders Nilsson's ideas contained so many dimensions of disobedience that his advocacy of the Danish Crown Prince was not even the most sensational one. However, there were other examples of highly concrete challenges to the king's authority. Albrecht von Duhn, a burgher in Ystad, chose to completely pass over his own Magistracy and instead turn to a foreign crown. Feeling unfairly treated in a conflict with the National Board of Trade, he had directed a supplication to the Danish King, petitioning for help in pursuing his case against the Swedish authorities. In an accurate assessment of the prevailing power relations, he asked Christian VI to send a letter of recommendation to the Estates of the realm – not to the King. In other words, he wanted the aid of a foreign head

---

1805' (in German); D 171:1, Schröderheims historiskt-politiska samlingar/ The Schröderheim historio-political collections, KB 1: 1590–1787 (in Swedish), KB.

of state in his attempt to influence the joint representatives of the realm. The truly serious thing, however, was the symbolic aspect of his course of action: that he had been deficient in his deference as a loyal subject and 'passed over Your Royal Majesty as his by law crowned and benevolent King'.[45]

Several such examples can be found in Finland, which was an extra-sensitive matter because this part of the kingdom, during the two occupations of the eighteenth century, had had experience of another Magistracy. During the first Russian occupation, Provost Sergeant Knut Koivistolainen, in a conflict over property with the yeoman Pehr Ruokolainen, had 'exclaimed these highly offensive words; the Devil takes care of the King of Sweden, but I have nowadays no help or aid from him'. According to other witnesses he had added, 'I serve whoever is in charge', thus implying that it did not matter to him whether he was subject to a Swedish or a Russian Magistracy.[46]

In the summer of 1724, a few years after the occupation had been lifted, the regiment of Ostrobothnia marched through the village of Jurva on their way to the newly founded town of Fredrikshamn (Hamina in Finnish). To feed the soldiers, the local sheriff wished to requisition an ox from the yeoman Mats Korpi in return for due payment. Korpi refused, however, and was enthusiastically supported by his wife, Margareta Johansdotter, who angrily said that 'Sweden will have to feed its people on its own when it doesn't give any money; the Russians fed their people otherwise.' She had spiced this statement by calling Sweden 'Satan's member'.[47] The same thing happened in the early spring of 1725 when the vicar Thomas Betulinus tried to talk some sense into the yeoman Erik Matsson Muolila. He was an old man who had not been to church for a long time, and when Betulinus called at his house to ask how he was doing, Muolila had complained and referred to the generally bad times. Betulinus urged him to instead thank God for being liberated from their enemies, for the consoling peace and for having

---

45 1744.XI.24/117 ('gått Eder Kongl. Maij:t, såsom sin Lag Krönte och hulda Konung, förbi'). In the catalogue of The National Archives, the erroneous date of 29 November is registered for this case.

46 1728.I.17/33 ('utbrustit i dessa högsförgripelige ord; Fanen skiöter om Konungen i Swerige, iag har dock af honom nu för tiden ingen hielp eller bistånd' and 'den tienar iag under hwilken iag är').

47 1725.VI.18/42 ('Swerige må föda sitt folck sielf, när det intet gifwer penningar, annorledes födde Ryssen sitt folck' and 'Satans lem').

'returned us to a godly and Christian Magistracy'. To this Muolila replied,

> Those who have use thereof may give thanks; 'twould be better to be under the Russians; under Russian rule one was never tormented with such severe taxes as we now are; then one could give what one wanted and be let off with that, but things are different now, now people are becoming completely destitute.[48]

Neither of these statements actually mentioned the person of the King, but since he embodied the legal state authority all these cases were considered crimes of lese-majesty. In the prosecution against Mats Korpi and Margareta Johansdotter, it was said that they had defamed 'the exalted Magistracy and the government of Sweden'.[49] It was probably often the case that what were actually general complaints were clad in national terms, and that Russian rule was idealised because of a more or less articulated displeasure with the government of the time. In the 1750s, and without any direct connection to the occupations, the crofter Michel Jacobsson of Löfsala parish in Finland still claimed that 'the false Swedish lords' were responsible for the high prices. He therefore hoped that the rumour of a Russian attack would be true: 'May God grant that the Russian should come so that one may eat.'[50] In return, both the Russian and the Swedish Magistracy were attacked in a legal case from Russia in 1750. During a visit to Russian Kexholm (present-day Priozersk), Henrik Matikainen, a Finnish yeoman, had said that he shat on both the Russian Empress and the Swedish King. Interestingly enough, the Swedish local sheriff who was informed of the case did not wish to prosecute Matikainen but handed him over to the Russian authorities.[51]

---

48 1725.III.19/51 ('gifwit oss åter en Gudfruchtig och Christelig öfwerhet' and 'Den må tacka som hafwer nytta deraf, bättre wore wara under Ryssen; Under Ryska wäldet blef man intet med så swåra uthlagor plågad, som nu skier, då fick man gie hwad man wille och slap dermed, men annor går det nu til, nu blifwa Menniskorna aldeles utblåttade').

49 1725.VI.18/42 ('Höga Öfwerheten och Sweriges Regering').

50 1757.XII.14/51 ('de falska swenska Herrarne' and 'Gud gife Ryssen skulle komma så finge man mat'). The protocol of the Judicial Review Division of 14 December 1757, RA, fols 844ʳ–845ᵛ.

51 Rustemeyer, pp. 376–77.

Opinions about the form of government

The source material provides no basis for making statistical statements about opinions. Even though there are quite a few statements in support of the existing form of government, it is hardly surprising that there were many more who argued in favour of a reinforced royal authority. The uneven distribution of the source material is a contributory factor, but this state of things also corresponds with what we know from other investigations. In an older study, the political scientist Erik Fahlbeck identified three main currents in the political intellectual life of the Age of Liberty: (1) the republican parliamentarian orientation; (2) various forms of power-distribution theories; and (3) a reinforcement of the royal authority. Within these currents, views regarding details may have varied.[52] In the discussion below, these ideological directions are distinguished from one another on the basis of empirically established subdivisions. Statements about the form of government can be subdivided according to the following continuous scale:

(a) Support for the Constitution
(b) Criticism of parliamentary rule
(c) Criticism of the power of the Council (rule of the lords)
(d) Advocacy of a strengthened royal authority
(e) Advocacy of absolutism

Fahlbeck's first current corresponds to category (a), and the third to (d) and (e); between these, (b) and (c) represent variants of the second current. Even if the intensity of the opinions cannot be assessed, the material is suitable at least for narrowing down the range of attitudes.

In the following investigation, the focus is not exclusively on the royal authority. As the form of government has to be considered a holistic system or a closed entity, occasional analyses of other parts of the aggregate state authority should be permissible. Obviously, views on the King as a person can also be included among political opinions; but these will be discussed separately in the following chapter. Criticism directed against the Council and the Riksdag could be aimed at bad decisions of a specific or general character without for that reason questioning the form of government

---

52 Erik Fahlbeck, 'Studier öfver frihetstidens politiska idéer', part 1, *Statsvetenskaplig tidskrift för politik, statistik, ekonomi*, 18 (1915), 325–45 (p. 331).

as such. Such opinions – which nevertheless are in a minority in the material – have not been included in the present analysis, which instead investigates criticism that more or less expressly concerned perceived systemic constitutional errors. The five individual categories above are an ideal-typical distillation of opinions which were more complex in reality. To mention a single example, criticism of the power of the Council and the rule of the Riksdag was usually combined with support for an expanded royal authority.

Support for the Constitution

An open, systematic support for the Constitution is the most difficult to find in the source material, at least when one is studying the party defending it. Even if the preservers of the system become visible from time to time, they naturally enough do not dominate in the sources. This is a question of representativeness to which one should not attribute too great a significance. The supporters of the system are perhaps rather to be found in the areas discussed in previous chapters, and we can thus already presume their existence. General and appreciative comments made in passing can however be noted, and several of these have already been mentioned. Often these appear as objections to injurious statements. When the parish smith Johan Petter Råbock of Fåglö on Åland commended the Swedish absolute kings of yore who so often had fought and bled for the fatherland, the vicar Andreas Backman had to object:

> they have done nothing good for Sweden, we are better off now than if an absolute king were to rule, for if an absolute king minds the talk of a toad-eater, an innocent man may often end up being made shorter by the head.[53]

It is not in itself surprising that the members of the courts often spoke positively about both the government and the royal authority. Associate Judge Johan Fredrik de Bruce of the Göta Court of Appeal spoke of 'our beneficial form of government, and the liberty which we through this experience with joy'. In 1730 Associate Judge Bering of the Göta Court of Appeal argued that 'for a time now the desire to speak highly injurious words against His Royal Majesty's own illustrious person and the most gracious

---

53 1757.VII.20/37 ('de hafwa intet giordt Swerige godt, wi äro nu lyckligare än om en Souverain Konung wore rådande, ty om en Souverain Konung achtar på en lismares tal, kan åfta den oskyldiga få räcka halsen til').

Magistracy has, to far too great an extent, got the upper hand'.[54] Not long thereafter the president of the same Court of Appeal, Germund Cederhielm, made a similar observation, which inspired him to produce the following exposition concerning principles:

> It is God's clear commandment and order that everyone in general, and each and every one in particular, shall honour their Magistracy; this is prescribed also by natural law, and by the regulations and ordinances of all other peoples, and it should so much more be heeded by us, because we have both all of us together and each of us individually the greatest reason to love, cherish and serve our most gracious King, who on all occasions clearly allows his love and benevolence for his loyal subjects to shine forth.[55]

As early as the beginning of the 1730s, the doctrine of natural law had thus had a total breakthrough even at the level of implementation, including the courts of the realm. To submit to the Magistracy was thus no longer simply a religious duty; it could be justified both by the demands of natural law – which were common for all peoples – and by all secular laws.[56] The theologically based duty of obedience of the Caroline era had hence been left behind, and the door was open to an equally static social declaration based on

---

54 On de Bruce: 1759.III.28/85 ('wårt hälsosamma Regerings sätt, och den frihet, hwarutinnan wij dymedelst och, med hugnad, besinna'). On Bering: 1730.VI.17/32 ('lusten har alt för mycket på en tijd tagit öfwerhanden, att med högstförgripelige ord emot Hans Kongl. Maij:tts egen Höga Persohn och högstnådiga Öfwerheten sig uthlåta').

55 1730.XII.09/15 ('Det är Guds Klara bud och befallning att alla i gemen, samt hwar och en i synnerhet skal hedra sin öfwerhet, det föreskrifwer ock den Naturliga Lagen, så wäl som och alla andra Folks stadgar ock Förordningar, och bör det så mycket mera hos oss i akt tagas, som wi hafwa så wäl alla tillsammans som hwar för sig högsta ordsak at älska, wörda och tiena wår nådigste Konung, som wid alla tilfällen låter klarl:n lysa sin Kiärlek och ömsinnighet för sine trogne undersåtare').

56 On the introduction and significance of the tripartite doctrine of natural law during the Age of Liberty, see Jonas Nordin, *Ett fattigt men fritt folk: Nationell och politisk självbild i Sverige från sen stormaktstid till slutet av friehtstiden* (Eslöv: Symposion, 2000), pp. 328–37; Jonas Nordin, 'Om kärleken till fäderneslandet och dess utövning', in *Nationalism och nationell identitet i 1700-talets Sverige*, ed. by Åsa Karlsson and Bo Lindberg, Opuscula Historica Upsaliensia, 27 (Uppsala: Historiska institutionen, 2002), pp. 113–26 (pp. 121–22); Jonas Nordin, 'Frihetstidens radikalism', in *Riksdag, kaffehus och predikstol: Frihetstidens politiska kultur*, ed. by Marie-Christine Skuncke and Henrika Tandefelt (Stockholm: Atlantis, 2003), pp. 55–72 (pp. 63–64).

treaty law. To revere the Magistracy in word and deed and promote
the justice and security of the realm, as a similar declaration of
principles from the Hundred Court in Hällestad proclaimed, were
obligations innate to all people. The court was therefore astounded
when compelled to observe that 'a kingdom under a mild and
benevolent Magistracy' contained 'such monsters' who spoke in
disparaging terms about their lawfully crowned king and incited
the general public to disobedience.[57] The way constitutional law
in the Age of Liberty developed during the Age of Liberty, the
accepted social contract remained as firm and above criticism as the
religiously motivated one had ever been.

In 1745, the postal inspector in Vasa (Vaasa in Finnish) discovered an anonymous letter addressed to the King and the Council,
signed by the pseudonym 'An Honest Finn' ('Ärlig Finne'). This case
illustrates the constant vigilance of the authorities, who took every
cautionary measure as soon as there was talk about the Instrument
of Government or the royal authority, because the letter-writer was
not at all critical of the form of government. On the contrary, he
felt that those who blamed the political system for the misfortunes
suffered by the kingdom ever since the death of Charles XII had
'an insufficient understanding of the excellent Constitution and
governing laws of the realm'. The true causes of the misfortunes
of the kingdom were in fact 'a lapsed Christianity' and 'the abuse
of our liberty for self-indulgence', which, if they were allowed to
spread, could overthrow 'all the excellent measures put in place for
the prevention of the reintroduction of an unlimited absolute rule
in the realm'. In the absence of hard evidence, the letter-writer did
not dare to name any such schismatics – an unverified report could
strike back at the informer – but urged the King and the Council
to be on their guard in a spirit of loyal veneration. The province
governor Gustaf Creutz, who reported the letter to His Royal
Majesty, declared that he had never encountered ideas like this
among the subjects in the province. In addition, one may be certain
that the intent of the letter-writer aroused greater concern than
the repudiators of the faith and abusers of liberty he had warned
about. The view of 'An Honest Finn' corresponded in letter and
spirit to the ideas that were publicly promoted through the Church
and the official proclamations; but when they were uttered by an

---

57 1748.VII.06/A3 ('uti et Rike under en mild och nådig Öfwerhet skulle
finnas sådane missfoster').

anonymous subject, they immediately awakened the suspicion of the authorities.[58]

Several people overinterpreted the freedom provided by the Constitution. The tailor Johan Forsman in Stockholm was enraged that the burgher guard had been ordered to protect the city while the life guards were ordered to Pomerania. Neither the king nor the Council was authorised to issue such an order, he felt, and 'he who went further than he should and wanted to was a rascal, since they were a free people'. The ombudsman Johan Ljunggren, who had heard the statement, then objected that the king and the Council obviously had the authority to give orders, and that Forsman should on the contrary thank God for that he lived under a blessed government. Certainly they were a free people, agreed Ljunggren; but they were also citizens bound by law with rights as well as obligations. Before the court, Forsman alleged as an excuse that his statement had been made without premeditation and without any real intent to incite disobedience against His Royal Majesty. Conversely, he maintained that he had acted as an honourable and loyal subject at the latest session of the Riksdag, and that he never wished to break that to which 'subjects are duty-bound in such a fortunate form of government'.[59]

Oppositionists who believed that they were the true interpreters of the form of government, and who accused the lords of abusing the Instrument of Government, were something of an exceptional case. Captain Börje Philip Schecta, who had been sentenced to life imprisonment for having attempted to recruit peasants in support of the royal court, focused on the discrepancy between the actual implementation of the form of government and the mediated image of it. The crime, he said in an appeal, consisted of his having spoken against 'the Government' ('Regeringen'); but he then requested an explanation of the meaning of that word. As far as he knew, sections 13–15 of the Instrument of Government, which had been established and generally accepted by the people, stipulated 'that the lawfully crowned King of Sweden alone is the

---

58 1745.XII.04/B8 ('otillräckeligit begrep om Rikets härliga Grund- samt Styrslolagar'; 'en förfallen Christendom'; 'wår Frihets misbrukande til sielfswåld'; and 'alla the förtreffeliga anstallter som til hämmande af ett oinskränckt Enwålds Regementes återinförande i Riket giorda äro').

59 1757.VIII.17/31(−40) ('den wore en Canaille, som gingo längre än han borde och sielf wille, då de woro fritt folk'); 1757.XII.01/3 ('undersåtare äro skyldige i ett så lyckeligit Regeringssätt').

ruling king according to the law, and no one else'. The Riksdag
Act, Schecta had noted, in addition left an opening for the Estates
to jointly change the Instrument of Government for the benefit and
security of society. The nobleman Schecta, who through his Estate
'by God and Nature is freely given the right to be a member of the
Riksdag', therefore did not see it as a crime, but rather as a duty,
to have promoted the letter of the Constitution at the assembly of
the Estates. As his question about the meaning of the word 'government' was left without an answer, he sent a new letter whose
content said that he thereafter only feared God and honoured the
King, but '[would] not recognise anybody else for the Magistracy of
the kingdom'.[60] Schecta felt that the true meaning of the Instrument
of Government had been his sole guiding principle.

Criticism of the form of government often meant a polarised
view of the king and the Council, where the person in question
supported one or other of these parties. Even though criticism of
the Council and the lords was widespread, it did not completely
predominate. Many people thought it necessary to have a counter-
force that could balance the royal authority. There were also those
who defended the political system on the basis of idealistic convictions and felt that the balance between the king and the Council
created harmony between parties who had the welfare of the realm
at heart. The defenders of the system were, of course, not primarily
among those who were tried in a court of law; but an additional
example can be provided.

One substantial case concerned the hearing of Petter Lundberg,
an innkeeper from Vadstena, who had – apparently on his own
initiative – formulated an extensive but poorly spelled proposal
for political reforms in thirteen points.[61] Dated 10 July 1733, it
was addressed to the King personally. The specific bad conditions
that had aroused Lundberg's dissatisfaction were explained in a
detailed preamble. While greed and selfishness had always been
prevalent in all the Estates in the fatherland, he said, now, 'since the

60 1758.X.25/52 ('at Swea Lagkrönte Konung är allena efter lagen Regerande
   Konung, och ingen annan'; 'af Gud och naturen är frij skänkt den Rättighet
   at wara RijksdagsMan'; and 'ärkiänner ingen annan för Rijkets öferhet').
   On Schecta and his crimes, see Malmström, Sveriges politiska historia, IV,
   pp. 160, 169–70, 242. He was convicted by the extensive 1755–56 estate
   commission for political crimes: R 5651–5665, RA.
61 The following description is based in its entirety on the material in 1734.
   VI.20/31.

royal authority was changed', they were completely out of control,
threatening to bring both town and country to rack and ruin. Stories
from abroad testified to hellfire breaking out in several towns and
villages, and it was possible that God in his anger wanted to bring
forward the vengeance spoken of in Revelation 6. 10. Godless self-
interest was expressed in concrete terms, in that manorial farms
(*frälsehemman*) had been absolved from the fees that had previously been paid in aid of the Crown; the nobility had appropriated
all offices; the fees for various services had been arbitrarily raised
through the charging of perquisites; and the law of Sweden, 'which
is a foundation of and a guiding principle for all those things
which should be undertaken and done in all Estates', had become
so bloated with ordinances and decrees that it could no longer be
deciphered by the simple multitude. In a sober analysis of the new
form of government, Lundberg noted that

> the royal authority has been changed here in this our Swedish
> kingdom so that His Royal Majesty shall be able to exercise nothing
> other than that which concerns the exalted and royal office in par-
> ticular; but shall not as before be able to be the protector of the
> lower Estates, *et cetera*[.][62]

Lundberg thus seems to have embraced the limitations of the royal
authority, among other things with the argument that the political
awareness of the lower social orders would be promoted as a consequence. At the same time, he expressed the corporatist idea that
each Estate had its own particular interests to safeguard. For this
reason, Lundberg believed that all spiritual and temporal offices
had to be limited to those that a person's office, the law of God
and secular law required. The interesting thing about Lundberg's
proposal is that from beginning to end, he demonstrated an understanding of and knowledge concerning the true meaning of the
Instrument of Government. He wished to distribute the proposal in
good time before the next session of the Riksdag, so that 'His Royal
Majesty and the esteemed Council and Estates of the Realm' would

---

62 1734.VI.20/31 ('sedan dhen Kongl: myndigheten blefwet ändratt'; 'som är
   ett fondamäntt ock Rättesnöre till altt dhett som i alla stånd företagas ock
   giöras bör'; and 'dhen Kongl. Myndigheten är ändradt här utj uår Suea
   Rike på dhet sättett att Hans Kongl. Maijtt icke mera skal kunna uträtta
   än allenast huad dhett Hög och Kongl. Embetett i synnerhett uijdkom-
   mer; män icke som till förene skall kunna uara dhe nedrige stånddens
   förmyndare mäd mera').

all have an opportunity to consider the suggestions contained in his proposal. Although Lundberg expressed an awareness of the limitations of the royal authority, the proposal was nevertheless addressed to the King personally, not to the king in Council. This is confirmed not least by the preserved envelope of the original letter: 'The most powerful and most gracious King of Sweden Frederick the first is most humbly petitioned in Stockholm with this proposal.' Lundberg's specification of the mandate of the royal authority also corresponded well with accepted doctrine:

> His Royal Majesty who by God and the inhabitants of the kingdom of Sweden is the anointed and lawfully appointed King on the Swedish throne[.][63]

Lundberg was obviously well aware of and favourably disposed towards the fact that absolutism was over. On the other hand, it remains unclear whether he saw Frederick as a constitutionally limited or as a completely powerless monarch. The fact that the proposal was addressed to Frederick in person suggests that Lundberg actually attributed greater influence to him than he really possessed. This interpretation is supported by the continuation of the case.

For Lundberg, sending this missive to the King was only the beginning of the story. Two days later, on 12 July 1733, Lundberg sent a copy of the same proposal to the province governor of Östergötland, Erik Ehrenkrona. In that context, he explained the true intent behind his proposal. Some time before, Lundberg had, according to his own statement, struck up a conversation with seven Dalecarlians on a journey from Småland. When he asked what they thought about their country, they complained of high taxes and declared that they had a mind to 'go up to Stockholm in full numbers and help the royal authority rise again to what it formerly was'.[64] The Dalecarlians said that they expected help from disgruntled private soldiers of the guard, who had laid up a store of rifles for them. On hearing this tale, Lundberg had

---

63 1734.VI.20/31 ('Hans Kongl: maijtt ock Riksens högll: Råd ock ständer'; 'Swäriges Rikes stormäktige aldra nådigaste Konung Frjdrik dhen första upwaktas mäd dhetta i Stockholm aldra underdånigast'; and 'Hans Kongl: maijtt som af Gud ock suäriges Rikkes Jnbygare är smord och lagell: tillförordnadtt Konung på dhen suänska Thronen').

64 1734.VI.20/31 ('man ok huse gå up till stokholm ock jälpa dhen Kongl: myndigheten up igen som han till förne warit').

urged them to consider the damage to the land and the realm that 'absolute' ('siälfrådande') kings had caused not too long ago in consequence of the long war. (Lundberg used the plural for the kings, but the singular for the war. Apparently all crowned heads were cast in the same mould and equally guilty of the protracted wars of Charles XII.) Therefore, he promised them to draw up a proposal of his own instead, one he thought would be much more constructive, for consideration before the next session of the Riksdag. He then went home to draw up his thirteen points. A short while later he had met two other Dalecarlians, previously unknown to him, who had gratefully promised to convey his text to Dalecarlia. He also claimed to have given a copy to an unknown man from Växjö.

In other words, the real purpose of Lundberg's proposal, which he now communicated to the province governor in copy, was to prevent a rebellion geared to strengthening the royal authority. By perfect chance, his proposal intended to rectify precisely those bad conditions that the guardsmen had complained about. In a post-script to the province governor, Lundberg explained that he had not stated the true reasons in his letter to the King, but hoped that the province governor would now warn the administrative boards in Stockholm so that they could forestall the attempted rebellion through love, loyalty and the establishment of unity.

The province governor Ehrenkrona was alarmed when reading this letter and immediately had Lundberg brought in for questioning. The matter was reported to Stockholm, and a comprehensive process was initiated to gain some clarity in the matter. After extensive investigations in Småland, Östergötland and Dalecarlia, two Dalecarlians from Gagnef who had received Lundberg's text were finally identified. Because they were illiterate they had, on their return home, handed it over to a local lay assessor (nämndeman). But because the assessor had not been able to make anything of the contents either, he had planned to pass the text on to Olof Danielsson in the parish of Djura and Leksand, a former member of the Riksdag. He had, however, left it lying in his cottage, whence it was confiscated by the province governor of Kopparberg, Nils Reuterholm, after almost three months. According to Reuterholm's assessment, the yeomen involved were neither cunning nor crafty, and the text had probably not done any harm. Lundberg's story about the planned rebellion of the Dalecarlians could not be verified. Instead, it turned out that Lundberg had tried to distribute his suggestions for reform long before the alleged occasion; according to the testimony of one witness, he had worked on them for three years.

The political petition of Lundberg the innkeeper was long and convoluted, and it demonstrated that he possessed good knowledge of the political system. It even contained a short enquiry into the rationality of the royal authority. In spite of his evidently good insight into the form of government, he attributed actual political influence to the King. This was precisely the result that the lords hoped to achieve by conveying the impression of a powerful king: subjects who were happy with the balanced form of government and at the same time relieved to be spared absolutism. It is impossible to say how widely disseminated such ideas were. No news is good news, and the supporters of the Constitution did not normally attract any attention. The somewhat naïve Lundberg was careless enough to combine his liking for the Instrument of Government with extra-parliamentary suggestions and a general spreading of rumours.

The Judicial Review Division did not rule on this case until 20 June 1734, one year after it had begun: Petter Lundberg was sentenced to fourteen days in prison on bread and water, while his neighbour Nils Lundberg, who had helped him write the text, was sentenced to eight days. As usual, the most important thing seems to have been to avoid drawing attention to the case. This attitude had paradoxical consequences for the reasoning of the Chancellor of Justice, Johan Cederbielke: on the one hand, he gave no credit to Lundberg's story about the planned rebellion of the Dalecarlians, and the entire responsibility therefore fell on Lundberg alone. On the other hand, the punishment was comparatively mild, because a stricter execution would have compelled the court to take the planned rebellion seriously, and then the Dalecarlians mentioned by Lundberg would also have had to be traced and punished. In view of the meagre descriptions of them, this would have been all but fruitless, and the only result of the investigations would have been to draw additional attention to the case.

Criticism of the rule of the Riksdag

Criticism directed against the rule of the Riksdag was different from other kinds of political discontent because the Estates represented the people and were not included in the Magistracy. The Riksdag was an old institution whose legitimacy was long established, and it had functioned as a popular body of implementation even during the absolute monarchy. According to the old way of thinking, the Estates were corporatist associations that balanced one another's immunities and constituted parties of negotiation vis-à-vis the Magistracy. The people had a right to be consulted concerning their freedoms whereas His Royal Majesty governed. Criticism might therefore concern decisions that had been made, but equally often it had to do with the Riksdag as a whole or individual Estates and members placing themselves above their peers and assuming Magistracy status. In a much-talked-about petition in support of an improved balance among the three branches of government – king, Council and Riksdag – Claes Wilhelm Grönhagen objected to this distorted view at the House of Nobility:

> It is surely also true that the common people are not called the subjects of the Estates of the Realm, while the king owns the entire majesty, which the Estates of the Realm have completely relinquished. [...] Indeed, can the freedom of a subject consist in being able to interfere as a principal in the government of the realm? We may be, and be called, men of liberty; but we must never forget that we are also subjects.[65]

The power of the Estates was thus, according to this way of looking at things, an abnormality, with respect to both symbolism and realpolitik: subjects could by definition not exert any influence over the governance of the kingdom, which was a regality; and as institutionalised special interests, the four Estates could not govern the kingdom with the required impartiality.

The yeoman Per Olsson objected to the participation of officials in the Riksdag. If district court judges, lay assessors and mayors

65 'C. W. Grönhagens memorial om Ärlig svensk', in *Sveriges ridderskaps och adels riksdags-protokoll från och med år 1719*, 32 vols (Stockholm: Norstedts, 1875–1982), XIX:1: *1755–1756* (1923), appendix 45, pp. 133, 137 ('Det är ock väl sant at menigheten ei kallas Riksens Ständers undersåtare, emedan Konungen äger hela maijestätet, hvilket Riksens Ständer aldeles afklädt sig. [...] Kan väl en undersåtes frihet bestå deruti at såsom principal kunna blanda sig i riksstyrelsen? Vi må vara och hete frie män, men få ändå ei glömma at vi tillika äro undersåtare'). Regarding this memorandum, see Ludvig Stavenow, 'De politiska doktrinernas uppkomst och första utveckling under frihetstiden', in *Historiska studier: Festskrift tillägnad Carl Gustaf Malmström den 2 november 1897* (Stockholm: Norstedts, 1897), pp. 1–50; Malmström, *Sveriges politiska historia*, IV, pp. 145, 246. For yet another example of the same opinion, see *En redlig swänsk patriots politiska tros bekiännelse*, articles 17–18.

followed their own interests when they acted as lawmakers, to whom could a person then turn when he had been wronged? he asked. The crofter Per Jönsson, who himself lacked the right to vote but supported the Peasant Estate, expressed traditional conflicts among the Estates when he argued that the Nobility and Clergy had already deserved their places in hell by oppressing Peasants and Burghers. More sweeping but just as crude in his utterances was Bengt Benzin, who in the marketplace in Karlstad had wished the Devil's curse on the Estates, which he felt had 'duped this old Sweden completely'.[66] The crown bailiff Eric Berggren had views on individual members of the Riksdag. He feared that if the influential and pro-royal 'Johan Pehrson would be evicted from the Estate, the peasants would become crofters under the Nobility', and was of the opinion that 'Skålmo Olof Ersson was a scoundrel and a rebel and the other peasants were stupid bastards'.[67] The yeoman Eric Holstensson felt 'that all members of the Riksdag should be in the clink and gaol', and Anders Palm, a journeyman wig-maker from Stockholm, wished that 'the Devil would take those who have now sat in the Riksdag'. The town representative from Kalmar, Lars Åbrandt, returned disillusioned from the Riksdag with the view that all decisions were made on a short-term basis and without consideration of the law. The members of the Riksdag had only one guiding principle, he said: 'we serve our friends'. The yeoman Jacob Esaiasson thought that his own representative was a knave and a bribe-taker who had done as much work as the fifth wheel on a wagon, while the soldier Lund felt that the realm could not possibly be governed as long as there was a king in every village. The skipper Niklas Lind spoke disparagingly about the powerful trade mayor of

---

66 On Per Olsson: 1771.X.24/29½c. On Per Jönsson: 1757.III.03/5. On Benzin: 1758.X.25/53 ('grundlurat thetta gamla Swerige').

67 1756.IX.08/23 ('Johan Pehrson wräktes utur Ståndet, skulle bönderna blifwa torpare under adeln' and 'Skålmo Olof Ersson wara en skälm och en uprorsmakare och de andra bönderna dumma dieflar'). Johan Pehrson had acted as the leader of the Court party in the Peasant Estate. With reference to some prosecutions that were at bottom politically motivated, the Council in 1755 refused to approve his letter of commission to the Riksdag, and he was therefore denied admission into the Estate. He then continued to work for the interests of the Court by wining and dining and lobbying, which led to his arrest. He died in gaol before sentencing; Malmström, *Sveriges politiska historia*, IV, pp. 49, 128–29, 159–60, 169, 184–85, 242. Olof Ersson, like Johan Pehrson, represented the province of Kopparberg, but has not left any significant mark in the records.

Stockholm and Speaker of the Burgher Estate, Gustaf Kierman, and said that 'Mr Mayor now governs pretty much the whole kingdom.' This statement was an affront to royal authority, and the administration regarded it as criticism of the Constitution in general.[68]

The criticism voiced against the Riksdag and its members was varied, as this series of examples shows. The basic argument was that the Estates were the representatives of the people and could not act as the Magistracy. Accusations of self-interest and Estate egotism also recurred. 'The members of the Riksdag may well drink wine and ride in coaches', opined Johan Pettersson, a painter in Jönköping, 'but poor people do not have enough to buy a loaf of bread.' The Estates, the critics felt, defended the individual or corporate self-interests of the members instead of looking after the common good. Precisely the latter was, according to traditional political thinking, something for which only the royal authority could work. Nor had Johan Pettersson the painter anything to say against the King; on the contrary, he had emphasised that 'we have a gracious King, may God preserve me if I should say something against His Royal Majesty'.[69]

Only a prince was without and above all special interests, and this was something that the authors of the Constitution had admitted when they drew up the Instrument of Government. The Riksdag did not rule on its own, but safeguarded its immunities through its control of the executive power. The Council did not have a mandate to govern, but moderated the royal exercise of power. The king in his turn sanctioned the impartiality of the collective decision-making through his signature. In reality, this balance was eliminated soon after the entry into force of the Instrument of Government, but the model survived in the conceptual world of the subjects. Although the actual design of the national government seems to have been obvious to many people, both defenders and detractors of the form of government abided by its principles, albeit

---

68 On Holstensson: 1748.IV.09/F1 ('at alla Riksdagsmän borde sittia i Kurran och Arrest'). On Palm: 1763.I.20/30½a ('fanen wäl ta dem, som nu hållit Riksdag'). On Åbrandt: 1772.VII.30/57 ('wi tjena wåra wänner'). On Jacob Esaiasson: 1754.VII.10/19. On Lund: 1757.XII.16/72. On Lind: 1760. VI.18/28 ('Herr Borgmästaren styrer rätt nu hela Riket').

69 1744.I.11/19 ('Riksdagsmennerne må wäl dricka win och åka i Caretter, men then fattige har icke så mycket, som han kan kiöpa sig en kaka bröd före' and 'wi hafwa en nådig Konung, Gud beware mig, att tala något på Hans Kongl. Maij:t').

for opposite reasons: the former saw the balance of power as an important basic principle to defend, the latter saw it as a construction to restore.

The questioning of the Appropriation Ordinance (*bevillnings-förordning*) of 1748 by the peasant miner Hans Hansson is interesting because of the principle involved. He did not know what value or effect this ordinance had, because it had been issued by the Estates and lacked the King's signature. According to Hans Hansson, who spoke for all the common people of Främshyttan, the King sat as a charity lodger (*nådehjon*) at the behest of the Estates, and Hans Hansson wondered what the point was of having a king at all, if he was not allowed to order appropriations. Nor did the Estates have the right to command, he emphasised, because they were not a Magistracy. However, the crown bailiff who communicated the ordinance emphasised that the Estates had issued the appropriation out of concern for the fatherland, and that a decision made in their name had the same weight as if it had borne the King's signature. In the eyes of the Court of Appeal, the seriousness of Hans Hansson's crime consisted in the King being referred to as a charity lodger. In fact, though, this had not been said with disparaging intent, but constituted Hans Hansson's matter-of-fact description of the power relations in the kingdom. His actual criticism was directed against the Riksdag, which was in his opinion controlled by inept young men. That he had really called the King a charity lodger could not be proved, and he was convicted only of having questioned the justification of having a king who had no power to control taxes. In this context it may be pointed out that the appropriations, as the Swedish term implies (*bevillning*, related to the verb *bevilja*, to approve, to grant), always required approval of the Riksdag – even during absolutism. Not until 1712 was this immunity revoked, and for a short period until the death of Charles XII six years later, the right of taxation was, by way of exception, an exclusively royal prerogative.[70]

---

70 1748.X.12/A5. On the appropriations during absolutism, see Gösta Hasselberg, 'De karolinska kungabalksförslagen och konungens makt över beskattningen', *Karolinska förbundets årsbok 1943* (1943), 54–90 (pp. 85–90).

Criticism of the power of the Council

Many of the cited statements about the Riksdag were made by people who themselves lacked representation. This may be a coincidence; but generally speaking, political discontent will have been in inverse proportion to the opportunity to do something about the situation. However, precisely because the Riksdag was the representative of the people, it frequently escaped criticism: it was an assembly which the subjects themselves could influence. It was more common for discontent to be directed against the lords in the Council. True, they were supposed to be representatives of the Estates; but among the people, the relationship was often perceived to be the opposite. This was primarily because the Council was regarded as an open vessel which corresponded with the House of Nobility.[71]

Carl Arvedson, a tradesman from Nyköping, criticised both the Riksdag and the Council. During a visit to the capital, Arvedson had approached a couple of soldiers from the Royal Guard who were posted outside the church while the Riksdag sermon was being read out. He asked what purpose the large troop of soldiers served. During the time of Gustav I there had been no need for a strong guard, he maintained, and it should be superfluous now as well, if the King was truly safe among his subjects. He felt that the King's lack of security was linked to the rule of the Council, although it is unclear exactly why this was the case: 'if it were not for too many lords ruling, things would be done in a better manner'. When Arvedson was later asked to explain this statement, he claimed to know well that royal absolutism was in conflict with temporal law; but on the other hand he found it compatible with the law of God. Previously he had himself been an opponent of the autocracy, but because the King now had three princes, he thought that it was both cheaper and better for 'one person to rule than many'. That would entail saving the large costs of the Riksdag assemblies, he declared.[72]

A common accusation against the lords was that they could not provide the protection that was the most important duty of the Magistracy. The noblemen in the Council were generally blamed for

---

71 See, e.g., 1756.VIII.25/44; 1756.IX.08/23.
72 1752.VI.01/6–7 ('om det ej wore för många Herrar, som regerade, gingo det bättre till' and 'at en regerade än många').

the two failed wars of aggression that had been started during the Age of Liberty. Some years after the War of the Hats of 1741–1743, the vicar Gottfried Hoffberg delivered an intercession-day sermon where he pointed his finger at those who had been responsible for the war debacle. The old deserving Councilmen who had spilt their blood for Charles XII had been removed from office, he thundered, while those who were now in the Council were ignorant cockerels who worked more for war than for peace so that 'little Count Baron' ('lilla Grefwen Baron') could have a military career. In days of yore a Swede could beat ten Russians, declared Hoffberg, but these days foreigners easily defeated Swedish soldiers.[73] To Hoffberg, general morals were closely linked, if not expressly to the form of government as such, then at least to those who dominated that form of government. The Council was a corporation of the Nobility defending its own interests, governed by self-interest and without an ounce of piety. The examples it set had a deleterious effect on social morals, on military discipline and on the welfare of the kingdom.[74]

Similar complaints recurred during the Pomeranian War. Johan Petter Råbock, a parish smith from Åland, felt that 'it would be better to serve one master than twenty-four' (exaggerating the number of Councillors); and the war in Germany, he opined, would never have had such an unfortunate outcome with someone like Charles XII at the helm of state. Besides, the infallibility of the monarch was confirmed by Råbock's contention that it had been the King's adviser Count Piper, rather than Charles XII himself, who had caused the defeats in the Great Northern War.[75] Christian Gnospelius, a coffee-maker in Stockholm, went so far as to hope

---

73 The ratio of one to ten harks back to the battle of Narva in 1700. That 8,000 exhausted Swedes defeated 80,000 well-entrenched Russians was emphasised already in the first victory bulletin: *Kårt doch sanfärdig berättelse om den glorieuse och i manna minne oförlijklige seger, hwarmed den aldrahögste Gud den 20. november hafwer behagat wälsigna Kongl: May:tx af Swerige rättmätige wapn emot den trolöse fiende czaren af Muscow.* Narva *Narva den 28. novemb:1700* ([n.p.]: [n. pub.], [n.d.]). See also Sylwan, p. 90; Olov Westerlund, *Karl XII i svensk litteratur från Dahlstierna till Tegnér* (Lund: Gleerups, 1951), pp. 23–26, 87; Nordin, *Ett fattigt men fritt folk*, p. 260.

74 1748.IX.15/A11; 1752.II.14/33.

75 1757.VII.20/37 ('det bättre wore at tiena en husbonde än 24'). Carl Piper was captured after the battle at Poltava and died in Russian captivity in 1716.

that the Pomeranian War would have a negative outcome for Sweden. That would be a serious chastisement for the Councillors who alone bore the responsibility for the unnecessary aggression. Addressing a smaller group, he also said that at a visit to a gentleman's residence, he had been shown a list of 125 people who were to be held responsible and executed, or be punished in some other way, for their support of the war. Among these were several lords of the Council, members of the Riksdag and members of the 1756 great commission dealing with political crimes.[76]

Obviously there were many people who contrasted the rule of the Council with a strong royal authority. A stranger had told Henrik Nyman, a drummer of the Dalecarlian regiment, that the Prussian king had sent troops that would help Adolf Frederick 'get the better of the lords, who had been obstructing His Royal Majesty's government'. The Swedish troops who had been summoned to defend the country were said to offer symbolic resistance only; and the Council of the Realm, duly alarmed, had therefore travelled to the King in the countryside in order to offer him absolute rule. The King had declined the offer, though, because he preferred to rely on the aid of the Prussian soldiers. According to the same source, the high prices in the country had been caused by the lords; and this could be rectified only if the King were to become an absolute monarch. Nyman had understood that the man who told him this was a charity lodger and not a freeholder, but he also assumed that the man was a former soldier because he had been so bold and outspoken.[77]

All things considered, it appears to have been relatively common to direct criticism at the Council. However, it is one of the many paradoxes of the form of government that such criticism was rarely expressed in the source material examined. Because of the structure of the public exercise of power, with an impersonal 'His Royal Majesty', the law did not differentiate between blame directed at the Council and blame directed at the king. The many statements that were properly directed against the lords of the Council were parried by being interpreted as a questioning of His Majesty. In this way, the Council shared in the political immunity of the king. This was unquestionably one of the most important functions of the

---

76 1759.II.16/18. See also 1760.IX.24/31.
77 1757.VII.27/74 ('at taga rätt på Herrarne, som warit Hans Kongl. Maij:t uti Regementet hinderlige'). See also 1757.VII.22/36.

royal authority according to the lords in government, and it is an important explanation of their stubborn adherence to a symbolic figure who was difficult to deal with for a variety of reasons.[78]

Advocacy of a strengthened royal authority

Petter Enström, a foundry inspector from the area around Säter in Dalecarlia, seems to represent the next step on the scale in his advocacy of a somewhat modified balance between the state authorities. He felt that 'His Royal Majesty should have more power, and more votes in the Council'. It is not clear how far he believed the expansion of the royal authority should go; but it was unreasonable, he said, that the king, 'being the Master', did not have greater influence. Gnospelius the coffee-maker was also dissatisfied with the government and the Constitution of the realm. He felt that 'the King should have and exercise more power', although he also steered clear of clarifying how extensive that power should be.[79]

Eric Berggren, a crown bailiff from Säter, was more specific, however. In his view, royal absolutism was loathsome; but he thought that the King should at least have six votes in the Council. In the present situation, the noblemen had too much influence, and they prioritised their own children before the commoners in appointments to public offices. On one occasion, though, Berggren had claimed that the Instrument of Government and absolutism were the same thing. The actual meaning of this cryptic statement escaped the prosecutor, but his conclusion was nevertheless clear:

> To make absolutism and the Instrument of Government one and the same would in itself be as impossible as it would be reprehensible for an honest Swedish subject, and it was a statement that accurately characterised the partiality Berggren certainly had for absolutism.[80]

The crown bailiff was a servant of the Crown, an official and a local representative, and he should be included in the elite of the local

78 Cf. Sennefelt, *Den politiska sjukan*, p. 111.
79 On Enström: 1757.II.04/8 ('Kongl. Maj:t borde hafwa mera makt, och flera röster i Rådet'). On Gnospelius: 1759.II.16/18 ('Konungen borde hafwa och få utöfwa mera makt').
80 1756.IX.08/23 ('At giöra souvereinite och Regeringz Form till ett och det samma, wore i sig sielf så omöijeligit, som det för en redelig Swensk undersåte, skulle wara lastwärdigt, och woro thet en utlåtelse, som noga utmärckte den smak och tycke, Berggren skall hafwa för enwäldet').

community when it came to influence and education. In his official oath he had, like all servants of the Crown, forsworn absolutism.[81] In spite of this, Eric Berggren claimed that the bailiff's office did not own a copy of the Instrument of Government, and that he for his own part had never seen one. It is impossible to know if this was said in self-defence or if it was actually true. However, one of the witnesses, assistant vicar Lars Frögelius, said that the two of them had once discussed the Instrument of Government, and Berggren had then asked if Frögelius thought that the King should have more power. 'God save us from that', Frögelius had answered, 'it would contribute to the introduction of absolutism, which we have forsworn'.[82] The better-informed Frögelius had furthermore pointed out that the King actually did have authority according to the existing Instrument of Government, and had said a few things about its contents. Berggren had listened thoughtfully to this.

In any case, the prosecutor did not accept Berggren's alleged ignorance. If Berggren had never read the Instrument of Government, he could not have understood the oath forswearing absolutism that he had taken either. If he made absolutism and the Instrument of Government one and the same, forswearing absolutism actually amounted to forswearing the Instrument of Government. Consequently, the prosecutor concluded, Berggren did not know 'what form of government we have', and this was unacceptable for an official of the Crown.[83]

During Berggren's hearing, The deputy district judicial officer (*vice landsfiskal*) Olof Wallman had been especially curious about any connections to some recently published pamphlets on the implementation of the Constitution.[84] These pamphlets concerned the dissimilar interpretations by the King and the Council of the foundational laws, and whether His Majesty had a right to review a majority opinion of the Council before a decision was made.

---

81 Maria Cavallin, *I kungens och folkets tjänst: Synen på den svenske ämbetsmannen 1750–1780* (Gothenburg: Historiska institutionen, 2003), pp. 69–73.
82 1756.IX.08/23 ('Gud beware oss derifrån, det skulle bidraga till souverainitetens införande, som wi afswurit').
83 1756.IX.08/23 ('hwad Regeringz sätt wij hafwa').
84 *Handlingar om grundlagarnes wärkställighet, tryckte på riksens höglofliga ständers befalning wid riksdagen år 1756* (Stockholm: Kungl. tryckeriet, [n.d.]). Regarding this political trial of strength between the King and the Council, see Malmström, *Sveriges politiska historia*, IV, pp. 146–59.

The definite view of the Council that this was not the case was subjected to the arbitration of the Estates, and the friction within the government authority was thus brought out into the public sphere. The issue itself concerned the assessment of merit versus ancestry when appointing officials, and this conflict marked the beginning of the dispute between the Estates that grew in strength until the end of the Age of Liberty. Following the lobbying of the commoner Estates, the Caps abolished the public ranking order (which imposed an authorised hierarchy among various state officials) and the Nobility's exclusive right to higher offices according to this order during the 1765–1766 session of the Riksdag. What was soon to become official policy was still considered subversive in the 1750s. The commoner Estates' resistance to the Nobility was often connected with royalist expressions in a traditional manner; the King was still considered the primary safeguard against the power of the lords. During the Riksdag sessions of the 1760s, the commoner Estates achieved considerable success with respect to civil rights; but ironically enough, Gustav III would abolish all the ordinances that had promoted equality among the Estates a short time after his coup d'état.[85]

In a handwritten pamphlet, which was found and may have circulated in the province of Jönköping in the summer of 1757, the issue of privileges was expressly linked to the royal authority. The anonymous pamphlet was addressed to the three commoner Estates, which 'are placed under the yoke of thraldom; for indeed things have now gone so far that the nobleman wants you to believe that all others are born to serve him'. The barb was directed against the rule of the lords – 'they do whatever they want both with the King and the Crown, and the other three Estates' – and the recommended reforms were politically cautious but socially

---

85 For these issues, see Nordin, *Ett fattigt men fritt folk*, pp. 392–428, and Nordin, 'Frihetstidens radikalism' and the literature quoted therein. At the abolition of the ranking, a symbolic exception – significant in this context – was made: 'With respect to the etiquette at the royal court, Your Royal Majesty's highness and the dignity of the realm require that this remains according to the earlier usual practice'; see 'Kungl. förordning angående lagarnas verkställighet den 12 november 1766', in *Frihetstidens grundlagar och konstitutionella stadgar*, ed. by Axel Brusewitz (Stockholm: Norstedts, 1916), pp. 218–19 ('hvad beträffar etiqvetten vid thet k. hofvet, så fordrar E. K. Maj:ts höghet och rikets värdighet, att thermed förblifver efter förra vanligheten').

revolutionary. Three of the four points promoted against an inherited nobility, for a limitation of the privileges of the Nobility and for merit as the sole basis for appointments to offices. The text was structured as a proposal to the next session of the Riksdag, and that was probably the reason for the pragmatic and modestly visionary proposals. Although the text had a royalist tone and was permeated with indignation at the Nobility, the opening point which dealt with the royal authority contained moderate demands:

> It should be arranged so that the king's power is increased somewhat, i.e. so that he in addition to the proposals by the officers in question, such as colonels, can within the framework of the army award the ranks of ensign and cornet, including the commission and rank of lieutenant, but he should not go higher with his power, in the appointment of posts, within the framework of the land army.[86]

The text was no doubt connected to the so-called committee report on appointments (*tjänstebetänkandet*) that had been issued in November 1756, and the issue was by no means an insignificant one: it was the King's refractoriness in such matters that had caused the reintroduction of the royal signature stamp six months earlier. The report also said that 'the appointment of posts is a rather urgent matter of national importance, which is closely connected to liberty'. The lower officer ranks could be awarded by the King in Cabinet – i.e. in the presence of two Councillors of the Realm – on the basis of proposals from the respective regimental commanders. The committee report on appointments did not suggest any changes in this praxis.[87] Conversely, the anonymous pamphlet proposed

---

86 1757.VII.12/16 ('äre stadde under träldoms oket; ty det har nu rätt gådt så långt at adelsmannen will man skall tro at alle andre äro födde at tiena honom'; 'de giöra hwad de wilja både med Kong och Crono, samt de öfrige 3 Stånden'; and 'Bör lagas, at Konungens makt något ökas, nemligen, så at Han utom förslaget af wederbörande Chefer, som Öfwerstar, kan under milicen gifwa bort Fändrike och Cornette, inclusive tillika och med Lieutenants beställning och tienst, men ei högre bör han gå med sin macht, wid tiensters bortgifwande, under milicen til lands').

87 The King's right of appointment was regulated by RF 1720, § 40, and above all by the Accession Charter 1751, § 9. The issue of appointing lower officers' ranks is discussed in the committee report on appointments of 23 November 1756, § 17. See *Frihetstidens grundlagar*, pp. 38–40, 76–77, 202, quotation on p. 192 ('tjensternes bortgifvande är ett ganska angelägit och riksvårdande ärende, som med friheten har en nära förknippad gemenskap'). See also Fredrik Lagerroth, *Frihetstidens författning: En*

that the King should have a right of appointment alongside the lists. The impression that a specific case had dictated the wording is close at hand, but there is also a principal dimension that can be inferred from the context. Even if skill should be the only ground for promotion, the regimental commanders, who were almost without exception noblemen, might be assumed to favour their peers from the same Estate when drawing up proposals. In other words, it was assumed that if the King had a free right of appointment it would favour skilled commoners, and here the old idea of the impartial king as a friend of the common people resurfaces.[88]

The charity lodger Olof Håkansson and the yeoman Anders Johansson, who had seen the letter and were questioned in consequence, claimed not to have understood its contents. Olof Håkansson was not even literate. The sober and pragmatic political attitude to which the text gave voice is otherwise quite unusual in the source material. It should be borne in mind that all popular and extra-parliamentary involvement in national politics was considered inappropriate, so this does not really have anything to do with more moderate proposals being allowed to pass without further ado. Even so, there is no conclusive evidence to the effect that the lower orders in general advocated an absolute monarchy. There is, however, reason to claim that this idea had widespread support. *En Ärlig Swensk* severely rejected any and all ideas of an extension of the royal authority, maintaining that any such change would in the long run unerringly lead to absolutism. In one such discussion, special reference was made to the 1723 petition of the Peasant Estate, which had spoken in favour of increased power

---

studie i den svenska konstitutionalismens historia (Stockholm: Bonniers, 1915), pp. 474–75.

88 The King himself also alluded to this image. In an open letter to the Estates, Adolf Frederick emphasised that one of his first and foremost endeavours since his accession had been to curb the corrupt purchase of appointments, and as the basis for appointment to public offices he wished to consider only 'the greatest skill and true merit' ('största skickeligheten och wärkelig förtienst'). The biased councillors wanted to deprive him of this royal right and benevolence, he claimed. See Adolf Frederick's open letter to the Estates of the Realm of 6 November 1755, transcript in D 182, Politiske skrifter (Political writings), KB. By the middle of the 1760s only a little over 10 per cent of the officers from the rank of major and up were commoners; Sten Carlsson, *Ståndssamhälle och ståndspersoner 1700–1865: Studier rörande det svenska ståndssamhällets upplösning*, 2nd edn (Lund: Gleerups, 1973), chapter 5, esp. table 15.

and authority for the king. It was underscored that although the intention behind the petition had certainly not been to reinstate absolutism, that would be its inevitable consequence.[89] Throughout, the discussions in *En Ärlig Swensk* referred to what were said to be generally held opinions at the time.

Advocacy of absolutism

Formulaic statements in support of autocracy are abundant in the source material. Carl Henric Grevesmühl, a tradesman from Stockholm, believed there would be no order in the kingdom 'until there is one sheepcote and one shepherd'. The crofter Per Jönsson complained about the privations of the peasantry and thought that 'things would not be good until they had an absolute monarch'. Bud Per Andersson of Mora for his part felt that 'there should be one God and one king, who ruled and alone had government'. As things were now, the King did not even have the power to control the upbringing of his own children, said Bud Per. This was in 1756, when the Riksdag had recently prescribed a new tutor for the Crown Prince. That the choice of tutor had been contrary to the wishes of the royal family seems to have been well known; this piece of information recurs in several stories and caused general perturbation.[90] Of course it had a strong symbolic value that the person who was supposed to be *pater patriae* was not even *pater familiae* – that the head of the kingdom was hardly the master of his own family.

Bud Per Andersson claimed that he had been associating with gentlefolk and had then learned a thing or two about both politics

---

89 *En Ärlig Swensk*, pp. 196–99, 666, 682, 932. Out of respect for the individual Estates it was impossible to attribute a collective political ill will or ignorance to them; cf. the discussion on the rebellious Dalecarlian peasants who were said to have been misled but had not at all wished a reintroduction of absolutism, *ibid.*, pp. 66–68. Whenever there were collective expressions of discontent during the Age of Liberty, unidentified but nefarious forces were always supposed to have acted in the background, because there was an axiomatic idea (at least officially) that the subjects liked and approved of the national government and the political system.

90 On Grevesmühl: 1758.X.25/51 ('förrän det blifwer et Fårahus och en Herde'). On Per Jönsson: 1757.III.03/5 ('det blefwo icke godt, innan de fingo souverain'). On Bud Per Andersson: 1756.VIII.25/44 ('at thet borde wara en Gud och en Konung, som regerade och hade styrelsen allena'). On the tutor of the Crown Prince, see also 1757.II.04/8.

and how to comport himself. He therefore knew that one should be careful to avoid all manner of spreading rumours. He could, however, in confidence report what he had heard on his work treks to the south of the country to the provincial sheriff Carl Tillberg, who was, it is true, a servant of the Crown but also 'a political man, who was wise'. Thus he could report 'that His Royal Majesty wanted to make war on Russia and reclaim what had been lost in Finland, but that the lords were against it'. He could also reveal how members of the Riksdag from the Peasant Estate felt about the previous war, and which of them had received bribes from the Queen or the lords to give away their votes. To some soldiers, he also said that a civil war was at hand because the lords objected to the King's war plans. This might be changed, though, because two thirds of the Nobility were allegedly in favour of absolutism and only a third were against. On a later occasion, he recalled that the relationship was the opposite. In any event, it was a general truth that 'the noble brats were too numerous'.[91]

To most listeners, Bud Per Andersson would probably have appeared a very initiated and well-informed man. His story contained a lot of detail, and in several cases the information was based on actual circumstances, albeit distorted after passing through many stages and twisted to suit his own view of the world. He could tell of the doings of Johan Pehrson of Tuna at the 1740–1741 session of the Riksdag; he knew that war was imminent, even if he identified the wrong enemy; and he was aware that the Crown Prince had been given a new tutor who had been appointed by the Estates. When the yeoman Per Aronsson asked whether Carl Gustaf Tessin was no longer a tutor for the Crown Prince, Andersson also knew the answer: Tessin had been sent on a diplomatic mission to St Petersburg, where the Russians had done away with him. This was a baseless rumour that spread through the country by several routes, contributing to the general picture of dissolution and misrule. All this disorder and confusion led Bud Per Andersson to a foregone conclusion: things were bad in Stockholm, and 'if His Royal Majesty had more power and could govern alone, things would be better'.[92]

---

91 1756.VIII.25/44 ('en politisk karl, som wore klok'; 'at Kongl. Maij:tt wille hafwa krig med Ryssland och taga igen thet som wore förlorat i Finland, men att Herrarne stodo theremot'; and 'adelsungarne wore för månge').

92 On the case against Bud Per Andersson: 1756.VIII.25/44 ('om Kongl. Maij:tt ägde mera makt och finge hafwa styrelsen allena skulle thet gå bättre').

The wars and other major political events had effects on the opinions found among the lower orders. The royalist conspiracy of 1756 had lengthy repercussions and is often referred to in the source material.[93] After the plot had been averted, information began to circulate that the perpetrators of the coup had intended to burn down the capital, that the King's life had been in danger and that the lords were probably most immediately responsible for the whole scheme. It was an especially serious rumour that there had been an attempt against the life of the King. Because of the popularity he enjoyed among the people, such talk could easily stir up those feelings in support of the royal authority that were a prerequisite for the attempted coup. A few days after the revolution had been averted, the province governor Bernhard Reinhold von Hauswolff reported that rumours had begun to circulate in Dalecarlia. To prevent rumours from spreading further, the Council therefore caused a general day of thanksgiving to be arranged on 11 July 1756. On that occasion, the priests were supposed to read out a special issue of *Riksdags-Tidningar* where the official version of the chain of events was reported. This issue became an enormous commercial success, and according to Carl Christoffer Gjörwell it had 'a wonderful effect on the people in the city [Stockholm], whose eyes were enlightened and who experienced first-hand what damaging effects a change of the Instrument of Government and an introduction of absolutism would entail'.[94]

Information via the pulpit was the normal route for the state authority to staunch the spread of rumours and communicate its own interpretations. The method was highly effective by the standards of the time. Obligatory church attendance made sure that virtually everyone in the general public was made aware of the proclamations.[95] However, one possible uncertainty in

See also 1756.II.18/40, and 1755.XII.17/43, where it is instead stated that the Russian minister in Stockholm had been murdered.
93 1756.IX.08/23; 1756.X.20/36½; 1757.I.27/37; 1757.VII.27/74; 1757. XII.16/72; 1758.X.04/2; 1759.I.31/65; 1759.II.16/18; 1760.V.08/42.
94 [Gjörwell], 'Anteckningar af Carl Christopher Gjörwell', pp. 101–15, quotation on p. 106 ('en härlig effect bland folket i staden [Stockholm], som fick uplysta ögon och kunde med händerna taga på hvad skadeliga påföljder ändring i regeringsformen och souverainitetens införande skulle hafva med sig').
95 See Bergström, pp. 117–24; Elisabeth Reuterswärd, *Ett massmedium för folket: Studier i de allmänna kungörelsernas funktion i 1700-talets*

the system was the ability or attitude of each individual clergyman. From Finland there were recurring protests when the ordinances, which were often written in Swedish, were given a stumbling simultaneous interpretation from the pulpit; and if the issue was ideologically sensitive, the political sympathies of a clergyman might have an effect on how the message was conveyed, as in the case of Thomas Kihlmark.

In 1756 Thomas Kihlmark, a rural dean in Tensta in Uppland, was an eighty-year-old man and a well-known supporter of the Caps who, when he had read the proclamation on the day of thanksgiving for the averted coup, had 'garbled' it and spoken in such a low voice that the congregation could not understand its contents. According to several parishioners, he had neglected to read out *Riksdags-Tidningar* on the pretext that it had been 'so elegantly printed that he had not been able to read any of it'. Instead he had given the congregation his own interpretation of the contents, which was that the perpetrators of the coup, who had been prosecuted in Stockholm, had in no way sought to take the King's life but had, on the contrary, 'wanted to change the form of government and [...] give more power to the King'. Kihlmark had then dwelt on his own interpretation of the Constitution, and from his explanations the congregation had derived the erroneous idea that 'the crimes of the instigators were no worse than that they would soon be set free'. The assistant vicar Olof Broman, who was supposed to deliver the sermon on the day of thanksgiving, had not been informed in advance by Kihlmark about the special purpose of the day and had therefore been unable to prepare a suitable speech. By way of explanation, Kihlmark later stated that there had not been a battle, and consequently there was no victory to celebrate.[96]

It is relevant that Kihlmark's parish was part of the domain of Salsta manor, which belonged to Erik Brahe, who had been identified as the leader of the attempted coup and was one of the eight

---

samhälle, Studia historica Lundensia, 2 (Lund: Historiska institutionen, 2001), chapter 2; Anna Maria Forssberg, *Att hålla folket på gott humör: Informationsspridning, krigspropaganda och mobilisering i Sverige 1655–1680*, Stockholm Studies in History, 80 (Stockholm: Almqvist & Wiksell, 2005), chapter 2.

96 1751.I.27/37 ('oredligt'; 'af så grant tryck, at han det intet kunnat läsa'; 'welat giöra ändring uti regeringssättet och [...] skaffa Konungen mera makt'; and 'som wore uphofsmännens brott icke skadeligare, än at de snart kunde lösgifwas').

who were eventually executed. Kihlmark had recounted how the perpetrators of the coup had been manhandled in prison, and many of the parishioners – especially those who worked at or for the manor – had therefore thanked God that their master would soon be set free. In other words, Kihlmark inverted the rumours that were going about and made the sentence that was subsequently pronounced by the royal commission appear a miscarriage of justice against an innocent royalist and patriot.[97]

When the same day of thanksgiving was proclaimed in Kalmar, Sergeant Carl Gustaf Skytte, of the Queen's life guard regiment that was stationed there, had burst out that the Devil should break the necks and legs of those who had revealed the attempted coup, and if only his regiment had been on site in Stockholm, 'we would have shown them what's what'. Similar talk could be heard among the soldiers. After the day of thanksgiving, Private Hallberg said that 'it would be better if things had transpired as had been intended in Stockholm'. He also argued that absolutism was something that everybody wanted, and if the Burghers were opposed to it the soldiers had sharp ammunition ready.[98]

Even though those who indulged in idle talk about the form of government did not always promote royal absolutism as such, that – and not an expanded but nevertheless limited and constitutional royal authority – was almost always foregrounded as the alternative to the existing Instrument of Government. This was true regardless of whether the speaker himself promoted change or merely quoted what he had heard from other people. For instance, the assistant vicar Pehr Weisman from the province of Jönköping stated that he

> had heard it said in company that the upcoming summoning of the Riksdag would take place because His Royal Majesty wanted more power for the royal authority, and that Weisman on being asked whether the King wanted to have absolute power had answered yes.[99]

---

97 1751.I.27/37. See also *Upsala ärkestifts herdaminne*, ed. by Joh. Er. Fant and Aug. Th. Låstbom, 3 vols (Uppsala: Wahlström & Låstbom, 1852–45), III (1845), pp. 126–27.

98 1757.XII.16/72 ('så skulle wi hafwa wisat them annat' and 'at thet warit bättre, om thet gått för sig, som tillärnat war i Stockholm').

99 1770.IV.24/26½h ('uti ett sällskap hördt omtalas, at then tå tillstundade Riksdagens sammankallande skulle therföre skje, at Kongl: Maj:t wille hafwa mera wälde uti Konunga myndigheten, samt at Weisman uppå skjed fråga om Konungen wille hafwa souverainitéten, thertil swarat ja').

It was the Hats who were behind the planned changes, Weisman could report. He did not himself share these views, but explained that he had merely quoted what he had heard from others. When Gustav III eventually restored the power of initiative to the royal authority with his coup d'état, this move encountered wide if not unanimous support.[100] In only two cases did protests against the so-called revolution seem to have led to legal proceedings, but because both of these cases lack trial documents, the details of the underlying circumstances cannot be determined. Late in the autumn of 1772, the yeoman Mattis Jonsson, a member of the Riksdag, was held legally responsible for having displayed a 'criminal discontent with the form of government that had been adopted during the latest completed session of the Riksdag, through His Royal Majesty's gracious and wise actions and the unanimous approval and consent of the Estates of the Realm, for the consolidation of the general and individual weal'. To judge from the short summary in the decisions of the Göta Court of Appeal, he rather seems to have spoken against the Council and in support of the change – for example, Mattis Jonsson had 'concluded by wishing God's blessing on his Royal Majesty, and that the Supreme Being might support His Royal Majesty in the difficult burden of government'. The original trial may have contained other statements that are not quoted in the grounds for the court's decision. However, it is more likely that the judicial authorities erred on the side of caution and cracked down on all talk concerning the government of the realm during the period immediately after the coup d'état. The Judicial Review Division also requested that Mattis Jonsson be put in gaol so that a confession could be coerced from him regarding malice aforethought.[101]

---

100 See, e.g., Herman Schück, *Gustaf III:s statsvälvning 1772 i berättande källor och äldre litteratur*, Historiskt arkiv, 4 (Stockholm: Vitterhetsakademien, 1955), pp. 40–43, and Erland Alexandersson, *Bondeståndet i riksdagen 1760–1772* (Lund: Gleerups, 1975), p. 207.
101 1772.XII.15/(52); Justitierevisionens protokoll (Rådsprotokoll i justitieärenden)/Minutes of the Judicial Review Division (Council minutes regarding judicial cases), 15 December 1772, RA, fols 2306–13 ('straffbart missnöje med thet Regeringssätt, hwilket wid sidst öfwerståndna Riksdag, genom Kongl: Maij:ts nådiga och wisa försorg, samt Riksens Ständers enhälliga bifall och samtycke, till befästande af allmänt och enskilt wäl, blifwit antagen' and 'sluteligen önskat Guds wälsignelse öfwer hans Kongl: Maij:t, och at then Högsta måtte wara Hans Kungl. Maij:ts bistånd, uti then dryga Regeringsbördan').

From the other case, a few petitions for mercy have been preserved in which the prosecuted man, Second Lieutenant Tore Toresson, expressed at least a partial acceptance of the accusations against him. He argued that the alleged criminal statements remained to a great extent unverified; but if he at any time had happened to lapse into 'anything that might have hinted at the slightest disparagement or censure of Your Royal Majesty's, in a blessed moment altered and now present, fortunate form of government', it had not been deliberate. Tore Torsson received a full pardon from His Royal Majesty.[102]

The origins of the royal authority

The issue of the scope of the royal authority is linked to the issue of its origins. Did it spring from a divine order or from a treaty among people? The question has been mentioned in passing above; for instance, the innkeeper Petter Lundberg was aware of the tripartite division of law according to natural law, and he thought that the people as a contracting party should decide on the competences of the royal authority. The trader Carl Arvedson also knew that autocracy was in opposition to the temporal law, but had 'found it to be in accordance with God's law'. Among the peasantry, the idea of the God-given kingdom also seems to have been prevalent. Ifwar Lafwason of Lyngby, a cavalry-provision yeoman (*rusthållare*), expressly called the King 'God's highest official and representative on Earth'.[103]

Such ideas could be overlooked as long as they were merely formulaic, because they were in accordance with how the royal authority was spoken of officially. The boundary between formality and principle was a subtle one, though, and it was constantly debated during the Age of Liberty. The clergyman Benedict Wettersten found himself in trouble over his sermon in the Finnish Church in Stockholm in 1758. His exposition concerned an ageless subject: the general dissolution of the norms of society.

---

102 1773.XI.18/54 ('i thet som kunnat påsyfta ringaste förklenande, eller tadlande af Eders Kongl. Maj:ts, i en wälsignad stund förändrade och nu warande sälla regeringssätt').
103 On Arvedson: 1752.VII.01/6–7 ('funit det wara enligt med Guds Lag'). On Lafwason: 1753.X.25/55½a ('Guds Högsta Ämbetsman och företrädare på jorden').

Wettersten had been reported by a man in the audience, the ombudsman Johan Ljunggren, who had heard Wettersten speak of the obedience subjects were obliged to show to the Magistracy. He had especially noted the view that the king should be revered in the same way as King David, 'with kneeling and prostrating upon the ground'. He had also perceived downright revolutionary strains in Wettersten's reproaches. The preacher allegedly claimed that the king's decrees and orders were no longer obeyed; 'the wealthy despise them, and only the poor have their hides tanned'.[104] According to Ljunggren, there was no doubt that these accusations were directed against both the Council and the Estates. An Old Testament-like worship of kings that was understood literally and included kneeling was also in violation of the official image of the royal authority, for instance the way it had been expressed in the educational programme of the Crown Prince two years earlier. Among other things, that document stated that

> royals are not created better than other people; they are as wretched in the beginning of their lifetime, as frail during its continuance, as mortal at the end of it, and before God on the Day of Judgement as humble and condemnable for their vices and misdemeanours.[105]

Against the background of this official view, it was not difficult for Ljunggren to make the prosecutor support his line of argument. The handwritten sermon was appended to the documents of the investigation, and in it the following passage on the subjects' love for the Magistracy had been marked out specially. According to Wettersten's exposition, the subjects

> first had to be thoroughly cognizant of the perfections of our Magistracy, which greatly differentiate him from other people: such as that *they* [i.e. kings] *by God in Heaven and no one else are chosen and appointed to their exalted and sacred office*, and God in Heaven

---

104 1758.VI.21/38 ('med knäböjande och nedfallande på jorden' and 'utan de rike föraktade dem, och de fattige allena måste släppa skinnet till').

105 *Utdrag utur alle ifrån den 7. decemb. 1718.[–1794] utkomne publique handlingar, placater, förordningar, resolutioner och publicationer*, ed. by Reinhold Gustaf Modée, 15 vols (Stockholm: Lorentz Ludwig Grefing; Kungl. Tryckeriet, 1742–1829), VI (1761), p. 3887 ('Kongl. Personer icke äro af finare slag skapade än andra menniskor, lika eländige uti början af deras lifstid, lika skröplige under fortgången, uti ändalyckten lika dödelige med dem, och in för Gud på domsens dag lika ringe och fördömelige för deras laster och odygder').

and *no one else* has placed *the crown* on *their* heads and *the sceptre in their* hands.[106]

This attitude was completely contrary to the established explanation according to which 'the people's choice is the basis of their [the kings'] highness'.[107] According to the prosecutor in the urban district court (*kämnärsrätten*), Wettersten had thus 'excluded the contribution of the Estates of the Realm' and spoken in a highly dubious fashion about 'the liberty of the realm'. This was especially serious because the ideas had been presented to the congregation that Wettersten in his capacity as a clergyman had been installed to teach, and it was also said that his sermon had created some commotion.

Wettersten was a Doctor of Theology and an educated man, and when the case was heard in the Court of Appeal he defended himself by saying that the Lord Jesus Christ had also sometimes angered the general public with his sermons. The Court of Appeal reasoned in a similar fashion. They felt that the explanation that God alone put kings on the throne was presented in a theological sense; it had support in the Bible and could hardly be said to be against the Constitution. On the other hand, Wettersten should be reprimanded by the consistory and admonished to be careful when choosing subjects for his sermons. However, one of the members, Chief Judge Dubbe, entered a dissenting opinion to the decision. A necessary prerequisite for a reprimand from the consistory was that some error had been committed, but the appended sermon did not reveal anything 'that would run counter to God's words or our constitutional or government laws'. On the contrary, Wettersten had exhorted his listeners to show their obedience to the exalted Magistracy without protest or calumny and to voluntarily contribute taxes and dues. And these were, according to Dubbe, 'the main obligations on the part of the subjects, to be able to contribute to [a] peaceful and blessed government'.[108]

---

106 1758.VI.21/38 ('först wäl känna och weta wår Öfwerhets fullkomligheter, som wida wägnar skiljer honom ifrån andra menniskjor: såsom at *de, af Gud i Himmelen, och ingen annan, äro utkorade och utsedde til sitt höga och dyra Embete*, och Gud i Himmelen och *ingen annan* har satt *Kronan* på *deras* hufwud och *spiran i des* händer'). The italicised words are under-lined in the original.

107 *Utdrag utur*, VI, p. 3887 ('folkets wal är grunden til deras höghet').

108 1758.VI.21/38 ('som skulle löpa emot Guds ord eller wåre Grund- och Regerings Lagar' and 'the hufwudsakeligaste skyldigheter å Undersåtares sida, at kunna bidraga til [ett] stilla och lycksaligt Regemente').

The Judicial Review Division found that the rough draft Wettersten had handed in differed from the witnesses' testimonies on several points, and during its hearing the division chose to believe the latter. The injurious statements Wettersten had disseminated were damaging enough if they had been spoken in private, and even more so when this happened in a public sermon. It was significant that the Judicial Review Division pronounced its judgement on Midsummer Day, 21 June; the judgement contained a special reminder that two years earlier, the Estates had made this day into a day of remembrance for the restoration of liberty, and the clergy were then required to remonstrate against all nefarious plotting. As a punishment for Wettersten, and as a warning to other people, Wettersten was therefore removed from his office as a clergyman and all appurtenant duties for a period of two years; and before he was allowed to be reinstated, he was to be given a serious reprimand by the consistory. It may be noted that the Judicial Review Division decided twenty-three cases on that particular day, and that this was the only one in which the King himself neither participated in the deliberations nor signed the decision.[109]

This example demonstrates the difficult balancing act that both authorities and subjects had to manage when discussing constitutional issues. The two contradictory messages, that all Magistracy was of God and that the social contract was dictated by the people, were fundamentally incompatible, and a choice between them had to be made on each individual occasion. For Wettersten as a clergyman, it was natural to start from a basic theological assumption. On an abstract theoretical level, and as long as it was not claimed that 'God had immediately placed His Royal Majesty on the throne', this view was accepted by the authorities.[110] Indeed, the authorities were in favour of its being embraced by the common people, because it corresponded with the general duty of obedience that was an important foundation for the royal authority.

The political awareness of the people

These paradoxes raise a question about the general political awareness of the lower orders, and how far the Magistracy could

---

109 Registry of the Judicial Review Division, 21 June 1758, RA.
110 1758.VI.21/38 ('Gud omedelbart igen upsatt Kongl. Maijt på Konunga stohlen').

go in maintaining a false image of the scope of the royal authority. The question is essentially impossible to answer, and only a few reflections can be made here.

In 1758, the Finnish yeoman Thomas Mårtensson was made to answer in detail the question of what he knew about the form of government and the Council of the Realm. Mårtensson said that he had been well informed concerning these issues for a long time. He had also heard that the common folk of Dalecarlia in Sweden had been restless during the latest Russian occupation and that they had tried to change the form of government. Since that time, there had been idle talk about the government among the common people in Finland as well. After being pressured several times, Mårtensson admitted that he had occasionally uttered the wish that God might give the King absolute power so that he alone would rule; but as an excuse, he added that such talk was fairly common. Around Christmas 1757, for instance, he had heard two burghers from Nystad (Uusikaupunki) say that the lords nowadays had governance, and the King did not rule. Mårtensson attested before the court that he did not at all understand the nature and consequence of speaking in this way, and he himself had only spoken from thoughtlessness.[111] His views were thus somewhat vague. He certainly seems to have been familiar with the principal features of the form of government, and he knew by way of rumour about the main events in the kingdom; but he did not express a consistent comprehensive political viewpoint.

In other cases, however, political awareness was remarkably strong. The case of the journeyman miller Johan Bromberg has already been mentioned. Not only was he critical of the Queen Dowager; he also seems to have singled her out, rather than the Magistracy in general, as being responsible for irregularities in the finances of the realm. He was able to identify several reasons for this profligacy, and he also had an idea of how great the expenses had been for the extravagant life of the court.[112]

On the whole, the lower orders appear to have been fairly well informed of the main events in the capital and in the kingdom in general. Knowledge was often spread by way of rumour and was somewhat distorted at each stage through which it passed. The correctness of the information that influenced the political opinions of

111 1758.V.10/16.
112 1774.II.04/9.

the common people might hence vary, but this did not make the opinions they formed less adamant. Nor was it a given beforehand how the information would be interpreted. As always, rumours and information were adapted to fit political preconceptions, and differences in opinion among the common people were as fierce as within other social classes.

In general, peasants and other members of the lower orders were believed to be unreliable in their relationship to the form of government. By contrast, the leadership of the state took the loyalty of the nobility practically for granted; that attitude is clear not least from their asking local people of rank to act as informants when they learned about unrest in the countryside. The nobility was considered reliable because it had material, social and political interests to defend, but another contributing factor was the deeper insights into the advantages of the form of government that were occasioned by a higher level of education. The spreading of false rumours by Sergeant Herman Gillman during the Pomeranian War was considered less serious because he had not talked to the lower orders but only spoken to people of rank, 'in whom they [the rumours] had been capable of making so much less of an impression because they [people of rank] had immediately noticed their insignificance'.[113] For the same reasons, officials of the Church and the Crown were also usually regarded as reliable people.

This lack of trust was reciprocal; and when the common people sent out rallying calls or the like, their messengers were told to make sure that the communications were not seen by a clergyman or a local sheriff.[114] Because the peasants were regarded as ignorant and uneducated, that view could protect them from being held responsible. Some rumours that were in circulation were simply considered too advanced to have emanated from the lower orders; someone must have planted these ideas in their minds.[115] Their own political simplicity was also used as an excuse by the peasants themselves, forming a common and generally useful tactic to escape accountability. Even Olof Håkansson, Speaker of the Peasant Estate for many years, wished to explain away his support for

---

113 1758.XI.22/45 ('hos hwilcka de så mycket mindre något intryck kunnat giöra, som de genast förmärkt deras owichtighet'). On persons of rank as informers: Judicial Review Division, 1756.VIII.16/33½a. See also Sennefelt, *Den politiska sjukan*, pp. 79, 85–86.
114 1756.VIII.16/33½a; 1756.VIII.25/44; 1757.01.14/12.
115 See, e.g., 1758.VIII.23/45.

the Hats' unsuccessful war of aggression against Russia, claiming after the event that he had not understood the deliberations and had believed that military action (*aktivitet*) meant military caution (*aktsamhet*).[116]

With regard to the main issue and the attitude of the lower orders to the royal authority, the aim behind the publicly manifested image seems to have failed. Taken altogether, the present analysis suggests that knowledge of the true scope of the limited royal authority was widespread. The subjects were well aware that power actually resided with the lords and the Estates, and that the king was a puppet. However, this assumption does not warrant the conclusion that there was one particular dominant attitude towards the Instrument of Government among the common folk. All views could be found there, from approval to disapproval. Nevertheless, it is possible to find a fair number of statements in support of a strengthened royal authority.

116 Malmström, *Sveriges politiska historia*, III, p. 210.

6

Public opinion on the monarch

In addition to opinions on the political functions of the king, there were a number of views regarding the personal characteristics of the monarch. The ruler was traditionally surrounded by a great variety of popular myths that elevated him above ordinary people. Ideas and epithets followed ingrained figures of thought and recurred with small variations across the entire European continent. Peter Burke has summarised these images of rulers on the basis of a few common types. He speaks especially of the victorious conqueror and the righteous judge. In both cases, the safeguarding functions of the king were crucial. A variant of the figure of the judge was the omniscient friend of the people who travelled incognito across the kingdom in order to examine and impeach corrupt officials. This conception was typically the antithesis to the tyrant ruler. The actual monarch could often be contrasted with the ideal image; and in the same way as the old and time-honoured possessed an indisputable quality when it came to laws, the rulers of old had had obvious virtues and skills that their more recent successors were not necessarily able to live up to.[1]

'The king was unconditionally righteous. With the king, the farmer would be given his due' is the historian Claus Bjørn's summary of the popular image in Denmark. The fact that Danish peasants generally felt slighted and poorly treated could not dislodge this idea. If only the king were to learn of the injustice and oppression, he would set everything to rights. The problem was simply that he was so desperately far away, and 'the greats' ('de store') prevented the abuse that they themselves perpetrated from coming to his attention. A prerequisite for the survival of the

---

1 Peter Burke, *Popular Culture in Early Modern Europe* (London: Temple Smith, 1978), pp. 150–55.

king's righteousness as a figure of thought was that it never needed to be put to the test. The distance from the just power enabled abuses to both arise and persist. Bjørn also makes an observation that turns Burke's line of argument on its head. The measures of the ruling King were always interpreted in a positive spirit, thereby smoothing over the mistakes of his predecessors. That the King abolished the so-called *stavnsbånd* was interpreted in line with the general and timeless righteousness of the ruler and obscured the fact that it was another king who had once introduced this form of serfdom.[2]

Consequently, there are opportunities for arguing in different directions with respect to the practical consequences of these popular notions; but among scholars there is nevertheless consensus to the effect that the king was surrounded by a positive aura and possessed a legitimacy that few other social institutions could match. While the image of the personal qualities of kings sketched by Burke and Bjørn is certainly not very detailed, the same components recur in the legal material that has formed the basis of the analysis in previous chapters of the present book. In this chapter, the same material will be used in order to investigate ideas about the king's personal characteristics rather than his political status and function. Although the image that emerges is broadly similar to that discussed previously, it was not an unambiguously appreciative one. Even though the favourable attitude dominated among the subjects, it cannot be denied that critical voices were heard among the chorus. The people did not indiscriminately accept the image of the king's sublime character that was conveyed through the official channels of information.

---

2 Claus Bjørn, *Bonde, herremand, konge: Bonden i 1700-tallets Danmark* (Copenhagen: Gyldendal, 1981), pp. 59–66, quotation on p. 59 ('Kongen var ubetinget retfærdig. Hos Kongen ville bonden få sin ret'). Cf. Michael Bregnsbo, *Folk skriver til kongen: Supplikkerne og deres funktion i den dansk-norske enevælde i 1700-tallet; En kildestudie i Danske Kancellis supplikprotokoller* (Copenhagen: Selskabet for Udgivelse af Kilder til Dansk Historie, 1997), pp. 133–38, on how the king's legal protection of ordinary people could work in practice. A previous form of serfdom, the *vornedskab*, which existed only on Zealand, had been abolished in 1702. The *stavnsbånd* was introduced in the whole of Denmark in 1733 as a new means for landlords and the military to control the male rural workforce.

The king's intelligence and capacity

At times the king's intelligence was questioned when unwise decisions and ordinances had been issued. These cases are interesting because they frequently portray the King as a ruling agent. The yeoman Hans Simonsson dismissed an ordinance about the construction of dry-stone walls with the statement that the King must be foolish, unwise or ignorant (the court was unsure of the exact translation of the Finnish utterance) to send out such regulations.[3]

The eighteen-year-old farmhand Axel Simonsson complained about the lowering of dragoon salaries: 'The Magistracy is wise; since they have got enough men, the salary has been reduced by that bugger the King.' Here the Magistracy was given a general and collective as well as a concrete and personal meaning. In Axel Simonsson's statement the Magistracy was first spoken of as 'they', but after that the King alone was specified. (In the hearing in the hundred court, the words were written down as follows: 'His Royal Majesty promises a good deal at first and that bugger the King gives less.') This is a typical example of the translation problems faced by the courts. This statement, like Hans Simonsson's, had been uttered in Finnish; and the Court of Appeal was primarily interested in the issue of whether the very coarse expression *hundsfott* (literally 'bitch's cunt'; here translated as 'bugger') had been used in the singular and had thus referred to the King, or in the plural and had hence referred to the dragoons, as Axel Simonsson claimed in his defence. One of the witnesses testified that although he 'had not heard Axel mention His Majesty the King, he had nevertheless not understood anything other than that the illustrious person of His Royal Majesty, who had issued the ordinance, had been intended thereby'. This was also the conclusion of the Court of Appeal.[4] In contrast, the provincial sheriff Otto Nordvall had his sentence reduced in another case because his statement was considered to

3 1737.IV.27/59. For the format of references to the cases of appeal and application/adjudication documents of the Judicial Review Division, see Chapter 5, n. 13.
4 1726.V.11/23 ('Öfwerheten är Klook, sedan de fådt manskap tillfyllest blifwer Lönen förminskad af Konungen den hunsfåtten'; 'Kongl. Maij:t låfwar mycket i förstone och Konungen den hunsfåtten gifwer mindre'; and 'intet hört Axel nämbna Hans Maij:t Konungen har han lijkwäl intet annat förstådt, än Kongl. Maij:ts Höga Person, som Förordningen utgifwit, där wid warit ment').

have concerned His Royal Majesty's gracious ordinance, and not really to have insulted the King's illustrious person.[5]

Even so, it was as common to ascribe a superhuman intellect to the King as it was to question his intelligence. The omniscient and omnipotent king who knew the needs of all his subjects and did everything in his power to alleviate their distress was an old figure of thought. '*Si le prince savoit*, dit le peuple: ces paroles sont une espece d'invocation', as the French *Encyclopédie* put it.[6] Since the king was the foundation of law and of politics, he also possessed complete insight into all the affairs of the kingdom. If there was a deficiency in his knowledge about the state of the realm, it was due to the bad advisers who surrounded him. The reason why the Peasant Estate more than any other Estate was weighed down by heavy burdens, according to a member of the Riksdag, Pål Svensson, was that there was nobody who could present their views to the King:

> When His Royal Majesty is travelling in the countryside and a person wants to complain about his distress or present a humble supplication, His Royal Majesty is so surrounded by lords that it is impossible for the pauper to get through and get an opportunity to speak that which he, perchance with difficulty, has formulated. In all this no blame falls on our most gracious King, because, God be thanked, we may be sure that he is in every way happy to attend to our distress, wants to be our father, keeps us under his illustrious protection and by his grace protects us from all unreasonable oppression.[7]

---

5 1764.X.24/63.

6 'If only the prince knew, say the people. These words are a kind of invocation'; *Encyclopédie, ou Dictionnaire raisonné des sciences, des arts et des métiers, par une société de gens de lettres*, 35 vols (Paris: Briasson, David, Le Breton, Durand, Panckoucke, Stoupe & Brunet; Neuchatel: Faulche; Amsterdam: Rey, 1751–80), X: *Mam–My* (1765), 'Monarque, s. m. (Gouvernement.)', p. 637.

7 'Pål Svenssons i Hallands län memorial om ett ombud i Stockholm för Allmogen', in *Bondeståndets riksdagsprotokoll*, ed. by Sten Landahl, 13 vols (Uppsala: Almqvist & Wiksell; Stockholm: Gernandts; Bok- och reklamtryck; Norstedts, 1939–86), VII: *1751–1756* (1963), pp. 379–80 ('Reser Hans Kongl. Maiest. utti lansorterna och någon wil sin nöd klaga eller genom underdånig siuplickue föreställa, så är Hans Kongl. Maiestätt så med herar omgifwen, at den fattige omögeligen kan tränga igenom och få telfälle, hwad han törs hända med möda fåt upsat, afgifwa. Utti alt detta har wår allernådigste Konung ingen skul[d], ty wii kuna Gudi lof wara

The king's all-encompassing knowledge was a theoretical necessity for his status as the beginning and end of law to be true. Without this fixed point, all politics risked being overthrown. This omnipotence was also the basis for the people's love, which was well expressed in a festive speech by the young student John Jennings on the King's birthday in 1749:

> Our gracious King must inevitably with a rather palpable pleasure see us embrace one another with sincere friendship, he who so evenly shares his love and care for us all, and so scrupulously prevents everything that may cause anxiety in the least of his subjects. For this reason, it has also happened that our most gracious King on the one hand is considered by all Swedish children their most benevolent safeguard and surest protection, and that he on the other hand with all safety can rest his head in whatever lap he desires, so that he for his highness's but not for his safety's sake needs a Drabant corps and life regiments. His Majesty knows that he has as many bodyguards as he can count Swedish subjects[.][8]

In practice, though, the situation was different; and the subjects certainly perceived that the king made bad judgements and errors. However, this was because he had been misled. One conspicuous feature of eighteenth-century politics is that no group or individual could really be openly blamed for unfortunate decisions. This circumstance was due in equal measure to a strict culture based on honour, an unconditional duty of obedience to all authority and an idealistic striving for consensus. In the same way as the insubordination of the people had always officially been blamed on the

---

säckre, at han på alt sätt giärna tager sig wår nöd an, wil wara wår fader, hafwa oss uti sit höga hägn och emott alt oskieligt förtröck af nåde hägna').
8 John Jennings, *Undersåtelig fägnad, wid Hans Kongl. Maj:ts Friederich, 1. Swea, Göthes och Wendes konungs &c. &c. &c. födelse-dag betygad wid kongl. academien i Upsala den 17. april MDCCXLIX* (Stockholm: Lars Salvius, 1749), p. 34. On this speech, see Jonas Norrby, *Jennings* (Köping: Vattenfall, 1991), pp. 21–23 ('Wår nådige Konung måtte nödwändigt med ett ganska känbart nöje se oss omfamna hwarannan med upriktig wänskap, Han som så jämt delar sin kärlek och wård til oss alla, och så sorgfälligt hämmar allt, hwad then minsta af sina undersåtare till oro wara kan. Theraf är ock skedt, att wår Nådigste Konung å ena sidan af alla Swea barn såsom theras huldaste wärn, och säkraste beskydd, anses, och Han å then andra med all säkerhet kan luta sitt hufwud i hwad knä Honom täckes, att Han för sin Höghet, men ej för Sin säkerhet behöfwer Drabanter, ock Lifregementen. Så månge Swenske undersåter som Hans Maj:t täljer, så manstark lifwackt wet Han sig hafwa').

evil influence of outsiders (subjects were loyal by their very nature), the king's erroneous decisions were always caused by bad advisers. This image was naturally not conveyed by the lords, but it was all the more vivid among the subjects.

The cavalry reserve soldier (*vargeringsryttare*) Josef Jonsson, who had been sentenced to three years of hard labour, wanted to have the King's written confirmation of his sentence. His belief was that the King would never approve of such an unfair decision. It is obvious that he referred to the King in person and not to the king in Council. If the written resolution should fail to appear, he declared that he, after having served his sentence, would look up the King to seek justice.[9] He apparently assumed that his petition would be hidden away and never come before the King's eyes. This case illustrates the idea of the just king who is misled by his advisers, but who would make everything right if only he learned of the true circumstances.

Sometimes the stories of the good and just king almost acquired the character of folk legends. An unknown woman from the area around Gothenburg spoke openly at an inn in Skänninge about having gone to Stockholm to recover a *rusthåll* (a farm that equipped and maintained a cavalry horseman) from a certain Major Ribbing, who had defrauded her by means of a false promissory note. According to the story, a relative had conveyed her supplication to the King and the Queen. She had been granted an audience, had knelt before their majesties and had subsequently had her farm returned to her. This story of royal favour and good will gives the impression of having been invented to create a stir. The story of the captain's daughter who walked on foot to Stockholm in order to have her cause justly adjudicated by the King and the Queen is like a fairytale and would probably have served that function in conversations at the inn. A number of other fantastic details about noise and unrest in Stockholm were attached to this woman's story: thirty-two Russian ships of the line lay at anchor in Strömmen, the harbour basin of the capital; the Empress of Russia was to ensure absolute power for the King; the nobility had fled the capital; retail trade had ceased; and the royal couple was guarded by the burgher guard. The innkeeper had believed the woman to be feeble-minded and had not immediately reported the matter for that reason.

---

9 1752.VIII.19/29, with the note to the King written by Josef Jonsson in his own hand.

A maid at the inn, on the other hand, had not noticed anything
unusual about the woman's sanity.[10]
One man, Captain Gabriel Du Rietz, felt that he had been
improperly treated by the Councillors of the Realm, and in a coffee
house he cried out in public that Sweden was ruled by injustice,
violence, tyranny and barbarism. At the same time, he had shown
the coffee-house patrons a resolution that awarded him economic
compensation for a loss he had sustained. However, the authorities
had paid no heed to this decision. When a lawyer present in the
coffee house had pointed out that the resolution actually bore the
King's signature, Du Rietz answered that the King had not been
informed of the matter and that the Councillors of the Realm had
tricked him into signing. Apparently, great importance was attached
to the King's personal signature. The reason was the ethos of the
monarchy, i.e. that the king was the foundation of the exercise of
power and the administration of justice, and the guarantor of their
incorruptibility. Their lords the Councillors of the Realm, on the
other hand, acted as though they wielded absolute power; but their
plurality could, according to Du Rietz, easily be purchased for
money. What is more, he pointed out that the Councillors of the
Realm were subjects just as he was, and that he had sworn his oath
of loyalty only to the King, the Queen and the Crown Prince.[11]
Du Rietz created a scene at the coffee house on 19 November
1756, a mere six months after the Estates had decided to reinstate
the royal signature stamp. The Council and the Estates had
explained that a document that was stamped had the same dignity
and legal effect as one that had been signed by the King in person
(see above, pp. 59–64). This nonchalant attitude to the royal
signature does not seem to have been embraced by the subjects in
general. In spite of the temporal connection, Du Rietz cannot at any
rate have been referring to a document signed by a stamp, because
the stamp was not delivered by the engraver until 22 December
1756, a little over a month after this incident. In any event, the
King's signature was an issue that, in Du Rietz's mind, was closely
connected to the legitimacy of the decision.[12]

---

10 1756.IX.15/51. See also 1756.X.27/37½c, with a report on the arrest of the
    unknown woman. It has been impossible to follow the case further.
11 1757.VII.06/6.
12 Carl Gustaf Malmström, *Sveriges politiska historia från konung Karl XII:s
    död till statshvälfningen 1772*, 2nd edn, 6 vols (Stockholm: Norstedts,
    1893–1901), IV (1899), p. 190–91; Birger Wedberg, '"Kongl. Maj:ts

The warrior king

As has been pointed out several times above, bearing arms in defence of the kingdom was perhaps the foremost duty of the king in the eyes of the people. However, there were different ideas about exactly how far the king should go in order to fulfil this obligation. According to semi-official perceptions, Charles XII was a brave warrior, but he had loved war too much. His 'rare qualities and heroism left the kingdom in a plight which another person's lesser [qualities and heroism] would probably have prevented', wrote Councillor of the Realm Gustaf Bonde.[13] This view was common among the masses, too; and at bottom, it was the primary reason for the Constitution of the Age of Liberty. Frederick was often contrasted to Charles XII, but it was not a given that the comparison was disadvantageous to the former. For instance, the yeoman Henrik Knapi felt that it would have been better if Charles XII had ended up in hell early on. He was a cruel and dreadful warrior who had conducted bloody wars and forced the soldiers to march until the blood was squeezed out of their toes. Knapi had experienced this himself when all able-bodied men had been mobilised during the Russian invasion of Finland in the 1710s. Conversely, Knapi had blessed King Frederick on his knees, cap in hand, and wished him a long life and happy government, for he was truly benevolent towards his subjects and loved peace and quiet.[14] In Knapi's world, the King alone bore the responsibility for war and peace.

If warlike absolute rulers of the calibre of Charles XII terrified the lords as much as they did the common people, the King's

---

höga namns stämpel": Några anteckningar', *Statsvetenskaplig tidskrift för politik, statistik, ekonomi*, 27 (1924), 369–87 (p. 370). Du Rietz was gaoled for his crime in the fortress of Varberg, where he died in 1773.

13 Gustaf Bonde, *Sverige, under Ulrica Eleonora och Fredric I, eller ifrån 1718 till 1751: Efter den, af framledne hans exellens, riks-rådet herr grefve Gustaf Bonde författade handskrift med ett Tillägg om fredsunderhandlingarna i Åbo 1741–1742, af r.r. herr gr. H. Cedercreutz; Ett bihang till skriften:* Tessin och Tessiniana (Stockholm: Ecksteinska tryckeriet, 1821), e.g. pp. 76, 83–85, 100, 136 ('rara egenskaper och hjeltemod lemnade Riket i den situation, som en annans mindre hade förmodligen förekommit'); Jonas Nordin, *Ett fattigt men fritt folk: Nationell och politisk självbild i Sverige från sen stormaktstid till slutet av frihetstiden* (Eslöv: Symposion, 2000), pp. 232–33.

14 1734.VII.05/12.

approval was, in return, considered indispensable when the Hat party government wanted to declare war on Russia in 1741; without that approval it would have been impossible to gain that of the Peasants. Indeed, early in the summer of 1742, when the recruits of the Dalecarlian regiment were in Stockholm ready to be shipped out, they refused to go aboard the ships unless the King led the campaign, as earlier monarchs had done. In addition, they demanded that he carry the crown and the sceptre with him, so that they knew for whom they were sacrificing their lives. They definitely did not want to fight for the nobility.[15]

Several people, not least among the soldiers, would later blame the defeat in the war in Finland on Frederick's absence. In June 1743, Private Erik Näs of Umeå had, following the capitulation of the Swedish army but before the conclusion of peace, asked where the King was. In a general proclamation, the King had promised that he would march with the army; but he had not been seen in Finland, and he was not with the troops in Sweden. 'If only we had a real king, we would be a plucky people', Näs declared, adding that the outcome in Finland would have been completely different if only the King had been with the troops in the field.[16] Exactly which proclamation Näs referred to is not clear. It was probably rather a matter of the general impression of the decision-making process that was communicated to the subjects, because the Council of the Realm always concealed their decisions behind the name of the King. The official declaration of war had presented the war as the King's personal affair, describing 'how his Royal Majesty [...] has felt himself unavoidably called upon to take up arms, invoking the merciful aid of the Supreme Being'.[17]

That a Swedish soldier could accomplish great deeds when led by his king was an old mantra that had been drummed into

15 Bonde, pp. 129, 132, 161; Bjarne Beckman, *Dalupproret 1743 och andra samtida rörelser inom allmogen och bondeståndet* (Gothenburg: Elanders, 1930), pp. 48–49.
16 1744.VI.20/GA ('Om wi hade allenast en ricktig Kung, så skulle wi ock wara kiäckt folck'). See also *En redlig swänsk patriots politiska tros bekiännelse* ([n.p.]: [n. pub.], [1743]).
17 His Royal Majesty's proclamation regarding a war on the Tsar of Russia, 24 July 1741, quoted in *Utdrag utur*, III, p. 1683 ('huru som Kongl. Maj:t [...] sedt sig oumgängeligen föranlåten, at under anropande af den Högste Gudens nådiga bistånd, gripa til wapen').

generations of Swedish subjects.[18] Frederick's war experience had also been an important aspect when the Estates had accepted him as the chosen king. In the same way as was later the case with the French field marshal Jean Baptiste Bernadotte, who was elected Swedish successor to the throne in 1810 and began a new dynasty, the expectations were that a general who had earned distinction abroad would be able to provide great service to the kingdom. But where the political and military goals of Bernadotte would develop in a different direction from those that had been anticipated, Frederick was not allowed to have any aspirations at all in either of these areas. When the plans for the war in Finland were drawn up, Frederick immediately announced his desire to personally lead the army in the field, probably both out of eagerness to practise his former craft and because he saw this as an excellent way to improve his reputation. In contradistinction, the Council of the Realm was, precisely for this latter reason, extremely anxious for him to play no military role whatsoever. In a way this was a double-edged sword, because a more visible royal participation, through the king's infallibility, could have saved the Council and the military leadership from blame after the failure. Now, however, the entire planning of the war was so audacious that there was hardly any reflection on a possible defeat. In the feverish atmosphere before the war, with all the euphoric hope, a royalist boost was a more tangible threat, and the lords had no wish to share their successes with an undeserving king. In the end, the Council managed to wriggle away from assuming any responsibility by foisting blame onto a few individual scapegoats.[19]

The grumbling of soldiers recurred when Sweden entered the Seven Years War under its next King. Before being shipped off to

---

18 Cf. Karin Tegenborg Falkdalen, *Kungen är en kvinna: Retorik och praktik kring kvinnliga monarker under tidigmodern tid*, Skrifter från institutionen för historiska studier, 5 (Umeå: Institutionen för historiska studier, 2003), pp. 142–51.

19 Wilhelm Gabriel Lagus, *Anteckningar rörande 1741 och 1742 års finska krig jemte Henr. Magn. von Buddenbrocks äreräddning* (Helsinki: Finska litteratursällskapet, 1853), pp. 9–12; Malmström, *Sveriges politiska historia*, II, pp. 426–27, 447; cf. *ibid.*, III, pp. 163–64; Walfrid Holst, *Fredrik I* (Stockholm: Wahlström & Widstrand, 1953), pp. 210–14, 221; Oskar Sjöström, 'De sekreta bihangen 1741 och deras idépolitiska bakgrund', *Sjuttonhundratal: Nordic Yearbook for Eighteenth-Century Studies 2008* (2008), 5–24.

the theatre of war in Pomerania in 1758, Lars Andersson Tupp of Mora Company from Dalecarlia said to his friends that 'it would not be advisable to ship out before they had a real ruler, and were given an absolute monarch'. Kråk Erik Olofsson had asked him to be quiet, protesting that they had a benevolent Magistracy and that it was not their place to speak of such things. Tupp then pointed his finger at Kråk Erik and said that he spoke like a fool. The soldiers in Pomerania had no one to lead them, according to Tupp, and this was a generally known fact.

Several statements along similar lines had come to the awareness of the authorities. There were even rumours circulating that the lords had started the war for the sole purpose of preventing absolutism. The yeoman Thomas Mårtensson had learned something about the causes of the war from Smed, a soldier, and Hertolin, the parish tailor. Thomas did not understand everything that had been said, but he had grasped enough to realise that Prussia had not displayed any hostility at all towards Sweden, and that the war was hence unprovoked. Another rumour said that the King of Prussia was unconcerned about the Swedish hostilities, because he considered the Swedish soldiers fatherless.[20]

However, even if the king was not an absolute monarch, he could still be held responsible by those who objected to the war. The aid in the form of grain that the Crown had sent to alleviate destitution in the province of Hälsingland was therefore interpreted as a way of purchasing the loyalty of the soldiers. 'Is the flour that the King has given to the farmers here intended to buy him soldiers?', Private Anders Ström of Hälsinge regiment had asked. Another time, Ström volunteered to be 'the man who shall go out [to war] for the flour'.[21] Lack of food and aid had contributed to the uprising of the Dalecarlian peasants fifteen years earlier. Now the emergency aid that was offered was instead interpreted as a royal bribe to silence the criticism of the people.

In 1760, the office of the province governor in Västerås reported an anonymous leaflet, transcripts of which had circulated and been read out during several parish meetings in the province.

20 On Tupp and others: 1758.IV.03/1 ('det ej wore rådeligit at gå ut, innan de hade en riktig Regent, och fingo en sielfrådande Konung'); 1758.V.24/27. On Thomas Mårtensson: 1758.V.10/16. On fatherless soldiers: 1758. XI.22/45.
21 1757.VIII.17/24 ('Är det miöl, som Konungen skjänkt hit till bönderna, at Han kan få soldater före' and 'karlen som skall gå ut för miölet').

The pamphlet had fifteen articles or points and bore the title 'Conjecture or prophecy about the peasantry's complaints' ('Gissning eller Spådom om allmogens beswärs puncter'). The majority of the points articulated in the pamphlet concerned issues that were pertinent to the peasants, such as distillation of schnapps for personal use, grain prices, fees for members of the Riksdag, the cost of courts of law and so on. This connection to matters of importance to the rural population suggests that the pamphlet may actually have originated among the peasantry. At least it was to this group that its message was directed, and the copy that had been seized and turned over to the authorities had been addressed to the peasant miner Gustaf Andersson of Vansbro. Particularly interesting here are points five to eight, which discussed the Pomeranian War and the responsibility for it. The official explanations stated that Sweden had been forced into the war as a guarantor of the Peace of Westphalia. Consequently, the pamphlet asked whether that treaty really had any legal effect after more than a century, and whether it had not ceased to be valid when Germany had refused to render aid when Sweden had been attacked by enemies. Besides, Gustav II Adolf had wanted to protect fellow Protestants in Germany, whereas this time Sweden fought in an alliance with Roman Catholics against an Evangelical prince. The young Swedish men who now died in Germany would have done more for the welfare of the kingdom if they had contributed their labour to their native country instead. Here the writer expressed the pragmatic-pacifist ideas that were emerging at this time, ideas to which Anders Nordencrantz devoted his principal attention in the approximately contemporaneous exposition *Tankar om krig i gemen och Sweriges krig i synnerhet* ('Thoughts on War in General and the Wars of Sweden in Particular').[22] The author of the pamphlet had a clear understanding of the political decision-making process; and by

---

22 [Anders Nordencrantz], *Tankar om krig i gemen och Sweriges krig i synnerhet, samt hwaruti Sweriges rätta och sanskyldiga interesse består: Skrifwit år 1758, och hörer til et större wärk, som på hög wederbörlig befallning blifwit författadt, men icke förr kunnat komma i dagsljuset*, 2 vols (Stockholm: Grefing and Carlbohm, 1767–72); Olov Westerlund, *Karl XII i svensk litteratur från Dahlstierna till Tegnér* (Lund: Gleerups, 1951), pp. 126–27, 134–39; Nordin, *Ett fattigt men fritt folk*, pp. 367–70; Jonas Nordin, 'L'esprit de paix ou la naissance d'une opposition contre la guerre en Suède au XVIIIe siècle', *Revue d'histoire nordique*, 14 (2012), 97–130.

referring to the applicable sections in the Instrument of Government
and the Riksdag Act, he wished to hold those who were directly as
well as indirectly responsible accountable for the outbreak of the
war. Responsibility was not imputed to the King but primarily
to those who had contributed 'pernicious advice' ('förderfwelige
rådslag') and those who had not actively opposed the attack. An
interesting point – and here further ideas strongly reminiscent of
Nordencrantz were presented – is the addition in the last section:

> Because absolute monarchs usually have ambitious and fickle inten-
> tions which aim for war and the violent expansion of their borders,
> in which their allies will also become embroiled, the peasantry
> desires that the Estates of the Realm should forestall and prevent
> all such relations through which the kingdom may be drawn into
> wars that are destructive to the country, and that alliances should
> be entered into exclusively with such foreign powers and peoples as
> are solicitous about peace and liberty, and try only to defend their
> countries and possessions in Europe.[23]

The gist of the text was thus that absolute monarchs were governed
by old warlike and expansive ideals, and that the leadership of the
kingdom should therefore make an effort to seek alliances with
countries that had constitutions based on liberty. The interests
of the people were assumed to be different and more peaceful
than those of kings. This view was widespread at the time and
may for instance be found as a foundational idea in the work of
Montesquieu concerning the spirit of laws.

Opprobrious statements

A large number of the trials regarding lese-majesty concerned
opprobrious statements about members of the royal family. This
requires a little clarification. Only the comprehensive term 'injurious
statements' ('förgripliga utlåtelser') or 'highly injurious statements'

---

23 1760.IX.24/31 ('Som Enwålds Konungar merendels hafwa äregirige och
     föränderliga afsichter hwilka syfta på krig och deras gränsers wåldsamma
     utwidgande, deruti deras bundsförwanter äfwen warde inwecklade, så
     åstundar allmogen at Riksens Ständer måtte förebygia och afstyra alla
     sådane förbindelser hwarigenom Riket kan råka i landförderfwelige krig,
     och endast förbund slutas med sådane utrikes machter och folkslag som
     äro måna om frijd och frihet, samt söka endast at förswara sina länder och
     besittningar i Europa').

('högstförgripliga utlåtelser') is to be found in the legal sources. This concept included all illicit speech about the Magistracy and could vary from criticism of the Instrument of Government to coarse and offensive utterances about the person of the King. The expression 'injurious statement' was used in the courts, but not in legal texts. 'Opprobrious statement' is used only in this text and for the analytic purpose of foregrounding expressions of downright abuse and insolence directed against the King or other members of the royal family. These are often specified in the material as *highly injurious and depraved statements about His Royal Majesty's own illustrious person* ('högstförgripliga och lastbara utlåtelser om Hans Kungl. Maj:ts egen höga person').[24]

What are characterised here as opprobrious statements take up a very large proportion of the material.[25] In most cases they occur in connection with other, more concrete charges; the accused may have been dissatisfied with a tax ordinance and given emphasis to his anger by denying the King's honour and integrity. Occasionally, though, the statements occur on their own or without any tangible connection to law or politics, seemingly having functioned almost as a type of superlative. In order to express real indignation people resorted to the crudest expressions they knew and directed them against God or the Magistracy.

When the city guard of Stockholm attempted to arrest Private Casper Lindgren for being drunk and disorderly, he resisted. One of the soldiers tried to encourage him to change his mind and

---

24 For example in 1746.VII.08/A3.
25 1726.V.11/23; 1726.V.11/24; 1727.XII.06/24; 1728.I.17/33; 1730.XII.09/15; 1731.IV.27/44; 1734.VII.05/12; 1737.IV.27/59; 1740.VII.10/GA-17; 1741. XI.19/52; 1743.XII.08/21; 1744.VI.20/GA; 1745.III.15/41; 1746.VII.08/ A3; 1747.VII.16/B11; 1748.VII.06/A3; 1748.VIII.17/B25; 1749.II.09/B3; 1749.V.03/B9; 1749.V.03/B11; 1749.V.31/F16; 1749.VI.21/C20; 1749.IX.20/ GA; 1750.XII.12/A10; 1751.III.15/72; 1751.VI.28/46; 1751.VII.17/45; 1751.X.18/45; 1752.I.10/8; 1752.V.27/53; 1752.IX.23/27; 1752.XII.03/6; 1753.II.12/20½a; 1753.III.16/38½a; 1753.III.21/39; 1753.IV.04/7½a; 1753. IV.04/7½b; 1753.IV.04/7½c; 1753.X.24/45; 1753.X.25/55½a; 1754.II.27/76; 1754.VII.08/7; 1754.VII.10/19; 1755.VII.23/48½d; 1755.VIII.27/42; 1757. VII.20/37; 1758.IV.19/71; 1759.VII.04/2; 1760.II.07/3; 1760.III.05/1; 1760. XII.10/51; 1761.XII.02/3; 1764.I.12/14; 1764.VI.20/25; 1766.XI.28/124; 1767.I.15/14; 1768.XII.01/2; 1770.III.28/101; 1771.II.08/20; 1771.VII.05/5; 1771.XI.06/6; 1771.XII.04/9; 1772.XI.06/17½a; 1773.XI.18/54; 1773.XI. 18/66; 1774.II.04/9.

told him that he was making himself miserable by challenging the
King's guards. To this Lindgren replied that he wished that 'the
Devil [would] take the guards and the King'. The likewise inebriated Private Petter Aspelund, who had beaten a couple of peasants
and a boy with his bayonet during a journey in the province of
Östergötland and had in addition coerced them to give him money
to stop the abuse, behaved in a similar manner. In the detention
cell he had damned and cursed everybody present 'and eventually
in his insolence claimed to have no respect for anyone, either high
or low, not even for the King himself'. During his hearing, to make
matters worse, he had 'denied the great God and His righteousness, and also denied that there was a hell, or at least that it was
as dreadful as it is described'.[26] Neither Lindgren's nor Aspelund's
tirades actually concerned the King's person; but the curses were
apparently thought to gain extra force when combined with the
King's name, and this idea was shared by the delinquents and
the courts. These cases illuminate another interesting fact: when
there were multiple charges, the crime of lese-majesty was always
considered the principal one – this was true not only with respect
to crimes of property and violent crimes, but also with respect to
crimes of blasphemy. Aspelund's attack against the King was thus
more aggravating than his denial of the existence of God. With
the 1608 appendix of Charles IX to the Law of the Realm, which
incorporated commandments from the Old Testament, blasphemy
against God and defamation of the king were included in one
and the same legal section and were distinguished by the courts
as crimen læsæ majestatis divinæ and crimen læsæ majestatis
humanæ, respectively.[27] If both categories of crime occurred in the
same case, the latter was considered the more serious of the two.

26 On Lindgren: 1740.VII.10/GA-17 ('gifwer den wackten och Konungen
   Fanen'). On Aspelund: 1751.VI.28/46 ('och äntligen under sitt öfwerdåd,
   sagt sig ej akta någon, hwarken högre eller lägre, och icke Konungen sielf'
   and 'förnekat then store Guden och thess rättfärdighet, samt at något
   helfwete woro till, eller ock åtminstone, at thet ej wore så swårt som
   beskrifwes').
27 Henrik Munktell, 'Mose lag och svensk rättsutveckling: Några huvuddrag',
   Lychnos: Lärdomshistoriska samfundets årsbok 1936 (1936), 131–50;
   Jan Eric Almquist, 'Karl IX och den mosaiska rätten', Lychnos:
   Lärdomshistoriska samfundets årsbok 1942 (1942), 1–32; Ruben Josefson,
   Guds och Sveriges lag: Studier i den lutherska socialetikens historia,
   Uppsala universitets årsskrift, 1950:8 (Uppsala: Lundequistska bokhandeln;

Several cases have been registered where the accused had made opprobrious statements about the person of the King for no particular reason. In most of these cases, the offence seems to have been the result of some provocation or have been spoken in anger in some private dispute or other. No such circumstances were noted in the case against Vice Judge-Advocate (*viceauditör*) Georg Vult, though. At a tavern in Nyköping he had, probably in a state of inebriation, exclaimed 'that if one saw the King standing on the furthest brink of hell, he should be pushed off into the deep abyss'. When the patrons of the tavern responded with protests, he excused himself by claiming merely to have repeated what one Cornet Schönström had previously said.[28]

Levelling curses at the authorities and the Magistracy was no doubt part of a general popular culture of protest. We know from international studies that opprobrious statements could be both politically motivated and expressions of general insubordination.[29] Cursing or poking fun at the king and the lords was, within reasonable boundaries, perceived as acceptable by the general public. For example, it seems to have been an everyday occurrence for a number of years that the rock-blaster Per Olofsson swore crude oaths against both God and the Magistracy without anybody raising their eyebrows.[30] With respect to such instances, which were probably only exceptionally reported to the authorities, the number of unrecorded cases is of course high. In other words, it is impossible to say how common they were. Regardless of their incidence, many of these curses nevertheless belie the idea that the King was universally and unqualifiedly popular among the common folk: in the eyes of many people, he was merely another lord.

Leipzig: Otto Harrassowitz, 1950), esp. pp. 14–36; Sven Kjöllerström, *Guds och Sveriges lag under reformationstiden: En kyrkorättslig studie*, Bibliotheca theologiae practicae, 6 (Lund: Gleerups, 1957), pp. 91–100; Rudolf Thunander, *Hovrätt i funktion: Göta hovrätt och brottmålen 1635–1699*, Rätthistoriskt bibliotek, 49 (Lund: Institutet för rättshistorisk forskning, 1993), pp. 52–67.

28 1760.III.05/1 ('at om man såge Konungen stå på yttersta helfwetis brädden, borde Konungen skjutas ned i djupa afgrunden'). For other examples, see 1752.XII.03/6; 1753.III.21/39; 1753.IV.04/7½a.

29 Angela Rustemeyer, *Dissens und Ehre: Majestätsverbrechen in Russland (1600–1800)*, Forschungen zur osteuropäischen Geschichte, 69 (Wiesbaden: Harrassowitz, 2006), pp. 40–45.

30 1764.VI.20/25.

This becomes even more apparent when the statements were mixed with concrete discontent and the King was made a target and held responsible for various political and legal missteps. The dismissed Staff Sergeant Torsten Ryberg thus refused to drink to the King's health with the justification that 'he [the King] has not rewarded his old servants particularly well; he has paid me and other people poorly'. As a dismissed non-commissioned officer, he evidently had a tangible reason for his dissatisfaction. The cavalry-provision yeoman (*rusthållare*) Ifwar Lafwason of Lyngby, on the other hand, gave vent to a more misdirected anger. Discovering that the lord of the nearby manor of Maltesholm had made a hole in his fence, Lafwason lashed out with crude (but unspecified) utterances against the King. For his behaviour to make any sense, one would have to see it as directed against a vague lordly authority that was thought to defend its own interests and bear a permanent grudge against the peasantry. The King was the foremost of these antagonists, and the squire of Maltesholm was the visible local representative. Mrs Ingeborg Börjesdotter expressed a similar idea when she prayed to God to save her from all levies and afflictions. Asked who tormented her so badly, she repeatedly answered, 'both the King and the Magistracy'.[31]

In certain cases, the discontent of subjects concerned the King's failure to intervene. The interim local sheriff (*interimslänsman*) Carl Björkequist, who was apparently also a cavalry-provision yeoman, ended up in a dispute with the dragoon Johan Starck about the maintenance of the latter. Because His Royal Majesty had provided both the horse and the equipment, the cavalry provisioner should, according to Starck, feed his dragoons better. 'May the Devil thank the King; but not I, who have been given nothing', answered Björkequist. Private Anders Westerling expressed similar dissatisfaction. When the Crown Prince had left Karlskrona after a tour of inspection, Westerling had said, 'may he go to hell, he had done nothing good here, because he did not give them the right to keep their equipment'.[32]

---

31 On Ryberg: 1730.XII.09/15 ('han [kungen] har intet så wäl lönt sine gamle betienter, han har illa aflönt mig med flera'). On Lafwason: 1753.X.25/55½a. On Ingeborg Börjesdotter: 1749.V.03/B9 ('thet gjör både Konungen och Öfwerheten').

32 On Björkequist: 1726.V.11/24 ('Fanen tacka Konungen; men icke jag, som intet fådt'). On Westerling: 1749.IX.20/GA ('han måtte fara åt helfwete, han hade intet godt giordt här, eftersom han intet skaffat them rätt, at få behålla sin mondering').

The evil disposition of the Magistracy was perhaps most concretely expressed in the liquor ordinances, which deprived the common people of the little comfort they had in their misery. The former cavalryman Erik Kapperman and his wife Sara Persdotter had violated the liquor ordinance of 1747. When this was pointed out to them, Kapperman had 'lashed out with highly criminal and execrable utterances against Almighty God and His sacred mercy, and against the highest temporal Magistracy and its useful ordinance'. The former sawyer Bertil Jöransson reacted in the same way when he was caught in *flagrante delicto* at his still. In these cases, the King was made responsible for the legislation that interfered in the everyday lives of the peasantry. In the case of Bertil Jöransson the sentence was, unusually enough, reduced because of his ignorance about the punishment for so serious a crime.[33]

The same compassion was not shown towards Nils Hvaling, imprisoned for life at Jönköping castle. At the coronation of Adolf Frederick in 1751 a proclamation of pardons was issued, as was the custom. But when Hvaling learned that he himself was probably not included, he expostulated, 'Unless I, too, with several other prisoners, may be released, I curse the crown and the sceptre and the one who bears [them] as well.' Though Hvaling's guilt was proved by means of four impartial witnesses, he refused before the court to admit to having made this statement. Because he had not shown the necessary remorse, he was sentenced to death by the Court of Appeal.[34] Hvaling (who was later pardoned) had assigned responsibility to the King for the welfare of prisoners, and when it came to crimes of lese-majesty he was not altogether wrong, as will be discussed in greater detail below. As far as can be judged on the basis of the historical sources, the King actually does seem to have had the final word in the Council when such matters were considered.

The same coronation provoked another crude statement, this time from the Finnish yeoman Johan Carlsson. When the ordinance regarding coronation and funeral aid was proclaimed in church, he had taunted 'that poor wretch the King', who demanded financial

---

33 On Kapperman: 1751.VII.17/45 ('utbrustit i the högst straffbara och wederstyggelige utlåtelser, emot then alsmäktige Guden och thes dyra Nåd, samt then werdslige Högsta Öfwerheten och thes hälsosamma förordning'). On Bertil Jöransson: 1754.07.08/7.

34 1753.II.12/20½a ('Om intet äfwen jag med flere fångar kan slippa ut, gifwer jag Kronan och Spiran Fanen och den som bär henne med').

assistance from his subjects. When 'my father died', he declared, 'I buried him myself, without begging for funeral aid from anyone'.[35] The statement is interesting for another reason as well: it suggests that the prescribed succession order of the hereditary kingdom had been internalised by its subjects. True, the sentence may be read differently depending on whether the stress is put on 'my' or on 'father'; but that Frederick I could be perceived as the father of Adolf Frederick among the lower orders is also supported by Lax the boatswain, who referred to the two of them by saying that he had 'served both the father and the son'.[36] The public ordinances also contained expressions that easily lent support to the belief in a crown handed down from father to son. For example, in 1751 Adolf Frederick complained about the loss of 'His late honoured Majesty's precious person such a tender father'. By this, of course, he meant a general father of the country who should 'serve as a model for natural parents'; but the wording could easily have been understood literally.[37]

His Royal Majesty's request for coronation and burial aid coincided with Adolf Frederick's royal tour of the country, which

---

35 1752.IX.23/27 ('Konungen den stackarn' and 'enär min Fader blef död så lät jag begrafwa honom sielf, utan at jag tigde någon begrafnings hjelp af någon'). As a parenthesis it can also be mentioned that it took almost three and a half months from the signing of the Riksdag resolution on 13 March until the proclamation was read out in Nyland on Midsummer Day. This length of time would have been fairly normal, even if it must have been possible to disseminate more urgent proclamations, such as summonses to the Riksdag, more rapidly. Cf. *Sweriges rikes ständers bewilning til en begrafnings och krönings hjelp, gjord och fastsäld wid riksdagen uti Stockholm then 13. martii år 1752.* (Stockholm, Kungl. tryckeriet [n.d.]) (official proclamation, annual print series). See also Elisabeth Reuterswärd, *Ett massmedium för folket: Studier i de allmänna kungörelsernas funktion i 1700-talets samhälle,* Studia historica Lundensia, 2 (Lund: Historiska institutionen, 2001), pp. 107–09.

36 1761.XII.02/3 ('tiendt både Fadren och Sonen'). That Johan Carlsson really believed Frederick to be the father of Adolf Frederick is supported by other testimonies, which reproduce his statement as 'I have also buried my father' or 'I have also had my father buried'; 1752.IX.23/27.

37 *Kongl. Maj:ts placat om en allmän klagodag, som öfwer högstsalig Hans Kongl. Maj:t konung Fredrich then förste, [...] högtideligen hållas och begås skall. Gifwit Stockholm i råd-cammaren then 16. april 1751* ([n.p]): [n. pub.], [n.d.]) (official proclamation, annual print series). ('Högstsalig Hans Maj:ts Dyra Person en så ömsint Fader' and 'tjena naturliga Föräldrar til efterdöme').

took him to Finland in June 1752. When the arrival of the King was announced in Johan Carlsson's native region, his spontaneous comment was, 'Haistacon Kuningas minum perseni.' This may be translated as 'The king can kiss my arse', and it is indicative of the language skills of the court officials that they dared to spell out a Finnish statement in the records whereas it was censored in Swedish. The same thing applies to the even coarser statement made for the same reason: 'If the King were to come into my house, and I have no schnapps to give him, I'll give him my wife's S:V: c:t.' (The abbreviation S.V. – *salva venia*, roughly 'pardon the expression' – is the recording clerk's addition.) It was not considered as sensitive to write out 'vajmoni wittun' in Finnish. According to the witnesses, Johan Carlsson had said this 'insolently, loudly and harshly', and without apparent cause.[38]

This was not quite true, though, for there was a relatively concrete reason for Johan Carlsson's discontent. The twenty-four-year-old widow Kirstin Simonsdotter could recall his long statement in its entirety:

> The King did not come here to take pity on us, or show us any mercy, but to take large sums of money from young and old, widows and fatherless children, to use as burial aid; I have also had my father buried, but did not ask anybody for any burial aid[.][39]

He had concluded this complaint by saying several times, 'to hell with such a King, he can kiss my arse!' According to the hundred court, Johan Carlsson was equipped with a good deal of insolence, and he failed to evince due humility towards people of rank and the Magistracy. This explains why the judicial authorities took this type of crime so seriously: when the king, through his office, guaranteed the incorruptibility of government authority and the administration of justice, all attacks on him risked calling the very foundations of the state system into question.[40]

---

38 1752.IX.23/27 ('Om Konungen kommer i mitt hus, och jag icke hafwer Brännwijn at gifwa honom, så gifwer jag honom min hustrus S: V: f:a' and 'öfwerdådigt, högt och hårdt').
39 1752.IX.23/27 ('Konungen kom intet hit at förbarma sig öfwer oss, eller at wisa oss någon Nåd, utan at af unga och gamla, änkor och faderlösa barn taga stora penningar til Begrafnings-hjelp, jag har ock låtit begrafwa min fader, men af ingen begjärt någon begrafnings-hjelp').
40 The custom of equating attacks on a ruler's officials with attacks on the ruler himself supposedly had its origin in Justinian's late Roman compilation of

This latter observation is also vital to an understanding of the crime of lese-majesty and its prosecution. It was a political crime against the state, and, as was mentioned above, the only punishment prescribed in law for this type of offence was capital punishment. Even so, it was not a crime for which people were executed; instead the aspect of social discipline was wholly at the forefront. Normally the sentence was reduced, on condition that the delinquent showed due remorse and promised reformation. Preferably the criminal should also admit his own lack of knowledge and how little he understood of matters of national importance.

In the assessment of the punishment against the shopkeeper Carl Arvedson, who had read out a text composed by himself which advocated absolutism, the Court of Appeal employed interesting lines of argument in order to allow him to escape the death penalty. The arguments concerned both the consequences of the crime and the effect of the punishment on the criminal. The sentence in which absolutism had been mentioned was found towards the end of the injurious document, and it could not be ascertained whether Arvedson had had time to read out the contents in full. According to the reasoning of the court, the crime mainly consisted in the act of making the text public, not in the notions that someone might hold covertly. It is true that a medical examination of Arvedson had not discovered any signs of insanity, but the court nevertheless felt that such a confusing text could not have been written by someone in full possession of his senses. And if it was the case that Arvedson was balancing on the brink of madness, his corporal punishment should not be too severe either, because that might aggravate his mental condition.[41]

If one disregards the eight conspirators who were decapitated for participating in the attempted royal coup of 1756 – and who are not included in the source material used for this study because they were sentenced by a commissorial court – only one person, the vagrant Fredrik Wimmercrantz, appears to have been executed for

laws, *Corpus juris civilis*. Montesquieu condemned such pseudo-legislation as the worst kind of miscarriage of justice; see Montesquieu, *De l'esprit des lois* (1748), book 12, chapters 7–10, esp. chapter 8. See Charles-Louis de Secondat de Montesquieu, *Œuvres de Monsieur de Montesquieu, nouvelle edition, revue, corrigée, & considérablement augmentée par l'auteur*, 7 vols (Amsterdam and Leipzig: Arkstée & Merkus, 1758–72), I (1758), pp. 259–63.
41   1752.VII.01/6–7.

the crime of lese-majesty during the Age of Liberty. Wimmercrantz had been denied a schnapps at an inn with reference to the current ordinances. When he asked who had issued these ordinances, the innkeeper had answered: God and the Magistracy. Wimmercrantz had then stood in the middle of the floor, cursed 'and exclaimed these words, which the court shudders to have entered into the records – may the Devil take the one who has issued such ordinances and the one who has received them'.[42]

While Wimmercrantz's crime is certainly not the most heinous offence in the source material, he displayed obvious contempt for the entire legal process and refused to show the necessary repentance and awareness of his guilt. The hundred court described him as an abomination, a notorious idler and a superfluous member of society, and the Court of Appeal recommended that he should not only be decapitated, but afterwards be broken on the wheel and have his head put on a stake. In addition to the alleged offence, he had spread false rumours to the effect that King Frederick had died, but the death was being kept secret by the lords in Stockholm. Come summer, though, the peasantry would march to the capital in order to 'make the young Prince an absolute monarch by force'. Wimmercrantz was sentenced for a crime in accordance with the opening sections of chapters 5 and 6 of the Misdeeds Code (*Missgärningsbalken*), that is, for depraved speech and disobedience to the king. The death sentence was carried out, although both the Court of Appeal and the Judicial Review Division had judged that there had been no real malice aforethought. Plainly put, this means that the lawyers did not regard his exhortations to rebellion as seriously intended; but they felt that his behaviour was so offensive that it had passed the limit of what was tolerable and excusable.

The foreign Kings

One special category of opprobrious statements consisted of those that referred to the foreign origins of the King or the royal family. The wine transporter Johan Åman's offence was brought up in the beginning of the previous chapter, but he was far from alone

---

42 1748.VII.06/A3 ('samt utbrustit i desse orden, som domstolen darrar wid at låta föras i Minnesboken – Fanen fare i den som sådane Förordningar gifwit ut, och den som dem tagit emot').

in making this kind of statement. There are plenty of surviving examples, and there is reason to believe that many more like these existed in the records that were destroyed by the Court of Appeal and the Judicial Review Division. Insinuations about the foreign birth of a king were a sensitive matter because they referred to a circumstance that could not be changed or easily explained away. Adolf Frederick, of the house of Holstein-Gottorp, was distantly related to the old Vasa dynasty. This relationship was often exploited by his son Gustav III, who liked to emphasise it for propaganda purposes. Apart from his union by marriage, Frederick I had no family relationship whatsoever to the older native dynasties, even though attempts were actually made to prove his descent from the early medieval Yngling dynasty.[43] At all events, he was in this respect at a clear disadvantage in comparison to his early rival, Charles Frederick, Duke of Holstein-Gottorp, who was the nephew of Charles XI. Charles Frederick was partly raised in Sweden, spoke Swedish and was considered a native prince by his followers. The same idea was subsequently attached to his son Charles Peter Ulrich – 'Charles XIII' as he was called by his sympathisers – when he was proposed as successor to the throne in 1742. For example, the yeoman Lars Persson from the province of Västernorrland thought it important to leave the throne to someone 'who is related to and of the blood of a native Swedish king', and then the only safe choice was the Duke of Holstein, 'who is descended from the great and most venerable Gustavian and Caroline families'.[44] Charles Peter Ulrich was unanimously elected by the Estates, but the decision was annulled when it became known that he had adopted the Greek Orthodox faith and been designated Empress Elizabeth's successor to the throne of Russia. He acceded as Emperor of Russia

43 [Kilian Stobæus], *Schema genealogicum serenissimi et potentissimi D. N. Friderici, Svethorum, Gothorum, Vandalorumque regis &c. stemma augustissimum ab Ynglingis, Skioldungis, Carolingis, Folkungis, antiquissimis et illustrissimis totius septentrionis, imo orbis familiis repetens et rite deducens* ([n.p.]: [n. pub.], [n.d.]), one sheet in broadside.
44 'Lars Persson från Västernorrlands län memorial om successionen', 16 October 1742, in *Bondeståndets riksdagsprotokoll*, ed. by Sten Landahl, 13 vols (Uppsala: Almqvist & Wiksell; Stockholm: Gernandts; Bok- och reklamtryck: Norstedts, 1939–86), V: *1742–1743* (1954), pp. 520–22, quotation on p. 521 ('slå in unga Printsen till Souverain' and 'som härstammar af de stora och glorwyrdigste Gustavianiske och Carolinske familierne').

in January 1762, but was deposed after a mere six months and died in captivity shortly thereafter. The old Law of the Realm, which was still in effect when the Instrument of Government was written, did not contain any prohibitions against electing foreign kings. On the contrary, such an election was actually a prerequisite, although this was not clearly stated anywhere. If the ruling dynasty had no legitimate heirs, a new king would almost by necessity have to be sought abroad. Because he should be descended from a princely dynasty, he could not be chosen from inside the country. The alternative, which was to raise a native noble family to a rank above their peers, would have been inconceivable.[45] True, this had been a natural practice in the time of the elective monarchy, when the pretenders to the throne backed up their candidacies with client relationships and real instruments of force, and it had worked one final time when Gustav Eriksson Vasa had been elected king of Sweden; but two centuries later, it would have been impossible for this procedure to provide the symbolic dignity that was the primary asset of the royal authority during the Age of Liberty. When Isac Faggot mentioned the procedure of royal elections, he said – without discussing it in detail – that the Estates on such occasions presented an enquiry to 'the high-born prince'. In a royal birthday tribute at the House of Nobility in 1729, Colonel Bror Classon Rålamb spoke of 'an elevated birth' and 'a majestic manner' as necessary royal qualities.[46] It was understood that princely rank, that is to say a congenital status, was a necessary condition for being considered for the royal office.

In similar contexts, Karin Tegenborg Falkdalen has spoken of 'the royal uniqueness' ('den kungliga särarten'). That kings

45 For instance, the rumours circulating about one of the perpetrators of the coup of 1756, Erik Brahe, who was said to covet the throne, were spoken of with derision; see [Carl Christopher Gjörwell], 'Anteckningar af Carl Christopher Gjörwell om sig sjelf, samtida personer och händelser 1731–1757', in *Samlingar utgifna för De skånska landskapens historiska och arkeologiska förening*, ed. by Martin Weibull, 9 vols (Lund: Berlings, 1874–80), III: *1875* (1874), pp. 31–142 (pp. 114–15).
46 [Isac Faggot], *Swea rikes styrelse efter grund-lagarne* (Stockholm: Johan Georg Lange, 1768), p. 57 ('den Högborne Furstan'); Bror Classon Rålamb, *Ett panegyriskt taal öfwer ten stormektige och allernådigste Sweries- Götes- och Wendes kånung Friederic ten förstas födelse-dag den XVII. aprilis åhr M.DCCXXIX, hållet samma dag vti Swea ridderskaps och adels Riddare-hus sal* (Stockholm: Kungl. tryckeriet, 1729), p. 13 ('Hög Afkomst' and 'ett Majestätiskt Sätt'); see also p. 19.

elevated themselves above ordinary people was important, not least when consolidating the hereditary kingdom. For that reason, Gustav I was eager to ennoble his offspring by marrying and producing a successor to the throne with a queen from an established princely dynasty. This royal uniqueness was a method of dynastic defence since it reduced the number of potential contestants for the throne. In order to ensure the survival of the royal dynasty, female succession to the throne was even introduced as a last line of defence. In many places, a female ruler was considered an anomaly. In addition, it was emphasised that the kingdom risked being engulfed by another state, were the queen to marry a foreign prince. On the other hand, female succession may be considered a monarchical principle since it formed an extra security for the royal dynasty. The female succession that was introduced in 1590 was therefore abolished by the Riksdag in 1650 as a condition for elevating Charles Gustav to hereditary prince, but it was reintroduced by the autocratic Charles XI in 1683. With similar consistency, it was again abolished in the 1719 Instrument of Government (RF 1719 and 1720, § 3), which adhered to republican principles. The Estates claimed that the right of election had reverted to them, and therefore Ulrika Eleonora's right of inheritance must also be invalidated.[47]

In many other countries, for instance France, there were native princely families in addition to the royal family, and these had a remote right of inheritance according to more or less established genealogies, were the ruling dynasty to die out. There were *fils de France* and *petit-fils de France*, who were the legitimate sons and grandsons of kings; *princes du sang*, princes descended from Louis IX (Saint Louis); and *princes étrangers* from autonomous princedoms with connections to France. As time went by, all these people formed an extensive network around the court; at the outbreak of the Revolution there were, for instance, twelve families that belonged to the first group alone. Even though only a few of these princely families could claim any actual right of inheritance to the crown, they were all potential power factors. The interpretation made of the early medieval Salic law also excluded

---

47 Tegenborg Falkdalen, pp. 37–54. This pattern continued repeating: with RF 1772, § 3, the opportunity for female succession was again opened up, while it was closed with the reintroduction of constitutionalism in RF 1809, § 1. It did not return in RF 1974, but it was reintroduced in the 1980 revision of the 1810 Act of Succession.

both women and foreign princes from all right of inheritance to the French crown.[48]

In Sweden praxis was different. When exigent circumstances occurred, the crown had primarily been handed down to a royal daughter, secondarily to a foreign prince. In the latter case, however, family relationships with the Swedish royal family were pursued. As late as the end of the eighteenth century, people thus still spoke of the Gustavian dynasty as having ruled in unbroken succession since the last Danish king had been thrown out of the kingdom (see Figure 24).

No native princely families other than the royal family came into being during this time. With the three sons of Gustav I, it would have been possible for the dynasty to branch off as it did in France; but none of them left any families close to the throne and within the kingdom. It was not until Charles X Gustav died, leaving a younger brother still alive, that such a situation could arise in Sweden; but neither Duke Adolph John himself nor his two sons ever had an opportunity to lay claim to the throne. However, the youngest of his sons, Gustavus Samuel Leopold, succeeded Charles XII as the ruling Duke of Zweibrücken, homeland of the Palatinate dynasty. When he died without heirs, the dukedom passed to the House of Palatinate-Birkenfeld, which was descended from one of the uncles of Charles X Gustav. Christian IV of Birkenfeld was also presented as the candidate of France and the Hat party in the struggle over the succession to the throne in 1742–1743. His family relationship with the older Swedish dynasties was thus remote, but at least he was of princely birth.

Frederick I had two so-called natural sons with Hedvig Taube. These were elevated to German imperial counts of Hessenstein, and in November 1772 the elder of the two, Frederick William, became a German prince of the Empire. Frederick I had been given the Swedish crown only as a personal possession: the House of Hesse-Kassel lacked any claim. As illegitimate children, his sons – even though they were nominally of princely birth – had no right of inheritance whatsoever, and it was even a criminal act to call the Count of Hessenstein a Swedish prince.[49] The adjective 'Swedish'

---

48 Yves-Marie Bercé, 'Les monarchies de l'âge moderne', in *Les monarchies*, ed. by Yves-Marie Bercé, Histoire générale des systèmes politiques (Paris: Presses universitaires de France, 1997), pp. 227–322 (pp. 235, 261–64).

49 Cf. 1768.12.01/2.

did not refer to his nationality in this context but should be understood precisely as implying that he lacked any right to the Swedish crown. The proposals that were presented following the death of Ulrica Eleonora to the effect that Frederick might acquire legitimate heirs by remarrying do not seem to have met with any significant support or to have been particularly seriously intended.[50]

In other words, there was no prohibition as such against foreign kings; but there were several limitations that were meant to prevent the unfavourable consequences that might follow from electing a king from abroad. The Law of the Realm expressly prohibited foreign men from being appointed Councillors of the Realm and, strictly speaking, from holding any domestic offices at all. For compelling reasons, these regulations had been dispensed with during Sweden's period as a great power, but they were increasingly strictly implemented following the changes in government after the death of Charles XII. The Council of the Realm and the Estates made sure that the Accession Charter, the Instrument of Government and other laws effectively prevented any attempts on King Frederick's part to bring officials from his German country of origin into the realm. There was also a suspicious vigilance concerning all possible attempts to open up the right of inheritance for Hessian princes.[51]

Regardless of formal rules, there was what might be called an intuitive distrust of foreign princes, even though it cannot be said to have prevailed everywhere. Religious aspects must be included among the objections that could be raised against foreign kings. The ideal would be that both king and queen were native Lutherans, but this basic requirement was not so strict that the Reformist Frederick was prevented from putting off his conversion until the week before

---

50 Bonde, pp. 177–78.
51 Accession Charter 1720, §§ 14, 17; Bonde, pp. 68–69; Carl Tersmeden, *Amiral Carl Tersmedens memoarer*, ed. by Nils Sjöberg and Nils Erdmann, 6 vols (Stockholm: Wahlström & Widstrand, 1912–19), [IV]: *Ur frihetstidens lif* (1917), p. 81; Malmström, *Sveriges politiska historia*, I, p. 418, n. 1, p. 487; *ibid.*, II, pp. 174, 252–53; *ibid.*, III, p. 122; Holst, *Fredrik I*, pp. 133, 137–38, 192, 227; Nordin, *Ett fattigt men fritt folk*, pp. 104–05, 112–13. Great Britain wished to put forward the brother of Frederick I, William of Hesse, or his son as a candidate for the Swedish throne in 1743, but the King refused to consent to this plan, which was in opposition to his previous affirmations; see Malmström, *Sveriges politiska historia*, III, p. 140.

finally being elected king. Officially, his conversion was considered sincere and seen as proof of the true strength of Lutheran doctrine.

Before the election of a successor in 1742, Major Henrik Wrede nevertheless demanded in the House of Nobility that a special statute be issued requiring any pretender to the Swedish crown to be both born into and raised in the pure Evangelical faith. This matter caused several days of animated discussion in all the Estates. The petition was finally adopted by the Nobility. The Peasants liked this proposal and went one step further: according to them, the same strict requirements with respect to religion must also apply to any future queen. Remarkably, the most cautious Estate was the Clergy. They said that they agreed with the spirit of Wrede's petition, but did not feel that the issue was important enough to require a particular statute; such a ruling merely risked delaying peace negotiations and the election of the successor to the throne. The Burghers chose to support the Clergy's line, and consequently the entire proposal was defeated.[52] All fundamental principles notwithstanding, people were often pragmatic when it came to assuming actual positions. In 1742, the rebellious Dalecarlians also expressed themselves in a typical manner when they demanded a king who was Swedish and who had the best interests of his subjects at heart. Still, if they were obliged to content themselves with the King who was already on the throne, his power should be increased so that he could accomplish good things.[53]

Foreign birth, then, did not automatically disqualify a monarch, even though a native king was always preferable. In addition, there was always the unfavourable aspect to consider: in case discontent with the monarch arose, his foreign status could be added to the list of grievances, as often happened with respect to Frederick, who was frequently vilified in memoir literature; it happened less often with Adolf Frederick. Soon after Frederick's ascension to the throne,

---

52 *Sveriges ridderskaps och adels riksdags-protokoll från och med år 1719,* 32 vols (Stockholm: Norstedts, 1875–1982), XIII:1: 1742–1743 (1890), pp. 149–58, 172–86, 191–92, 195–99; *Prästeståndets riksdagsprotokoll,* ed. by Lennart Thanner and others, 16 vols (Stockholm: Riksdagsförvaltningen, 1949–), XI: 1742–1743 (1999), pp. 50, 58–64; *Borgarståndets riksdag-sprotokoll från frihetstidens början,* ed. by Nils Staf and others, 12 vols (Uppsala: Almqvist & Wiksell; Stockholm: Riksdagsförvaltningen, 1945–), VIII:1: 1742–1743 (1982), pp. 101–08; *Bondeståndets riksdagsprotokoll,* V: 1742–1743 (1954), pp. 73–76, 83; Malmström, *Sveriges politiska historia,* III, pp. 122–24.
53 Malmström, *Sveriges politiska historia,* III, p. 102.

the Danish traveller Jacob Bircherod felt that many 'feared, or at least had an *aversion* to a foreign king'. That he was a foreigner prevented him from becoming a great king, and 'at bottom he did not love the nation', wrote Carl Christopher Gjörwell one generation later.[54] In July 1742 Eric Alstrin, a clergyman born in Leksand, was, on the basis of his local reputation, commissioned by the Council to negotiate with the restive Dalecarlian peasants. Among his instructions was to emphasise 'the great benevolence which His Royal Majesty has at all times evinced towards this nation, for which His Royal Majesty has come to feel much love and regard'. Respect for Frederick remained fairly constant, but the peasantry nevertheless maintained the demand that 'a person of Swedish blood would be elected and appointed the successor to the Swedish royal throne'.[55] A Swedish-born prince was presumed to be more familiar with Swedish circumstances and identified with Swedish interests as a matter of course.

In the examples that appear in the sources from the courts, foreignness was used as an immediate invective in many cases and did not necessarily hold any carefully considered meaning or evoke a deeper subtext. Still, when used in critical situations it was something that would generally make a statement coarser. Calling the Queen a 'German bitch', as in one of the examples below, was more serious than merely calling her a bitch. In the same way, the addition of 'bitch' was necessary in order to emphasise the derogatory aspect of the adjective 'German', which, if taken alone, could

---

54 Jacob Bircherod, *Jacob Bircherods Rejse til Stockholm 1720*, ed. by Georg Christensen (Copenhagen: Aschehoug, 1924), p. 66 ('frycktede, eller i det ringeste hafde *aversion* for een udenlands Konge'); [Gjörwell], 'Anteckningar af Carl Christopher Gjörwell', pp. 89–91, quotation on p. 89 ('i botten älskade han ej nationen'). See also Fredrik Axel von Fersen, *Historiska skrifter*, ed. by R. M. Klinckowström, 2nd edn, 8 vols (Stockholm: Norstedts, 1867–72), I (1867), pp. 182–83.

55 Alstrin's memorandum, § 11, in *Handlingar rörande Skandinaviens historia*, ed. by Kungl. Samfundet för utgifvande af handskrifter rörande Skandinaviens historia, 60 vols (Stockholm: Elmén & Granberg and others, 1816–60), III (1817), p. 211 ('den store nåd, som Kongl. Maj:t uti alla tider haft för denna Nationen, hvaraf Kongl. Maj:t fattadt för dem mycken kärlek och nåd'). On the King being of Swedish blood: Humble petition from 'all the inhabitants of the Dalelagen' ('samtelige Invånare här i Dalelagen'), 2 March 1743, § 2, in *Handlingar rörande Skandinaviens historia*, III (1817), pp. 227–28 ('någon af Svensk blod måtte til Successor på then Svenska Kongl. Thron utvald och antagen blifva').

be a neutral statement of fact. When Private Hallberg, a soldier, said that 'there are German masters [officers] in our regiment who could rule better than the Swedish [Councillors]', it was not intended as a declaration of loyalty to his superiors but as a rude rejection of the competence of the Council. Even German officers might be better rulers, he seems to have wanted to say.[56] Johan Åman's offence, with which the previous chapter began, could possibly be included in the same category. That the kingdom fared badly under German kings was a sweeping accusation that expressed a general discontent without any actual substance, even though the specific issue – that a son of the Burgher Estate had been recruited to the life guards in violation of burghership privileges – certainly had a superficial connection to the king.

In another, somewhat older example, which has been mentioned in passing above, the circumstances were reversed: here it was the accusation that was sweeping while the King's German birth was given special explanatory value. In 1731 Jonas Norlin, a tailor in Växjö, lashed out with such highly criminal statements against the King that the Court of Appeal – at the command of His Royal Majesty – appointed an extraordinary court that would work in camera and under an oath of silence. Characteristically, the injurious utterance has been crossed out in all the records, and the wording used to justify the censorship is the same as that which recurs in many other court cases. However, in Norlin's case his statement can actually be reconstructed. One of the witnesses present, the upper-secondary-school pupil Elias Fult, had enough of his wits about him to immediately write down the injurious statement on a piece of paper. Although attempts have been made to expunge the writing on this note by crossing it out in ink, it can be read with some difficulty.

The circumstances behind the crime have become overshadowed by the rudeness of Norlin's statement and are therefore somewhat unclear. However, the origin seems to have been that Norlin, in an inebriated state, had gone to the burgher Nils Sörman in order to receive some kind of payment, but had refused to accept any money that bore the name of King Frederick. In that context, he had said that the Devil could take the King's money. It was true that he lacked money, he had shouted, but not the King's money, and he

---

56 1757.XII.16/72 ('här äro tyska Herrar [officerare] wid wårt Regemente, som kunna bättre regera, än the Swänska [rådsherrarna]').

added that 'the King is good for nothing other than lying at home with hussies; he is good for nothing when it comes to making war because he is in no way born of Swedish blood'.[57] This statement attacked those character traits which were perceived as Frederick's personal weaknesses in more ways than one. Even before he began his liaison with Hedvig Taube in the spring of 1730, Frederick had had several casual love affairs. As the first public royal mistress in Sweden, Hedvig Taube was the cause of quite a few protests, not least from the clergy.[58] The King's behaviour violated the general understanding of morals, and could easily be given an explanatory power: his debauchery made him neglect his duties and rendered him incapable of ruling. In Norlin's accusation, Frederick's effete licentiousness was also contrasted with the manly power that previous Swedish kings had shown by leading their troops in battle. Nor could anything else be expected from an enfeebled German, Norlin seems to have meant.

Those who had been displeased with the German Frederick were not relieved when it became clear who had been elected his successor. After all, this had been one of the reasons for the

---

57 The words according to Elias Fult's note in 1731.IV.27/44 ('at konungen duger intet annat til än at liggia hemma hos kieringar intet Duger han til at föra nogot krig för det at han intet är af swenskt blod födder'). The entire statement except for the words 'is good for nothing' has been carefully crossed out.

58 Carl Gustaf Tessin, *Framledne riks-rådet, m. m. grefve Carl Gustaf Tessins dagbok. 1757* (Stockholm: Ecksteinska tryckeriet, 1824), p. 175; [Gjörwell], 'Anteckningar af Carl Christopher Gjörwell', pp. 89–91; Fersen, I, pp. 182–83; Holst, *Fredrik I*, pp. 170, 191, 194, 199, 202, 208–09; Walfrid Holst, *Ulrika Eleonora d.y.: Karl XII:s syster* (Stockholm: Wahlström & Widstrand, 1956), pp. 262–64. The court preacher Johan Nordman's birthday sermon to Frederick in 1739 contained rather unabashed admonitions: 'The example of the Magistracy has a strong influence over the habits of the subjects. The virtue of the Magistracy is the strongest encouragement for virtue, and the sin of the Magistracy the greatest temptation to sin' ('Öfwerhetens exempel hafwer stark influence i Undersåtarenas seder. Öfwerhetens dygd är then kraftigaste upmuntring til dygd, och Öfwerhetens synd then största retelse til synd'). This reminder was drummed into the audience with a number of biblical examples, both commendable and cautionary ones; see Johan Nordman, *Underdånig lyckönskan på Hans Kongl. Maj:ts wår allernådigste konungs födelse-dag, then 17 april 1739* (Stockholm: Peter Jöransson Nyström, 1739). In Ulrika Eleonora's own annotated copy (National Library of Sweden, ex. B) the words 'the sin of the Magistracy' are underlined.

Dalecarlian uprising; and both during the intervening period and still at the following session of the Riksdag in 1746–1747, there were those who opposed the elevation of Adolf Frederick.[59] Nils Persson, a Peasant member of the Riksdag, went to see his Estate brother Olof Assarsson in his overnight lodgings in order to make him withdraw a petition directed against Olof Håkansson, Speaker for the Peasants. This matter was part of a series of rather convoluted party-political twists and turns that do not need to be described here. The petition had, in violation of the Riksdag Act, been submitted to the Clerical Estate, and Nils Persson wondered indignantly what Olof Assarsson had been thinking and from whom he was hoping to find support. Olof Assarsson answered that he sought the support of God in Heaven, of His Royal Highness – i.e. the Crown Prince, Adolf Frederick – and of all other Magistracy. It may be that you intend to seek the support of the Crown Prince, retorted Nils Persson, 'but you do not consider the fact that his Royal Highness is an alien and so is the Crown Princess'. Now it was Olof Assarsson's turn to become upset, and he warned Nils Persson in God's name against speaking in this way. However, Nils Persson persevered:

> If the country were to end up at war, His Royal Highness would lead the army! Perchance His Royal Highness would take the army and leave, without him or the army ever returning, and what would then become of the country?[60]

Since October 1743, Adolf Frederick had been the highest military commander in the country except for the King (Figure 55). In March 1747, his operative competence was extended for the purpose of curbing the discipline-subverting tendencies in the armed forces. In a variant of the time-honoured argument about the bravery of the Swedish soldier when led by his king, Colonel Hans Henrik von Liewen believed that order was best maintained through royal authority.[61] Protecting the kingdom by force of arms

---

59 Cf. 1747.VII.09/F11 and the related cases 1746.XII.12/F21 and 1747. IV.08/B16–17.

60 1747.VII.16/B11 ('men tu besinnar intet at Hans Kongl. Höghet är en Främling och KronPrinsessan med' and 'Om här skulle komma ofred på Landet, skulle ju Hans Kongl. Höghet föra Arméen! Kan hända Hans Kongl. Höghet toge Armeen och ginge sin wäg, utan at han eller Armén komme här mera, huru stode då landet?').

61 Birger Steckzén, 'Adolf Fredrik under kronprinstiden', *Historisk tidskrift*, 54 (1934), 342–55 (pp. 343, 346–47). See 'Ödmiukt memorial' presented

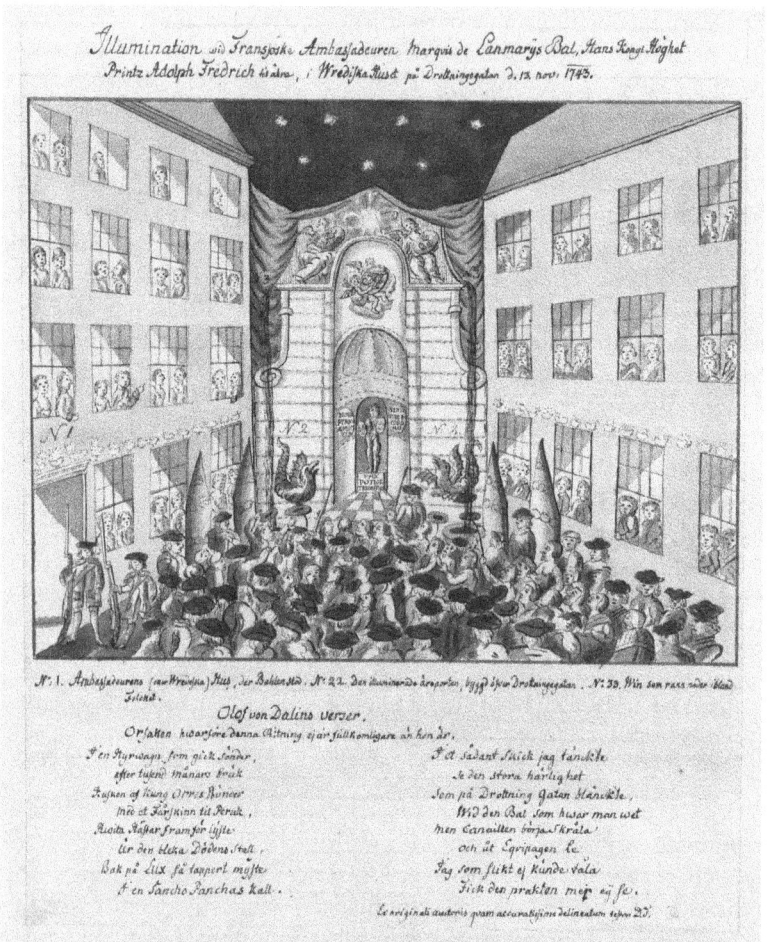

Figure 55 Popular royalism. The month after the new successor to the throne Adolf Frederick had arrived in Stockholm, the French ambassador gave a ball in his honour in the Wrede Palace on Drottninggatan. The guests at the ball are seen in the windows to the left, and above the street an illuminated triumphal arch has been erected, with the coats of arms of Sweden and France and the Crown Prince's monogram. The people are competing to catch the wine flowing from the sides of the triumphal arch. Tinted pencil drawing by Olof von Dalin, contemporaneous copy by Daniel Tilas. Photo: Björn Green, KB.

was still the primary obligation of the king, at least symbolically; and distrust in the successor to the throne could not be phrased any more clearly than in Nils Persson's accusation. His statement reflected the demands of the Dalecarlian rebels 'that no German or foreign man may be used in Swedish service at the regiments, and even less be trusted with a supreme command', and 'that no foreigners, only native Swedes, may hold Swedish honorary offices, in order that any treason may be prevented'.[62]

Arendt Israel Nordenlöf, a member of the Riksdag who shared overnight lodgings with Nils Persson during the session, was similarly harassed. On two occasions, Persson insistently, and in tears, pleaded with Nordenlöf not to side with the Crown Prince. After all, His Royal Highness had 'very rapidly been named the successor, and besides he was an alien who could not be trusted with anything', was the argument. Nils Persson mentioned his fear that the Crown Prince would abscond with the army he commanded to Nordenlöf as well. During his trial, Nils Persson tried to specify what he had said without diminishing his crime. He claimed to have been misquoted and maintained that his true words had been as follows: 'that one could not have any confidence in His Royal Highness if there was a war, because he was an alien' and 'that His Royal Highness, in the event that he would lead the army, could then march off with it, never to return again'.[63]

---

by Liewen in the Defence Deputation (försvarsdeputationen), 13 January 1747, in R 2894, Sekreta utskottet/Secret Committee, 1746–47, vol. 32, Defensionsdeputationens handlingar angående krigsväsendet till lands/ Documents of the Defence Deputation regarding the organisation of the land army, annex no. 60, RA, where he voiced criticism of the discipline within the armed forces citing historical examples taken from the Greek and Roman republics.

62 Humble petition from 'all the inhabitants of the Dalelagen' ('samtelige Invånare här i Dalelagen'), 2 March 1743, § 4, in Handlingar rörande Skandinaviens historia, III, p. 228 ('At ingen Tysk eller utlänsk man måtte vid Regementerne brukas i Svensk tienst, fast mindre anförtros något öfver-commando'); 'Dalekarlarnas Postulata vid allmänna Landztinget 1742', § 12, ibid., p. 223 ('att inga utlänningar, utan Svenska infödda, måtte bekläda Sveriges Rikes Ähretjenster, på thet alt förräderij måtte afböjt blifva').

63 1747.VII.16/B11 ('mycket hastigt kommit till Successionen och thesförutan wore en Främling, som man intet skulle kunna lita på'; 'at man, therest thet blefwe Krig af, ei kunde hafwa något förtroende til Hans Kongl. Höghet, så wida han wore en främling'; and 'at Hans Kongl. Höghet, i then händelsen han skulle föra Arméen, kunde thermed rycka bort, och icke komma mera igien').

Nils Persson's utterances were in fact considered so serious
that an extra legal commission was appointed to judge the case.
This court eventually sentenced him to death, a sentence which
was reduced by His Royal Majesty to thirty days' imprisonment
upon bread and water, in itself a very harsh starvation penalty.[64]
(Thirty days was the maximum duration of this form of punishment, which was considered closest to the death penalty in terms of
severity.)
Another episode inverts Swedishness in an interesting way.
When the artillery officer (*överfyrverkare*) Lars Wijnbladh had
vented his anger about how little he could stand the person of Adolf
Frederick, he had been rebuked by the lawyer Claes Hoffman, who
reminded him 'both of the sacredness of a king and the obligation of a subject, and of the benevolence His Majesty feels for all
things Swedish'. That the King was of foreign descent was thus not
something that prevented him from having a sincere love for his
kingdom and new homeland. When the case ended up in the Court
of Appeal, the court maintained that Wijnbladh had neglected his
duty 'as a Swedish subject, to speak of our gracious Magistracy
with all imaginable reverence'. In other words, Adolf Frederick
had completely embraced his new *Wahlheimat*, and as King he
felt a benevolent love for all his subjects. Conversely, Wijnbladh
had disregarded his innate duties towards his fatherland. For this
reason, he had 'made himself unworthy as a subject of the kingdom
to continue to enjoy His Royal Majesty's gracious safeguard and
protection' and was exiled from the realm for life.[65]

---

64 ÄK 57, Kommissarialrätt över bonden och riksdagsmannen Nils Persson/
Proceedings of the legal commission against Nils Persson, yeoman and
member of the Riksdag, 22 April 1747, RA. The commission was
appointed on 27 April 1747 and the whole case is connected to the major
prosecution against Christopher Springer and Abraham Hedman, who
through extra-parliamentary methods had tried to influence the members of
the Peasant Estate. Regarding this issue, see Malmström, *Sveriges politiska
historia*, III, pp. 278–79, 322–25 and *passim*. Assarsson's petition is printed
in *Bondeståndets riksdagsprotokoll*, VI: 1746–1747 (1957), pp. 763–64;
see also the protocol on pp. 160–64. Nils Persson was convicted by the
commission for his statements. The Judicial Review Division case in reality
concerned a member of the Riksdag, one Jonas Nilsson, who according
to Nils Persson had planted the statement with him. Owing to a lack of
witnesses, Jonas Nilsson was completely exonerated.
65 1752.I.10/8 ('så wäl om en Konungs helgd som en undersåtes skyldighet,
samt utaf hwad nådigt sinne [Hans] Maj:t är emot alt thet swensk hette';

The spatial distances between the royal family and the inhabitants of the small capital were not great, as has been pointed out
before. Regular city dwellers were welcome to the morning service
in the chapel at the Royal Palace, and to this service went the
widowed mayor's wife Gertrud Ziegler early in the summer of 1755.
Having partaken of the spiritual nourishment, she went to obtain
some corporeal nourishment together with Schederman, singer to
His Majesty the King, and the chamber clerk Anders Bygdeman.
During their walk, the latter – somewhat in passing – reproached
Ziegler for not standing up like the rest of the congregation when
the Queen arrived at the church, thereby failing to show the respect
due to a crowned head from a subject. Ziegler had answered
Bygdeman with a torrent of abuse, but had especially emphasised
that she herself 'was an old honest wife who did not have to rise
for the foreign bitch'.[66] Ziegler thought that this comment was so
witty that she repeated it later on at least three different occasions,
according to other informants. Bygdeman, of course, felt that the
statement was both appalling and offensive, but in addition it must
have conveyed a certain racy titillation, because he delightedly
related the episode to anyone he chanced upon during the following
weeks. Nevertheless, he eventually decided to bring the matter
before a court of law with the express aim of having the old widow
Ziegler beheaded.

He was successful to some extent, and the Court of Appeal,
according to legal praxis, sentenced Ziegler to death for her
statement. However, adducing a number of mitigating circumstances, the court recommended that the punishment be reduced to
three weeks' imprisonment upon bread and water, and following
the personal intercession of both the Queen and the King, this
sentence was confirmed. The same Court of Appeal sentenced
Bygdeman to two weeks in prison upon bread and water for having
publicly spread the injurious statement further. In the end, these
two punishments were almost the same, because the widow was

'honom såsom en swensk undersåte, ålåge, at med all uptänkelig wördnad
tala om wår nådiga Öfwerhet'; and 'giort sig owärdig, at widare såsom
undersåte i Riket, [Hans] Kongl. Maij:ts nådiga hägn och beskydd åtniuta').
Wijnbladh entered military service in Russia, where he was again deported,
this time to Kamtjatka for a different crime.
66 1755.VIII.27/42 ('wore en gammal hederlig fru, som ej behöfde upstiga för
then utländska markattan [literally "vervet monkey"]').

released after only fifteen days.[67] This, however, was not the end of the story.

Even though the widow Ziegler had had her death sentence commuted to time in prison, she seems to have taken the punishment she had suffered to heart. Two years later, in the summer of 1757, she was again put on trial for insulting the Queen. On several occasions, she had spoken of the torment she had endured for the Queen, whom she called a rascal's whore ('kanaljehora'), and she had also claimed that the Queen was responsible for the deaths of the co-conspirator lords after the attempted royalist coup in the previous year. Ziegler felt that in her previous court case she had had as many friends as she had had enemies, and she claimed that the Councillors of the Realm had been obliged to stifle their laughter behind their handkerchiefs when she had described her statements before the Judicial Review Division. When the trial was over, they had admitted – all according to Ziegler's own claim – that she had hit the mark in her characterisation of the Queen, and when she was released from prison they had sent her bottles of wine. Ziegler told several witnesses that the King and Queen had also sent money to alleviate her distress during her time of imprisonment, but that she had rejected this gift of grace. She continued her insolent behaviour after being set free. It was a great honour to have been imprisoned for the Queen, she joked on one occasion. For this reason she wanted to drink to Her Royal Majesty's health, and called for the piss pot.[68]

Ziegler's story about the amused members of the Court of Appeal may have a fairly low value as a source; but the claim in itself, just like the whole story in general, suggests that the type of drastic comments that she made might have resonated with many people. Not only Ziegler herself but also other informants retold the episodes in different situations and to a number of familiar and unfamiliar people. Apparently the juicy statements were not considered so criminal that they could not be repeated rather nonchalantly in a variety of contexts. They will have been titillating for having bordered on, but not transgressed, what was socially acceptable. How such injurious statements were judged must have been entirely dependent on the people involved and the occasion.

---

67 1755.VIII.27/42.
68 The hearing and decision of Svea Court of Appeal, dated 6 July 1757, in 1755.VIII.27/42.

The individuals who overheard Ziegler's utterances belonged to the higher burghership and the circles of public officials. This means, on the one hand, that they were sufficiently distanced from the court for rude jests about the royal family to be acceptable. In a context closer to the court, the same statements could easily have embarrassed those who had personal ties to the royal couple and would therefore not have been perceived as comical at all. On the other hand, Ziegler and the circles in which she moved were sufficiently established for her statements not to risk being seen as subversive. If the same people had heard similar statements from more common people, they would probably have perceived them as disquieting rather than amusing.

After her second offence Ziegler had, according to regular praxis, made herself liable for a strict execution of her punishment. However, the summoned character witnesses claimed that she had seemed unbalanced and mentally deranged when her trials were mentioned. Because of this, and with consideration for her advanced age, the court could not 'in good conscience' ('med godt samwete') sentence her to the punishment prescribed by general law, that is to say death. Instead they recommended imprisonment upon bread and water followed by two years of preventative detention with a discharge review. Ziegler was incarcerated at the asylum of Danviken, from where she sent in a petition for mercy in September 1758. After the case had been reviewed and the vicar and the warden at Danviken had testified to her cognitive abilities and her pious way of life, she was released in November of the same year.[69]

The gracious Magistracy

Both the King and the Queen had spoken on Ziegler's behalf and pleaded for a mild sentence for her crime. This intervention draws our attention to another important feature of the general view of the royal authority: the image of the merciful king. Mercy and benevolence were important components both in popular ideas and in the mediated image of the monarch. It was of course a basic prerequisite for legitimacy that the king was believed to feel solicitude for his subjects. It was not really the absolute power in itself that had invalidated the previous form of government but how the monarch

---

69 See the pardon case in 1758.XI.09/9.

used it. Charles XI had used his power for the general good, *salus publica*, whereas Charles XII had put the glory of the majesty before the security of the people. The celebration of the former and condemnation of the latter during the Age of Liberty were therefore practically rather than principally motivated, regardless of the justifications that were stated in public.[70]

The idealised image was spread in proclamations and public documents. In those contexts, the adjective 'gracious' and the adverb 'graciously' were used in both the first and the third person: 'We have graciously granted ...', 'His Royal Majesty's graciously approved ...', 'His Royal Majesty's gracious will ...' ('Vi haver i nåder förunt ...', 'Kungl. Maj:ts i nåder beviljade ...', 'Kungl. Maj:ts nådiga vilja ...') and so on were turns of phrase in regular use. A randomly chosen but altogether typical turn of phrase occurred in the sermon of the prosecuted but eventually acquitted priest Benedict Wettersten:

> We see with joy and delight a devout, wise, benevolent and just Magistracy sitting on our royal throne, who with all requisite tenderness, wisdom and caution rules over and protects his people.[71]

However, there was also a purely concrete clemency that was shown not least in the contexts discussed here, namely His Royal Majesty's right to pardon criminals. The death penalty was, according to the statute book, the only sentence for the crime of lese-majesty; but in practice, this was a crime for which people were rarely executed. For this reason, His Royal Majesty frequently had to make use of his so-called right of mitigation (*leuterationsrätt*), meaning the right to 'improve' a judgement by reducing the severity of an otherwise peremptory legal provision. This right was to be exercised subject to the advice of the Council, and it was regulated in the second section of the Instrument of Government. When it came to crimes of lese-majesty, though, the King often seems to have had the last word; it was he – or some other 'member of the royal family – who had been personally abused and who was the party most immediately concerned. Exactly how common it was for the King to settle the final verdict cannot be determined,

---

70 Cf. Nordin, *Ett fattigt men fritt folk*, pp. 229–33.
71 1758.06.21/38 ('Wi se med glädje och fägnad en Gudfruktig, wis, mild och rättrådig Öfwerhet sittja på wår Konungastol, som med all forderlig ömhet, klokhet och försiktighet regerar och wårdar sitt folk').

because it is often unclear in the records whether the term 'His Royal Majesty' refers to the King in person or to the king in Council. Still, it was definitely a recurring practice, at least during the reign of Adolf Frederick.[72]

Hans Möller, book-keeper at Bofors ironworks, had drunkenly uttered 'injurious and depraved statements about Their Majesties our most gracious King and Queen', and had been sentenced by Göta Court of Appeal to 'forfeit his life and be beheaded for this his severe crime, as a well-earned punishment to himself and as a deterrent and warning to others'.[73] The immediate details of the crime are not clear from the documents, but the case was unusual in that the Court of Appeal had not already petitioned for a suitable mitigation of the penalty. The offence must have been especially severe because the Councillors of the Realm also wanted to confirm the judgement, but here the King intervened personally: 'because His Royal Majesty declared himself willing to show this man Möller clemency; therefore Their Excellencies claimed to have reason to humbly support [the decision of] His Royal Majesty'. This wording leaves no doubt as to who is the agent behind His Royal Majesty.[74] Similar turns of phrase occur in other cases. In the judgement against the yeoman Johan Johansson, the lords of the Council had nothing to object to in the reduction proposed by the Åbo Court of Appeal, 'to which end this case will be humbly reported to His Royal Majesty'. A few years later, the King also

---

72 In Carl Fredrik Scheffer's normative textbook for Crown Prince Gustav, the king was also given considerable control over the institution of pardon: 'The king alone can provide mercy. However, the Council is entitled to humbly reject the same, in case the crime would be of a nature that mercy could not be offered' ('konungen allena kan gjöra nåd. Dock äger rådet i underdånighet afstyrcka densamma, i fall brottet wore af den beskaffenhet, att nåd icke kunde äga rum'); Fredrik Lagerroth, 'En frihetstida lärobok i gällande svensk statsrätt', *Statsvetenskaplig tidskrift för politik, statistik, ekonomi*, 40 (1937), 185–211 (pp. 192, 207).

73 1757.V.18/53 ('förgripelige och lastbare utlåtelser om Theras Majestäter Wår Allernådigste Konung och Drottning' and 'för detta sitt grofwa brott, sig sielf till wälförtjent straff och androm till skräck och warning, lif sitt mista och halshuggas').

74 Justitierevisionens protokoll (Rådsprotokoll i justitieärenden)/Minutes of the Judicial Review Division (Council minutes regarding judicial cases), 18 May 1757, fol. 748ʳ, RA ('emedan Hans Kongl. Maij:t förklarade Sig wilja giöra thenne Möller nåd; Ty yttrade Theras Excellencier sig häraf hafwa anledning, at i underdånighet styrka Kongl. Maij:t').

wished to exempt Michael Lundgren, a burgher from Sigtuna, from any punishment 'by favour and grace'.[75]

While the case of the journeyman miller Johan Bromberg falls chronologically somewhat outside the framework of this investigation, it may still be mentioned because it provides a good snapshot of how the royals wished to present themselves. As we have seen (above, p. 268), Bromberg had accused the Queen Dowager Louisa Ulrika of wasting the funds of the kingdom, and in that context he had used offensive expressions. This happened in August 1773, that is, a year after the royal coup d'état. It seems that following this event, the courts of appeal – to err on the side of caution – judged crimes of lese-majesty rather more severely: it is true that only six cases after the change of government have been studied, but the courts of appeal pronounced a death penalty in half of these cases and unusually strict sentences in the remainder.[76] That courts of appeal pronounced death penalties in such cases was an exception during the Age of Liberty. Even so, this did not entail a more severe application of the law after the coup d'état; the lenient Gustav III commuted all death penalties in accordance with earlier practice.

Since Bromberg's offence primarily concerned the Queen Dowager, the King ordered that she should be allowed to have a say in the matter. She on her part wished to exonerate Bromberg completely. The Councillors of the Realm then remonstrated that exempting Bromberg from all liability could have dangerous consequences. The Queen Dowager understood the objection but stood her ground. In addition, she felt that it would have a much stronger effect and provoke sincere regret if Bromberg were to be taken to the Royal Palace in order to be given the message

75 *Ibid.*, 19 April 1758, fol. 547^{r-v} ('Til hwilken ända detta mål hos Kl. Maijt kommer i underdånighet at anmälas'); *ibid.*, 4 December 1771, fols 1341–43 ('af Gunst och Nåde'), RA. See also, e.g., 1766.XI.28/124.

76 On the death sentences passed: 1773.X.04/26; 1773.XI52.17 and 1774. II.04/9 (concerning the same case); 1773.XI.18/54. On other sentences: 1772.XI.06/17½a, in which the accused was declared feeble-minded and was sentenced to be committed to a lunatic asylum pending further notice or until he regained his senses; 1772.XII.15/52, in which the accusation could not be proved with sufficient evidence to secure a conviction, and therefore the defendant was ordered to prison in order to force a confession from him; 1773.XI.18/66, in which the defendant was sentenced to death, but it was suggested that the sentence be commuted to thirty days in gaol upon bread and water.

by the Queen Dowager herself. The King approved of this and made arrangements for Bromberg, through the agency of the governor of Stockholm (*överståthållare*) and under appropriate guard, to be taken to the palace to see the Queen Dowager. From her hand he would then receive the letter of pardon, which not only annulled the death sentence but completely spared him any punishment.[77] This was a well-thought-out strategy for provoking the regret of the delinquent and his guilty love for the majesty. It has not been possible to find precedents of this example, and Louisa Ulrika thanks her son for having shown her the grace of letting her decide the matter. The basic pedagogical idea of portraying the majesty as indulgent and always forgiving in his elevation was well established, though. For instance, Adolf Frederick stipulated – as was reported in, among others, *Dagligt Allehanda* – that no punishment be executed in the new square in Stockholm that was to bear his name.[78] Gustav III also acted mercifully after his coup d'état and avoided taking revenge on those who had opposed him, a conciliatoriness that he ostentatiously emphasised.

As early as the 1730s, Judge of Appeal (*hovrättsråd*) Jakob Clerck felt that the practice of always mitigating sentences brought serious consequences. The pernicious habit of speaking offensively about the Magistracy was increasing, he claimed, and the reason for this vice was that 'the general public in their assemblages and gatherings are induced by the mercy shown them by the King to not consider the crimes particularly serious'.[79] Even if the material is not quite germane to this type of quantification, there is nothing that directly suggests that crimes of lese-majesty increased in number, at least not in the form of those opprobrious statements that Clerck referred to in this case. However, these circumstances raise the question of the context of lese-majesty crimes and why such firm legal measures were taken against them. While the scope of the present discussion does not permit a thorough investigation

---

77 1774.II.04/9.
78 *Dagligt Allehanda*, no. 37 (29 January 1768); Johan Elers, *Stockholm*, 4 vols (Stockholm: H. Nordström junior, 1800–01), III, p. 32. In 1959, the name Adolf Fredriks torg ('Adolf Frederick's Square') was changed to Mariatorget ('Maria Square').
79 1730.XII.09/15 ('at gemene man i sine lag ock sammankomster taga sig anledning af den nåd, som Konungen dem bewisar ock förbrytelserne icke så högt anser').

of the legal treatment and function of the crime of lese-majesty, the ensuing pages offer some brief reflections on this topic which have a bearing on the relationship between the people and the royal authority.

Legal measures against crimes of lese-majesty: context and function

At bottom, crimes of lese-majesty should be viewed as political crimes; but this is not the principal impression formed after a review of these legal cases. Rather, a socially disciplining function is foregrounded. Numerous cases within this category of crime fall under the heading 'opprobrious statements', and they come across as everyday crimes – commonplace offences where ordinary people expressed their discontent and aired their frustrations. Many of these episodes give reason to believe that from a social perspective, it was a completely accepted form of protest, and that the incidents which became known to the authorities were merely the tip of the iceberg. Opprobrious statements about the royal family seem to have been reported only by way of exception, and in many cases it was not the statement itself that was the actual reason for the report.

Coarse statements about the King and the Queen could be made in large gatherings without any thought of legal consequences, but the same statements could become issues of life and death if they were overheard by an outsider or if enmity were to arise. In several cases, a long time passed between the statement and the report. This suggests that such statements may have been common and not at all perceived as remarkable when they were made. Much later, though, they might be reported by way of revenge in some other, and completely different, conflict. Captain Gustaf Bagge felt that he was innocent and had been wrongly reported by his adversaries, and in his case the preliminaries regarding the issue of conflict of interest took almost three years to investigate.[80] There were also cases where the informer openly admitted that the aim was revenge against the accused by reporting an injurious statement. Applications for an

---

80 1759.VII.04/2. In February 1724, Åbo Court of Appeal delivered a judgement upon a crime committed at Midsummer in 1719; see 1724. II.19/42. Other similar examples: 1751.VI.28/45; 1756.XII.08/28; 1766. XI.28/124; 1768.XII.01/2.

economic reward for one's efforts also occurred, even though the reward was not necessarily the incentive for the report.[81] Using the legal system for the implementation of actions that people lacked the capacity or courage to undertake themselves was not unheard of during the eighteenth century. A parallel can be found in so-called suicide by crime, which occurred within the framework of prosecutions for infanticide or sodomy in the sense of sexual intercourse with animals. Suicide was a sin that was considered to have serious consequences for one's afterlife; but by making – or at least reporting – oneself guilty of some crime that was punishable by death, the execution became an indirect way of taking one's own life without any unfortunate consequences for the salvation of one's soul.[82]

The fact that lese-majesty was a serious crime that was severely punished but at the same time lacked an actual victim made it a useful instrument for personal vendettas. Johan Hasselgren, the crown bailiff of Lagunda Hundred, was reported for having called Crown Princess Louisa Ulrika a 'chit of a girl who could not tie her own shoelaces, much less state an opinion on important matters'. Here the underlying matter was a family drama. A few months before, Hasselgren's wife, Magdalena Sibylla Erman, had taken legal action against her husband before the cathedral chapter of Uppsala for the rudeness and physical abuse she had been forced to endure for twenty years. When Hasselgren did not observe the settlement that had been made in this matter, she had, together with their son Alvar, 'invented some other contrivance to convict him, which he would get into trouble for, namely that he was to have defamed the Princess'. Regardless of whether the statement was authentic or not, the undertaking failed this time, and both wife and son were instead convicted of false incrimination.[83]

---

81 1756.IX.08/23: 'Their aim was to gamble his employment off him' ('theras syftemåhl woro att spela tiensten af honom'). On rewards: e.g. 1757. VIII.31/56.

82 Jonas Liliequist, 'Brott, synd och straff: Tidelagsbrottet i Sverige under 1600- och 1700-talet' (unpublished doctoral thesis, Department of History, Umeå University, [1991]), pp. 108–13; Arne Jansson, From Swords to Sorrow: Homicide and Suicide in Early Modern Stockholm, Stockholm Studies in Economic History, 30 (Stockholm: Almqvist & Wiksell, 1998), chapter 3.

83 1748.V.11/A7 ('Flickslyngla, hwilcken icke kunde knyta til skoremmarne, långt mindre sig öfwer wigtiga saker utlåta' and 'hittat på ett annat råd at

A very special case concerned the clerk Peter Tallberg of
Nyköping, who had written letters in the name of the subsequently
famous painter of miniatures Peter Adolf Hall, in which the King
and the Queen were accused of being sodomites. Weeping and
wailing, Tallberg explained to the Judicial Review Division that it
had happened only with the intent of getting rid of Hall, because
Tallberg had perceived him as a rival for the woman he loved.[84]
The risk of informing on enemies for the crime of lese-majesty
was that it might backfire on the informer. Since there was usually
no technical evidence, the whole prosecution rested on testimony;
and if a crime could not be proved, the informer instead risked
being punished for making false accusations. For a conviction, sufficient evidence in the form of 'full proof' (fullt bevis) was required,
i.e. two unanimous witnesses, but the person who reported the
crime was not allowed to testify.[85] Sometimes it happened that
an informant preferred to be summoned as a witness so that
there would be sufficient evidence to convict.[86] In some cases the
witnesses did not dare report irregularities to the administrative
authority out of fear of repercussions on themselves. This was an
obvious dilemma for the authorities, and occasionally the court had
to acquit late reporters so as not to discourage other people from
making reports.[87]

Personal conflicts with the accused could also disqualify a witness.
This circumstance was exploited with cold but erroneous calcula-
tion by the widow Gertrud Ziegler, whose case has been described
above. On one of the occasions when she had spoken offensively
about the Queen, she had slapped the people present in the hope
of later being able to declare them disqualified because of a conflict
of interest. This ruse failed, though, and the law was prepared for
such tactics. Conversely, her informer Anders Bygdeman himself
ended up in a quandary when the Court of Appeal discovered that

---

fälla honom, som han skulle komma i olyckan före, nemligen, at han skulle
hafwa förtalt Printsessan').
84 1766.XI.28/124.
85 The Civil Code of 1734: Sveriges rikes lag gillad och antagen på riksdagen
    år 1734, reprint of 1780 edn, Rättshistoriskt bibliotek, I:37 (Stockholm:
    Institutet för rättshistorisk forskning, 1984), 'Rättegångs balk' (Code of
    Judicial Procedure), 10:24, 17:29.
86 E.g. 1760.III.05/1.
87 See, e.g., the records of the Judicial Review Division of 25 August 1756,
    RA, fols 425ᵛ–427ʳ; 1756.VIII.25/44; 1756.IX.15/51; 1761.I.22/23.

he had repeated her statement to other people, not without relish at the sensation he caused, and thus himself spread 'this poison among the general public'. He had thereby made himself guilty of the same offence as Ziegler and was convicted both of committing the crime and of not immediately reporting her statements to the proper authorities.[88]

There is reason to consider the aspect of class, even though the protection offered by a superior social position should not be exaggerated. Noblemen, high officers and other persons of rank appeared among those who were convicted of the crime of lese-majesty, but they were comparatively few. Quantification will not get us far, though, because noblemen are actually likely to have been overrepresented in relation to their share of the population (about 1.5 per cent). Rather, it is the character of the cases that differs between the higher and lower segments of the population.[89] The type of everyday verbal insubordination that was punished among the lower orders is conspicuous by its absence in cases where people from the higher orders were accused. Those cases were apt to involve a more seriously intended defiance of the authorities, including activities that must be characterised as downright rebellious. Many cases concerned the spreading of injurious writings, which had been more far-reaching and deliberate than the rash verbal statements for which the common people could be prosecuted. The charges differed, then; but when people of rank were eventually brought to trial, there is nothing to suggest that they received a different or more lenient legal hearing. Under the principle that the criminal should be tried only by his peers and according to Estate privileges, a nobleman had the right to be tried in the Court of Appeal as the court of first instance. In practice, when it came to the crime of lese-majesty, this was also the case for commoners. Consequently, common people frequently experienced a more qualified judicial process than they would normally have had; and at least for this type of crime, the assessments were in general increasingly lenient the higher up in the court hierarchy the case went.

---

88 Code of Judicial Procedure, 17:7, 15. 1755.VIII.27/42 ('thetta förgift ibland menigheten utspridt').

89 Cf. Jan Sundin, *För Gud, Staten och Folket: Brott och rättskipning i Sverige 1600–1840*, Rättshistoriskt bibliotek, 47 (Lund: Institutet för rättshistorisk forskning, 1992), pp. 438–39.

Men appear much more frequently in the material than women. This discrepancy is accounted for by the fact that lese-majesty crimes generally occurred in either a political or a public context. Injurious statements may have been made at tax-collection meetings and parish meetings, where women were not present, or in public establishments such as taverns and inns, where women did not have an obvious place in the conversational culture. However, the crime in itself does not appear to have been tied to gender in the sense that assessments differed on the basis of whether the accused was a woman or a man. The gender aspect was otherwise unmistakable in the two crimes that most commonly led to a death penalty during the eighteenth century: infanticide and sodomy (in the sense of bestiality). Together they constituted around half of all executions, and in the former category almost exclusively women were executed and in the latter almost exclusively men.[90] Nevertheless, where crimes of lese-majesty were concerned, the penal value seems to have been the same regardless of whether a man or a woman was prosecuted. Since the crime had political implications, it might otherwise have been natural to assume that men would be punished more severely than women, who were not political subjects. However, many of those who were prosecuted and convicted came from groups that lacked representation, and that circumstance had no effect on the assessment of the punishment. Crimes of lese-majesty had primarily to do with obedience and social stability, and only in the second place with politics.

The examples that most clearly emphasise the function of social discipline in the prosecution of crimes of lese-majesty are the

---

90 In the period 1751–1760 a total of 428 executions were performed (the statistics are unreliable with respect to details). Of these barely 20 per cent (82 men) were executed for the crime of sodomy, and barely 30 per cent (120 women, 6 men) for the crime of child murder. Other common crimes that were punished by death were murder, manslaughter and incest. More sporadically there were thieves and fraudsters among the executed. See table IV in Knut Olivecrona, *Om dödsstraffet*, 2nd rev. edn (Uppsala: W. Schultz, 1891), pp. 110–23, and cf. pp. 155 and 157. The ratios were roughly the same until the 1770s, even though the number of executions that were actually carried out gradually diminished. The social aspects of child murder and child smothering are discussed in Eva Bergenlöv, *Skuld och oskuld: Barnamord och barnkvävning i rättslig diskurs och praxis omkring 1680–1800*, Studia historica Lundensia, 13 (Lund: Historiska institutionen, 2004); the crime of sodomy is discussed by Liliequist, 'Brott, synd och straff'.

numerous cases where it was not the king himself but his officials who had been criticised. Although the eighteenth century was a period of profound changes in and reinterpretations of society, there was a slow process before these permeated all parts of politics and the justice system. In spite of all the civic rhetoric and an intensified struggle for civil rights, hierarchical social thinking lived on, at least with respect to views on the political foundations of the state. When the commoner Estates delivered proposals for common civic rights at the end of the Age of Liberty – a 'general Swedish rights of men', which would have obliterated most of the privileges of the Nobility – they were still formulated as decrees issued by the king and directed to his subjects. The radicalism of these proposals was seen in the far-reaching demands for civil rights, not in the rhetoric. The proposals would have adapted the legal system to many of the social changes that occurred during the century, but their aim was not to change the foundations of the political order.[91] New political thinking was only allowed to be implemented responsibly, on certain conditions and in certain contexts. If an ordinary subject left the theoretical discussion aside and questioned the established order, the entire arsenal of the state and the justice system was mobilised in defence of the traditional and established hierarchies. In this hierarchy, the king was placed at the top as the beginning and end of politics and the legal system. Questioning even the lowliest of his servants or the smallest of his orders was therefore an attack on the one who was both the head of state and its fixed foundation. In spite of his alleged powerlessness, the king retained this symbolic position throughout the Age of Liberty.

---

91 Jonas Nordin, 'Von "fremder Unterdrückung" zur "Freiheitszeit": Die Vorstellung von *frihet* im frühneuzeitlichen Schweden', in *Kollektive Freiheitsvorstellungen im frühneuzeitlichen Europa (1400–1850)*, ed. by Georg Schmidt, Martin van Gelderen and Christopher Snigula, Jenaer Beiträge zur Geschichte, 8 (Frankfurt am Main: Peter Lang, 2006), pp. 145–58 (pp. 153–56).

Conclusion

The investigation presented in this book has not resulted in an unequivocal picture of the Swedish monarchy during the Age of Liberty. It is incorrect to claim that the royal authority was inconsequential and insignificant, but neither is it accurate to call it completely indispensable. The king, both as an office and as a person, had an important role to play, and he was treated with respect and indeed reverence by most groups. At the same time, the political system could probably have managed very well without the king as a symbolic figure and still have functioned in an efficient manner. What is significant is that this question never seems to have been asked, and that, in its turn, is another confirmation of the secure position of the monarchy in society during the Age of Liberty.

The public image of the king is also ambiguous. On the one hand, he was depicted in ceremonies, proclamations and other public contexts as a powerful figure with a firm grip on the governance of the realm. On the other hand, no attempt was made to conceal the successive limitations that were placed on the royal authority during the Age of Liberty. Although a fair measure of education was required in order to correctly interpret and understand the meaning of legal texts, information about the design of the governance of the realm slowly trickled down to the broader segments of the population. In return, there is reason to believe that the symbolic respect for the king that was also maintained by the lords was in some sense genuine. It is easy to dismiss this reverence as hypocrisy, as has frequently been done in research, and the realpolitik often seems to reveal its fundamentally false basis. At the same time, the royal authority was surrounded by the remnants of an earlier mystique which may be difficult to understand today, but which was deeply ingrained in eighteenth-century subjects. Loyalty to the king can perhaps be compared to a code of morality or etiquette that was internalised by high and low alike. Like all everyday norms, it was exhortative without being mandatory; and there were types of behaviour that were allowed in certain contexts and from certain people, but not in and from others. Reverence for the majesty was dependent on the context. That the lords in their capacity as subjects showed respect for their monarch did not prevent them from carefully guarding their political rights and immunities, and both aspects were equally important in the holistic social thinking of the time. It was a system built on a balance among complementary interest groups, and this stability required mutual respect among the parties. The king was the ultimate, fixed point – the very foundation.

Among ordinary people royalism appears to have been widespread and unwavering. This did not prevent voices of discontent from being heard, though; and it seems to have been among the common subjects, if anywhere, that genuinely bold ideas were expressed. Here one could find those who would be willing to dispense with the king entirely, as well as with all those lords who tormented the powerless. Even so, such agitators seem to have been the exception. The old idea of one lord being preferable to a hundred remained alive; and in spite of the extended popular participation in the political system during the Age of Liberty, there were still many subjects who were afraid to contemplate matters of national politics: it was not for the common people to have opinions about the form of government. In any case, formulaic tributes to the king were widespread; and from a sociological point of view, the members of the royal family gradually took on an increasingly important role in the minds of the subjects. In them people found delight, to them people's prayers were dedicated, and around them feast days were organised.

The ethos of the monarchy

The primary function of the monarchy was to guarantee the outward independence of the realm and to provide legitimacy and stability for the government authority and the administration of justice. To this was added the more complementary role of being a cultural rallying point.

The form of government of the Age of Liberty was not fixed in and by the 1720 Instrument of Government, but was the subject of significant factual as well as theoretical adjustments. The royal authority was intended to be an important government body.

Through various changes in praxis and later also constitutional amendments, it was nevertheless pushed into the background to such a degree that its participation became superfluous in the governance of the realm. Still, this did not automatically lessen the prestige of either the monarchy or the royal family. Continental theorists of constitutional law had long treated the monarchy as an institution whose symbolic value did not necessarily have a direct connection with the scope of the royal authority. In Germany, according to the historian Horst Dreitzel, people primarily experimented with three models of a limited monarchy. The first of these, *monarchia pura*, meant that the royal authority was restricted only by constitutional limits that established a framework for the monarch's room to manoeuvre. The second, *monarchia mixta*, meant that there were several government bodies that competed with or counterbalanced one another, each of which had an equal right to an allotted share of the state authority. According to this conception, the regalities were allocated to various government bodies of equal stature. The third model, *monarchia limitata*, meant that the monarch needed to cooperate with various administrative bodies when governing, but was the sole holder of state authority. This required certain additional provisions: that the legislature had transferred parts of its liberty to the monarch but in other respects retained its immunities; that the monarch accepted his or her limited power, which was established in the constitutional laws that had been adopted; and that the limitations on the right to exercise power did not reduce the monarch's (symbolic) monopoly on power.[1]

The ideas that shaped Swedish constitutional law in the Age of Liberty were undoubtedly comparable to this last-mentioned model. The intact power position of the king was foregrounded both in constitutional documents and in expositions concerning the form of government. He and no one else wielded the power of governance – albeit with the assistance of the Councillors of the Realm and with the Estates, who safeguarded their rights. On a formal level, the monarch embodied the entire state authority. 'The king alone represents the entire realm and all the commoners of the realm, with all their privileges and rights', *En Ärlig Swensk* declared. 'From this follows the king's independence of other realms and powers, as does

---

1 Horst Dreitzel, *Monarchiebegriffe in der Fürstengesellscahft: Semantik und Theorie der Einherrschaft in Deutschland von der Reformation bis zum Vormärz*, 2 vols (Cologue, Weimar and Vienna: Böhlau, 1991), I: *Semantik der Monarchie*, pp. 94–99.

his *egalité* or equality to other kings and potentates. This majesty of his is sacred and inviolable.'² The same periodical explained that the king, being placed above political parties, had the power to exterminate arbitrariness: 'indeed, according to the constitutional laws of the realm, the King of Sweden holds as much power and authority as the most powerful absolute prince on earth'.³ At the same time, reinterpretations were made during the Age of Liberty, and constitutional law seems to have become more ambivalent. In the 1750s, for example, the power to make laws, which the Instrument of Government had bestowed on the king, was declared to be a right that belonged solely to the Estates. Thus the Riksdag was theoretically elevated to be a state body equal in stature to the king, in a form reminiscent of a *monarchia mixta*.

Nevertheless, the king was indispensable in all the interpretations that were made. Nor did the Swedish system appear particularly unusual; on the contrary, it was, theoretically speaking, firmly established in European constitutional law, even though hardly any other kingdom could actually produce an equally impotent monarch at this time. The great French *Encyclopédie* describes Sweden succinctly as a 'monarchie limitée' in line with the British form of government and contrary to the Danish one.⁴ On paper, then, there was nothing to prevent the Swedish monarchy from fulfilling one of its most important rationales – guaranteeing the independence of the realm.

While it is reasonable to imagine that the powerless Swedish monarchs were viewed with a certain degree of disdain by other powers, this was not allowed to affect diplomatic protocol. Diplomacy and realpolitik are two different things, though, and it is well established that the neighbours of the Swedish kingdom saw

---

2 *En Ärlig Swensk* (Stockholm: Historiographi regni, 1755), p. 465 ('Konungen allena repræsenterar hela Riket och hela Rikets Menighet, med alla des tilhörig- och rättigheter. Härutaf följer Konungens independance utaf andra Riken och Magter, såsom ock des Egalité eller jämlikhet med andra Konungar och Puissancer. Detta des Majestät är heligt och inviolabelt').

3 *Ibid.*, p. 286 ('så äger ju Swea Konung efter Rikets Grundlagar all den magt och myndighet, som den mägtigaste Enewålds Herre på jorden'); see also, e.g., pp. 290–91, 328–29.

4 *Encyclopédie, ou Dictionnaire raisonné des sciences, des arts et des métiers, par une société de gens de lettres*, 35 vols (Paris: Briasson, David, Le Breton, Durand, Panckoucke, Stoupe & Brunet; Neuchatel: Faulche; Amsterdam: Rey, 1751–80), X: *Mam–My* (1765), p. 637.

366 Monarchy in the Age of Liberty

its form of government during the Age of Liberty as an important means of forestalling Swedish military revanchism.[5] In any case, the international reputation of the royal family and the extent to which Sweden was dependent on the king's prestige for the country's relations with foreign powers are issues beyond the scope of the present book. That the independence of the kingdom was jeopardised by the powerlessness of the monarchy – as Gustavian propaganda would later claim – is unlikely, however. On the contrary, if anything caused concern and activity in the outside world, it was the portents of Gustav III's plans for a coup d'état.[6]

At all events, the foreign-political situation had a relatively small impact on the outcome of the Gustavian coup d'état of 1772. The decisive factor was the domestic prestige that the royal family still enjoyed among the masses. To a large extent, this prestige coincided with the second component in the ethos of the monarchy, that of being an arbitrator among conflicting special interests. Among many necessary preconditions for the success of the coup d'état, the intensified struggle among the Estates was the most important. When the Nobility saw its privileges threatened by the onrush of the commoners, it abandoned its traditional antagonism against the royal authority. Likewise, the commoners – in spite of their growing confidence, albeit facing a struggle with an uncertain outcome to abolish the privileges of the foremost Estate of the realm – felt that it was better to be safe than sorry and instead allied with the ever benevolent and gracious king. One essential reason for the fact that this ethos of the monarchy still permeated popular awareness lies in the public image of the king that was manifested throughout the Age of Liberty.

---

5 In section 7 of the Treaty of Nystad 1721, the Tsar had pledged to respect the Swedish Instrument of Government and Act of Succession, something that was in reality used as a pretext for Russian interference in Swedish domestic politics.

6 Michael Roberts, 'Great Britain and the Swedish Revolution 1772–73', *Historical Journal*, 8 (1964), 1–46; Knud J. V. Jespersen and Ole Feldbæk, *Revanche og neutralitet 1648–1814*, Dansk udenrigspolitiks historie, 2 (Copenhagen: Danmarks Nationalleksikon, 2002), pp. 226–27, 328–42; Olof Jägerskiöld, *Den svenska utrikespolitikens historia*, 10 vols (Stockholm: Norstedts, 1951–61), II:2: *1721–1792* (1957), pp. 236–38.

Manifestation and communication

The royal family was the cultural centre of the realm. At this time, publicly financed culture was an integral part of the exercise of power.[7] When power did not *a priori* originate in a popular mandate, it had to be fortified *a posteriori* by the Magistracy being ritually separated from the subjects. Consequently, cultural investments were as much a prerequisite for as an aim of the public manifestation of the royal authority. The Council of the Realm, which may be said to have been the actual government authority, did not have its own executive mandate but acted as and through the king. It was not possible for this corporation of the Nobility to represent the government, nor were they, as ordinary subjects, able to administer the public resources and cultural capital that should support the international standing of the realm. The public authority still required personal representatives, and the time for collective national manifestations and monuments had not yet arrived. The royal family was thus necessary as a rallying point for the cultural manifestations that placed Sweden in the ranks of civilised nations.

Externally, the authority and reputation of the royal authority were always maintained. Public rituals such as coronations had a similar format and were just as lavish as during the seventeenth century. In the royal portraits, the same symbols of power were used as for the absolute monarchs of the continent. When public proclamations and the semi-official newspapers described the governance of the realm, no room was given to anything other than the activities of the king. The symbolic core of politics hence remained largely unchanged.

Even so, it should be emphasised that no attempts were ever made to actually conceal the organisation of the state authority. The Instrument of Government was duly published and distributed across the realm, and the reintroduction of the signature

---

7 Theodore K. Rabb, 'Politics and the Arts in the Age of Christina', in *Politics and Culture in the Age of Christina: Acta from a Conference Held at the Wenner-Gren Center in Stockholm, 4–6 May 1995*, ed. by Marie-Louise Rodén, Suecoromana, 4 (Stockholm: Swedish Institute in Rome, 1997), pp. 9–22; *Iconography, Propaganda, and Legitimation*, ed. by Allan Ellenius (Oxford: Clarendon Press, 1998); T. W. C Blanning, *The Culture of Power and the Power of Culture: Old Regime Europe 1660–1789* (Oxford: Oxford University Press, 2002).

stamp during the reign of Adolf Frederick was announced without obscuring this message to any significant degree. As the symbolic respect for the king was always maintained, it was nevertheless hard for ordinary people without deep theoretical insights to really grasp the character of the form of government. The emphasis with which the image of the royal governmental authority was maintained prevented the development of true republicanism and of a political basis for legitimation based on the power of the people. Consequently, it was difficult to give the citizens – or the subjects, as they continued to be – the necessary justification for the power of the Riksdag.

Although extensive attempts were made in academic and political circles to theoretically place sovereignty with the people, this idea does not seem to have taken root in the awareness of the general public. Fear that actual governance by the people would be distinguished by self-interest and arbitrariness was still widespread; and though the Age of Liberty entered a qualitatively new phase in political terms in the mid-1750s, uncertainty regarding political developments was strong enough that when a reinforced royal authority gratuitously stepped in with the coup d'état of Gustav III, reactions spanned from resignation by way of relief to expectant enthusiasm. For natural reasons, the outspoken critical voices were few in number; but it is significant that many of the most eager republicans of the Age of Liberty placed their services and pens at the disposal of the King at an early point during the post-revolutionary autumn of 1772. This was true of politicians such as Anders Johan von Höpken, academics such as Anders Schönberg and agitators such as Daniel Helsingius, and it happened in spite of the fact that Gustav III, through his dictatorial behaviour, soon squandered the capital of trust with which he had begun his reign. The opposition that soon emerged against him was in part nourished by the new political currents of the time, but also by ideas that belonged organically to the Age of Liberty. General Carl Fredrik Pechlin, who was among the sworn opponents of Gustav III from the coup d'état to the murder of the King twenty years later, was one of the most consistent republicans produced by the era; but it is hard to believe that he was the only one who retained sympathies for the rule of the Estates. That circumstance brings us back to the issue of the attitudes of subjects towards the king.

Imago regis

Even though significant changes in ideas and conceptions occurred over the course of the eighteenth century, it often took a long time for them to find general acceptance. The ethos of the monarchy was deeply rooted among the common people when it came to issues concerning the impartial and conciliatory role of the king in and above the disputes among subjects. The personal characteristics of the king were also normally, if not as generally, described in deferential terms. This book has not discussed Kings as such; the analysis has focused on *the image of the king* and the royal authority, or *imago regis*, to borrow a Latin concept that eighteenth-century people liked to use in both an abstract and a concrete sense. In modern psychoanalysis, C. G. Jung introduced the concept of the *imago* to denote an intuitive ideal image projected by a child onto a person in its immediate surroundings, usually one of its parents. 'The imago is built up of parental influences plus the specific reactions of the child; it is therefore an image that reflects the object with very considerable qualifications. Naturally, the simple soul believes that his parents are as he sees them.'[8] This distorted ideal image, Jung claimed, unconsciously influences a child's identity and sense of self by providing exemplary patterns for norms. It is shaped by the parents but perhaps even more so by the child himself or herself, who creates his or her own expectations about how adults are supposed to behave. With appropriate adaptations, the king may be described as such an *imago* that possessed a number of redeeming qualities. He was all-wise, gracious and forgiving (Figure 56). Bad decisions were the result of incompetent or evil advisers, not of the king's lack of ability. This *imago* worked in two directions, both as an instrument of legitimation before the subjects and as a memento of the kings. On the one hand, it was not possible – not even formally – to hold an incompetent monarch in veneration; the hereditary kingdom presupposed that the head of state could always master the tasks that belonged to the office. On the other hand, this ideal image also functioned as a mirror for princes and provided ethical standards for the behaviour of the king

---

8 C. G. Jung, 'The Relations between the Ego and the Unconscious', in *Two Essays on Analytical Psychology*, trans. by R. F. C. Hull, The Collected Works of C. G. Jung, 19 vols (New York: Pantheon, 1966 [1928]), VII, p. 186. In analytical psychology, the concept has been replaced by 'primordial image' and 'parental archetype'.

Figure 56 Apotheosis of Adolf Frederick along with the royal virtues of
justice, valour, peace and benevolence. Engraving by Gustaf Precht (?),
approximately 1759. Photo: Björn Green, KB.

vis-à-vis his subjects. Kings were trained to behave in accordance
with the expectations placed on them.

Although the king was a central figure in the political notions of
the lower orders, their thoughts on such matters rarely included the
theoretical foundations of the rule of kings that were pondered by
scholars. The question of whether the monarchy was theologically
based or bound by contract is unlikely to have engaged the subjects
in general; but if anyone ever reflected on it, the former interpretation was probably still the one closest at hand for the majority.
However, the primary foundational motivation for the elevation of
the king would have been an ingrained idea of ancient custom. The
presence of the king in government life was not reflected upon; it
went without saying.

The *imago* of the king was probably the most significant aspect
of his public image. It was not only in the visual media that
royalty was more important than personality in depictions of the
monarchy: that was true of all public representations. The subjects

might have had ideas about the qualities of a Good King, but they rarely harboured an image based on the reality of the ruling agent's character and qualities of as a ruler. It can justly be claimed that the democratically elected politicians of today are probably also judged more on the basis of their media profiles than on their competence in day-to-day government work.

The public image and the general respect that followed from it – that which this book has referred to as the sociological aspect of the monarchy – was the primary asset of the royal authority, and it was independent of the actual power of the King. The form of government worked smoothly as long as he *appeared* to be a ruling agent. On the other hand, a perception of the King being a hostage of the Council gave rise to a lack of correspondence between the norm and the reality that undermined the legitimacy of the government, because no attempts were ever made to portray the Council and the Riksdag as bodies authorised to exercise public power. They were primarily safeguarding instances that protected the immunities of the subjects against encroachment by the public authority, the Magistracy, the Crown, the king.

Whether the authority of the Council and the Riksdag would have been able to gain legitimacy of their own if the form of government had been given a different public rationality can only be the subject of guesswork. It is true that there was a lack of correspondence between the constitutional legitimacy enjoyed by the king, the position of power attributed to him in public proclamations and popular support for the monarchy. This discrepancy, which manifested itself in several ways, actually undermined the legitimacy that the Council and the Estates possessed in their own right – not as governing but as consultative and implementing bodies. They enjoyed stronger support as counterparts of the king than as his superiors. Even among the supporters of the rule of the Estates, resistance to the coup d'état of Gustav III was therefore surprisingly feeble. The general idea appears to have been that in spite of everything, the revolution did not mean a complete death blow to, but merely an adjustment of, the balance of power among state bodies, each of which possessed its own legitimacy.

Concluding remarks

When I began working on this book, I wanted to find an answer to the question of whether and to what extent the king was, or was perceived to be, an important political actor. Here, at the end of this investigation, I have reached the conclusion that this question is incorrectly posed. The king was a natural, obvious, and for this reason (as has been pointed out many times above) indispensable figure in the politics and views on society of the time. His self-evident position could be neither overestimated nor questioned; indeed, it could hardly even be reflected on. Again, it should be borne in mind that the 1809 Instrument of Government was the first to expressly establish that Sweden was a monarchy. In all previous constitutional documents this state of affairs had been taken for granted.

The question of whether the king, in spite of his relative power-lessness, had a role to play must unreservedly be answered in the affirmative. His significance, as has been explained in the investigations above, was partly on a symbolic level, partly on a real political level. Because of the firmly established position of the monarchy, the king always enjoyed a *potential* political influence. Not least the king's role as holder of the balance of power ensured that his position and opinions could never be ignored. The monarchy also had a legitimacy that no other form of government even came close to possessing. Through practical experience, the masses might gradually become aware of the idea that representative parliamentary governance promised increased political influence for them; but the relative gains that were achieved in this respect were nevertheless not so great that people did not allow themselves to be drawn back into the safe embrace of monarchism as soon as an opportunity arose. This was the case in 1772 and again in 1789, when Gustav III made himself absolute monarch following a second coup d'état; and in 1809, the importance of the royal authority in social thought was still so fundamental that it was given a necessary balancing role among the government authorities. No matter how many bad kings people had experience of, the alternatives always frightened them more. Another reason for the lasting acceptance of the royal authority will be the entrenchment of corporatist thinking. Politics, it was believed, could never be anything other than a zero-sum game in which some groups lost what other groups gained. The royal authority was the only institution that stood above this continuously ongoing struggle among different interests.

Glossary

Accession Charter – *Konungaförsäkran*
Act of Succession – *successionsordning*
adjudication documents – *utslagshandlingar*
annual print series – *årstrycket*
Appropriation Ordinance – *bevillningsförordning*
attorney counsel – *advokatfiskal*
baron – *friherre*
billeting order – *kvartersordning*
cases of appeal and application – *besvärs- och ansökningsmål*
cavalry-provision yeoman – *rusthållare*
cavalry reserve soldier – *vargeringsryttare*
Chamberlain – *kammarherre*
Chancellor of Justice – *justitiekansler*
Chancellor of the Realm – *rikskansler*
Chancery College – *kanslikollegium*
Chancery President – *kanslipresident*
charity lodger – *inhysehjon, nådehjon*
chief judge – *lagman*
city court, town court – *rådstugurätt*
Code of Judicial Procedure – *Rättegångsbalken*
commissorial court – *kommissionsdomstol*
conscripted soldiers – *indelta soldater*
Councillor of the Realm – *riksråd* (also State Councillor)
count – *greve*
Court Chancellor – *hovkansler*
Court of Appeal – *hovrätt*
court protocol – *hovordning*
crown bailiff – *kronofogde*
Deputation on the Construction of the Royal Palace –
    slottsbyggnadsdeputationen
Directorate of the House of Nobility – *riddarhusdirektionen*

district judicial officer – *landsfiskal*
Estate commission court – *ständerkommission*
the Estimates – *riksstaten*
the Finance Chamber – *kammarkollegiet*
Greater Secret Deputation – *stora sekreta deputationen*
House of Nobility – *Riddarhuset*
Instrument of Government – *regeringsformen*
Judge-Advocate – *auditor*
Judge Advocate General – *generalauditören*
Judge of Appeal – *hovrättsråd*
Judicial Review Division – *Justitierevisionen*
Law of the Realm – *Landslagen*
lay assessor – *nämndeman*
legal commission – (*dömande*) *kommission, kommissionsdomstol*
licence, licentiation – *licentiering*, dismissal of a Councillor of the
    Realm
local sheriff, provincial sheriff – *länsman*
Lord High Steward – *drots*
Lord Marshal – *lantmarskalk*
Magistracy – *överheten*
manorial farms – *frälsehemman, frälsejordbruk*
Marshal of the Realm – *överstemarskalk*
Misdeeds Code – *Missgärningsbalken*
National Board of Trade – *kommerskollegium*
province governor – *landshövding*
provincial sheriff, local sheriff – *länsman*
Riksdag Act – *riksdagsordningen*
Royal Elections Act – *kunglig valakt*
the Secret Committee – *sekreta utskottet*
Staff Sergeant – *rustmästare*
State Councillor – *riksråd* (also Councillor of the Realm)
State Deputation – *statsdeputationen*
State Secretary – *statssekreterare*
Superintendent of the King's Buildings – *överintendent*
town court, city court – *rådstugurätt*
trade mayor – *handelsborgmästare*
urban district court – *kämnärsrätt*

Bibliography

Unprinted sources and popular prints (*kistebrev*)

Riksarkivet/Swedish National Archives, Stockholm (RA)

Handlingar angående Fredrik I:s och Adolf Fredriks namnstämplar/
Documents regarding the signature stamps of Frederick I and Adolf
Frederick, vol. 9

Inrikes civilexpeditionen/Office for domestic civil matters

A 1 a, Rådsprotokoll i renskrift, huvudserie/Fair copies of Council minutes,
main series, vol. 87, September–December 1768
B 1 a, Registratur, huvudserien/Registry, main series, vol. 70, 1768

Justitierevisionen/Judicial Review Division

Lappkatalog/Slip catalogue: Revisionsakter/Review documents and Utslags-
handlingar/Adjudication documents. Ämnesindelade serien/Series classified
according tosubject. Högmålsbrott/Political crimes against the state, 62:
1700–56; 63: 1757–89
Registratur/Registry, 1720–44, 1758
Besvärs- och ansökningsmål (utslagshandlingar)/Cases of appeal and application (adjudication documents), 1721–74
Generalauditörsmål/Cases before the Judge Advocate General, 1740, 1744
Justitierevisionens protokoll (Rådsprotokoll i justitieärenden)/Minutes
of the Judicial Review Division (Council minutes regarding judicial
cases), July–December 1756; January–June 1757; July–December 1757;
January–June 1758; January–June 1760; July–December 1771; July–
December 1772

Kommissionshandlingar/Commission documents

ÄK 57, Kommissarialrätt över bonden och riksdagsmannen Nils Persson/ Proceedings of the legal commission against Nils Persson, yeoman and member of the Riksdag, 22 April 1747

Riksdagshandlingar/Riksdag documents

R 2392, Documents of the year 1720, vol. 1

R 2894, Sekreta utskottet/Secret Committee, 1746–47, vol. 32, Defensionsdeputationens handlingar angående krigsväsendet till lands/Documents of the Defence Deputation regarding the organisation of the land army

R 5614, Protokoll och handlingar i saken över kommissarien Osthof/ Minutes and documents regarding the case of Commissioner Osthof, vol. 1

R 5615, Protokoll och handlingar i saken över kommissarien Osthof/ Minutes and documents regarding the case of Commissioner Osthof, vol. 2

Rådsprotokoll (det odelade kansliet)/Council minutes (the undivided chancery)

Vol. 127, December 1718–March 1719

Vol. 131, January–March 1720

Vol. 132, April–June 1720

Rådsprotokoll i koncept/Rough draft of Council minutes

Vol. 27, January–June 1719

Tessinska samlingen/Tessin Collection

Vol. 17 (E 5731), Brev till Carl Gustaf Tessin/Letters to Carl Gustaf Tessin

Kungliga biblioteket/National Library of Sweden, Stockholm (KB)

B 762, [David Nehrman (Ehrenstråle)], 'Inledning till Thet Swenska Jus Publicum Förklaradt i Publiques Lectioner af David Nehrman Juris Patrii & Romani Prof: Reg: &. ord: in Academ: Carolin: Gothor:'

B 766, 'Profess. Jur. Patr. et Rom. David Nehrmans Inledning till Jus Publicum, eller Swenska Etats Lagfarenheten, efter Sweriges äldre och nyare Stadgar, Regierings-Former, försäkringar, Riksdags beslut, Collegiers Instructioner, Resolutioner på beswär, etc. upsatt. 1748'

D 158:1, 'Assessor Höppeners samlingar rörande Sweriges stats hwälfningar ifrån 1719 til 1805'

D 171:1, Schröderheims historiskt-politiska samlingar/The Schröderheim historio-political collections, 1: 1590–1787

D 182, Politiske skrifter/Political writings

D 837, [David Silvius], 'Oförgripelige påminnelser angående Successions Rättigheten i Sweriges rike'

D 842, Strödda handlingar rör. Sveriges historia under Ulrika Eleonora/ Miscellaneous documents regarding the history of Sweden in the reign of Ulrika Eleonora (transcripts)

D 845, Hist. Sv., Frederick I., 'Försäkr. til Swea rikes ständer' [title on spine]

D 847, Erik Gammal Ehrencrona, 'Berättelse om 1719 års Riksdag. Diarium öfver det, som wijd rijksdagen a:o 1723 passerade på Riddarhuset i Stockholm'

Engeströmska handskriftsamlingen/Engeström manuscript collection

B.II.2.13, Anmärkningar över tillståndet och förändringen i Sverige efter konung Karl XII:s död/Observations on the situation and change in Sweden following the death of Charles XII

B.II.2.14, Handlingar rörande drottning Ulrika Eleonoras regering/ Documents regarding the reign of Queen Ulrika Eleonora

B.II.2.19, Handlingar rörande konung Fredriks regering/Documents regarding the reign of King Frederick, 1

Kistebrev/Popular prints

Series 37, Gävle

Series 38, Gothenburg

Series 43, Stockholm and Nyköping and no stated place of printing, eighteenth century

Series 61, Copenhagen

Series 62, Nyköping

Series 63, Sweden, late eighteenth century

Nationalmuseum/National Museum, Stockholm

Svenska Porträttarkivet/Swedish Portrait Archives ((SPA)

Kungliga porträtt från frihetstiden/Royal portraits from the Age of Liberty

Printed primary sources

Adelcrantz, Carl Fredrik, *Tal om de fria konsters värde och nytta; hållit för Kongl.* *Vetenskaps Academien vid præsidii nedläggande, den 23 julii, år 1757* (Stockholm: Lars Salvius, 1757)

Adlerbeth, Gudmund Göran, *Historiska anteckningar*, ed. by [Elof Tegnér], 2 vols (Stockholm: Beijers, 1892)

Alla riksdagars och mötens besluth, samt arfföreningar, regements-former, försäkringar och bewillningar, som, på allmenna riksdagar och möten, ifrån år 1521. intil år 1727. giorde, stadgade och bewiljade äro; med the för hwart och ett stånd utfärdade allmenna resolutioner, ed. by Anders Anton Stiernman, 3 vols (Stockholm: Johan Henrik Werner, 1728–33)

Arckenholtz, Johan, *Memoires concernant Christine, reine de Suede, pour servir d'eclaircissement a l'histoire de son regne et principalement de sa vie privee, et aux evenemens de l'histoire de son tems civile et literaire*, 4 vols (Amsterdam and Leipzig: Jean Schreuder and Pierre Mortier le Jeune, 1751–60), I (1751); III (1759)

Aristotle, *Politics*, with an English translation by H. Rackham (Cambridge, MA, and London: Harvard University Press, 1944)

Bång, Jonas, *Hans Kongl. Höghets af Swerige Adolphi Friederici ättartal* (Stockholm: Peter Momma, 1743)

Bellman, Carl Michael, *Öfwer Hans Kongl. Maj:ts tal på Riks-salen d. 25 jun. 1771: Författat den 26 jun. följ.* (Stockholm: Carlbohm, Kungl. finska boktryckeriet, 1771)

Berättelse om Hännes Kongl. Maj:ts wår regerande allernådigste drottnings, drottning Ulricæ Eleonoræ Sweriges, Giöthes och Wändes drottning &c. &c. &c. smörjelse- och krönings-act, med allmän fägnad begången uti Upsala dom-kyrkia, den 17. martii, åhr 1719 (Stockholm: Kungl. tryckeriet, [n.d.])

Bergstrand, Carl-Martin, *Ur västgötaprästers bouppteckningar från tiden före 1761* (Skövde: Skövde antikvariat, 1977)

——, *Ur västgötaprästers bouppteckningar från tiden 1761–1800* (Skövde: Skövde antikvariat, 1978)

The Bible: Authorized King James Version, ed. by Robert Carroll and Stephen Prickett (Oxford: Oxford University Press, 1997; 2008 reissue)

Bircherod, Jacob, *Jacob Bircherods Rejse til Stockholm 1720*, ed. by Georg Christensen (Copenhagen: Aschehoug, 1924)

Bodin, Jean, *Les six livres de la republiqve* (Lyon [= Geneva]: Gabriel Cartier, 1593 [1576])

Bonde, Gustaf, *Sverige, under Ulrica Eleonora och Fredric I, eller ifrån 1718 till 1751: Efter den, af framledne hans exellens, riks-rådet herr grefve Gustaf Bonde författade handskrift med ett Tillägg om fredsunderhandlingarna i Åbo 1741–1742, af r.r. herr gr. H. Cedercreutz; Ett bihang till skriften:* Tessin och Tessiniana (Stockholm: Ecksteinska tryckeriet, 1821)

Bondeståndets riksdagsprotokoll, ed. by Sten Landahl, 13 vols (Uppsala: Almqvist & Wiksell; Stockholm: Gernandts, Bok- och reklamtryck, Norstedts, 1939–86), I: *1720–1727* (1939); V: *1742–1743* (1954); VI: *1746–1747* (1957); VII: *1751–1756* (1963); X: *1765–1766* (1973)

Borgarståndets riksdagsprotokoll från frihetstidens början, ed. by Nils Staf and others, 12 vols (Uppsala: Almqvist & Wiksell; Stockholm: Riksdagsförvaltningen, 1945–), I: *1719–1720* (1945); VIII:1: *1742–1743* (1982); IX:1: *1746–1747* (2003)

[Busser, Johan B.], *Historisk berättelse, om alla kongliga kröningar uti Swerige* (Stockholm: Wennberg & Nordström, 1771)

——, *Utkast til beskrifning om Upsala,* 2 vols (Uppsala: Johan Edman, 1769–73), I: *Om Upsala stad, dess äldre och nyare öden, samt förnämsta märkvärdigheter* (1773)

Cicero, *De re publica: De legibus,* trans. by Clinton Walker Keyes, Loeb Classical Library (Cambridge, MA: Harvard University Press; London: William Heinemann, 1953)

Dalin, Olof [von], *Svea rikes historia ifrån dess begynnelse til wåra tider,* 3 vols. (Stockholm: Lars Salvius, 1747–62)

De Lolme, John Louis, *A Parallel between the English Constitution and the Former Government of Sweden; Containing Some Observations on the Late Revolution in that Kingdom; and an Examination of the Causes that Secure us against Both Aristocracy, and Absolute Monarchy* (London: Almon, 1772)

Divine Right and Democracy: An Anthology of Political Writing in Stuart England, ed. by David Wootton (Harmondsworth: Penguin Classics, 1986)

Elers, Johan, *Stockholm,* 4 vols (Stockholm: H. Nordström junior, 1800–01)

En Ärlig Swensk (Stockholm: Historiographi regni, 1755)

Encyclopédie, ou Dictionnaire raisonné des sciences, des arts et des métiers, par une société de gens de lettres, 35 vols (Paris: Briasson, David, Le Breton, Durand, Panckoucke, Stoupe & Brunet; Neuchatel: Faulche; Amsterdam: Rey, 1751–80), V: *Do–Esy* (1765); X: *Mam–My* (1765)

En redlig swänsk patriots politiska tros bekiännelse ([n.p.]: [n. pub.], [1743])

[Faggot, Isac], *Swea rikes styrelse efter grund-lagarne* (Stockholm: Johan Georg Lange, 1768)

Fersen, Fredrik Axel von, *Historiska skrifter,* ed. by R. M. Klinckowström, 2nd edn, 8 vols (Stockholm: Norstedts, 1867–72), I (1867); II (1868); III (1869)

Filmer, Sir Robert, *Patriarcha and Other Writings,* ed. Johann P. Sommerville (Cambridge: Cambridge University Press, 1991)

Fischerström, Johan, *En gustaviansk dagbok: Johan Fischerströms anteckningar för året 1773,* ed. by Gustaf Näsström (Stockholm: Bröderna Lagerström, 1951)

Floding, Pehr, *Solemnités, qvi se sont passés à Stockholm, capitale du royau.me de Svede, dans les années 1771 et 1772, consistantes en des décorations, emblemesm inscriptions, plans, élevations et processions, tant à l'enterrement de feu Sa Majesté le roi Adolphe Frederic à l'Église de Riddarholmen, qu'au sacre de Leurs Majestées regnantes le roi Gustave III. et la reine Sophie Magdelaine à l'Église de S.t Nicolas, avec l'acte de l'hommage. On y a joint le discours de Sa Majesté le roi, lors de la nouvelle forme de gouvernement récuë et jurée par les états dy royaume; avec le plan de la Salle des États à cette occasion, &c.a* (Stockholm: [n. pub.], 1772)

Florerande general Europæ land- och regente-spegel som kort-tydeligen wisar och repræsenterar de i dag, d. 1 januarii, 1740, warande förnämsta europæiska (Stockholm: Lorentz Ludwig Grefing, 1740)

Förarbetena till Sveriges rikes lag 1686–1736, ed. by Wilhelm Sjögren, 8 vols (Uppsala: Almqvist & Wiksell, 1900–09), I: *Lagkommissionens protokoll 1686–1693* (1900); II: *Lagkommissionens protokoll 1694–1711* (1901); III: *Lagkommissionens protokoll 1712–1735* (1901); IV: *Lagkommissionens förslag 1686–1697* (1902); VII: *Utlåtanden öfver Lagkommissionens förslag* (1908)

[Forsskål, Peter], *Tankar om borgerliga friheten* (Stockholm: Lars Salvius, 1759)

Forsskål, Peter, *Thoughts on Civil Liberty: Translation of the Original Manuscript with Background*, ed. by David Goldberg, trans. by Gunilla Jonsson and others (Stockholm: Atlantis, 2009)

Frihetstidens grundlagar och konstitutionella stadgar, ed. Axel Brusewitz (Stockholm: Norstedts, 1916)

[Frölich, Charlotta], *Swea och Götha christna konungars sagor, sammanfattade til underrättelse för Sweriges almoge och menige man, som af dem kunna lära, huru deras k. fädernesland ifrån flera hundrade år tilbakars blifwit regerat, samt se, huru på gudsfruktan, laglydnad, dygd och enighet altid följt Guds wälsignelse; men deremot synd, lagens och eders öfwerträdelse, samt oenighet, haft til påföljder swåra landsplågor, blodsutgiutelser, förödelser m. m.* (Uppsala: Kongl. Akademiska tryckeriet, 1759)

[Frondin, Birger], *Riksdags-manna rätt: Til dess grund och beskaffenhet föreställd* (Stockholm: Lars Salvius, 1747)

[Funck, Johan], *Genwäg til kundskap och utöfning af swensk lagfarenhet* (Stockholm: Kungl. tryckeriet, 1761)

Geijerstam, Emanuel af, *Emanuel af Geijerstams levernesbeskrivning*, ed. by Ingvar Andersson, Källpublikationer och studier till Uddeholms historia, 1 (Stockholm: Norstedts, 1954)

Gibbon, Edward, *Memoirs of my Life*, ed. by Georges A. Bonnard (London: Nelson, 1966)

Gjörwell, Carl Christoffer, 'Anteckningar af Carl Christopher Gjörwell om sig sjelf, samtida personer och händelser 1731–1757', in *Samlingar utgifna för De skånska landskapens historiska och arkeologiska förening*, ed. by Martin Weibull, 9 vols (Lund: Berlings, 1874–80), III: *1875* (1874), pp. 31–142

——, *En Stockholmskrönika ur C. C. Gjörwells brev, 1757–1778*, ed. by Otto Sylwan (Stockholm: Bonniers, 1920)

Grosses vollständiges Universal-Lexicon aller Wissenschaften und Künste, welche bishero durch menschlichen Verstand und Witz erfunden und verbessert worden, ed. by Jacob August Franckenstein and others, 68 vols (Leipzig and Halle: Johann Heinrich Zedler, 1731–54), XXI: *Mi–Mt* (1739)

Gustave III par ses lettres, ed. by Gunnar von Proschwitz (Stockholm: Norstedts; Paris: Jean Touzot, 1986)

Gyllenborg, Gustaf Fredrik, *Mitt lefverne, 1731–1775: Själfbiografiska anteckningar*, ed. by Gudmund Frunck (Stockholm: Seligmann, 1885)

Hamilton, Adolf Ludvig, *Anekdoter till svenska historien under Gustaf III:s regering*, ed. by Oscar Levertin, Svenska memoarer och bref, 4 (Stockholm: Bonniers, 1901)

Handlingar angående revolutionen i Sverige 1718–1719, ed. by Lennart Thanner, Historiska handlingar, 36:1 (Stockholm: Kungl. Samfundet för utgifvande af handskrifter rörande Skandinaviens historia, 1954)

Handlingar om grundlagarnes wärkställighet, tryckte på riksens höglofliga ständers befalning wid riksdagen år 1756 (Stockholm: Kungl. tryckeriet, [n.d.])

Handlingar rörande Skandinaviens historia, ed. Kungl. Samfundet för utgifvande af handskrifter rörande Skandinaviens historia, 60 vols (Stockholm: Elmén & Granberg and others, 1816–60), III (1817); VI (1818)

Handlingar uti swenska historien, utgifne utur Upfostrings-sälskapets bibliothek, ed. by Carl Christoffer Gjörwell, 1 (Stockholm: A. J. Nordström, 1786)

Hermansson, Johannes (*praeses*) and Brehmer, Christopher J. (respondent), *Dissertatio historico-politica, de regalibus regni Sveo-Gothici* (Stockholm: Johan Henrik Werner, 1733)

Hertig Adolph Friedrichs intog til Sweriget och hufwud staden Stockholm beskrifwen på gammalt sätt i en wisa helt ny: År 1743 ([n.p.]: [n. pub.], [n.d.])

[Hesselius, Andreas, Americanus], *Swea- och Götha-rikens underdånige fägne-ljud, hördt wid Hans Kongl. Höghets, Sweriges rikes arf-furstes hertig Adolph Fredrichs högstönskelige intog, uti kongl. residence-staden Stockholm, then 14 octobris åhr 1743; Siunges som: Rest hafwer jag öfwer watn och land, &c.* (various edns from Linköping, Stockholm and Strängnäs, 1743)

Hoffbro, Petter Lorens, *Kort Beskrifning öfwer alla Swea och Götha Konungars Regemente i en [...] som regerade 88. åhr efter syndafloden, til wår allernådigste K[...] FREDRICH I* (Stockholm: Petter Lorens Hoffbro, [n.d.])

——, *Kort Beskrifning öfwer alla Swea och Götha Konungars Regemente ifrån Magog til wår allernådigste Konung Adolph Fredrich*, 2 variants (Stockholm: Petter Lorens Hoffbro, [n.d.])

Homer, *Iliad, Books 1–12*, trans. by A. T. Murray, rev. by William F. Wyatt, Loeb Classical Library, 170 (Cambridge, MA: Harvard University Press, 1999)

Höpken, Anders Johan von, *Riksrådet grefve Anders Johan von Höpkens skrifter*, ed. by Carl Silfverstolpe, 2 vols (Stockholm: Norstedts, 1890–93), I: *Minnes-anteckningar, tal, bref*

Jennings, John, *Undersåtelig fägnad, wid Hans Kongl. Maj:ts Friederich, 1. Swea, Göthes och Wendes konungs &c. &c. &c. födelse-dag betygad wid kongl. academien i Upsala den 17. april MDCCXLIX* (Stockholm: Lars Salvius, 1749)

Kant, Immanuel, 'What is Enlightenment?' (1784), in *Foundations of the Metaphysics of Morals and What is Enlightenment?*, trans. and ed. by Lewis White Beck, Library of Liberal Arts, 113, 2nd ed. (Upper Saddle River: Prentice-Hall, 1997), pp. 83–90

King Magnus Eriksson's Law of the Realm: A Medieval Swedish Code, trans. and ed. by Ruth Donner, Acta Societatis Fennicae Iuris Gentium, 2 (Helsinki: Ius Gentium Association, 2000)

Klagan jämte tröst, då den i lifstiden stormäcktigste herre Svea, Götha och Wendes konung, konung Friedrich den förste, med skjäl kallad den Milde, Svea barns hulldaste fader, odödelig, til dess dödeliga del i konunga-grafwen jämte de odödeliga Carlar bisattes den 11. april. 1751. Framgifwen af B.V. ([Stockholm]: Kungl. tryckeriet, [n.d.])

Klein, Carl Ernst, *Samtal emellan afledne deras Kongl. Majestäter, Hennes Maj:t drottning Ulrica Eleonora Sweriges, Göthes, och Wendes drottning &c. &c. &c. landt-grefwinna til Hessen &c. &c. &c. som sidstledne d. 24. novembr. här i Stockholm j herranom afsomnade; och dess fru moder, Hennes Maj:t drottning Ulrica Eleonora Sweriges, Göthes och Wendes drottning &c. &c. &c. arf-printzessa til Dannemark och Norrige &c. &c. &c. hwilken högstsaligen afled d. 26. julii 1693 på Carlbergs slott; hwarutinnan bägge deras Kongl. Majestäter hwarannan berätta den mycket märkwärdige historien af deras lefwerne* (Stockholm: Lars Salvius, 1742)

König, Christian, *Lärdoms öfning; sjunde tomen, om stats-kunskapen, Swerges rikes ungdom, til tjenst* (Stockholm: Lars Salvius, 1748)

——, *Lärdoms-öfning: Tredje tomen angående lagfarenheten i kyrko-saker, bergs-saker och några missgerningsmål* (Stockholm: Lars Salvius, 1746)

Kongl. stadgar, förordningar, bref och resolutioner, jfrån åhr 1528. in til 1701. angående justitiæ och executions-ährender, med een förteckning på stadgarne främst, och ett fulkommeligit orda-register efterst wid wercket öfwer thes innehåld; uppå Hans Kongl. May:tz allernådigste befalning och privilegier, til thet almänne bästas tienst, och hwars och ens särskilte nytto, sålunda med flijt samlade, och genom trycket i dagzliuset befordrade, ed. by Johan Schmedeman (Stockholm: Johan Henrik Werner, 1706)

Kort beskrifning öfwer alla SVEA och GÖTHA Konungar, ifrån Magog, som regerade 88 år efter syndafloden, till närwarande tid. Af de trowärdigaste Skribenters Krönikors innehåll utdragen (Gothenburg and Surbrunn: Anders Lindgren, 1847)

Kort historia, om den kongl. gustavianska familien, ifrån glorwyrdigst i åminnelse konung Gustaf den förste, intil wår nu regerande allernådigste konung Gustaf III: Jämte de höga kongl. personernas portraiter (Stockholm: J. C. Holmberg, 1786)

Kort historia om den kongl. gustavianska familien, ifrån glorwördigst i åminnelse konung Gustaf den förste, intil wår nu regerande allernådigste konung Gustaf IV Adolph: Jämte de höga kongl. personernes portraiter, 2nd edn (Stockholm: J. C. Holmberg, 1797)

La Motraye, Aubry de, *Travels through Europe, Asia, and into Part of Africa; with Proper Cutts and Maps* (London: the Author, 1723)

——, *Voyages du sʳ. A. de La Motraye, en Europe, Asie & Afrique*, 2 vols (Haag: T. Johnson & J. van Duren, 1727), II

Landslagen: *Swerikes rijkes lands-lag, som af rijksens råd blef öfwersedd och förbättrat: Och af k. Christofer, Swerikes, Danmarks, Norikes, Wendes och Götha konung, palatz-grefwe widh Reen, och hertigh af Beijeren, årom efter C. b. 1442. stadfäst: Så ock af menige Swerikes rijkes ständer samtyckt, gillat och wedertagen, efter then stormächtige, höghborne furstes och herres, herr Carls then nijondes, Swerikes, Göthes, Wendes, finnars, carelers, lappars i Norlanden, the caijaners, och esters i Lifland &c. konungs, nådige befalning, åhr 1608. af trycket utgången: Nu å nyo andra gången med anmärckningar uplagd* [with commentaries by Petter Abrahamsson] (Stockholm: Johan Henrik Werner, 1726)

Leben und Tod Carls des XII. der Schweden/Gothen und Wenden &c. Königes, nach denen merckwürdigsten Umständen kürtzlich zusammen gefasset, und biß auf die Krönung der Königin Ulricæ Eleonoræ inclusive in diesem geschmeidigen Format mit schönen Kuppffern gezieret, beschrieben, von einer unpartheyischen Teutschen Feder (Nuremberg: Buggel & Seitz, 1719)

Leopold, Carl Gustaf, *Samlade skrifter af Carl Gustaf af Leopold*, ed. by Knut Fredlund and others, 8 vols (Stockholm: Svenska Vitterhetssamfundet, 1911–96), I:1: *Ungdomsskrifter (1770–1784)* (1912)

Linnaeus, Carl, *Wästgöta-resa, på riksens högloflige ständers befallning förrättad år 1746: Med anmärkningar uti oeconomien, naturkunnogheten, antiquiteter, jnwånarnes seder och lefnads-sätt, med tilhörige figurer* (Stockholm: Lars Salvius, 1746)

Locke, John, *Oförgripelige tankar om werldslig regerings rätta ursprung, gräntsor och ändamål*, trans. by Hans Harmens (Stockholm: Kungl. tryckeriet, 1726)

——, *Two Treatises of Government*, ed. Peter Laslett, Cambridge Texts in the History of Political Thought (Cambridge: Cambridge University Press, 1988)

Louis XIV, *Mémoires de Louis XIV pour l'instruction du Dauphin*, ed. by Charles Dreyss, 2 vols (Paris: Didier, 1860), II

Mechel, Chretien de, *Oeuvre du chevalier Hedlinger ou recueil des medailles de ce celebre artiste, gravées en taille douce, accompagnées d'une explication historique et critique, et précédes de la vie de l'auteur: Dedie a S. M. Gustave III roi de Suede* (Basel: the Author, 1786)

Möller, Johann Georg Peter, *Die Verdienste der königlichen schwedischen Gustave aus dem Wasastamm um die Wissenschaften und Künste in einer feierlichen akademischen Rede auf die zu Stockholm vollzogene königliche Krönung den 29sten Mai des Jahrs 1772 zu Greifswald entworfen: Nebst einer historischen Nachricht von den Feierlichkeiten und Gebräuchen die in ältern Zeiten beim Antrit der Regierung schwedischer Könige erfordert wurden und einer Beschreibung der vornehmsten Krönungsinsignien* (Stralsund: Christian Lorenz Struck, 1772)

Montesquieu, Charles-Louis de Secondat de, *Œuvres de Monsieur de Montesquieu, nouvelle edition, revue, corrigée, & considérablement augmentée par l'auteur*, 7 vols (Amsterdam and Leipzig: Arkstée & Merkus, 1758–72), I (1758)

Nicander, Anders, *Guds staf i Gustafs hand skal hägna Svea land: Hans tal til riksens ständer har fägnat Svea länder: I et heroiskt skalde-quäde, underdånigst yttrat* (Stockholm: Henric Fougt, 1771)

[Nordencrantz, Anders], *Tankar om krig i gemen och Sweriges krig i synnerhet, samt hwaruti Sweriges rätta och sanskyldiga interesse består: Skrifwit år 1758, och hörer til et större wärk, som på hög wederbörlig befallning blifwit författadt, men icke förr kunnat komma i dagsljuset*, 2 vols (Stockholm: Grefing and Carlbohm, 1767–72)

Nordman, Johan, *Underdånig lyckönskan på Hans Kongl. Maj:ts wår allernådigste konungs födelse-dag, then 17 april 1739* (Stockholm: Peter Jöransson Nyström, 1739)

Norrköping den 3. junii 1772 (Norrköping: Johan Benjamin Blume, [n.d.])

[Oelreich, Niclas von], *Tankar öfwer et högmål uti swenska jure-publico, eller rikets styrelse-lagar, nämligen om Kongl. Maj:t med regeringens nedläggande imellan riksdagarne försätter kongl. collegier och kronans ämbetsmän uti en fullkomlig inactivité och det i stöd af rikets grundlagar, med mera* (Stockholm: Carl Stolpe, 1769)

Öfwer Hans Kongl. Höghets hertig Adolph Fredrichs lyckeliga ankomst til Stockholm, den 14. octobris 1743 (Stockholm: Peter Jöransson Nyström, [n.d.])

Pontoppidan, Erich, *Den danske Atlas eller Konge-Riget Dannemark, med dets naturlige Egenskaber, Elementer, Jndbyggere, Væxter, Dyr og andre Affødninger, dets gamle Tildragelser og nærværende Omstændigheder i alle Provintzer, Stæder, Kirker, Slotte og Herre-Gaarde: Forestillet ved en udførlig Lands-Beskrivelse, saa og oplyst med dertil forfærdigede Land-Kort over enhver Provintz, samt ziret med Stædernes Prospecter, Grund-Ridser, og andre merkværdige Kaaber-Stykker*, 7 vols (Copenhagen: Godiche, 1763–81), I (1763)

Prästeståndets riksdagsprotokoll, ed. by Lennart Thanner and others, 16 vols (Stockholm: Riksdagsförvaltningen, 1949–), V: *1719–1720* (1980); XI: *1742–1743* (1999); XVI:2: *1765–1766* (2022)

Pufendorf, Samuel, *The Whole Duty of Man According to the Law of Nature*, 2nd edn (London: Motte/Harper, 1698 [1673])

Rålamb, Bror Classon, *Ett panegyriskt taal öfwer ten stormektige och allernådigste Sweries- Götes- och Wendes kånung Friederic ten förstas födelse-dag den XVII. aprilis åhr M.DCCXXIX, hållet samma dag vti Swea ridderskaps och adels Riddare-hus sal* (Stockholm: Kungl. tryckeriet, 1729)

Reuterholm, Axel, *Axel Reuterholms dagboksanteckningar under riksdagen i Stockholm 1738–39*, ed. by Göran Nilzén (Stockholm: Kungl. Samfundet för utgivande av handskrifter rörande Skandinaviens historia, 2006)

Samling af danske Kongers Haandfæstninger og andre lignende Acter (Copenhagen: Bianco Luno, 1856–58)

Scheffer, Carl Fredrik, *Tal, hållit för Kongl. Vetenskaps academien, vid præsidii afläggande, den 2 augusti, år 1755* (Stockholm: Lars Salvius, 1755)

Sellstedt, Peter, *En ung drängs glädje-sång öfwer Hans Kongl. Maj:t kong Gustaf den tredje, när han, år 1772 den 19 augusti, hade den nåden, at första gången se Hans Kongl. Maj:t, hwilket upwäckte en owanlig och besynnerlig stor glädje i honom, at han däröfwer sammanskref följande, under melodie*: Hwar man må nu wäl glädja sig, &c. (Stockholm: Wennberg & Nordström, 1772)

Serenius, Jacob, *An English and Swedish Dictionary: wherein the generality of words and various significations are rendered into Swedish and Latin, forms of speech, proverbs and terms of art in husbandry and gardening especially, observed, above 2400 English words traced from their true original Gothick, and the mistakes of Junius, Menagius and other etymologians remarked. Thereunto is added a large collection of terms of trade and navigation and an herbal or index of plants common: to both nations*. The second edition with large additions and amendments. (Harg and Stenbro: Peter Momma, 1757)

Silvius, David, *Påminnelser angående successions-rättigheten i Sweriges rike, samt det så kallade souveraine wäldet, upsatte i januarii månad 1719* (Stockholm: Johan Henrik Werner, 1720)

Stadslagen: Swerikes stadz-lagh, effter den stormächtige, högborne furstes och herrer herr Gustaff Adolphs, Sweriges, Göthes och Wendes, &c. konungs, storfurstes til Finland, hertigs vthi Estland och Carelen, herres vthöfwer Jngermanland, &c. befallning, vthgången af trycket åhr 1618: *Ny åter å nyo med anmärckningar vplagd* [by Israel Arnell] (Stockholm: Anders Björkman's widow, 1730) [Stobæus, Kilian], *Schema genealogicum serenissimi et potentissimi D. N. Friderici, Svethorum, Gothorum, Vandalorumque regis &c. stemma augustissimum ab Ynglingis, Skioldungis, Carolingis, Folkungis, antiquissimis et illustrissimis totius septentrionis, imo orbis familiis repetens et rite deducens* ([n.p.]: [n. pub.], [n.d.])

Svenska riksrådets protokoll, ed. by Severin Bergh, Handlingar rörande Sveriges historia, 3rd series, 12 vols (Stockholm: Norstedts, 1886–1920), XIV: *1650* (1916)

Sveriges regeringsformer 1634–1809 samt konungaförsäkringar 1611–1800, ed. by Emil Hildebrand (Stockholm: Norstedts, 1891)

Sveriges ridderskaps och adels riksdags-protokoll, 17 vols (Stockholm: Norstedts, 1855–1910), XIII: *1680* (1896)

Sveriges ridderskaps och adels riksdags-protokoll från och med år 1719, 32 vols (Stockholm: Norstedts, 1875–1982), I:1: *1719* (1875); I:2: *1720* (1875); II:1: *1723* (1876); XIII:1: *1742–1743* (1890); XVIII:1: *1751–1752* (1908); XIX:1: *1755–1756* (1923); XX:1: *1760–1762* (1934); XXIV:1: *1765–1766* (1958); XXIV:3: *1765–1766* (1960); XXIX:1: *1771–1772* (1969)

Sveriges rikes lag gillad och antagen på riksdagen år 1734, reprint of the 1780 edn, Rättshistoriskt bibliotek, I:37 (Stockholm: Institutet för rättshistorisk forskning, 1984)

Tabula Chronologica eller Kort beskrifning öfwer alla Swea och Götha konungars regemente, i en wiss ordning, ifrå Magog, som regerade 88 åhr efter syndafloden, till wår allernådigste regerande konung, k. Carl den XII. utdragen af de trowärdigste scribenters chrönicor ([n.p.]: [n. pub.], [n.d.])

Tersmeden, Carl, *Amiral Carl Tersmedens memoarer*, ed. by Nils Sjöberg and Nils Erdmann, 6 vols (Stockholm: Wahlström & Widstrand, 1912–19), [IV]: *Ur frihetstidens lif* (1917); [V]: *Gustaf III och flottan* (1918)

Tessin, Carl Gustaf, *Framledne riks-rådet, m. m. grefve Carl Gustaf Tessins dagbok: 1757* (Stockholm: Ecksteinska tryckeriet, 1824)

Tidningar utgifne i Upsala år 1774, second annual volume (Uppsala: Johan Edman, 1774)

Tilas, Daniel, *Anteckningar från riksdagen 1769–1770*, ed. by Olof Jägerskiöld (Stockholm: Kungl. Samfundet för utgivande av handskrifter rörande Skandinaviens historia, 1977)

Underdånig lyck-önskan til Hennes Kongl. Maj:t Sweriges Göthes och Wändes stormächtigste drottning Ulrica Eleonora då huldnings-acten blef firat i Stockholm den 7 april åhr 1719 (Stockholm: Kungl. tryckeriet, 1719)

Utdrag af de emellan Hans Konglige Majestät och cronan Swerige å ena och utrikes magter å andra sidan sedan 1718 slutna alliance-tractater och afhandlingar, ed. by Reinhold Gustaf Modée (Stockholm: Lorentz Ludwig Grefing, 1761)

Utdrag utur alle ifrån den 7. decemb. 1718.[–1794] utkomne publique handlingar, placater, förordningar, resolutioner och publicationer, som riksens styrsel samt inwärtes hushållning och författningar i gemen, jämwäl ock Stockholms stad i synnerhet, angå; med nödige citationer af alle paralel-stellen, som utwisa, hwad ändringar tid efter annan i ett eller annat mål kunnat wara giorde: Hwarförutan uti desse handlingar åberopade äldre acters innehåll korteligen anföres, så ofta nödigt warit; Följande efterst wid hwar del ett fullkomligit orda-register öfwer des innehåll, ed. by Reinhold Gustaf Modée, 15 vols (Stockholm: Lorentz Ludwig Grefing; Kungl. Tryckeriet, 1742–1829)

Warmholtz, Carl Gustaf, *Bibliotheca historica Sveo-Gothica; eller Förtekning uppå så väl tryckte, som handskrifne böcker, tractater och skrifter, hvilka handla om svenska historien, eller därutinnan kunna gifva ljus; med critiska och historiska anmärkningar*, 15 vols (Stockholm: Anders Jacob Nordström and Uppsala: Zeipel & Palmblad, 1782–1817), V (1790)

Verzeichnüß und Conterfeÿen aller Könige in Schweden wie solche Ordentlich nacheinander gefolget von den Ersten biß auf den jetzt Regierenden ([n.p.]: [n. pub.], [n.d.])

Voltaire, *Œuvres historiques*, ed. by René Pomeau, Bibliotheque de la Pléiade, 128 (Paris: Gallimard, 1957)

Royal ordinances (annual print series) in chronological order

Kurtze Beschreibung wie Jhre Königliche Mayt. zu Schweden Carolus XI. zu Upsahl ist gekrönet worden. Auß dem schwedischen ins hochteutsche übersetzet. Anno M. DC. LXXVI ([n.p.]: [n. pub.], [n.d])

Kurtze Beschreibung wie Jhr. Königl. Majest. zu Schweden Carolus XI zu Upsahl ist gekrönet worden. Aus dem schwedischen verdeutschet ([n.p.]: [n. pub.], 1676)

Kort berättelse om Hans Kongl. May:tz wår allernådigste konungs och herres konüg Carl den tolftes, Sweriges, Giöthes och Wändes konungz, &c. kongl. hyldningh, ock der på fölliande smörielse-act, med heela rijkets, sampt alla trogne och redelige undersåtare största hugnad och förnöyelse, anstäld och begången uti kongl. residentz-staden Stockholm den 13 och 14 decembr. åhr 1697 (Stockholm: Kungl. tryckeriet., [n.d.])

Kårt doch sanfärdig berättelse om den glorieuse och i manna minne oförlijklige seger, hwarmed den aldrahögste Gud den 20. november hafwer behagat wälsigna Kongl: May:tz af Swerige rättmätige wapn emot den trolöse fiende czaren af Muscow. Narva den 28. novemb: 1700 ([n.p.]: [n. pub.], [n.d.])

388   Bibliography

Allmännelig böön, efter predikan och böne-stunder at brukas i församlingarne; utgången den 7 decemb. 1718 (Stockholm: Kungl. tryckeriet, 1718)

En noga underrättelse om alt hwad, som wijd Hans Kongl. Maj:[s] wår allernådigste konungs och herres, konung Friedrich den förstes, Swerjes, Göthes och Wändes konung &c. &c. krönings-act, j acht tahgas bör, så i det Kongl. Palais, som wijd processen til och ifrån Store Kyrkian, samt ceremonierna uti sielfwa kyrkian, uppå krönings-dagen här i Stockholm, den [3] maji, åhr 1720 (Stockholm: Kungl. tryckeriet, 1720)

Hennes Kongl. Höghets nådiga swar, gifwit på swenska til [ridderskapet och adelens/preste-ståndets/borgare-ståndets/bonde-ståndets] deputerade, tå the aflade theras underdåniga hälsning then 23. september 1746 (Stockholm: Kungl. tryckeriet, [s.d.])

Tacksäjelse efter högstsal. Hans Kongl. Maj:t ([Stockholm]: Kungl. tryckeriet, 1751)

Kongl. Maj:ts försäkran, gifwen Stockholm i råd-cammaren then 26. martii 1751 (Stockholm: Kungl. tryckeriet, [n.d.])

Underdånigst tal til Hans Kongl. Maj:t, hållit uti råds-salen wid öpna dörar then 26. martii 1751. af hans excellence herr riks-rådet, præsidenten uti Kongl. Maj:ts och riksens cancellie collegio, öfwerste marskalken, Hans Kongl. Höghets cron-printsens gouverneur, academiæ-cantzleren, riddaren och commendeuren af Kongl. Maj:ts orden, riddaren af Swarta örn, samt Cantzleren af alla Kongl. Maj:ts orden, högwälborne grefwe Carl Gustaf Tessin (Stockholm: Kungl. tryckeriet, [s.d.])

Kongl. Maj:ts nådiga swar uppå thet, af herr riks-rådet och cancelliepræsidenten, uti samtelige rådets namn, håldne talet. Then 26. martii 1751 (Stockholm: Kungl. tryckeriet, [n.d.])

Allmänelig bön efter predikan och bönestunder, at brukas i församlingarne; utgången then 26. martii 1751 ([Stockholm]: Kungl. tryckeriet, [n.d.])

Tro- och Huldhets ed. [26 March 1751] ([n.p.]: [n. pub.], [n.d.])

Publication angående sorgedrägts anläggande efter högst-sal. Hans Kongl. Maj:t. Stockholm af kongl. slotts-cancelliet then 27. martii 1751 (Stockholm: Kungl. tryckeriet, [n.d.])

Berättelse om högst sahlig Hans Kongl. Maj:ts konung Friedrich then förstes sidsta sjukdom och högstbeklageliga dödsfall, ed. E. Ribe ([Stockholm]: Kungl. tryckeriet, 1751)

Berättelse om thet, som observerades uppå högstsalig Hans Kongl. Maj:t konung Friedrich then förste, tå thess andelösa lekamen blef öpnad och balsamerad af lif-chirurgis assessorerne Ribe och Schützer, i närwaro af archiatrerne Ribe och Rosén, lif-medicis Bäck och Réef, stads-physico assessoren Strandberg, samt chirurgis Boltenhagen och Acrel, som hade then nåden, i högstsalig Hans Kongl. Maj:ts lifstid thess höga person at betjena och upwackta [30 March 1751] ([Stockholm]: Kungl. tryckeriet, [n.d.])

Bibliography 389

Reglemente, som wid högstsalig Hans Kongl. Maj:ts konung Friedrich then förstes, bisättnings-process ifrån Konungshuset til Ridderholms Kyrckan, som sker then [11] April. 1751. bör i akt tagas och eferföljas ([Stockholm]: Kungl. tryckeriet, [n.d.])

Kongl. Maj:ts placat om en allmän klagodag, som öfwer högstsalig Hans Kongl. Maj:t konung Fredrich then förste, Sweriges, Göthes och Wendes konungs &c. &c. &c. landtgrefwes til Hessen &c. &c. &c. högstbedröfwelige dödsfall, öfwer hela Sweriges rike, storfurstendömet Finland och alla Sweriges crono tilhörige och underliggande furstendömen, land och herrskaper högtideligen hållas och begås skall. Gifwit Stockholm i råd-cammaren then 16. april 1751 (Stockholm: Kungl. tryckeriet, [n.d.])

Tal hållit uppå ordens-dagen, then 17. april 1751. af hans excellence herr riks-rådet, præsidenten uti Kongl. Maj:ts och riksens cancelllie collegio, öfwerste marskalken, Hans Kongl. Höghets cron-printsens gouverneur, academiæ-cantzleren, riddaren och commendeuren af Kongl. Maj:ts orden, riddaren af Swarta örn, samt cantzleren af alla Kongl. Maj:ts orden, högwälborne Carl Gustaf Tessin (Stockholm: Kungl. tryckeriet, [n.d.])

Kongl. Maj:ts nådiga wilja och förklaring, huru med klädedrägter wid thess höga kongl. kröning förhållas må. Stockholm i Råd-cammaren then 14. maji 1751 (Stockholm: Kungl. tryckeriet, [n.d.])

Kungjörelse, uppå Kongl. Maj:ts nådigste befallning, angående högstsalig Hans Kongl. Maj:ts begrafning, med mera. Stockholm, af kongl. slottscancelliet then 3. sept. 1751 (Stockholm: Kungl. tryckeriet, [n.d.])

Ceremonial, som wid riksdagens början år 1751. kommer at i akt tagas ([Stockholm]: Kungl. tryckeriet, [n.d.])

På Kongl. Maj:ts wägnar, herr riks-rådets, cancellie-présidentens, öfwerste marskalkens, hans Kongl. Höghets Cron-Printzens gouverneurs, academiæ cantzlerns, riddarens, commendeurens och cantzlerens af Kongl. Maj:ts orden, samt riddare af Swarta örn, högwälborne grefwe Carl Gustav Tessins tal, hållit upp Riks-salen wid riksdagens början then 23. september 1751: Tryckt uppå Hans Kongl. Maj:ts befallning, och samtelige riksens ständers begäran (Stockholm: Kungl. tryckeriet, [n.d.])

Wid hög-salig Hans Kongl. Maj:ts konung Friedrich then förstes begrafning, som sker uti Riddarholms kyrkan, then 27. septembr. 1751. kommer följande at i akt tagas (Stockholm: Kungl. tryckeriet, [n.d.])

Til Hans Kongl. Maj:t[.] Landt-marskalkens, högwälborne grefwe Henning Adolph Gyllenborgs tal, hållit then 12. Octobr. 1751. å riksens samteliga ständers wägnar, uti theras wid samma tilfälle utsedde deputations närwaro ([Stockholm]: Kungl. tryckeriet, [n.d.])

Hans Kongl. Maj:ts nådige swar, gifwit samtelige riksens ständers deputerade, then 12. october 1751 (Stockholm: Kungl. tryckeriet, [n.d.])

Wid theras Kongl. Majestäters, Hans Kongl. Maj:ts, wår allernådigste konungs, konung Adolph Friedrichs, Sweriges, Göthes och Wendes

390 Bibliography

Maj:ts, wår allernådigsta drottnings, drottning Lovisæ Ulricæ kröning,
som sker then 26. november 1751. kommer följande at i akt tagas
([Stockholm]: Kungl. tryckeriet, [n.d.])

Wid Hans Kongl. Maj:ts wår allernådigste konungs konung Adolph
Friedrichs hyllnings-acht, som sker then 28. novembr. 1751. kommer
följande at i akt tagas ([Stockholm]: Kungl. tryckeriet, [n.d.])
Sweriges rikes ständers bewilning til en begrafnings och krönings hjelp,
gjord och faststäld wid riksdagen uti Stockholm then 13. martii år 1752
(Stockholm: Kungl. tryckeriet, [n.d.])

Ceremonial, wid riksdagens början 1755 ([Stockholm]: Kungl. tryckeriet,
[n.d.])
Tacksägelse och bön, at alla midsommars dagar upläsas i församlingarne
öfwer hela riket (Stockholm: Kungl. tryckeriet, [1757])
Ceremonial wid riksdagens början 1760 ([Stockholm]: Kungl. tryckeriet,
[n.d.])
Ceremonial wid riksdagens början 1765 ([Stockholm]: Kungl. tryckeriet,
[n.d.])

Hans Kongl. Maj:ts tal, til riksens ständer uppå riks-salen wid riksdagens
början den 25 junii 1771 (Stockholm: Grefingska, 1771)
Ceremonial wid Hans Kongl. Maj:ts höga kröning (Stockholm: Henric
Fougt, 1772)
Ceremonial, wid Hans Kongl. Maj:ts wår allernådigste konungs konung
Gustaf den III:s hyllnings-act, som sker then 1:sta junii 1772 (Stockholm:
Henric Fougt, 1772)

Newspapers

Dagligt Allehanda (Allehanda. Hörande til Stockholms Wekoblad),
1767–May 1769; 1771
Inrikes Tidningar, 1760–61, 1770–72
Riksdags-Tidningar, 1756, 1771
Posttidningar (Stockholmiske Post-Tijdender, Stockholmske Post Tidningar, Stockholms Post Tidningar, Stockholms Post-Tidningar), 1720–21,
1730–31, 1740–41, 1750–52, 1760, 1771

Secondary literature

Absolutism in Seventeenth Century Europe, ed. by John Miller (Basingstoke:
Macmillan, 1990)
Åhlén, Bengt, Ord mot ordningen: Farliga skrifter, bokbål och kät-
tarprocesser i svensk censurhistoria, ed. by Agneta Åhlén, Lillemor
Widgren Matlack and Christer Hellmark (Stockholm: Ordfront, 1986)
Åhlén, Bengt and Agneta Åhlén, Censur och tryckfrihet: Farliga skrifter i
Sverige 1522–1954 (Södertälje: Fingraf, 2002)

Alexandersson, Erland, *Bondeståndet i riksdagen 1760–1772* (Lund: Gleerups, 1975)

Alm, Mikael, *Kungsord i elfte timmen: Språk och självbild i det gustavianska enväldets legitimitetskamp 1772–1809* (Stockholm: Atlantis, 2002)

Almquist, Jan Erik, 'Karl IX och den mosaiska rätten', *Lychnos: Lärdomshistoriska samfundets årsbok 1942* (1942), 1–32

Åmark, Karl, *Sveriges statsfinanser 1719–1809* (Stockholm: Norstedts, 1961)

Anderson, Benedict, *Imagined Communities: Reflections on the Origin and Spread of Nationalism* (London and New York: Verso, 1991)

Anderson, Perry, *Lineages of the Absolutist State* (London: NLB, 1974)

Andrén, Åke, 'Kungakröningar och kröningsmässor', *Svensk teologisk kvartalskrift*, 34 (1958), 153–77

Armitage, David, 'Empire and Liberty: A Republican Dilemma', in *Republicanism: A Shared European Heritage*, ed. by Martin van Gelderen and Quentin Skinner, 2 vols (Cambridge: Cambridge University Press, 2002), II, pp. 29–46

Artéus, Gunnar, *Krigsmakt och samhälle i frihetstidens Sverige*, Militärhistoriska studier utgivna av Militärhistoriska avdelningen vid Militärhögskolan, 6 (Stockholm: Militärhistoriska förlaget, 1982)

Asker, Björn, *Hovet: Historien om ett kungligt maskineri* (Lund: Historiska media, 2022)

Baker, Keith Michael, 'Politique et opinion publique sous l'Ancien Régime', *Annales: Economies, sociétés, civilisations*, 42 (1987), 41–71

Banning, Knud, 'Fra symbol til antikvitet: En oversigt over symboltolkningen i danske kroningsprædikener 1537–1815', in *Kongens makt og ære: Skandinaviske herskersymboler gjennom 1000 år*, ed. by Martin Blindheim, Per Gjærder and Dag Sæverud (Oslo: Universitetets Oldsaksamling, 1985), pp. 123–28

Beckman, Bjarne, *Dalupproret 1743 och andra samtida rörelser inom allmogen och bondeståndet* (Gothenburg: Elanders, 1930)

Bercé, Yves-Marie, 'Les monarchies de l'âge moderne', in *Les monarchies*, ed. by Yves-Marie Bercé, Histoire générale des systèmes politiques (Paris: Presses universitaires de France, 1997), pp. 227–322

Bergenlöv, Eva, *Skuld och oskuld: Barnamord och barnkvävning i rättslig diskurs och praxis omkring 1680–1800*, Studia historica Lundensia, 13 (Lund: Historiska institutionen, 2004)

Bergström, Carin, *Lantprästen: Prästens funktion i det agrara samhället 1720–1800; Oland-Frösåkers kontrakt av ärkestiftet*, Nordiska museets handlingar, 110 (Stockholm: Nordiska museet, 1991)

Bertelli, Sergio, *The King's Body: Sacred Rituals of Power in Medieval and Early Modern Europe* (University Park: Pennsylvania State University Press, 2001)

Biografiskt lexikon öfver namnkunnige svenska män, 2nd rev. edn, 10 vols (Stockholm: Beijers, 1874–76), I (1874)

Bjørn, Claus, *Bonde, herremand, konge: Bonden i 1700–tallets Danmark* (Copenhagen: Gyldendal, 1981)

Blanning, T. C. W., *The Culture of Power and the Power of Culture: Old Regime Europe 1660–1789* (Oxford: Oxford University Press, 2002)

Bloch, Marc, *Les rois thaumaturges: Étude sur le caractère surnaturel attribué à la puissance royale particulièrment en France et en Angleterre*, 2nd edn (Paris: Gallimard, 1983 [1924])

Blom, Hans, 'Spinoza on *Res Publica*, Republics, and Monarchies', in *Monarchisms in the Age of Enlightenment: Liberty, Patriotism and the Common Good*, ed. by Hans Blom, John Christian Laursen and Luisa Simonutti (Toronto, Buffalo and London: Toronto University Press, 2007), pp. 19–44

Boesen, Gudmund, *Danmarks riges regalier* (Copenhagen: Gyldendal, 1986)

Boëthius, Simon Johannes, 'Några anmärkningar om uppkomsten och karaktären af Frihetstidens författning', *Historisk tidskrift*, 11 (1891), 233–70

Böhm, Wolfgang, 'Die hessischen Münzen des Landgrafen Friedrich (1730–1751): Eine Betrachtung über das Münzewesen in jener Zeit', in *Friedrich, König von Schweden, Landgraf von Hessen-Kassel: Studien zu Leben und Wirken eines umstrittenen Fürsten (1676–1751)*, ed. by Helmut Burmeister (Hofgeismar: Verein für hessische Geschichte und Landeskunde, 2003), pp. 309–42

Børresen, Kari Elisabeth, 'Christina's Discourse on God and Humanity', in *Politics and Culture in the Age of Christina: Acta from a Conference Held at the Wenner-Gren Center in Stockholm, May 4–6, 1995*, ed. by Marie-Louise Rodén, Suecoromana, 4 (Stockholm: Swedish Institute in Rome, 1997), pp. 43–53

Braconier, Jean, 'Suveränitetsbegreppets betydelse för det karolinska enväldet', in *Technica & humaniora: Festskrift till Anders Nevsten 1885 18/3 1950* (Malmö: Landby & Lundgrens boktryckeri, 1951), pp. 48–75

Bregnsbo, Michael, *Folk skriver til kongen: Supplikkerne og deres funktion i den dansk-norske enevælde i 1700–tallet; En kildestudie i Danske Kancellis supplikprotokoller* (Copenhagen: Selskabet for Udgivelse af Kilder til Dansk Historie, 1997)

——, *Samfundsorden og statsmagt set fra prædikstolen: Danske præsters deltagelse i den offentlige opinionsdannelse vedrørende samfundsordenen og statsmagten 1750–1848, belyst ved trykte prædikener; En politisk-idéhistorisk undersøgelse* (Copenhagen: Det Kongelige Bibliotek, Museum Tusculanums Forlag, 1997)

Bringéus, Nils-Arvid, 'Massmedium i miniformat: En översikt över den svenska kistebrevsproduktionen', *Rig: Kulturhistorisk tidskrift*, 91 (2008), 129–39

——, *Skånska kistebrev: Berlingska Boktryckeriet, N. P. Lundbergs Boktryckeri och F. F. Cedergréens Boktryckeri* (Stockholm: Carlssons, 1995)

Brown, Carolina and Merit Laine, *Gustaf Lundberg 1695–1786: En porträttmålare och hans tid*, Nationalmusei skriftserie, n.s., 19 (Stockholm: Nationalmuseum, 2006)

Brown, Jonathan and John Huxtable Elliott, *A Palace for a King: The Buen Retiro and the Court of Philip IV*, rev. and expanded edn (New Haven and London: Yale University Press, 2003)

Burke, Peter, *The Fabrication of Louis XIV* (New Haven and London: Yale University Press, 1992)

——, *Popular Culture in Early Modern Europe* (London: Temple Smith, 1978)

——, 'State-making, King-making and Image-making from Renaissance to Baroque: Scandinavia in a European Context', *Scandinavian Journal of History*, 22 (1997), 1–8

Burmeister, Helmut, *Der unbekannte König: Friedrich von Schweden* (Hofgeismar: Verein für hessische Geschichte und Landeskunde, 2012)

Cannadine, David, 'Introduction: Divine Rites of Kings', in *Rituals of Royalty: Power and Ceremonial in Traditional Societies*, ed. by David Cannadine and Simon Price (Cambridge: Cambridge University Press, 1992), pp. 1–19

Carlquist, Gunnar, 'Karl XII:s ungdom och första regeringsår', in *Karl XII: Till 200-årsdagen av hand död*, ed. by Samuel E. Bring (Stockholm: Norstedts, 1918), pp. 43–86

Carlsson, Alfred Bernhard, *Den svenska centralförvaltningen 1521–1809: En historisk öfversikt* (Stockholm: K. L. Beckmans, 1913)

Carlsson, Ingemar, *Frihetstidens handskrivna politiska litteratur: En bibliografi*, Acta bibliothecae universitatis Gothoburgensis, 9 (Gothenburg: Göteborgs universitetsbibliotek, 1967)

Carlsson, Sten, *Ståndssamhälle och ståndspersoner 1700–1865: Studier rörande det svenska ståndssamhällets upplösning*, 2nd edn (Lund: Gleerups, 1973)

Catherine the Great & Gustav III, Nationalmuseum Exhibition Catalogue, 610 (Stockholm: Nationalmuseum, 1998)

Cavallin, Maria, *I kungens och folkets tjänst: Synen på den svenske ämbetsmannen 1750–1780* (Gothenburg: Historiska institutionen, 2003)

Cederlund, Johan, *Skulptören Pierre Hubert L'Archevêque 1721–1778*, Nationalmusei skriftserie, n.s., 18 (Stockholm: Nationalmuseum, 2003)

Cederström, Rudolf, *De svenska riksregalierna och kungliga värdighetstecknen* (Stockholm: Livrustkammaren, 1942)

Claréus, Anders, 'På offensiven: Bondeståndet under slutet av frihetstiden', in *Riksdag, kaffehus och predikstol: Frihetstidens politiska kultur 1766–1772*, ed. by Marie-Christine Skuncke and Henrika Tandefelt (Stockholm: Atlantis, 2003), pp. 95–103

Clausen, V. E., *Det folkelige danske træsnit i etbladstryk 1565–1884*, Danmarks folkeminder, 85 (Copenhagen: Foreningen Danmarks Folkeminder, 1985)

——, *Folkelig grafik i Skandinavien* (Copenhagen: Berg, 1973)

Colley, Linda, *Britons: Forging the Nation 1707–1837* (London: Pimlico, 1994)

The Courts of Europe: Politics, Patronage and Royalty, 1400–1800, ed. by A. G. Dickens (London: Thames and Hudson, 1977)

Darnton, Robert, *The Forbidden Best-Sellers of Pre-Revolutionary France* (New York and London: Norton, [1995])

De Geer, Louis, 'Minne af Anders Johan von Höpken: Uppläst i Svenska Akademien den 20 december 1881', in *Valda skrifter*, 2 vols (Stockholm: Norstedts, 1892), I, pp. 60–188

Delblanc, Sven, *Ära och minne: Studier kring ett motivkomplex i 1700-talets litteratur* (Stockholm: Bonniers, 1965)

Den svenska mynthistorien: Frihetstiden och den gustavianska perioden 1719–1818 (Stockholm: Kungl. Myntkabinettet and Svenska numismatiska föreningen, 2007)

Den svenska pressens historia, ed. by Karl Erik Gustafsson and Per Rydén, 5 vols (Stockholm: Ekerlids, 2000–03), I: *I begynnelsen (tiden före 1830)* (2000)

Der Absolutismus – ein Mythos? Strukturwandel monarchischer Herrschaft in West- und Mitteleuropa (ca. 1550–1700), ed. by Ronald G. Asch and Heinz Duchhardt, Münstersche historische Forschungen, 9 (Cologne: Böhlau, 1996)

Dermineur, Elise M., *Gender and Politics in Eighteenth-Century Sweden: Queen Louisa Ulrika (1720–1782)* (London and New York: Routledge, 2017)

Dreitzel, Horst, *Absolutismus und ständische Verfassung in Deutschland: Ein Beitrag zu Kontinuität und Diskontinuität der politischen Theorie in der frühen Neuzeit*, Veröffentlichungen des Instituts für Europäische Geschichte Mainz, 24: Abteilung Universalgeschichte (Mainz: Philipp von Zabern, 1992)

——, *Monarchiebegriffe in der Fürstengesellscahft: Semantik und Theorie der Einherrschaft in Deutschland von der Reformation bis zum Vormärz*, 2 vols (Cologne, Weimar and Vienna: Böhlau, 1991), I: *Semantik der Monarchie*; II: *Theorie der Monarchie*

Duindam, Jeroen, *Vienna and Versailles: The Courts of Europe's Dynastic Rivals, 1550–1780* (Cambridge: Cambridge University Press, 2003)

Earenfight, Theresa, 'Without the Persona of the Prince: Kings, Queens and the Idea of Monarchy in Late Medieval Europe', *Gender & History*, 19 (2007), 1–21

Ekedahl, Nils, *Det svenska Israel: Myt och retorik i Haquin Spegels predikokonst*, Studia rhetorica Upsaliensia, 2 (Uppsala: Gidlunds, 1999)

Ekstrand, Gudrun, *Kröningsdräkter i Sverige* (Stockholm: Carlssons, 1991)

Elias, Norbert, *The Court Society* (New York: Pantheon, 1983)

Ellenius, Allan, *Karolinska bildidéer*, Ars Suetica, I (Uppsala: Almqvist & Wiksell, 1966)

Elliott, John Huxtable, 'Philip IV of Spain: Prisoner of Ceremony', in *The Courts of Europe: Politics, Patronage and Royalty, 1400–1800*, ed. by A. G. Dickens (London: Thames and Hudson, 1977), pp. 169–90

Ericsson, Peter, *Stora nordiska kriget förklarat: Karl XII och det ideologiska tilltalet*, Studia historica Upsaliensia, 202 (Uppsala: Historiska institutionen, 2002)

Fahlbeck, Erik, 'Studier öfver frihetstidens politiska idéer', part 1, *Statsvetenskaplig tidskrift för politik, statistik, ekonomi*, 18 (1915), 325–45; parts 2–3, 19 (1916), 31–54, 104–21

Forssberg, Anna Maria, *Att hålla folket på gott humör: Informationsspridning, krigspropaganda och mobilisering i Sverige 1655–1680*, Stockholm Studies in History, 80 (Stockholm: Almqvist & Wiksell, 2005)

Friedrich, König von Schweden, Landgraf von Hessen-Kassel: Studien zu Leben und Wirken eines umstrittenen Fürsten (1676–1751), ed. by Helmut Burmeister (Hofgeismar: Verein für hessische Geschichte und Landeskunde, 2003)

Geschichtliche Grundbegriffe: Historisches Lexikon zur politisch-sozialen Sprache in Deutschland, ed. by Otto Brunner and others, 8 vols (Stuttgart: Klett-Cotta, 1972–97), IV: *Mi–Pre* (1978)

Giesey, Ralph E., 'The King Imagined', in *The Political Culture of the Old Regime*, ed. by Keith Michael Baker, The French Revolution and the Creation of Modern Political Culture, 1 (Oxford: Pergamon Press, 1987), pp. 41–59

Grauers, Sven, *Riksdagen under den karolinska tiden*, Sveriges riksdag, I:4 (Stockholm: Victor Pettersons, 1932)

Grundberg, Malin, *Ceremoniernas makt: Maktöverföring och genus i Vasatidens kungliga ceremonier* (Lund: Nordic Academic Press, 2005)

Gundermann, Iselin, '"Ob die Salbung einem Könige nothwendig sey"', in *Dreihundert Jahre preußische Königskrönung: Eine Tagungsdokumentation*, ed. by Johannes Kunisch, Forschungen zur brandenburgischen und preussischen Geschichte, 6 (Berlin: Duncker & Humblot, 2002), pp. 115–34

Gustav Vasa tur & retur: Guide till svenska folkets kungaminnen (Stockholm: Livrustkammaren, 2003)

Hammersley, Rachel, *Republicanism: An Introduction* (Cambridge: Polity Press, 2020)

Hardman, John, *Louis XVI* (New Haven and London: Yale University Press, 1993)

Haskell, Francis, *History and its Images: Art and the Interpretation of the Past* (New Haven and London: Yale University Press, 1993)

Hasselberg, Gösta, 'De karolinska kungabalksförslagen och konungens makt över beskattningen', *Karolinska förbundets årsbok 1943* (1943), 54–90

Hatton, Ragnhild Marie, *Charles XII of Sweden* (London: Weidenfeld & Nicolson, 1968)

Hennings, Beth, 'Gustav III:s hovliv på Gripsholm', in *Fyra gustavianska studier* (Stockholm: Norstedts, 1967), pp. 95–127

Henshall, Nicholas, *The Myth of Absolutism: Change and Continuity in Early Modern European Monarchy* (London and New York: Longman, 1992)

Hildebrand, Bror Emil, *Sveriges och svenska konungahusets minnespenningar, praktmynt och belöningsmedaljer*, 2 vols (Stockholm: Vitterhetsakadmien, 1874–75), II (1875)

Hildebrand, Emil, *Svenska statsförfattningens historiska utveckling från äldsta tid till våra dagar* (Stockholm: Norstedts, 1896)

Hinrichs, Ernst, *Fürsten und Mächte: Zum Problem des europäischen Absolutismus* (Göttingen: Vandenhoeck & Ruprecht, 2000)

Hoffmann, Erich, 'Coronation and Coronation Ordines in Medieval Scandinavia', in *Coronations: Medieval and Early Modern Monarchic Ritual*, ed. by János M. Bak (Berkeley, Los Angeles and Oxford: University of California Press, 1990), pp. 125–51

Holm, Edvard, *Danmark-Norges Historie fra den Store Nordiske Krigs Slutning til Rigernes adskillelse (1720–1814)*, 7 vols (Copenhagen: Gad, 1890–1912), I: *Frederiks IV's sidste ti Regeringsaar (1720–1730)* (1891); III: *Under Frederik V (1746–1766)* (1897)

——, *Den offentlige Mening og Statsmagten i den dansk-norske Stat i Slutningen af det 18de Aarhundrede (1784–1799)*, Indbydelsesskrift til Kjøbenhavns Universitets Fest i Anledning af Hans Majestæt Kong Christian IX.'s Regeringsjubilæum, den 15. November 1888 (Copenhagen: J. H. Schultz, 1888)

——, *Om det Syn paa Kongemagt, Folk og borgerlig Frihed, der udviklede sig i den dansk-norske Stat i Midten af 18de Aarhundrede (1746–1770)* (Copenhagen: J. H. Schultz, 1883)

Holst, Walfrid, *Fredrik I* (Stockholm: Wahlström & Widstrand, 1953)

——, *Ulrika Eleonora d.y.: Karl XII:s syster* (Stockholm: Wahlström & Widstrand, 1956)

Horstbøll, Henrik, 'Defending monarchism in Denmark-Norway in the eighteenth century', in *Monarchisms in the Age of Enlightenment: Liberty, Patriotism and the Common Good*, ed. by Hans Blom, John Christian Laursen and Luisa Simonutti (Toronto, Buffalo and London: Toronto University Press, 2007), pp. 175–93

Hughes, Lindsey, *Russia in the Age of Peter the Great* (New Haven and London: Yale University Press, 1998)

Iconography, Propaganda, and Legitimation, ed. by Allan Ellenius (Oxford: Clarendon Press, 1998)

Ihalainen, Pasi, *Protestant Nations Redefined: Changing Perceptions of National Identity in the Rhetoric of the English, Dutch and Swedish Public Churches, 1685–1772*, Studies in Medieval and Reformation

Traditions: History, Culture, Religion, Ideas, 109 (Leiden and Boston: Brill, 2005)

Israel, Jonathan, *The Dutch Republic: Its Rise, Greatness and Fall 1477–1806* (Oxford: Clarendon Press, 1995)

Jackson, Richard A., *Vive le roi! A History of the French Coronation from Charles V to Charles X* (Chapel Hill and London: University of North Carolina Press, 1984)

Jansson, Arne, *From Swords to Sorrow: Homicide and Suicide in Early Modern Stockholm*, Stockholm Studies in Economic History, 30 (Stockholm: Almqvist & Wiksell, 1998)

Jenkinson, Sally, 'Bayle and Hume on Monarchy, Scepticism, and Forms of Government', in *Monarchisms in the Age of Enlightenment: Liberty, Patriotism and the Common Good*, ed. by Hans Blom, John Christian Laursen and Luisa Simonutti (Toronto, Buffalo and London: Toronto University Press, 2007), pp. 60–77

Jespersen, Knud J. V. and Ole Feldbæk, *Revanche og neutralitet 1648–1814*, Dansk udenrigspolitiks historie, 2 (Copenhagen: Danmarks Nationalleksikon, 2002)

Jespersen, Leon, 'Teokrati og kontraktlære: Et aspekt af de statsretlige brydninger ved Frederik 3.s kroning', in *Struktur og Funktion: Festskrift til Erling Ladewig Petersen*, ed. by Carsten Due-Nielsen, Knud J. V. Jespersen, Leon Jespersen and Anders Monrad Møller (Odense: Odense Universitetsforlag, 1994), pp. 169–86

Johannsen, Birgitte Bøggild and Hugo Johannsen, *Kungens kunst*, Ny dansk kunsthistorie, 2 (Copenhagen: Fogtdal, 1993)

Josefson, Ruben, *Guds och Sveriges lag: Studier i den lutherska socialetikens historia*, Uppsala universitets årsskrift, 1950:8 (Uppsala: Lundequistska bokhandeln; Leipzig: Otto Harrassowitz, 1950)

Josephson, Ragnar, 'Larchevêque och svenskarna', in *Septentrionalia et orientalia: Studia Bernhardo Karlgren dedicata*, Kungl. Vitterhets Historie och Antikvitets Akademiens handlingar, 91 (Stockholm: Almqvist & Wiksell, 1959), pp. 236–51

——, *Tessin i Danmark* (Stockholm: Bonniers, 1924)

Jung, C. G., 'The Relations between the Ego and the Unconscious', in *Two Essays on Analytical Psychology*, trans. by R. F. C. Hull, The Collected Works of C. G. Jung, 19 vols (New York: Pantheon, 1966 [1928]), VII

Jägerskiöld, Olof, *Den svenska utrikespolitikens historia*, 10 vols (Stockholm: Norstedts, 1951–61), II:2: *1721–1792* (1957)

——, *Hovet och författningsfrågan 1760–1766* (Uppsala: Almqvist & Wiksell, 1943)

——, *Lovisa Ulrika* (Stockholm: Wahlström & Widstrand, 1945)

Kantorowicz, Ernst H., *The King's Two Bodies: A Study in Mediaeval Political Theology*, with a new preface by William Chester Jordan (Princeton: Princeton University Press, 1997 [1957])

Karlsson, Eva-Lena, 'Regentserier', in *Ulrica Fredrica Pasch och hennes samtid*, ed. by Eva-Lena Bengtsson (Stockholm: Konstakademien, 1996), pp. 21–25

Katalog över statens porträttsamling på Gripsholm, 2 vols (Stockholm: Victor Pettersons, 1951–52), I: *Porträtt före 1809* (1951)

Kern, Fritz, *Kingship and Law in the Middle Ages*, trans. by S. B. Chrimes (Oxford: Basil Blackwell, 1956)

Kishlansky, Mark, *A Monarchy Transformed: Britain 1603–1714* (London: Allen Lane, Penguin Press, 1996)

Kjöllerström, Sven, *Guds och Sveriges lag under reformationstiden: En kyrkorättslig studie*, Bibliotheca theologiae practicae, 6 (Lund: Gleerups, 1957)

Klingensmith, Samuel John, *The Utility of Splendor: Ceremony, Social Life, and Architecture at the Court of Bavaria, 1600–1800* (Chicago: University of Chicago Press, 1993)

Koenigsberger, Helmut G., 'Republicanism, Monarchism and Liberty', in *Royal and Republican Sovereignty in Early Modern Europe: Essays in Memory of Ragnhild Hatton*, ed. by Robert Oresko, G. C. Gibbs and H. M. Scott (Cambridge: Cambridge University Press, 1997), pp. 43–74

Koselleck, Reinhart, 'Standortbindung und Zeitlichkeit: Ein Beitrag zur historiographischen Erschließung der geschichtlichen Welt', in *Vergangene Zukunft* (Frankfurt am Main: Suhrkamp, 1979), pp. 176–207

Krischer, André, 'Das diplomatische Zeremoniell der Reichsstädte, oder: Was heißt Stadtfreiheit in der Fürstengesellschaft?', *Historische Zeitschrift*, 284 (2007), 1–30

Kulturhistoriskt lexikon för nordisk medeltid från vikingatid till reformationstid, 22 vols (Malmö: Allhems, 1956–78), III: *Datering–Epiphania* (1958); VII: *Hovedstad–Judar* (1962); IX: *Konge–Kyrkorummet* (1964); XIV: *Regnebræt–Samgäld* (1969)

Kungl. Maj:ts kanslis historia, 2 vols (Uppsala: Almqvist & Wiksell, 1935), I: *Kansliets uppkomst, organisation och utveckling intill 1840*

Lagerqvist, Lars O. and others, *Sveriges och dess forna besittningars guldmynt och riksdaler från Gustav I till Carl XVI Gustaf: Samling Julius Hagander/Goldmünzen und Reichstaler Schwedens und seiner früheren Besitzungen von Gustav I. bis Carl XVI. Gustaf; Sammlung Julius Hagander* (Stockholm: Svenska numismatiska föreningen i Stockholm; Bern: Stämpfli + Cie, 1996)

Lagerroth, Fredrik, *Den svenska monarkin inför rätta: En författningshistorisk exposé* (Stockholm: Rabén & Sjögren, 1972)

——, 'Det rättsliga utgångsläget för de stora författningsändringarna i Sveriges historia', *Scandia: Tidskrift för historisk forskning*, 36 (1970), 1–63

——, 'Det svenska statsrådets ansvarighet i rättshistorisk belysning', *Scandia: Tidskrift för historisk forskning*, 12 (1939), 32–98

——, 'En frihetstida lärobok i gällande svensk statsrätt', *Statsvetenskaplig tidskrift för politik, statistik, ekonomi*, 40 (1937), 185–211

——, *Frihetstidens författning: En studie i den svenska konstitutionalismens historia* (Stockholm: Bonniers, 1915)

——, *Frihetstidens maktägande ständer 1719–1772*, Sveriges riksdag, I:5–6, 2 vols (Stockholm: Victor Pettersons, 1934)

——, 'Positiv rätt eller naturrätt? Ett statsrättsligt dilemma från svenskt 1700-tal', *Scandia: Tidskrift för historisk forskning*, 33 (1967), 270–312

——, 'Svensk konstitutionalism i komparativ belysning', *Historisk tidskrift*, 86 (1966), 129–57

Lagus, Wilhelm Gabriel, *Anteckningar rörande 1741 och 1742 års finska krig jemte Henr. Magn. von Buddenbrocks äreräddning* (Helsinki: Finska litteratursällskapet, 1853)

Laine, Merit, 'En drottning med "manna-wett"', in *Drottning Lovisa Ulrika och Vitterhetsakademien*, ed. by Sten Åke Nilsson (Stockholm: Vitterhetsakademien, 2003), pp. 17–39

——, *'En Minerva för vår Nord': Lovisa Ulrika som samlare, uppdragsgivare och byggherre* (Stockholm: M. Laine, 1998)

——, 'Kungliga slott som nationella byggnader under frihetstiden', in *Nationalism och nationell identitet i 1700-talets Sverige*, ed. by Åsa Karlsson and Bo Lindberg, Opuscula Historica Upsaliensia, 27 (Uppsala: Historiska institutionen, 2002), pp. 101–12

Lenhammar, Harry, *Individualismens och upplysningens tid*, Sveriges kyrkohistoria, 5 (Stockholm: Verbum, 2000)

Lenk, Torsten, 'Karl IX:s regalier', in *Karl IX*, ed. by Boo von Malmborg, Småskrifter utgivna av Svenska Porträttarkivet, Nationalmuseum, 2 (Stockholm: Nordisk Rotogravyr, 1959), pp. 41–43

Liliequist, Jonas, 'Brott, synd och straff: Tidelagsbrottet i Sverige under 1600- och 1700-talet' (unpublished doctoral thesis, Department of History, Umeå University, [1991])

Lindberg, Bo, *Den antika skevheten: Politiska ord och begrepp i det tidigmoderna Sverige*, Filologiskt arkiv, 45 (Stockholm: Vitterhetsakademien, 2006)

Lindblom, Andreas, *Fransk barock- och rokokoskulptur i Sverige: Studier* (Uppsala: Almqvist & Wiksell, 1923)

——, 'Pierre-Hubert L'Archevêques ryttarbild av Gustav Adolf: Några blad ur dess tillkomsthistoria', *Nationalmusei årsbok*, 5 (Stockholm: Gunnar Tisells Tekniska Förlag, 1923), 31–54

Lindgren, Torgny, *Sveriges mynt 1719–1776* (Stockholm: Kungl. Myntkabinettet, 1953)

Linnarsson, Lennart, 'Sveriges statsskick under frihetstiden: Några teser ur professor skytteanus Hermanssons föreläsningar i statskunskap på 1720-talet', in *Festskrift till professor Skytteanus Axel Brusewitz utgiven till 60-årsdagen den 9 juni 1941*, Skrifter utgivna av Statsvetenskapliga föreningen i Uppsala, 12 (Uppsala and Stockholm: Almqvist & Wiksell, 1941), pp. 3–19

Ludwigs, Folke, 'Namnstämplarna från frihetstiden', *Arkivvetenskapliga studier*, 6, ed.

by Lars Otto Berg, James Cavallie, Claes Gränström and Nils Nilsson ([Uppsala]: Landsarkivet i Uppsala, 1987), 247–53

Luebke, David Martin, *His Majesty's Rebels: Communities, Factions, and Rural Revolt in the Black Forest, 1725–1745* (Ithaca and London: Cornell University Press, 1997)

Lundberg, Gunnar W., 'Formskärar Hoffbro', in *Bellmansfigurer: Kulturhistoriska tidsbilder och personhistoriska anteckningar till Fredmansdikten* (Stockholm: Gebers, 1927), pp. 99–117

——, *Roslin: Liv och verk*, 3 vols (Malmö: Allhems, 1957), III: *Katalog och bilagor*

——, *Svenskt och franskt 1700–tal i Institut Tessins samlingar* (Malmö: Allhems, 1972)

Malmstedt, Göran, 'Frihetstidens karismatiska kungar', in *Maktens skiftande skepnader: Studier i makt, legitimitet och inflytande i det tidigmoderna Sverige*, ed. by Börje Harnesk (Umeå: Institutionen för historiska studier, 2003), pp. 75–89

Malmström, Carl Gustaf, 'Axel Fersen såsom memoarförfattare', in *Smärre skrifter rörande sjuttonhundratalets historia* (Stockholm: Norstedts, 1889), pp. 209–40

——, *Sveriges politiska historia från konung Karl XII:s död till statshvälfningen 1772*, 2nd edn, 6 vols (Stockholm: Norstedts, 1893–1901)

Mansén, Elisabeth, *Ett paradis på jorden: Om den svenska kurortskulturen 1680–1880* (Stockholm: Atlantis, 2001)

Matzen, Henning, *Danske Kongers Haandfæstninger: Indledende Undersøgelser*, Indbydelsesskrift til Kjøbenhavns Universitets Aarsfest til Erindring om Kirkens Reformation (Copenhagen: J. H. Schultz, 1889; reprint 1977)

Meinander, K. K., *Porträtt i Finland före 1840–talet* (Helsinki: Söderström, 1931)

Monarchisms in the Age of Enlightenment: Liberty, Patriotism and the Common Good, ed. by Hans Blom, John Christian Laursen and Luisa Simonutti (Toronto, Buffalo and London: Toronto University Press, 2007)

Monod, Paul Kléber, *The Power of Kings: Monarchy and Religion in Europe 1589–1715* (New Haven and London: Yale University Press, 1999)

Mousnier, Roland, *La monarchie absolue en Europe du Ve siècle à nos jours* (Paris: Presses universitaires de France, 1982)

Munktell, Henrik, 'Mose lag och svensk rättsutveckling: Några huvuddrag', *Lychnos: Lärdomshistoriska samfundets årsbok 1936* (1936), 131–50

Newton, William R., *La petite cour: Service et serviteurs à la cour de Versailles au XVIIIe siècle* (Paris: Fayard, 2006)

Nilsén, Per, *Att 'stoppa munnen till på bespottare'*: *Den akademiska undervisningen i svensk statsrätt under frihetstiden*, Rättshistoriskt bibliotek, I:59 (Lund: Institutet för rättshistorisk forskning, 2001)

——, 'Die problematische königliche Alleinherrschaft und die verständnislosen Ausländer: Über die Bedeutung Jacob Wildes (1679–1755) für die Entwicklung des schwedischen Staatsrechts bis 1772', in *Geschichte und Perspektiven des Rechts im Ostseeraum: Erster Rechtshistorikertag im Ostseeraum 8.–12. März 2000*, ed. by Jörn Eckert and Kjell Å. Modéer, Rechtshistorische Reihe, 251 (Frankfurt am Main: Peter Lang, 2002), pp. 45–58

Nilsson, Sten Åke, 'On Heroes and Traitors: The First Popular Prints in Sweden', in *Popular Prints and Imagery: Proceedings of an International conference in Lund 5–7 October 2000*, ed. by Nils-Arvid Bringéus and Sten Åke Nilsson, Kungl. Vitterhets Historie och Antikvitets Akademien, Konferenser, 53 (Stockholm: Almqvist & Wiksell, 2003), pp. 169–80

——, 'Petter Lorens Hoffbro och frihetstidens bildmanipulationer', *Vetenskapssocieteten i Lund, Årsbok 1976* (Lund: Gleerups, 1976), 5–34

——, 'Populärkonst som "kistebrev": De första exemplen i Sydsverige', *Rig: Tidskrift utgiven av Föreningen för svensk kulturhistoria i samarbete med Nordiska museet och Folklivsarkivet i Lund*, 60 (1977), 35–46

Nodermann, Maj, *Från Altranstädt till Delsbo: Bildtryck och bonader med Carl XII* (Stockholm: Nordiska Museet, 1984)

——, 'Kistan från Forssa', *Fataburen: Nordiska museets och Skansens årsbok* (1994), 145–58

Nokkala, Ere, 'Rewriting Eighteenth-Century Swedish Republican Political Thought: Heinrich Ludwig von Hess's *Der Republickaner* (1754)', *History of European Ideas*, 42 (2016), 502–15

Nordin, Jonas, 'Brevmålaren Petter Lorens Hoffbros regentlängder och deras förlagor', *Biblis: Kvartalstidskrift för bokvänner*, 43 (2008), 30–41

——, *Ett fattigt men fritt folk: Nationell och politisk självbild i Sverige från sen stormaktstid till slutet av frihetstiden* (Eslöv: Symposion, 2000)

——, *Frihetstidens monarki: Konungamakt och offentlighet i 1700-talets Sverige* (Stockholm: Atlantis, 2009)

——, 'Frihetstidens radikalism', in *Riksdag, kaffehus och predikstol: Frihetstidens politiska kultur*, ed. by Marie-Christine Skuncke and Henrika Tandefelt (Stockholm: Atlantis, 2003), pp. 55–72

——, 'L'esprit de paix ou la naissance d'une opposition contre la guerre en Suède au XVIIIe siècle', *Revue d'histoire nordique*, 14 (2012), 97–130

——, 'Mediating Images of Monarchy from Castle to Cottage in Eighteenth-Century Sweden', in *Media and Mediation in the Eighteenth Century*, ed. by Penelope Corfield and Jonas Nordin (Lund: Swedish Society for Eighteenth Century Studies/Division of Book History, Lund University, 2023), pp. 25–71

——, 'Om kärleken till fäderneslandet och dess utövning', in *Nationalism och nationell identitet i 1700–talets Sverige*, ed. by Åsa Karlsson and Bo Lindberg, Opuscula Historica Upsaliensia, 27 (Uppsala: Historiska institutionen, 2002), pp. 113–26

——, 'Von "fremder Unterdrückung" zur "Freiheitszeit": Die Vorstellung von *frihet* im frühneuzeitlichen Schweden', in *Kollektive Freiheitsvorstellungen im frühneuzeitlichen Europa (1400–1850)*, ed. by Georg Schmidt, Martin van Gelderen and Christopher Snigula, Jenaer Beiträge zur Geschichte, 8 (Frankfurt am Main: Peter Lang, 2006), pp. 145–58

Normann, Carl-E., *Prästerskapet och det karolinska enväldet: Studier över det svenska prästerskapets statsuppfattning under stormaktstidens slutskede*, Samlingar och studier till Svenska kyrkans historia, 17 (Stockholm: Svenska kyrkans diakonistyrelses bokförlag, 1948)

Norrby, Jonas, *Jennings* (Köping: Vattenfall, 1991)

Odhner, Clas Theodor, *Sveriges politiska historia under konung Gustaf III:s regering*, 2 vols (Stockholm: Norstedts, 1885–96), I: *1771–1778* (1885); II: *1779–1787* (1896)

Oja, Linda and Karin Sennefelt, 'En ny historia varifrån? Om perspektivvalet i forskning om tidigmodern tid', *Historisk tidskrift*, 126 (2006), 803–10

Olden-Jørgensen, Sebastian, '"At vi maa frycte dig af idel kjærlighed": Magdudøvelse og magtiscensættelse under den ældre danske enevælde', *Fortid og Nutid: Tidsskrift for kulturhistorie og lokalhistorie* (1997), 239–53

Olin, Martin, *Det karolinska porträttet: Ideologi, ikonografi, identitet* (Stockholm: Raster, 2000)

Olivecrona, Knut, *Om dödsstraffet*, 2nd rev. edn (Uppsala: W. Schultz, 1891)

Oresko, Robert, 'The House of Savoy in Search for a Royal Crown in the Seventeenth Century', in *Royal and Republican Sovereignty in Early Modern Europe: Essays in Memory of Ragnhild Hatton*, ed. by Robert Oresko, G. C. Gibbs, and H. M. Scott (Cambridge: Cambridge University Press 1997), pp. 272–350

Oscarsson, Ingemar, 'Från statstidning till akademitidning 1734–1809', in *Världens äldsta: Post- och Inrikes Tidningar under 1600-, 1700-, 1800-, 1900- och 2000-talen*, ed. by Karl Erik Gustafsson and Per Rydén (Stockholm: Atlantis, 2005), pp. 131–236

Östlund, Joachim, *Lyckolandet: Maktens legitimering i officiell retorik från stormaktstid till demokratins genombrott* (Lund: Sekel, 2007)

Ozouf, Mona, 'L'opinion publique', in *The Political Culture of the Old Regime*, ed. by Keith Michael Baker, The French Revolution and the Creation of Modern Political Culture, 1 (Oxford: Pergamon Press, 1987), pp. 419–34

Persson, Fabian, 'The Courts of the Vasas and Palatines c. 1523–1751', in *The Princely Courts of Europe: Ritual, Politics and Culture under the*

Ancien Régime 1500–1750, ed. by John Adamson (London: Weidenfeld & Nicolson, 1999)

——, *Servants of Fortune: The Swedish Court between 1598 and 1721* (Lund: Department of History, 1999)

——, *Survival and Revival in Sweden's Court and Monarchy, 1718–1930* (Cham: Palgrave Macmillan, [2020])

Pleijel, Hilding, *Karolinsk kyrkofromhet, pietism och herrnhutism 1680–1772*, Svenska kyrkans historia, 5 (Stockholm: Svenska kyrkans diakonistyrelses bokförlag, 1935)

Pocock, J. G. A., 'Monarchy in the Name of Britain: The Case of George III', in *Monarchisms in the Age of Enlightenment: Liberty, Patriotism and the Common Good*, ed. by Hans Blom, John Christian Laursen and Luisa Simonutti (Toronto, Buffalo and London: Toronto University Press, 2007), pp. 285–302

Popular Prints and Imagery: Proceedings of an International Conference in Lund 5–7 October 2000, ed. by Nils-Arvid Bringéus and Sten Åke Nilsson, Kungl. Vitterhets Historie och Antikvitets Akademien, Konferenser, 53 (Stockholm: Almqvist & Wiksell, 2003)

The Princely Courts of Europe: Ritual, Politics and Culture under the Ancien Régime 1500–1750, ed. by John Adamson (London: Weidenfeld & Nicolson, 1999)

Rabb, Theodore K., 'Politics and the Arts in the Age of Christina', in *Politics and Culture in the Age of Christina: Acta from a Conference Held at the Wenner-Gren Center in Stockholm, May 4–6, 1995*, ed. by Marie-Louise Rodén, Suecoromana, 4 (Stockholm: Swedish Institute in Rome, 1997), pp. 9–22

Rangström, Lena, *Kläder för tid och evighet: Gustaf III sedd genom sina dräkter* (Stockholm: Livrustkammaren, 1997)

Redelius, Gunnar, *Sigtuna rådshus: Byggnadsminne i Stockholms län* (Stockholm: Länsstyrelsen, 1997)

Redworth, Glyn and Fernando Checa, 'The Courts of the Spanish Habsburgs, 1500–1700', in *The Princely Courts of Europe: Ritual, Politics and Culture under the Ancien Régime 1500–1750*, ed. by John Adamson (London: Weidenfeld & Nicolson, 1999), pp. 43–65

Republicanism: A Shared European Heritage, ed. by Martin van Gelderen and Quentin Skinner, 2 vols (Cambridge: Cambridge University Press, 2002), I: *Republicanism and Constitution in Early Modern Europe*; II: *The Values of Republicanism in Early Modern Europe*

Republiken und Republikanismus im Europa der frühen Neuzeit, ed. by Helmut G. Koenigsberger and Elisabeth Müller-Luckner, Schriften des Historischen Kollegs, Kolloquien, 11 (Munich: Oldenbourg, 1988)

Reutersward, Elisabeth, *Ett massmedium för folket: Studier i de allmänna kungörelsernas funktion i 1700-talets samhälle*, Studia historica Lundensia, 2 (Lund: Historiska institutionen, 2001)

Riksarkivets beståndsöversikt, 9 vols (Stockholm: Riksarkivet, 1993–2012), I:1: *Medeltiden, Kungl. Maj:ts kansli, utrikesförvaltningen*, ed. by James

404 Bibliography

Cavallie and Jan Lindroth (1996); III: *Kommittéarkiv*, ed. by Helmut Backhaus, James Cavallie and Lars Wickström (1993)

Rivière, Marc Serge, '"The Pallas of Stockholm": Louisa Ulrica of Prussia and the Swedish Crown', in *Queenship in Europe 1660–1815: The Role of the Consort*, ed. by Clarissa Campbell Orr (Cambridge: Cambridge University Press, 2004), pp. 322–43

Roberts, Michael, *The Age of Liberty: Sweden 1719–1772* (Cambridge: Cambridge University Press, 1986)

——, 'Great Britain and the Swedish Revolution 1772–73', *Historical Journal*, 8 (1964), 1–46

Rogister, J. M. J., 'The Crisis of 1753–4 in France and the Debate on the Nature of the Monarchy and of the Fundamental Laws', in *Herrschaftsverträge, Wahlkapitulationen, Fundamentalgesetze*, ed. by Rudolf Vierhaus, Veröffentlichungen des Max-Planck-Instituts für Geschichte, 56 (Göttingen: Vandenhoeck & Ruprecht, 1977), pp. 105–20

Roling, Bernd, *Odins Imperium: Der Rudbeckianismus als Paradigma an den skandinavischen Universitäten (1680–1860)*, Mittellateinische Studien und Texte, 54, 2 vols (Leiden: Brill, 2020)

Rudelius, Karl-Elof, 'Författningsfrågan i de förenade deputationerna 1769', *Statsvetenskaplig tidskrift för politik, statistik, ekonomi*, 38 (1935), 331–65

Runeby, Nils, *Monarchia mixta: Maktfördelningsdebatt i Sverige under den tidigare stormaktstiden*, Studia historica Upsaliensia, 6 (Stockholm: Svenska bokförlaget, 1962)

Rustemeyer, Angela, *Dissens und Ehre: Majestätsverbrechen in Russland (1600–1800)*, Forschungen zur osteuropäischen Geschichte, 69 (Wiesbaden: Harrassowitz, 2006)

Sabatier, Gérard, 'Beneath the Ceilings of Versailles: Towards an Archaeology and Anthropology of the Use of the King's Signs during the Absolute Monarchy', in *Iconography, Propaganda, and Legitimation*, ed. by Allan Ellenius (Oxford: Clarendon Press, 1998), pp. 217–42

Salling, Emma, 'Frederiks plads: J. F. J. Salys ryttermonument for Frederik V', *Architectura*, 21 (Copenhagen: Selskabet for Arkitekturhistorie, 1999), 49–76

Sallnäs, Birger, *Samuel Åkerhielm d.y.: En statsmannabiografi* (Lund: Gleerups, 1947)

Schama, Simon, 'The Domestication of Majesty: Royal Family Portraiture, 1500–1850', *Journal of Interdisciplinary History*, 17 (1986), 155–83

Schück, Herman, *Gustaf III:s statsvälvning 1772 i berättande källor och äldre litteratur*, Historiskt arkiv, 4 (Stockholm: Vitterhetsakademien, 1955)

Seip, Jens Arup, 'Teorien om det opinionsstyrte enevelde' *Historisk tidsskrift* (Norway), 38 (1958), 397–463

Sennefelt, Karin, *Den politiska sjukan: Dalupproret 1743 och frihetstida politisk kultur* (Hedemora: Gidlunds, 2001)

——, 'Mellan hemligt och offentligt: Sven Hofman vid riksdagen 1765–66', in *Riksdag, kaffehus och predikstol: Frihetstidens politiska kultur 1766–1772*, ed. by Marie-Christine Skuncke and Henrika Tandefelt (Stockholm: Atlantis, 2003), pp. 209–27

Setterwall, Åke, Stig Fogelmarck, and Lennart af Petersens, *Stockholms slott och dess konstskatter* (Stockholm: Bonniers, 1950)

Signums svenska konsthistoria: Frihetstidens konst (Lund: Signum, 1997)

Sjögren, Iréne, *Nils Rosén von Rosenstein: Mannen som förlängde människolivet. En trilogi* (Stockholm: Carlssons, 2006)

Sjöström, Oskar, 'De sekreta bihangen 1741 och deras idépolitiska bakgrund', *Sjuttonhundratal: Nordic Yearbook for Eighteenth-Century Studies 2008* (2008), 5–24

Skinner, Quentin, *The Foundations of Modern Political Thought*, 2 vols (Cambridge: Cambridge University Press, 1978), I: *The Renaissance*; II: *The Age of Reformation*

Skuncke, Marie-Christine, *Gustaf III – Det offentliga barnet: En prins retoriska och politiska fostran* (Stockholm: Atlantis, 1993)

Smith, Hannah, *Georgian Monarchy: Politics and Culture, 1714–1760* (Cambridge: Cambridge University Press, 2006)

Snickare, Mårten, *Enväldets riter: Kungliga fester och ceremonier i gestaltning av Nicodemus Tessin den yngre* (Stockholm: Raster, 1999)

——, 'Kungliga fester och ceremonier', in *Carl Hårleman: Människan och verket*, ed. by Göran Alm and others (Stockholm: Byggförlaget, 2000), pp. 252–63

Solen och Nordstjärnan: Frankrike och Sverige på 1700-talet, Nationalmusei utställningskatalog, 568 (Höganäs: Bra Böcker, Wiken; Stockholm: Nationalmuseum, 1993)

Staden på vattnet, ed. by Lars Nilsson, Monografier utgivna av Stockholms stad, 159:1 (Stockholm: Stockholmia, 2002), I: *1252–1850*

Stålhane, Henning, *Gustaf III:s bosättning, brudfärd och biläger: Kulturhistorisk studie* (Stockholm: Nordisk rotogravyr, 1946)

Stavenow, Åke, *Carl Hårleman: En studie i frihetstidens arkitekturhistoria* (Uppsala: Almqvist & Wiksell, 1927)

Stavenow, Ludvig, 'De politiska doktrinernas uppkomst och första utveckling under frihetstiden', in *Historiska studier: Festskrift tillägnad Carl Gustaf Malmström den 2 november 1897* (Stockholm: Norstedts, 1897), pp. 1–50

Steckzén, Birger, 'Adolf Fredrik under kronprinstiden', *Historisk tidskrift*, 54 (1934), 342–55

Stollberg-Rilinger, Barbara, 'Honores regii: Die Königswürde im zeremoniellen Zeichensystem der frühen Neuzeit', in *Dreihundert Jahre preußische Königskrönung: Eine Tagungsdokumentation*, ed. by Johannes Kunisch, Forschungen zur brandenburgischen und preussischen Geschichte, 6 (Berlin: Duncker & Humblot, 2002), pp. 1–26

Stolpe, Sven, *Drottning Kristina: Efter tronavsägelsen* (Stockholm: Bonniers, 1961)

406 Bibliography

Strömberg-Back, Kerstin, *Lagen, rätten, läran: Politisk och kyrklig idédebatt i Sverige under Johan III:s tid*, Bibliotheca historica Lundensis, 11 (Lund: Gleerups, 1963)

Sturdy, David J., 'The Royal Touch in England', in *European Monarchy: Its Evolution and Practice from Roman Antiquity to Modern Times*, ed. by Heinz Duchhardt, Richard A. Jackson and David Sturdy (Stuttgart: Franz Steiner, 1992), pp. 171–84

Sundin, Jan, *För Gud, Staten och Folket: Brott och rättskipning i Sverige 1600–1840*, Rättshistoriskt bibliotek, 47 (Lund: Institutet för rättshistorisk forskning, 1992)

Sveriges riddarhus: Ridderskapet och adeln och dess riddarhus, ed. by Carl Hallendorf (Stockholm: Historiska förlaget, 1926)

Sylwan, Otto, *Svenska pressens historia till statshvälfningen 1772* (Lund: Gleerups, 1896)

Talvio, Tuukka, 'Sedlarnas århundrade: Mynt och pappersmynt från 1724 till 1818', in *Myntningen i Sverige 995–1995*, Numismatiska meddelanden, 40 (Stockholm: Svenska numismatiska föreningen, 1995), pp. 201–18

Tandefelt, Henrika, 'Prins Gustafs resa i Bergslagen år 1768: Kronprinsen som politisk aktör under frihetstidens slut', in *Riksdag, kaffehus och predikstol: Frihetstidens politiska kultur 1766–1772*, ed. by Marie-Christine Skuncke and Henrika Tandefelt (Stockholm: Atlantis, 2003), pp. 229–52

Tegenborg Falkdalen, Karin, *Kungen är en kvinna: Retorik och praktik kring kvinnliga monarker under tidigmodern tid*, Skrifter från institutionen för historiska studier, 5 (Umeå: Institutionen för historiska studier, 2003)

Tengberg, Niklas, *Konung Gustaf III:s första regeringstid till och med 1772 års statshvälfning: Fragment av Gustaf III:s historia.* ed. by Clas Theodor Odhner (Lund: Gleerups, 1871)

Thanner, Lennart, *Revolutionen i Sverige efter Karl XII:s död: Den inrepolitiska maktkampen under tidigare delen av Ulrika Eleonora d.y:s regering* (Uppsala: Almqvist & Wiksell, 1953)

Thunander, Rudolf, *Hovrätt i funktion: Göta hovrätt och brottmålen 1635–1699*, Rättshistoriskt bibliotek, 49 (Lund: Institutet för rättshistorisk forskning, 1993)

Tingström, Bertel, *Svensk numismatisk uppslagsbok: Mynt i ord och bild 1521–1972*, 3rd rev. edn (Stockholm: Numismatiska bokförlaget, 1972)

Twining, Edward Francis, *European Regalia* (London: B. T. Batsford, 1967)

Tydén-Jordan, Astrid, *Kröningsvagnen: Konstverk och riksklenod; En studie i barockens karossbyggnadskonst* (Stockholm: Livrustkammaren, 1985)

Upsala ärkestifts herdaminne, ed. by Joh. Er. Fant and Aug. Th. Låstbom, 3 vols (Uppsala: Wahlström & Låstbom, 1852–45), III (1845)

Upton, Anthony F., *Charles XI and Swedish Absolutism* (Cambridge: Cambridge University Press, 1998)

Valentin, Hugo, *Frihetstidens riddarhus: Några bidrag till dess karakteristik* (Stockholm: Gebers, 1915)

Världens äldsta: Post- och Inrikes Tidningar under 1600-, 1700-, 1800-, 1900- och 2000-talen, ed. by Karl Erik Gustafsson and Per Rydén (Stockholm: Atlantis, 2005)

Vegesack, Thomas von, *Smak för frihet: Opinionsbildningen i Sverige 1755–1830* (Stockholm: Natur och kultur, 1995)

Venturi, Franco, *The End of the Old Regime in Europe, 1776–1789*, 2 vols (Princeton: Princeton University Press, 1991), I: *The Great States of the West*

Wedberg, Birger, 'Drottning Ulrika Eleonora d. y:s första justitiesession', *Svensk juristtidning*, 29 (1944), 144–48

——, '"Kongl. Maj:ts höga namns stämpel": Några anteckningar', *Statsvetenskaplig tidskrift för politik, statistik, ekonomi*, 27 (1924), 369–87

Wennberg, Bo G., *Niclas Lafrensen den yngre* (Malmö: Allhems, 1947)

Westerlund, Olov, *Karl XII i svensk litteratur från Dahlstierna till Tegnér* (Lund: Gleerups, 1951)

Winberg, Kurt, 'Årstrycket: En avslutad historia', *Tal över blandade ämnen*, Collegium curiosorum novum, yearbook 1984–86 (Uppsala: Carmina, 1988), 223–40

——, 'Årstrycket och dess förteckningar: Projekt till en bibliografi', *Nordisk tidskrift för bok- och biblioteksväsen*, 62–63:4 (1975–1976), 114–26

Wiséhn, Eva, *Mynt till ära och minne: Svenska jubileums- och minnesmynt* (Stockholm: Sveriges riksbank, 2005)

Wollin, Nils G., 'Kungsträdgården i Stockholm. II', *Samfundet S:t Eriks årsbok 1924* (1924), 93–121

Zurbuchen, Simone, 'Theorizing Enlightened Absolutism: The Swiss Republican Origins of Prussian Monarchism', in *Monarchisms in the Age of Enlightenment: Liberty, Patriotism and the Common Good*, ed. by Hans Blom, John Christian Laursen and Luisa Simonutti (Toronto, Buffalo and London: Toronto University Press, 2007), pp. 240–66

Index

Page numbers in italics refer to illustrations. An 'n' after a page number refers to a footnote on that page. Titles serve only as a guide to the person's role in the present context and should not be understood as precise or exhaustive.

EU authorised representative for GPSR:
Easy Access System Europe, Mustamäe tee 50,
10621 Tallinn, Estonia
gpsr.requests@easproject.com